Emancipation's Daughters

Emancipation's Daughters / *Reimagining*

Black Femininity and the National Body

Riché Richardson

DUKE UNIVERSITY PRESS   *Durham and London*   2021

© 2021 Duke University Press
This book is licensed under a Creative Commons
Attribution-NonCommercial-NoDerivatives 4.0 International (CC BY-NC-ND
4.0) License, available at https://creativecommons.org/licenses/by-nc-nd/4.0/.
Designed by Matthew Tauch
Typeset in Minion Pro and Avenir Lt Std by Westchester Publishing Services

Library of Congress Cataloging-in-Publication Data
Names: Richardson, Riché, [date] author.
Title: Emancipation's daughters : reimagining black femininity and the national body / Riché Richardson.
Description: Durham : Duke University Press, 2021. | Includes bibliographical references and index.
Identifiers: LCCN 2020024441 (print) | LCCN 2020024442 (ebook) | ISBN 9781478009917 (hardcover) | ISBN 9781478010975 (paperback) | ISBN 9781478012504 (ebook) Subjects:
LCSH: African American women—Political activity—United States—History—20th century. | African American women—Political activity—United States—History—21st century. | African American leadership—United States. | Leadership in women—United States.
Classification: LCC E185.86 .R534 2021 (print) | LCC E185.86 (ebook) | DDC 305.48/896073—dc23
LC record available at https://lccn.loc.gov/2020024441
LC ebook record available at https://lccn.loc.gov/2020024442

ISBN 978-1-4780-9091-5 (ebook/other)

Cover art: Riché Richardson, *Rosa Parks, Whose "No" in 1955 Launched the Montgomery Bus Boycott and Was Heard around the World*. 2006–12. Dedicated to Georgette Norman. Photograph © Mickey Welsh—USA TODAY NETWORK

Publication of this open monograph was the result of Cornell University's participation in TOME (Toward an Open Monograph Ecosystem), a collaboration of the Association of American Universities, the Association of University Presses, and the Association of Research Libraries. TOME aims to expand the reach of long-form humanities and social science scholarship including digital scholarship. Additionally, the program looks to ensure the sustainability of university press monograph publishing by supporting the highest quality scholarship and promoting a new ecology of scholarly publishing in which authors' institutions bear the publication costs.

Funding from Cornell University made it possible to open this publication to the world.

Duke University Press gratefully acknowledges the support of the Hull Memorial Publication Fund of Cornell University, which provided funds toward the publication of this book.

For

JOANNE RICHARDSON, MY MOTHER

and in memory of

EMMA LOU JENKINS RICHARDSON, MY GRANDMOTHER

Preface / ix

{ CONTENTS }

Acknowledgments / xxi

Introduction: An Exemplary American Woman / 1

1   Mary McLeod Bethune's "My Last Will and Testament" and Her National Legacy / 39

2   From Rosa Parks's *Quiet Strength* to Memorializing a National Mother / 87

3   America's Chief Diplomat: The Politics of Condoleezza Rice from Autobiography to Art and Fashion / 128

4   First Lady and "Mom-in-Chief": The Voice and Vision of Michelle Obama in the Video *South Side Girl* and in *American Grown* / 178

Conclusion: Beyoncé's South and the Birth of a "Formation" Nation / 220

Notes / 235

Bibliography / 257

Index / 281

{ PREFACE }

Like many other Americans, I got my first glimpse of Condoleezza Rice on television when she appeared before a national audience as a speaker at the 2000 Republican National Convention (RNC), held in Philadelphia, Pennsylvania, during the presidential campaign of Texas governor George W. Bush. The event officially marked his selection as the party's nominee. During the television broadcast, I remember listening with rapt attention as Rice, who was at the time a professor of political science at Stanford University and the campus's former provost, reflected on the experience of her father, John Rice, of becoming a Republican in 1952, when the Democrats of segregated Jim Crow Alabama had prohibited him from registering to vote because of the color of his skin.

Her other personal story in the speech highlighted her grandfather, "Granddaddy Rice." It reflected on how he rose from farming in rural Alabama to attending Stillman College, where he eventually became a Presbyterian minister, a choice that provided him a scholarship to remain in school and that also opened the door for generations of her family members to become college educated. She underscores his story as "an American story" and as an illustration of hard work and perseverance in pursuing the American dream. The speech ends with a proclamation of her belief that "George W. Bush challenges us to call upon our better selves, to be compassionate toward those who are less fortunate, to cherish and educate every child, descendants of slaves and immigrants alike, and to thereby affirm the American dream for us all."[1]

Significantly, Rice frames herself as a "daughter" in relation to a longer history of blacks in the United States since slavery. Furthermore, she frames her own family—a black family—as a *representative* American family within a national body from which people of African descent have typically been excluded. These terms tacitly mediate and authorize her entry into the nation's public sphere.

Yet the Republican establishment's long-standing investments in the notorious southern strategy—developed after the civil rights movement to dismantle major civil rights legislative gains and social progress toward racial integration through agendas premised on race baiting—were also likely not lost on some who heard her speech and caught the irony. The nationalization of this reactionary political ideology under the auspices of the neoconservative movement flew in the face of the Republican Party's historical reputation as the party of Lincoln, which had opposed slavery, endorsed Emancipation, supported the project of Reconstruction during the post–Civil War era, and created a welcoming climate for earlier generations of black voters, such as Rice's father. In the wake of her speech, Rice emerged as a symbol of a new kind of conservatism that promised to be more inclusive of blacks moving forward than it had been in the past and as a primary proponent of the political platform of "compassionate conservatism," which George W. Bush was advocating as a cornerstone of his campaign.[2]

If this event, where she emphasized the influence of her paternal ancestors, gave Rice her most salient public exposure to a national audience on the Bush campaign trail, she became a familiar face in news and television media after Bush's controversial and widely disputed presidential election victory over Vice President Al Gore in 2000 and Bush's selection of Rice as national security adviser in his presidential cabinet, the first black woman to ever occupy this position, alongside Colin Powell as the nation's first black secretary of state. Powell had served under Bush's father, President George H. W. Bush, as the first black chair of the Joint Chiefs of Staff. The unprecedented high-ranking appointments of African Americans in George W. Bush's administration seemed all the more significant because they were leadership roles that no blacks had ever held in the nation's history, opening up new possibilities for these leaders to affect domestic and international affairs, including key policy decisions. In a way, the appointments also seemed to hearken back to the theme that Rice had introduced at the RNC, related to Republicans giving blacks access to opportunities that the Democratic Party—though no longer defined by the infamous segregationist Dixiecrat ideology premised on states' rights, which had dominated southern politics since 1948—had systemically denied, notwithstanding the Democratic Party's large and consistent African American voting base.[3] Based on a constitutional provision that accorded states rather than the federal government the power to make decisions, the states' rights doctrine had also been invoked by southern states invested in slaveholding to rationalize secession that led to the Civil War.

Although I did not share Rice's party affiliation or investments in neoconservative political agendas, I was definitely intrigued and excited to see her so regularly on the national stage after her historic appointment to Bush's cabinet. Rice stood out for me, as she did for a lot of other black women, because of the key role she played. Her symbolic power was undeniable. This fascination intensified all the more for me once Rice was appointed secretary of state in 2004, after President Bush was elected to a second term, for this appointment meant that Rice as a black woman held more power than any woman in the world. It made her the nation's primary representative in the realm of international affairs. Never had a black woman been as influential in a president's cabinet, as powerful in the realm of national and global politics, or had such a prominent national platform in my lifetime.

At the same time, the space for Rice to occupy such a prominent leadership position in the nation's government as a black woman had been established by a long line of predecessors. They had paved the way and established salient voices in politics in an effort to achieve a more democratic America for black people and all others who have been excluded from its opportunities. Among her predecessors were Mary McLeod Bethune, the founder of Bethune-Cookman College, who had established the National Council of Negro Women and served as the only woman in the Black Cabinet of President Franklin Delano Roosevelt. Rosa Parks's courageous choice to remain seated on the Montgomery bus in 1955 had launched the Montgomery bus boycott and was the tipping point for the desegregation of public buses in the city, while establishing foundations for the Freedom Rides, making her a national and global symbol. She also had an intimate connection to politics as the secretary of Congressman John Conyers in Detroit from 1965 until she retired in 1988. As someone born and raised in Montgomery, Alabama, during the post–civil rights era, I have been able to study and learn from her activist legacy in visceral ways.

Fewer people know that Pauli Murray, who had practiced passing as a boy during her teen years, was arrested for refusing to move to the back of a bus in Virginia in 1940, years before Parks, an incident that led Murray to become a civil rights lawyer. Murray, the first black woman ordained in the Episcopal church, was a lesbian who in more recent years has become legible as transgender. Such factors may help explain why Murray is not as widely celebrated in civil rights history for resisting discrimination and coining the term Jane Crow to describe the effects of systematized segregation on black women, or celebrated as a cofounder of the National Organization for Women and a foremost advocate for equal rights.

I was a baby when Shirley Chisholm—the first black woman ever elected to Congress—made her historic run for president in 1972 and emerged as a national symbol, establishing new precedents in the nation's political context as a black woman leader in the post–civil rights era, in the midst of the black power and women's liberation movements, as she promoted policies designed to help ensure the well-being of women and children. Indeed, when I was thirteen, my grandfather Joe Richardson recommended Shirley Chisholm to me as a black woman who had achieved great things and whom I should think of as a role model. Rice's role would have been inconceivable without the foundations established by Chisholm.

Carol Moseley Braun, who made history in 1993 as the first African American senator and the first woman elected in the state of Illinois, had also helped pave the way for Rice. The same could be said for Barbara Jordan's significance as the first African American elected to the state senate in Texas in 1966, establishing the foundations for the formidable political contributions of Representative Sheila Jackson Lee. As someone living in California, I was also deeply inspired by Maxine Waters, who was first elected to Congress in 1991 to represent California's Twenty-Ninth District, and who has become known to newer generations as Auntie Maxine for her bold and tireless advocacy in the national arena on behalf of the disenfranchised, alongside Barbara Lee, who was elected to represent California's Ninth Congressional District in 1998.[4]

The lives and legacies of all these women provide powerful testimonies of the transformative influence on national politics of black women, all of whom have been identified as liberal Democrats whose political philosophies radically differ from the neoconservatism espoused by Rice. Even as Rice often invoked civil rights histories, the policy agendas she advanced and supported in the national arena were recurrently reactionary and differed radically from the agendas associated with other black women leaders. The new heights to which Rice had risen in the national and global arenas in the new millennium, coupled with that intriguing paradox, made me interested in learning more about her, as well as about her black women predecessors. I wanted to study the public voices that black women have been able to establish in the national arena, along with their writings, notwithstanding the marginality, stereotyping, and othering of black women in the public sphere. This goal put me on the path to writing this book, which examines how such iconic black women leaders in the political realm have expanded national femininity beyond its conventional white definitions.

Indeed, in some ways, Rice's rise to such prominent positions under the auspices of the Republican Party at the dawn of the twenty-first century seemed ironic. On top of notoriously polarizing rhetoric in the political arena throughout the 1980s, characterizing young single black women with children who used forms of public assistance as "welfare queens," the Republican establishment had targeted several high-profile black women for propaganda attacks during the 1990s, in heated debates that arose over prominent leadership positions. In 1991, law professor Anita Hill experienced hostile interrogation before a Republican- and male-dominated Senate Judiciary Committee, chaired by Democratic senator Joe Biden, during hearings held in the months after she accused Clarence Thomas, a Supreme Court nominee of President George H. W. Bush and a colleague with whom she had worked at the U.S. Department of Education and the Equal Employment Opportunity Commission, of sexual harassment, prior to Thomas's confirmation to the Court.

As the neoconservative movement of the 1990s consolidated in the concerted effort to oppose newly elected Democratic president and former Arkansas governor Bill Clinton's administration, an increasingly hostile climate made high-profile black women, who were potential candidates for prominent posts because of their affiliation with Clinton, objects of public ridicule and spectacle. The targets included Clinton's nomination for secretary of education in 1992, Johnetta B. Cole, a noted anthropologist and esteemed president of the historically black, all-female Spelman College; his appointment of Joycelyn Elders as the first African American and second female surgeon general of the United States in 1993; and his nomination of University of Pennsylvania law professor Lani Guinier as assistant attorney general for civil rights in 1993.

The centrist positions of the Clinton administration were perceived as detrimental to African Americans, leading to the crime bill that expanded mass incarceration and to the dismantling of the welfare system, but they were also obviously inimical for black women leaders. Moreover, its centrist agendas held dire implications for the gay and lesbian population in sanctioning the notorious Don't Ask, Don't Tell policy in 1993. This Department of Defense directive prohibited discrimination and harassment in the military based on sexuality, but also threatened discharge for soldiers who disclosed information about their sexuality and same-sex relationships, expressly barring those who engaged in "homosexual acts." Such policies encouraged the closeting of sexual difference at a time when the field of queer studies was expanding, challenging conventional understandings of gender and sexuality, and queer identities were gaining more visibility in popular culture.

Unlike Cole, Elders, and Guinier, Rice's affiliation with the Republican Party made her an insider and afforded her some protection and immunity from the kinds of attacks that black women in the public sphere of politics had experienced in previous years. Her acceptance, however, was premised on complicity with policy agendas that were widely perceived to be reactionary. Her alliances with a political party perceived to be invested in advancing the interests of wealthy and white Americans often led critics to question her blackness and, in some cases, to even think about making more productive and strategic political alliances between blacks and conservatism.

I found it fascinating in daily life that as I circulated in public spaces in Sacramento, California, where I lived while working on the faculty at the University of California, Davis, and as I traveled, even on vacation to Jamaica, people began to compare me to Rice. They would mention that I reminded them of her. These everyday casual comparisons not only pointed to Rice's salience as one of the nation's most recognizable leaders but also underscored her iconicity and influence as a black woman on the national stage.

Like many others, I admired Rice's signature classic look, which regularly incorporated designer items such as St. John suits, Salvatore Ferragamo shoes, pearls, and a flipped bob hairstyle. I vividly remember excitedly calling my mother on the phone one evening as Rice walked into the House chamber for a State of the Union address wearing one of her St. John suits. Even before I could mention what I was calling about, my mother, Joanne Richardson, said, "I saw it," a moment that epitomized the collective admiring gaze that many black women in the nation were directing at Rice, even when others seemed not to be as invested in analyzing or talking about the masterful political showmanship embodied in her impeccable styling as a black woman circulating so saliently in the nation's public sphere. Rice's impeccable style was clearly connected to some degree to her iconic force and impact. I also grasped the power and influence of Rice's iconicity when my hairstylist at a Regis salon in downtown Sacramento, who prided himself on his deft cutting expertise, honed by a mentor trained at Vidal Sassoon, took to giving the ends of the chin-length bob I wore at the time an upward turn with the barrel of his curling iron to make my hairstyle resemble Rice's famous flip.

As fascinated as I was, I shared the serious concern of her critics about the reactionary neoconservative political platforms that she seemed to be endorsing so willingly. Like her fiercest critics, I questioned the veracity of Rice's claims on behalf of the Bush administration that Saddam Hussein possessed weapons of mass destruction, which culminated in the Iraq War in the months after the tragedy of September 11, 2001, when multiple groups of al-Qaeda terrorists hijacked four flights from Boston to crash into three primary targets—the World Trade Center in New York, the Pentagon, and the nation's capital—resulting in several thousand casualties. The bravery of a group of passengers on Flight 93, which crashed in a field in Pennsylvania, had thwarted the effort of the terrorists to reach the nation's capital. In numerous interviews and public speeches, to rationalize the war on terror in the post-9/11 era, Rice repeatedly mentioned her personal friendships and recollections related to Denise McNair, Addie Mae Collins, Carole Robertson, and Cynthia Wesley, the four black girls who were killed during the horrific bombing of 16th Street Baptist Church in Birmingham, Alabama, on September 15, 1963. The tragedy made international news, and the girls became iconic symbols of the nation's moral conscience in the wake of their tragic deaths.

Similarly, in 2005, I shared the public concern about the failure of the Federal Emergency Management Agency (FEMA) to send faster relief to New Orleans after the levees broke and flooded the city in the days after Hurricane Katrina, as thousands of people remained stranded in the city. I was deeply unsettled by stories alleging that Rice had been spotted shopping for Ferragamo shoes in New York City as the levees broke. During this period, I even remember puzzling inwardly and feeling frustration about why so many people kept comparing me to her in public, stubbornly insisting that I had absolutely nothing in common with "that woman." I finally felt compelled to do some serious self-examining about what if anything I really did have in common with her beyond the level of superficial appearances people typically mentioned.

As a child born in Alabama who had also earned a doctorate, eventually lived in California, and worked as a university professor, I began to think more about the places where our histories converged and diverged. I began to study and reflect on her story. I read every book available related to her, including biographies, and began to research her in earnest and to present academic talks on her fashioning and iconicity as a woman in the public sphere of politics. I began to analyze her conservative political alliances with a more open and objective mind to think about how I could put myself into her shoes and understand where she was coming from.

I began to ponder from a critical standpoint what it meant to witness so many people across genders, races, sexualities, ethnicities, regions, and nationalities citing Rice as an iconic figure in everyday life. She seemed to be both intensely fascinating and captivating as a point of reference in the minds of a diverse constellation of people I encountered in public spaces. Through Rice I began to grasp in a visceral sense how possible it is for a high level of symbolic capital to be associated with black women subjects in the national context, observations that also put me on the path to developing this study related to black women who have emerged as representative women in symbolizing and shaping definitions of national identity.

Like Rice, Michelle Obama seemed to signal new possibilities for black women's representation in the nation's public sphere of the twenty-first century. Just as I had been strongly affected when Rice spoke at the 2000 RNC, I remember being similarly fascinated the first time I heard of Michelle Obama on the night that her husband, Barack Obama, a veteran state senator in Illinois, community organizer, and law professor at the University of Chicago, spoke and stole the show as a keynote at the 2004 Democratic National Convention (DNC) in Boston, Massachusetts. To borrow the lingo of contemporary social media such as Facebook and Twitter, I began to "follow" her and track information about her once I became a member and contributor to the Barack Brigade, organized to support her husband's election to the U.S. Senate, and even well before she became an object of fascination in the national media while on the campaign trail during her husband's first bid for the presidency.

During these months, despite her committed work and powerful speeches on the campaign trail, a lot of propaganda seemed designed to distort Michelle Obama's public image. Her DNC speech in 2008 countered such misleading representations. Presented on a night with the theme "One Nation," Obama's speech was a watershed public address that gave her widespread salience on a national stage. Her delivery of this speech accomplished for her what her husband's captivating presentation had accomplished at the prior DNC in 2004, when he was campaigning for the U.S. Senate, enabling her to connect in a visceral way with a national audience while also revealing the depth and sincerity in her ideas and the extent of her rhetorical talents, taking her to a new level of popularity, recognition, and appreciation.[5] Chimamanda Ngozi Adichie aptly describes this moment: "All over America, black women were still, their eyes watching a form of God, because she represented their image writ large in the world."[6]

At a rhetorical level, this speech, more than any prior one, established her alignments with the values of the U.S. mainstream and identification with it as a woman, increasing her legibility and symbolic force as an emerging feminine icon in the national arena. This speech was foundational in shaping narratives related to her as a wife and mother that have since crystallized in the U.S. public sphere, including in some of the major policy initiatives that she has advanced. Her major initiatives included the Let's Move! campaign in

2010, which was designed to address childhood obesity in the United States in an effort to improve nutrition in schools and to encourage physical activity and exercise, and her work with Vice President Joe Biden in 2011 to introduce Joining Forces in support of military veterans and their families, centered on American families and children. These projects frame her as a premier mother in the nation and as a primary representative and advocate for these groups in the national arena, drawing on her political capital as the nation's First Lady.

When her husband was elected president, Michelle Obama became the first black First Lady in this nation's history, a role that expanded representational possibilities for black women in the national arena and placed a black woman front and center in the nation's consciousness. To be sure, her role as First Lady made her a new and unprecedented symbol of American womanhood in the twenty-first century. As a black woman, she introduced a new paradigm for the concept of the First Lady by reframing the position in relation to black feminine subjectivity and unsettling the position's conventional essentialist associations with white womanhood, just as Barack Obama's 2008 election unsettled the tacit white masculine subjectivity conventionally associated with the office of the president in the United States.

Once Michelle Obama emerged on the national stage, I had the experience of being compared to her a lot in public spaces as well. For me, witnessing this phenomenon all over again, as I had with Rice, underscored Michelle Obama's iconic force, increasing popularity, and legibility for everyday people and attested to her profound effect on the national imaginary. Rice and Obama are clearly positioned on opposite ends of the political spectrum, yet they share common ground for introducing themselves to national audiences through speeches at national political conventions while framing themselves as "daughters" and their families as representative American families, as well as invoking the interests of children. My research has shown me that their examples are far from unique. Reflecting on black women such as Rice and Obama, who became nationally prominent within contemporary politics of the twenty-first century, led me to raise questions about the role that black women have played historically in shaping notions of national selfhood within a diverse citizenry.

Condoleezza Rice and Michelle Obama stand on the shoulders of black women within a long cultural legacy, spanning back to the late nineteenth century, who have, in their speeches and writings, recurrently invoked notions of the nation as a "family" and prioritized the interests of children to affirm the place of black subjectivity within national narratives, which have conventionally excluded and othered black identities. This study traces the development of these themes in African American literary and cultural history by examining Rice and Obama within the continuum of black women leaders who have become emblems of the nation and who have persistently deployed such strategies in writing, speech, and public discourses in the political arena since Emancipation. In the process, I draw on some of the signal writings in which they have voiced their political agendas alongside some of the cultural texts that foreground representations as well as contestations over black women's scripts in relation to national femininity. Such black women are also connected to the story of "daughters of sorrow" chronicled by Beverly Guy-Sheftall.

In Stacey Abrams's historic bid to become governor of Georgia in 2018 and her work to address issues such as voter suppression, she has emerged as a national leader and stands at the vanguard of a new generation of black women in the twenty-first century who are helping to transform politics at the national level. Her example also moves us closer to the democracy advocated by Cathy Cohen, in which black youth voices are amplified and heard.[7] California senator Kamala Harris made history in 2020 when Democratic presidential candidate Joe Biden selected her as his vice presidential running mate, making her the first black woman and Asian American nominated for one of the country's top two offices by a major U.S. party. As black queer women who founded Black Lives Matter in the wake of George Zimmerman's acquittal in 2013 for murdering Trayvon Martin in Sanford, Florida, Alicia Garza, Patrisse Cullors, and Opal Tometi have mobilized grassroots communities across the nation to protest against issues such as police violence against blacks and racial profiling. At the same time, they have brought an intersectional view of race, class, gender, and sexuality to their agendas and challenged the conventional patriarchy and male-centered leadership in black political movements, as well as homophobia.

Similarly, Lori Lightfoot and Toni Preckwinkle challenged the infamous male-dominated political machine in Chicago in the historic 2019 election in which they faced off as two black lesbian women running for mayor. Lightfoot made history yet again as the city's first lesbian and woman elected mayor. Pamela Rocker's bid for the presidency as a black trans candidate in a field that included several other LGBTQ candidates also disrupts the conventional logics and optics of gender and sexuality within national politics, emphasizing the need for more inclusive narratives of selfhood in the nation.

Inroads into the mainstream political arena by black queer and trans leaders in the contemporary era, along with historical figures such as Murray, throw into relief the extent to which the most legible models of black national femininity have been limited, despite how provocatively they have challenged white- and male-centered models of national selfhood. They reflect the prevailing heterosexist models of gender and family, which marginalize and exclude black trans and queer subjects, whose role in constituting black womanhood's representations in the public sphere is also important to acknowledge as part of the national story. As Audre Lorde illustrated, outsider identities hold the greatest potential to challenge conventional stories and to bring about revolutionary change.[8]

{ ACKNOWLEDGMENTS }

While my first book focused on the role of the U.S. South in nationalizing ideologies of black masculinity, this project builds on it by looking at the role of the region in nationalizing models of black femininity. Cathy N. Davidson encouraged this book's potential from its early stages of development. I am also thankful to the scholars Houston A. Baker Jr.; his wife, Charlotte Pierce-Baker; and Valerie Smith for encouraging this study from the very beginning.

I appreciate the enthusiasm and feedback I received from colleagues and students when I presented an early version of my chapter on Condoleezza Rice at the University of California, Davis, in the English Department's Scholar's Symposium in 2008. At UC Davis, I especially want to thank Patricia A. Turner (now at UCLA), Clarence Major, and Clarence Walker. I also shared aspects of this project when I was hosted at UC Riverside's Center for Ideas and Society in 2008 by the late scholar Emory Elliott, and as an invited speaker at the conference on the hemispheric South at UC Santa Barbara in 2011, which was coordinated by Carl Gutiérrez-Jones and the late Clyde Woods.

This study continued to move forward in new and exciting directions once I joined the faculty at Cornell University in the Africana Studies and Research Center in 2008. I appreciate Salah M. Hassan's and Grant Farred's reading of my early work on Michelle Obama. Robert L. Harris's historical insights, along with his work as the national historian of Alpha Phi Alpha fraternity and contributions in the development of the Martin Luther King Jr. national memorial in the capital, added important perspective. I have valued and learned from dialogues with James Turner, Locksley Edmondson, Anne Adams, and Beverly Blackshear as veteran Africana colleagues. Moreover, I am thankful for dialogues with Margaret Washington, N'Dri Assie-Lumumba, and Carole Boyce-Davies on black feminism and womanism. Travis Lars Gosa passed along a rich ensemble of hip-hop songs dedicated to Michelle Obama. Furthermore, I have also valued Judith Byfield, Noliwe Rooks, Gerard Aching, Oneka LaBennett, C. Riley Snorton, Olufemi Taiwo, Siba Grovogui, Kevin Gaines, Adeolu Ademoyo, and Happiness Bulugu as colleagues in Africana. I extend my sincere thanks for the administrative staff support provided by

Treva Levine, Renee Milligan, and Donna Pinnisi. I have appreciated the support, collegiality, and insights of Kenneth McClane on campus in the African American literature field, along with those of Margo Crawford, Dagmawi Woubshet, Mukoma Wa Ngugi, Naminata Diabate, Lyrae Van Clief-Stefanon, Eric Cheyfitz, Shirley Samuels, and George Hutchinson. I am thankful for dialogues on this project with colleagues in the brilliant Mellon Diversity Group in 2016–17, especially Debra Castillo, Ella Diaz, Bobby Smith, Sara Warner, Anna Bartel, Gerald Torres, and Ed Baptist. I have also valued insights from Carol Kammen, Ken Glover, Russell Rickford, and Adrienne Clay. In 2017, it was an honor to share work from the conclusion of this study in the Rabinor Lecture in American Studies. I also benefited from the opportunity to dialogue with Lauren Berlant about this project when she was a scholar in Cornell's School for Criticism and Theory in 2012.

On the journey to this book's completion, I conducted research in the archives of the David M. Rubenstein Rare Book and Manuscript Library at Duke University, along with archival materials and institutions related to Rosa Parks and Mary McLeod Bethune. At Cornell, this project has been enabled by access to resources at the Cornell Law School, the Olin Library, and the John Henrik Clarke Library in the ASRC, as well as the support of Eric Acree, Sharon Powers, and Saah Nue Quigee. I thank my undergraduate and graduate students for dialogues in the classroom and beyond. I appreciate the work of Marshall Smith, Kristen Wright, and Lauren Siegel as research assistants for this project. I extend my deepest thanks to Courtney Berger at Duke University Press, a dream editor, as well as my anonymous reviewers.

On February 4, 2013, I was honored to be the invited speaker for Rosa Parks's gala one hundredth birthday celebration at Troy University's Rosa Parks Museum in Montgomery, Alabama, on the program with Mayor Todd Strange and other officials, and to be invited by postmaster Donald Snipes to participate in the city's historic unveiling of a postage stamp in her honor. I also gave extended versions of this talk, "Rosa Parks @100," at Cornell and Georgia State universities, with the latter coordinated by Gina Caison, who put together a rich seminar for me with Akinyele Umoja. In 2012, I was delighted to be an invited speaker in the English Department at the University of Pittsburgh in the lecture series New Directions in African American Literature and Culture, coordinated by William Scott. In 2014, I was hosted in the Critical Speaker Series in the English Department at the University of North Carolina, Chapel Hill, which was coordinated by David Baker. I drew on this book in my talk in the Arts and Humanities Colloquium at Colgate University as the 2019–20 Olive B. O'Connor Visiting Distinguished Chair in English and appreciate the feedback and intellectual support that I received during my semester there. I have also presented sections from this book at conferences and professional meetings. I thank GerShun Avilez for his generous feedback, along with Honorée Jeffers, Géraldine Chouard, Anne Crémieux, Steven Thrasher, Aliyyah Abdur-Rahman, Rebecca Wanzo, Anna Everett, Koritha Mitchell, Daryl Scott, Tara White, Cecily Jones, and Suzette Spencer.

On the home front, I am tremendously grateful for the support and insights provided by Georgette Norman, founding director of the Rosa Parks Museum in Montgomery, as I have developed this project, including access to exhibitions and archives at the museum. This aspect of my project, as a Montgomery native, feels particularly close to home. That civil rights heroine Rosa Parks and my great-aunt Johnnie Rebecca Carr, a longtime leader of the Montgomery Improvement Association, were best friends is background that has inspired me deeply as I have researched Mrs. Parks. Similarly, I am thankful for the support that my research on the civil rights movement received from the late actor Nick Latour, the son of E. D. Nixon. I am grateful to a dear family friend, the late Alma Burton Johnson, for sharing resources with me related to Nick and his father—her uncle. Mary Frances Whitt, who was mentored in the Youth Council led by Rosa Parks and sponsored by the National Association for the Advancement of Colored People (NAACP), also shared reflections, archival resources, and insights that I have valued in developing this project. I am thankful and feel blessed to have Rev. Robert Graetz and his wife, Jeannie Graetz, as my family's neighbors in Montgomery. I also thank Mathew Knowles, another fellow Alabamian, for his support of my Beyoncé Nation course at Cornell and encouragement of my research in Beyoncé studies.

Florida has been my grandmother Emma Lou Jenkins Richardson's second home, and it was beyond wonderful to discover that she and my grandfather Joe Richardson are both listed in the state's 1945 census. I enjoyed her memories and vivid stories about working with the National Youth Administration as a young woman, later in the navy yard in Pensacola, Florida, during World War II, as my grandfather worked in construction building barracks, and then moving on to Daytona Beach, Florida, where he helped to build beachfront homes. That she describes having seen figures like Mary McLeod Bethune in person during their time there, as well as First Lady Eleanor Roosevelt, brought the history related to these figures to life for me and inspired me to learn more about it.

I deeply appreciate my conversation with Elaine Smith on Mary McLeod Bethune. Similarly, meeting Bettye Collier-Thomas, who served as the founding executive director of the Bethune Museum and Archives, national historic site, from 1977 to 1989 and worked tirelessly within the National Council of Negro Women, inspired me as I began work on this project. My essay "Monumentalizing Mary McLeod Bethune and Rosa Parks in the Post–Civil Rights Era," which draws on both chapters 1 and 2 of this book, is featured in *Phillis: The Journal for Research on African American Women*, the landmark 2013 special issue co-edited by Darlene Clark Hine and Paula Giddings.

David Leverenz offered an encouraging response to an early chapter. Jon Smith read two early chapters of this study. Deborah Barker and Kathryn McKee offered helpful feedback on an early essay. I am thankful for the long-standing support I received from my professors at Spelman, including Beverly Guy-Sheftall, Donna Akiba Sullivan Harper, Gloria Wade-Gayles, A. J. Billingslea, Christine Wick Sizemore, Anne Warner, and June Aldridge. I am also thankful to Karla FC Holloway, Wahneema Lubiano, Richard Powell, C. T. Woods-Powell, Shireen Lewis, and the late Kenny J. Williams. I cherish my longtime friendships with Efua Paul and Denise Ross. I had major surgery in July 2018, on this book's path to completion; I applaud my primary care physician, Lloyd Darlow; hematologist, Timothy Bael; and surgeon, Michael Randell; along with the medical staff at Emory St. Joseph's Hospital in Atlanta, for providing such excellent care. I deeply appreciate the spiritual guidance of Rev. Janice Cooper as well as at St. Andrew's Methodist Church in Sacramento, California; Calvary Baptist Church in Ithaca, New York; and Maggie Street Missionary Baptist Church and Resurrection Catholic Church in Montgomery.

Finally, my family has provided continuing support and encouragement as I have completed this study. I have deeply appreciated the support of my uncle Joseph Richardson; my aunt Pamela R. Garrett; her husband, the Reverend Michael Garrett; my cousins—Keri Smith; Megan Smith-O'Neil; her husband, Patrick O'Neil; Norman Every and Kyrie Joseph Every; and Lamar Landon and Sharon Frazier, along with our extended family. My mother, Joanne Richardson, has cheered on this book from day one and enthusiastically welcomed the various chapter drafts as they have emerged. My grandmother Emma Lou Jenkins Richardson, whose regular requests for updates helped to keep me focused, encouraged me continually to keep moving toward the finish line and was a veritable coach as I worked on this book. I savored the soft and sweet soundtrack she provided with her beautiful singing voice many days as I worked on the manuscript during my visits home to Montgomery. I have dearly missed her. Regardless of where I have ever lived and traveled, my family gives me the greatest reminders in my life of words that the national heroine of Munchkinland famously immortalized on the cinematic screen in 1939: "There's no place like home."

Introduction

An Exemplary American Woman

In 2015 on social media, a groundswell of voices within the feminist movement, primarily represented by the Women on 20s corporation, raised concern about the absence of a woman on U.S. currency. They emphasized the urgency of including a woman on the twenty-dollar bill to replace the image of President Andrew Jackson by the 2020 centennial anniversary of the Nineteenth Amendment, which granted women the right to vote, and they launched a petition to President Barack Obama to order the secretary of the treasury to update the currency "to reflect the remarkable accomplishments of an exemplary American woman who has helped shape our Nation's great history."[1] In several rounds that unfolded over five weeks in 2015, multiple black women—such as Shirley Chisholm, Sojourner Truth, Rosa Parks, Barbara Jordan, and Harriet Tubman—were among the finalists. Harriet Tubman was ultimately declared the winner.

The public campaign spearheaded by Women on 20s aimed to challenge male-centered patriarchal views of American history by framing the highlighting of exclusively men on monetary currency as a symptom of a national history that has systematically erased, marginalized, and ignored the contributions of women. The movement unsettles conventional narratives of American selfhood that center men. The group comments, "We believe this simple, symbolic and long-overdue change could be an important stepping stone for other initiatives promoting gender equality," noting, "Our money does say something about us, about what we value."[2]

That this movement to update the twenty-dollar bill unfolded as former First Lady, New York senator, and secretary of state Hillary Clinton was on the campaign trail in the effort to become the nation's first woman president, who made history by being selected as the first woman presidential nominee of a major political party, reinforces its resonances with historical struggles for equal rights and voting rights for women. It is all the more significant that the movement emerged against the backdrop of political movements for social justice such as #SayHerName, which is designed to confront the pervasive silence and invisibility in black communities related to black girls and women in narratives about police brutality focused on black boys and men, and to promote intersectional approaches to thinking about race, class, gender, and sexuality, clarifying ways in which the categories are intrinsically interlocked. Women on 20s suggested the value in intersectionality in the sense originated by critical race theorist Kimberlé Williams Crenshaw and advanced by scholars such as Patricia Hill Collins, which challenges conventional politics' exclusion of black women.[3]

To be sure, the racial and ethnic diversity of the initial finalists, which, in addition to nine white women, also includes five black women and an Asian woman, is noteworthy when considering perceptions of the feminist movement in the American mainstream as being white-centered, exclusionary, and indifferent to issues concerning black women and other women of color. This public campaign suggests how black women have shaped notions of American selfhood, notwithstanding their historical devaluation, marginality, and invisibility in the national context since antebellum slavery. That two black women, Tubman and Parks, symbols of freedom in the nation in the nineteenth and twentieth centuries, garnered two-thirds of the votes to make the final list is quite remarkable for registering the influence of black women in shaping American identity. Tubman's selection in the popular vote as the woman of choice to appear on the new version of the twenty-dollar bill not only underlines the potential of black women to help represent and define the nation in this day and time, but also demonstrates their long-standing legacy as national emblems and the public voices they have established in the national arena, dating back to the antebellum era.[4]

Critics of this gesture, however, underscore the bitter irony of printing Tubman's face on American money considering she was once a slave classified as property, while leaving in place the prevailing capitalist economy and its profiteering imperatives, which originated in the modern slave trade. That Tubman was not awarded until her death the monthly pension of twenty dollars to which she was entitled for her service in the Civil War is a concern for critics, along with the deeper implications given the spirit of her work as an abolitionist whose heroism freed many slaves via the Underground Railroad. In an era when paper currency is no longer used or circulated as widely in national and global financial markets, the political, social, economic, and cultural impact of the new bill featuring a woman, even while holding great symbolic significance, will be inherently limited.

As Salamishah Tillet points out in her landmark study *Sites of Slavery: Citizenship and Racial Democracy in the Post–Civil Rights Imagination*, blackness has been characterized by civic estrangement from the prevailing notions of citizenship and democracy that have been premised on black exclusion since slavery.[5] Nobel laureate Toni Morrison's critical insights underscore that ideals of freedom and democracy, which fed the spirit of the American Revolution and were later foundational to the philosophy of the nation as a republic, stressing individual rights such as life, liberty, and the pursuit of happiness, were informed by a visceral awareness of what slavery meant given the routine subordination and dehumanization of those categorized as black during the period. In the slave society of colonial America, blacks were regarded as other, inferior, and subhuman; were equated with slavery; and were fully dissociated from notions of freedom and citizenship in the emergent nation, though paradoxically, America would never have been developed without the labor black slaves provided. Morrison reminds us that the foundational definitions of the nation were intrinsically informed by the black condition during the Revolutionary War era.[6] While the constitutive role of black subjects in helping to shape foundational notions of liberty and freedom in the nation has been evident from the time when the United States crystallized as a republic, the black influence on these principles has sometimes been repressed, denied, or downplayed.

Conventional patriarchal national narratives have typically focused on white men as the nation's "founding fathers," such as George Washington and John Adams for being patriots of the American Revolution and the nation's first and second presidents, along with Thomas Jefferson for being the third president and the principal author of the Declaration of Independence. This term implies that the new nation was symbolically a family and inherently patriarchal. In a critical sense, the pioneering scholarship of Dana D. Nelson has clarified how "national manhood" has been essentially linked to white male subjectivity and premised on the exclusion of racial and ethnic others outside the category "white" while prioritizing material property and wealth as terms of inclusion. All women were by definition excluded from this ideal. The new nation established a hierarchy within its citizenry based on race, gender, class, and sexuality, with white male elites solidly positioned as the superior and legitimate subjects.[7]

Purist, nativist ideologies of American identity have failed to accord legibility to black women, including black queer and trans women, and other women of color. While no narratives of "founding mothers" figure as saliently in the national imagination as those related to the "founding fathers," and white women have typically been marginalized and excluded in these patriarchal narratives, stories related to figures such as Betsy Ross, who by legend is reputed to have sewn the first American flag, have nevertheless been passed down frequently throughout American history. In the earliest years of the American republic, figures such as Ross and Dolley Madison emerged as national emblems of American patriotism. Black women, however, are far less likely to be linked to the prevailing national narratives or to the nation's sense of selfhood and what it means to be a representative American woman. Blackness, like queerness, has been an inadmissible and unthinkable quality in defining universal or normative notions of American subjectivity and citizenship.[8] I believe these factors make Tubman's selection by Women on 20s quite significant.

This study explores ways in which black women leaders have unsettled the conventional white- and male-centered narratives of American selfhood through recurring scripts in the public sphere—in speeches and in writing, along with some of their most salient cultural representations—as nationally representative women and in relation to notions of national family, while using their platforms to challenge prevailing pathological images and narratives related to black motherhood and children. It clarifies how and why maternal motifs have so significantly inflected black women's representations in the public sphere and scripts linking them to notions of national identity. The conditions for this phenomenon were established during antebellum slavery.

Beginning in the colonial era, black women were made synonymous with slavery, classified as property, and primarily associated with labor, including the process of birthing and reproducing the slave class in their children, who legally inherited status as slaves through their black mothers in light of the famous legal precedent in Virginia in 1662, *partus sequitur ventrem*, stipulating that the condition of the child should follow that of the mother. As scholars from history to literature have pointed out, the labor of black women was exploited and appropriated within this system in both work and reproduction, and their bodies were placed under forced and frequently violent subjection, including beatings, rape, and concubinage, as assaults on the black maternal body within modernity.[9] This context of sexual exploitation, which frequently held black women as captives and hostages, mainly benefited white males, who dominated this inherently patriarchal slave system. The silencing and subjugation of black women, along with their sexual and physical abuse in servant roles, typified their condition within the domestic sphere, even as black women's labor was primarily consigned to fieldwork alongside men, where their bodies were also subjected to horrific and brutal forms of routinized physical and sexual violence and abuse.

As Hortense Spillers observes in her classic essay "Mama's Baby, Papa's Maybe," the assault on black flesh within the slave system led to an "ungendering" of people of African descent, so that masculine and feminine gender categories were unsettled under slavery's subjection, as the primacy of the maternal linkage for black children was established as a result of the uncertain paternal lineage that slavery inaugurated.[10] C. Riley Snorton has related such conditions within the slave system to gender mutability, linking blackness and transness since the antebellum era, while linking the abusive experiments on black women's bodies of J. Marion Sims within nascent gynecology to the racial assault on blackness and its mutuality with transness.[11] Sexual pathologies linked to black women within the antebellum slave system were premised on the idea of black womanhood as being lascivious, seductive, and wanton to rationalize their rape and physical abuse by slave masters.

Such perceptions were typically internalized by black women's white slave mistresses, who were more likely to react with jealousy and blame toward them for such circumstances than to recognize their victimization. At the same time, the reigning ideology of the nineteenth century for white bourgeois women, the Cult of True Womanhood, exalted elite white women for embodying the ideals of purity, piety, submissiveness, and motherhood. These tenets by definition excluded poor women, along with black women, who were vulnerable to sexual abuse through their subordination within the slave system and its ongoing assault on black maternity, and because they were not permitted to marry legally as slaves given their categorization as property.

The particular forms of race- and gender-based abuse of black women within the slave system and the effects on black mothering were graphically highlighted by Harriet Jacobs, writing under the pseudonym Linda Brent, in *Incidents in the Life of a Slave Girl*, the first slave narrative written by a black woman, in 1861, and published in the weeks before the Civil War began.[12] In fiction, Toni Morrison offers the most compelling and sustained literary examination of the assault of slavery on the black maternal body and its continuing trauma through her character Sethe in the novel *Beloved* (1987). It draws on the history of Margaret Garner, an escapee from slavery who took the life of her daughter to prevent her children's recapture by her former master.[13] The exploitation of the black maternal body was further evident in black women's roles as "mammies," who tended and served as wet nurses for the children of the master class, a practice that obliged them to prioritize the suckling and nurturing of white infants as the nutritional needs of their own babies went unmet.

Slavery conditioned the groundwork for the salience of the black maternal body in constructing black femininity in the nation's public sphere, for the better in emblems like Truth, and for worse in stereotypes such as the mammy. These material conditions make it all the more remarkable and exceptional that the voices of black women emerged in the national context through writings and speeches within abolitionist and feminist discourses during the antebellum era. Black women have typically been cast as the quintessentially abject, subordinate, excluded, and "other" category within the prevailing national narratives in the United States. That the short list by Women on 20s includes Truth and Tubman, who had experienced the traumas of slavery firsthand, among nationally significant American women, along with Tubman's victory in the popular vote in social media, point to ways in which black women subjects have helped to shape notions of American selfhood since the era of slavery.[14]

As a scholar who now lives and works near Auburn, New York, which is where Harriet Tubman lived for the last half century of her life, I gained valuable knowledge by going on the annual tour of Harriet Tubman National Historical Park, led by historian Margaret Washington, a site that includes Tubman's residential home and the residence for seniors she managed. The project culminates an initiative that was more than twenty years in the making. Like the Women on 20s project, this public initiative demonstrates the continuing investment in Tubman as a national and global symbol.[15]

The symbolic constructions of Truth and Tubman have served different purposes at different times. Both women share common ground in having escaped to freedom, working prominently within the abolitionist movement during the antebellum era, and working within the movements for black citizenship and women's rights after slavery. Truth and Tubman used their public platforms as black women to advocate for freedom and women's rights, which informed the national narratives that coalesced around them as symbolic

American women and their emergence as national icons after Emancipation. In both instances, epistemologies on freedom and womanhood mediated the national narratives that coalesced around them, and they emerged as beacons in defining black womanhood and as symbolic American women by the era of Emancipation, while expanding early foundations in black feminist thought and black women's intellectual history.

In establishing public voices and gaining national recognition as black women, they joined their predecessors, such as Phillis Wheatley, the first person of African descent and second woman to publish a book in colonial America, and Maria Stewart, who was free and the first black woman to give a public speech to a racially integrated audience. Black women who made foundational and pioneering contributions in developing genres that constitute African American literary history established conditions for the emergence of black women's voices in the nation's public sphere and foundations for the development of black feminist thought in the African diaspora. Such early representations of black women in this nation made them, at the very least, foremothers in the African American context, who influenced the political landscape by establishing pioneering public voices in their speeches and writings during the antebellum era and in early epistemologies linking freedom and literacy to black feminine subjectivity. They established important foundations for the recurrent invocations of black women in constructions of American national identity that I am examining in this study, those who might be thought of as their "daughters" and heirs apparent in a symbolic sense, who were birthed as free women to a world no longer shadowed by slavery, in which black women and their children could be categorized as property.

This book considers how black women national leaders in the political arena since Emancipation have recurrently invoked images of the nation as a family and cited maternal motifs and children in their public speeches and writings to challenge the conventional exclusion of blackness from definitions of America. In the process, they have provided counternarratives to prevailing pathological narratives established during slavery of the black maternal body and black families. They reconfigure black family and the black maternal body in the public sphere and restore intimacy with black children. The dominant themes in these women's works and cultural representations are important to recognize and analyze in African American literary and cultural history, not only for their salience but also because they attest to the profound political legacy that black women have created in the nation, while underscoring its significance for literary studies.

Even so, such cultural models of black womanhood are limited to replicating the rhetoric of family associated with conventional national narratives, including motifs related to mothers and children, which reinscribe heteronormativity and the alienation of black trans and queer women from scripts of blackness and American selfhood, preconditioning their marginality and exclusion. Moreover, such erasures obscure how black queer and trans subjects have constituted black women's iconicity since the antebellum era and risk mirroring the material forms of violence and annihilation to which black queer and trans bodies have been routinely subjected. Roderick A. Ferguson is among scholars whose research underscores the indispensability of sexuality, including "queer of color" analysis, in thinking about discrimination.[16] The legibility and inclusion of black queer and trans women is vital for reimagining the national body and actualizing a vision of the United States in which all black lives are visible, valued, and indeed truly matter.

The Shadow of Aunt Jemima

In 1892, when Anna Julia Cooper was a teacher and principal at M Street High School in the nation's capital, she boldly proclaimed in *A Voice from the South* that the status of blacks collectively in the nation was contingent on the inclusion of black women, famously stating: "Only the black woman can say 'when and where I enter, in the quiet, undisputed dignity of my womanhood, without violence and without suing or special patronage, then and there, the whole Negro race enters with me.'"[17] Ironically, the image of black womanhood gaining the most public exposure in the national arena during this period was popularized because of her body size and national nostalgia for the southern mammy, and was premised on not having a voice at all. In 1889, Chris L. Rutt and Charles G. Underwood developed the Aunt Jemima logo for their ready-made pancake flour mix at the Pearl Milling Company, a logo inspired by Billy Kersands's minstrel song "Old Aunt Jemima."[18] By the 1890s, Aunt Jemima emerged as the most prominent stereotypical symbol of black womanhood in the national arena.

The Aunt Jemima logo was grounded in the mammy myth that emerged in the antebellum era and was further consolidated after the Civil War through Old South plantation nostalgia and romance, which typically represented this figure as an eager servant and caretaker for her master's family, who loved and doted on his children. In visual representations, in keeping with the mammy stereotype, Aunt Jemima is typically plump and asexual, wearing a bandanna headscarf.[19] Nancy Green was the first of a series of black women to bring Aunt Jemima to life by portraying her flipping pancakes in an oversized flour barrel at the World's Columbian Exposition in Chicago, Illinois, in 1893. In effect, Aunt Jemima, in the context of this historic event, was scripted as a prominent national and global emblem of black femininity. This spectacle proved to be one of the most popular exhibits.[20]

The irony could not have been more bitter considering that blacks, including political leaders who desired to represent a broader spectrum of black history and cultural contributions in exhibits they had developed, were excluded, an oversight that seemed like a slap in the face given the political repression blacks increasingly faced in the nation at the time. The antilynching crusader Ida B. Wells famously protested against this exclusion.[21] During this reactionary period of growing political repression for African Americans in the years after Reconstruction, when lynchings were on the rise, along with white rioting, Wells stood at the forefront in mobilizing national organizations such as the black women's club movement to resist social, economic, and political repression against blacks.

Michael Borgstrom has recognized that among racial stereotypes represented in the black characters in Harriet Beecher Stowe's *Uncle Tom's Cabin* (1852), including Aunt Chloe as the mammy figure and her husband, Uncle Tom, the queer subjectivity of the body servant Adolph has remained invisible and unacknowledged. Borgstrom's insights throw into relief the role of queerness in constituting the marginal legibility of characters such as Adolph in the novel.[22] The mammy is not only inherently sexualized through her markings as asexual, but she has also been routinely sexualized through cross-dressing and cross-racial performances linked to queer practices, as witnessed in *Birth of a Nation* (1915).[23] Indeed, in the 1890s, Aunt Jemima heralded such queer cinematic visual embodiments of the mammy that were steeped in minstrelsy. When circulated as the Aunt Jemima trademark, the mammy was hyperembodied and popularized through invention and spectacled public performances before a white audience. To this day, her residual traces in matriarchal figures, from Martin Lawrence's Big Momma to Tyler Perry's Madea, are premised on embodying performative models of black trans womanhood that have gained widespread currency and iconicity in the nation's popular culture, even as black trans and queer women remain excluded from the prevailing national models of black womanhood, which are paradoxically premised on heterosexual identification. Queerness and transness have been foundational in constituting the mammy, including manifestations as Aunt Jemima, and saliently inflect her ideological embodiments in the national context, while black queer and trans women have remained voiceless and invisible within national models of black womanhood.

The most significant and ubiquitous popular manifestation of the plantation ideal of black servants who knew and stayed in their place, Aunt Jemima was tacitly apolitical and a signpost of black complicity with the emerging Jim Crow social order. The Aunt Jemima figure began to appear prominently on a host of items circulated in American material culture, including paper and rag dolls, sheet music, needle books, recipe books, placemats, paper napkins, dinnerware, coloring books, aprons, posters, buttons, cigarette lighters, letter openers, and so on.[24] In *Ceramic Uncles and Celluloid Mammies*, the folklorist Patricia A. Turner examines the lingering fascination with items along these lines, which she classifies as "contemptible collectibles" for their grotesque, exaggerated imaging of the black body steeped in racist stereotypes.[25]

In a compelling piece in the *Atlantic*, "The Mammy Washington Almost Had," Tony Horwitz begins by making the link between Aunt Jemima pancake mix and the mammy as he discusses the famous campaign to erect a monument in the U.S. capital in honor of mammy and as a paean to the figure authorized by the U.S. Senate in 1923 "in memory of the faithful slave mammies of the South."[26] The campaign was largely spearheaded by the United Daughters of the Confederacy and was grounded in myths of the Old South that romanticized the work of slave women on southern plantations, including their relationships to the white children for whom they cared, while extolling their devotion and subservience to white masters and mistresses. The goal was to locate the monument blocks away from the newly dedicated Lincoln Memorial. The initiative sparked intense outcry and protests from blacks, including black women leaders at the national level, such as Mary Church Terrell of the black women's club movement in the National Association of Colored Women (NACW), and was never completed. Significantly, Horwitz frames the opposition to the monument as a precursor to civil rights activism later in the twentieth century.

The enthusiastic campaigns to erect this monument to mammy, like the infamous Aunt Jemima display at the World's Columbian Exposition, dramatize long-standing and highly racialized conventional scripts of black femininity that have figured black women as abject, subordinate, and alien within the national imagination. The outcry against this monument also spoke to long-standing contestations and conflicts over national representations of black women. At the same time, this controversy over mammy anticipated later contestations and challenges that have emerged related to memorializing and monumentalizing black women linked to national politics.

The Quaker Oats Company, which had purchased and established the Aunt Jemima logo as a trademark in 1925, advertised its products through promotions such as painted hard plastic salt shakers, a syrup container, spice containers, and a sugar bowl and creamer featuring Aunt Jemima, along with a fictive husband named Uncle Mose, produced by the F&F Mold and Die Works in Dayton, Ohio, from the 1930s to the 1950s (figure I.1). Archival materials related to Aunt Jemima and the Quaker Oats Company, which I examined at Duke University's David M. Rubenstein Rare Book and Manuscript Library, reveal a concerted effort in advertising from decade to decade to adapt the trademark to a changing nation in terms of both gender and race, along with more racially inclusive representations of family. For example, Aunt Jemima advertisements of the 1950s mirrored the popular television images of the era, which romanticized domesticity by prominently featuring white nuclear families, idealizing white womanhood in relation to the home and promoting domestic ideals in the years after masses of American women had entered industries to work during World War II. Such idealizations were also evident in ads of the early 1960s proclaiming, "The lovin'est moms make Aunt Jemimas!" and "The huggin'est moms make Aunt Jemimas!," which visually decenter and erase her body and rely on recollecting her iconic image and voice.[27]

The advertisements seemed premised on southern nostalgia, depicting images of white families sitting at the breakfast table juxtaposed with pancake boxes featuring Aunt Jemima, alluding to the labor of black women as servants, even as white women were taking on their own domestic work and the ranks of black women as domestic laborers were shrinking statistically. Such contradictions reveal the continuing role of the black maternal body in mediating anxieties related to race, gender, and sexuality in this nation after World War II. These materials reveal that during the 1960s, the Aunt Jemima advertising campaigns became more inclusive, as black nuclear families were featured in some advertisements, a trend that mirrored cultural shifts toward racial integration during the civil rights era. The records indicate not only a shifting and expanding discourse on national family but also the fantasy of a more inclusive one. Such archives are important, too, when recognizing how easily Aunt Jemima is written out of histories of advertising that center whiteness when discussing the significance of women, despite her longevity as a logo and trademark.

FIGURE I.1 Aunt Jemima kitchen items by F&F Mold and Die Works. Photograph by Dave Burbank.

The salience of the Aunt Jemima in the final years of the nineteenth century established foundations for her ubiquity in stereotyping black women throughout the decades that followed. Rebecca Sharpless points out in *Cooking in Other Women's Kitchens: Domestic Workers in the South, 1865–1960* that the romance of the Aunt Jemima stereotype obscured the material conditions under which black women worked as domestics and cooks after Emancipation. It ironically romanticized work that black women in reality were thankful to have escaped once slavery ended, even as it continued to shadow their lives as paid laborers over the next decades. Sharpless observes, "Between emancipation in 1865 and the civil rights movement in the 1950s and 1960s, African American women did domestic work, including cooking, to earn wages and support their families, biding their time until better opportunities opened," which acknowledges how profoundly this work continued to define the material conditions of black women after slavery.[28] In 2014, Kara Walker's provocative installation at the Domino Sugar factory in Brooklyn, New York, *A Subtlety, or the Marvelous Sugar Baby*, had a large sphinx-like sculpture of a mammy figure as its centerpiece and pondered the roots of this mammy stereotype in slavery. Significantly, it confronts asexual depictions by highlighting the mammy's sexual erotics, also hinting at her queer performances, through the breasts and buttocks prominently displayed in its sphinx-like positioning, pondering its continuing cultural impact. This interactive sculpture resembled earlier images of Aunt Jemima donning a scarf and confronted its audiences with internalized racism and oppression related to such images.

Yet as critics such as Lauren Berlant have stressed, the size and ubiquity of the mammy figure on the marquee as hyperembodied and circulated as a commodity through fictive national brands, such as Aunt Delilah in the 1934 film *Imitation of Life*, while bearing the trace of Aunt Jemima, came with no power.[29] It paradoxically underscored her subordination and abjection because of her race, gender, and sexuality, including her lack of voice and agency.[30] Specularity at this level has foreclosed voice and power to the extent that disembodiment has been the prerogative of liberal individualism from the age of Enlightenment, as quintessentially embodied in white male subjects who were elite and propertied and who epitomized rationality, a narrative fueled by scripts linking blackness to slavery, dehumanization, and notions of intellectual inferiority.[31]

Despite Aunt Jemima's visual iconicity as a spectacle in advertising and her hyperembodiment, a raced and gendered stereotype such as the Aunt Jemima image registers the powerlessness, marginality, and silencing of black women and lack of legitimacy in representing the national body, given that her popularity and currency are premised on a spectacled body and visual iconicity as a national fantasy in the vein of mammy as a holdover from slavery, a time when the black woman's role as a servant who knew her "place" was idealized. These qualities signal a lack of subjectivity, linking the Aunt Jemima figure to what Karen Shimakawa theorizes as "national abjection."[32] The relegation of blackness to subhumanity within evolutionary biology of the nineteenth century, which analogized women to children in intelligence, coupled with an emerging eugenics by the end of that century, added to contexts for Aunt Jemima's abjection in the public mind. Indeed, in some ways, it was ironic that the iconicity of Aunt Jemima crystallized in a period during which domestic practices such as cooking were being regimented through discourses of math and science, though her appeal and expertise were correlated with folk wisdom rather than intellectual ingenuity.[33]

In this study, I examine what happens when black women are able to gain voice and legibility at the national level and assert their subjectivity, to the point that they challenge conventional stereotypes of black womanhood like Aunt Jemima, while expanding definitions of womanhood, motherhood, and American identity. I began my investigation of the lingering repercussions of raced and gendered stereotypes established in the antebellum South, including their role in creating race and gender formations at the national level, in my first book, *Black Masculinity and the U.S. South: From Uncle Tom to Gangsta* (2007), which explores how the discourses of Uncle Tom have frequently been nationalized and invoked to pathologize black masculinities both within and beyond the U.S. South; black masculinity is frequently associated with an urban ideal.[34] Similarly, Aunt Jemima has been legible as one of the most nefarious images of the black female body, and as one of the longest-running trademarks in American advertising history, a history that I have long studied and have previously discussed in published work such as my 2003 essay "Southern Turns," which draws on this Aunt Jemima image as a historical context for pondering the phenomenon of Miss Cleo, a black Florida woman promoted by two white male entrepreneurs to masquerade as a Caribbean psychic in the 1990s.

On June 17, 2015, a young white supremacist male, Dylann Roof, who heavily identified with racist and fascist symbols, attended a Bible study at the historic Mother Emanuel AME Church in Charleston, South Carolina, and took the lives of eight African American congregants and the minister, South Carolina state senator Rev. Clementa Pinckney. Confederate flags and related merchandise have been widely regarded as symbols of racism and hate by many African Americans and as a primary aspect of southern heritage and culture linked to Civil War ancestors among many white southerners. The emblems were the subject of widespread public discussion in the immediate aftermath of this tragedy and were rapidly removed from commercial circulation by many top companies. Public pressure also led to their removal from some federal and state buildings. In a bold act of civil disobedience, the Black Lives Matter activist Bree Newsome bravely climbed the flagpole and removed the Confederate flag from public display on the property of the South Carolina state house ten days after this tragedy.

In the days thereafter, I was invited to write an opinion piece for the *New York Times* on what other problematic symbols need to go besides the flag. My op-ed piece, "Can We Please, Finally, Get Rid of Aunt Jemima?," addresses the linkages between Aunt Jemima, the mammy figure of the Old South, lingering Confederate nostalgia, and southern racism. It raises questions about what is at stake in the lingering visibility of this antebellum stereotype for advertising pancakes, syrup, and other breakfast foods in the twenty-first century. It provided a media platform for me to engage some of my research concerns at the national level in the context of an urgent public debate.[35]

On May 25, 2020, George Floyd died in Minneapolis, Minnesota, at the hands of four police officers, including the white officer Derrick Chauvin, who used the controversial knee-on-neck method to restrain Floyd for nearly nine minutes while ignoring Floyd's pain and pleas of "I can't breathe." This horrific incident was the tipping point igniting Black Lives Matter protests across all fifty states and around the world. These protests, which were on a broader scale and more diverse than any in recent history, called for an end to such violence and for radical changes in policing. The public dialogue about symbols and monuments linked to racism also resurfaced, including concerns about the Confederate flag, leading organizations such as NASCAR to ban it from public display at their events and the Mississippi legislature to take a historic vote to remove it from the state flag.

In the midst of the protests and after the singer Kirby's TikTok video criticizing the Aunt Jemima brand went viral, PepsiCo, the owner of the Quaker Oats Company, revisited the trademark and announced the decision to retire it. In light of my 2015 op-ed, NBC Universal interviewed me on the issue of Aunt Jemima and featured my commentary linking the symbol to racism and notions of black inferiority on programs such as the *Today Show* and the *Nightly News*; that interview led to others that ultimately reached an audience of more than 1.5 billion people.[36] Within the long history of critiques of Aunt Jemima among scholars and artists, I am thankful to have had the opportunity to contribute to this public conversation and to have been among the most recent voices advocating for this symbol's removal.

Since the nineteenth century, gender ideologies of southern origins, from the black male as a rapist and the black female as mammy to the white male as a southern gentleman and the white female as the southern lady and southern belle, have helped to constitute heteronormative national discourses on masculinity and femininity. Manhood and masculinity have been topics of increasing interest in studies of the U.S. South in recent years, to the point that numerous monographs and anthologies have been published in the field. The critical and theoretical work on masculinity and manhood that emerged in the 1990s, energized by developments in women's studies; queer, gay, and lesbian studies; cultural studies; critical theory; and critical race theory, fed the development of gender studies while advancing this field toward institutionalization. The U.S. South, even in our time, constitutes some of the prevailing representations of femininity in the cultural imagination, which also needs to be increasingly studied.

In this book, I am invested in examining the region's typically unacknowledged role in constituting black feminine models that have gained national iconicity in political contexts. The critical contributions that I am making in the current project continue my work to help expand the understanding of geography in shaping race and gender categories in this nation, with an emphasis on femininity. It adds to the growing body of scholarship on intersections between gender and region as related to women that has developed in fields such as southern history and southern literature and that has often been grounded in feminist frameworks.[37] This book also contributes to the growing critical enterprise focused on the U.S. South, gender, and sexuality. It adds to these conversations through its focus on femininity within a national framework. Dislodging femininity from any essentialist definitions, I frame it as a social construct and as performative. By examining questions related to the influence of black femininity on the national body, and acknowledging the marginalization of black and trans women in shaping them, this new study builds on my research project on black masculinity in the effort to expand epistemologies related to the effects of the U.S. South on processes of race, gender, and sexuality formation in the nation.

Because of its reliance on slave labor to sustain its primarily agricultural economy, the U.S. South was the region positioned at the forefront in developing and advancing slavery as a legalized and socially sanctioned institution in the nation during the antebellum era. The institution of slavery has also accorded the U.S. South a salient role in engendering, articulating, and legally defining black women as raced and gendered subjects. The mammy and her manifestations in figures such as Aunt Jemima, like Uncle Tom, is an ideological byproduct of the culture of plantation slavery in the antebellum South. Aunt Jemima epitomizes the fashioning of black women's subjectivity as an abject emblem of the national body. It is important to recognize this image, one of the most long-standing and familiar stereotypes of black femininity in the United States, as part of the ongoing pathologization of the black maternal body within the history of slavery and modernity and as one of its most accessible, salient, and ubiquitous public embodiments in American material cultural, beginning in the last decade of the nineteenth century and persisting to the present day. Aunt Jemima's serviceability and familiarity as one of the most egregious and grotesque emblems of the black feminine body was reinforced throughout the twentieth century by a range of other representations steeped in pathological invocations of the black maternal body in the nation's public sphere.

The Aunt Jemima stereotype is just one of the earliest illustrations of how the mammy figure established foundations for recurring citations of pathological images of the black maternal body throughout the twentieth century. These images have been central in mediating public dialogues about black women, to the point of affecting political policymaking, as evidenced in the Senate's endorsement of the initiative of the United Daughters of the Confederacy to enshrine a monument to mammy in 1923 in the nation's capital to celebrate her legacy of servitude spanning back to slavery. New twists on pathological representations of the black maternal body that built on this ubiquitous mammy stereotype were propagated roughly every generation. By the 1950s, amid the Great Migration to the urban North and growing poverty and crime in black communities resulting from deindustrialization, the matriarch emerged as an outgrowth of the mammy stereotype as the reigning pathological emblem of the black maternal body.

Patricia Hill Collins classifies the mammy and the matriarch among the primary "controlling images" of black women that proliferated in twentieth-century cinema designed to pathologize black motherhood. As she points out, "While the mammy typifies the Black mother in white homes, the matriarch symbolizes the mother figure in Black homes. Just as the mammy represents the 'good' Black mother, the matriarch symbolizes the 'bad' Black mother. The modern Black matriarchy thesis contends that African American women fail to fulfill their traditional 'womanly' duties."[38] Playwright Lorraine Hansberry offers what is perhaps the most redemptive portrait of the matriarch in her characterization of the long-suffering Lena Younger in her critically acclaimed 1959 play *A Raisin in the Sun*.

In 1965, Senator Daniel Patrick Moynihan famously framed the matriarch, in light of the proliferation of women-headed households, as the reason for the emasculation of black men, the delinquency of black children, and the dissolution of the black family in urban contexts, along with its dysfunction, revealing the salience of this stereotype in shaping national dialogues and public policy related to black families and its ubiquity in pathologizing black womanhood. In the 1980s, continuing investments in pathologizing black mothers at the national level were evident when the neoconservative Republican right wing popularized references to young black women on forms of government assistance, such as Aid for Families with Dependent Children, as "welfare queens," correlating the pervasiveness of out-of-wedlock births among black mothers and the absence of fathers in the home with an increase in crime and violence among black youth.

In Wahneema Lubiano's compelling essay "Black Ladies, Welfare Queens, and State Minstrels," she elaborates on how this reactionary ideological climate, animated by raced and gendered black stereotypes, affected constructions of law professor Anita Hill and Clarence Thomas during their testimony at the Senate Judiciary hearings in 1991, held after Thomas's nomination to the Supreme Court, regarding her allegations against him for sexual harassment. Lubiano emphasizes that the U.S. public sphere has most often been volatile and precarious for black female subjects and a context in which the notion of the "black lady" embodied by Hill was unfamiliar and unintelligible.[39] In the early 2000s, references to the "baby mama" in the political mainstream, which appropriate black slang among some black men to refer to the mothers of their children to whom they are not married, have been invoked by political reactionaries to emphasize the decline of marriage in black communities and to critique and pathologize black single mothers and fathers, along with their children. Most famously, when Barack Obama was on the campaign trail for president in 2008, Fox News invoked this term to refer to his wife, Michelle Obama, as a strategy for linking them to the stereotypes of black relationships as being noncommittal and common law and of black families, including black mothers and fathers, as being dysfunctional and inherently pathological. Such newer representations of black women as "welfare queens" and "baby mamas" accord with Collins's description of "controlling images" of black motherhood "portraying black women as stereotypical mammies, matriarchs, welfare recipients and hot mommas."[40] Terrion L. Williamson affirms the value of exploring these images within black feminist practice.[41]

Black women entering public life are inevitably shadowed by this history and challenged to create alternative and more agential scripts of the black woman subject. While Aunt Jemima is a familiar example of the conventional stereotypical imaging of black women in the national context, this book examines the role of black feminine models across multiple Souths that have posed a challenge to conventional exclusionary national narratives premised on white identity, including white femininity. The pathological representations of black womanhood elaborated here provide vital contexts and foundations for analyzing how the South in the broadest conceptual sense has functioned as a primary backdrop for black women's repetitive significations in relation to the national body, building on and extending cultural motifs that were established during the antebellum era by black women abolitionists such as Truth and Tubman. Aunt Jemima emerged by the end of the nineteenth century as a national brand and became the most ubiquitous and visible symbol of an abject and subordinate black womanhood in the national imaginary. Her glaring specularity was an ironic signpost and a harbinger of a more inclusive and complex representational politics of black womanhood, which increasingly defined this category in the modern national arena but was nevertheless premised on black queer and trans women's exclusion, as well as limiting the legibility of such subjects.

Black National Femininities

Precursors such as Truth and Tubman under the banners of suffragist and abolitionist movements provide valuable foundations for thinking about the litany of black women who have emerged as national icons in the twentieth century and into the new millennium of the twenty-first. The black female body has conventionally been ascribed low symbolic capital and has been marked as undesirable in defining and representing the national body, or else has been circulated as a primary marker of abjection and subjection, as we have seen in Aunt Jemima, along with related pathological images that distort black maternity. As Melissa Harris-Perry points out in her poignant study *Sister Citizen: Shame, Stereotypes, and Black Women in America*, the status of black womanhood in the United States has been continually associated with marginality, devaluation, and exclusion.[42] It is also important to examine ways in which black women leaders have developed counternarratives to abject constructions of black female identities premised on the subjection of the black maternal body. Monolithic, homogenizing, and reductive scripts of the black feminine as being always already nationally abject, outside, and othered obscure the ways in which black women have consistently challenged, unsettled, and ruptured conventional notions of national femininity and the national body. Familiar ideological images such as Aunt Jemima have functioned as the obverse of the representations that I examine in this study, in which I highlight black women as representative emblems of the national body.

Several fundamental questions energize this study: What happens in moments when the script is flipped, and black women emerge as central and even primary representatives of the national body? What happens when black female subjects move to front and center in shaping significations of America at the national level, to the point of transforming, expanding, deconstructing, and rescripting conventional narratives of American selfhood? What is the potential for subversion in moments when black women gain access to national platforms? How radically might we reconceptualize notions of the national body and expand its familiar definitions by scrutinizing the interstitial and compressed spaces where black women emerge within America's scripts of national femininity, renewing, realigning, and revising them? How might we identify models of black female subjectivity that potentially intrude on or disrupt the conventional national narratives that repress and exclude black women and privilege whiteness, by recognizing black women's historical symbolic impact in shaping them? What are the limitations in iconic models of black womanhood that have infiltrated national politics, come to voice, and been most visible? What potential do black queer and trans women hold to further unsettle and disrupt white- and male-centered representations by engendering a more radical, subversive, and inclusive model of black female subjectivity in the public sphere, and to make American scripts more democratic, beyond heteronormativity?

Emancipation's Daughters illustrates how consistently black women have challenged scripts of American identity premised on notions of black otherness through black women's framing as representatives of the national body. *National body* is one of those terms invoked frequently but seldom defined. For my purposes in this study, I define the national body as the collective U.S. citizenry in all its diverse contours as shaped, for example, by race, class, gender, nationality, region, and sexuality, whose human rights are invoked in the abstract and legally protected by the Constitution while being linked to the definition of democracy, even as subjects who contradict its tacitly white and masculine prerogatives are often classified and perceived as noncitizens, systemically alienated from the reigning national ideals, and work to deconstruct the premises underlying them. At the same time, the term affirms the agency of those who are legally excluded from or invisible within notions of American citizenship. The national body is often magnified and epitomized by prominent representatives of the collective citizenry and emblematized in the form of their literal bodies. It consists of citizens who are unseen and invisible, to the point of disembodiment altogether, as much as it is conceivably emblematized, and indeed, epitomized, through such ubiquitous and abstracted iconic figurings.

Concomitantly, this study challenges scripts of representative raced and gendered groups within the category black as male, highlighting the primacy of black women's voices and their salience to definitions of blackness. This study throws into relief ways in which black women leaders have consistently invoked black families, including black mothers and children, to frame blacks as being representative Americans and, in the process, have related them to notions of national family in their political speeches and writings. Such alternative scripts of the black mother unsettle the mammy myth. In the shadow of the Aunt Jemima stereotype and later ideological images such as the matriarch, which informed and mediated black women's representations in the public sphere, I consider alternative scripts and counternarratives of black womanhood that have linked blackness to notions of national family and framed black women as representative women while variously invoking them as national mothers. They are compelling from my perspective as a literary scholar and cultural critic to the extent that they envision more inclusive narratives of American selfhood and challenge ones that are premised on black exclusion, otherness, and pathology.

I examine how black women leaders in their speeches and writings, alongside many of their cultural representations, have consistently scripted black women as emblems of the national body not only in the realm of politics. At the same time, this motif is also important to recognize and think about in relation to African American literary and cultural history. I consider the manifestations of this motif as it has played out in a range of periods since Emancipation and within what some scholars frame as the long history of slavery, including the eras of the Depression, civil rights, post–civil rights within neoconservatism, and the early twenty-first century, dominated by notions of postblackness and the postracial. In these moments, Mary McLeod Bethune, Rosa Parks, Condoleezza Rice, and Michelle Obama, in differing ways, have all magnified contestations about black womanhood in relation to the national body and national family. Moreover, it is intriguing that rhetoric of the maternal is a common thread despite divergent political positionings associated with black women at the national level, which all challenge and unsettle pathologies of the black maternal body.

Just as the women's movement, beginning in the antebellum era, established the groundwork for constituting black women ex-slaves such as Truth and Tubman as national icons by the postbellum era, national black women's organizations, beginning with the black women's club movement, provided the earliest and most salient platforms on which black women became visible in the national political arena in the era after Emancipation. Black women's organizations were also pivotal in helping to challenge stereotypical representations by expanding the visibility of black women at the national level, beyond stereotypes sanctioned in contexts such as advertising, through the emphasis in organizations such as the National Council of Negro Women on establishing a voice in politics. Moreover, black women whom I examine in this study have primarily emerged as the most striking embodiments of U.S. identity in the public sphere and have been constituted in relation to major historical moments, including the New Deal of the Depression era, the civil rights era, neoconservatism, and the Obama era.

An outgrowth of the NACW, the National Council of Negro Women played a vital role in the national legibility of Mary McLeod Bethune, who emerged as a premier black woman leader during the Depression and was at the forefront in representing the voices of black women politically in the years leading up to the beginning of the modern civil rights era, which was inaugurated with the *Brown v. Board of Education* decision in 1954. Rosa Parks was articulated as a national icon of femininity during the civil rights era that followed. This terrain for black feminine subjects to signify in this sense was expanded through major legislative and legal hurdles such as the *Brown v. Board of Education* case in 1954, the Civil Rights Act of 1964, and the Voting Rights Act of 1965. By the post–civil rights era, the rise of second-wave feminism and the increasing cultural influence of black feminism measurably expanded this space. Rice gained prominence as a black woman at the national level through the right-wing conservatism of the early millennium. Michelle Obama has been its most salient signifier since the age of Obama began with her husband's election as president. In all instances, black women's national iconicity has been mediated by epistemologies related to freedom and civil rights. The growth of mass communications from the modern period, including television and video, expanded the space for disseminating and proliferating iconic narratives linking black women to national femininity, just as the rise of the internet and social media in more recent years has expanded the space for disseminating such representations exponentially and pluralizing notions of the public sphere.

I believe that we need to grapple with the significant body of work produced by these black women in speeches and writings. I regard them as cultural texts, all the more important to examine given that they have typically been overlooked within and excluded from dialogues in African American literature and have not been legible within its conventional canons. Increasingly, scholarship on race and class within areas such as black women's history and black women's literature and criticism has established foundations for my discussion in this study. Indeed, my work would be inconceivable without the pioneering contributions made by writers and critics within the black women's literary renaissance of the 1970s, women who prioritized the teaching and study of black women's literary history and explored black women's texts across multiple genres, while challenging exclusionary politics of mainstream feminism by grounding their work in black feminist methodologies, which emphasized interlocking variables that shaped black women's oppression in addition to gender, such as race, class, sexuality, and nationality.[43]

The discourses related to these figures have contested the reigning ideological images of black womanhood and black maternity that have been dominant in the nation's public sphere, including the mammy, matriarch, welfare queen, and "baby mama," which have emerged over the past century. This study throws this highly exceptional, seldom remarked on, and relatively invisible if consistent economy of black feminine representation into relief through a sustained critical discussion of figures that I consider across its chapters. Such black feminine representations have been serviceable across the liberal and conservative political spectrum, from Democratic to Republican, which is one reason that I consider in some cases, such as Condoleezza Rice's, both the liberatory and highly reactionary purposes they have variously served, along with the varied critiques and responses they have engendered.

My longtime studies of transnational feminism, nationalism, and nations have been indispensable as I have developed this project and established the conceptual groundwork for my critical reflections related to national identity, national femininity, and national family. This journey began with anthologies such as Chandra Talpade Mohanty, Ann Russo, and Lourdes Torres's *Third World Women and the Politics of Feminism* and Inderpal Grewal and Caren Kaplan's *Scattered Hegemonies: Postmodernity and Transnational Feminist Practices*.[44] Women who have become models of what I am describing as *national femininity* have typically made a profound social, cultural, and political impact at the national level through their leadership and pioneering contributions and, in some instances, have been linked to political movements and activism that helped to bring about social change. It is significant that the civil rights movement, public offices, and work in presidential administrations are primary contexts in which the symbolic capital of the women under investigation has been registered, affirmed, and acknowledged in national politics.

In invoking the term *national femininity*, I refer to how the national influence of such distinguished public and political women establishes conditions for their abstraction, in their singularity, as representatives and emblems of the national body in the public sphere, a representation that also sometimes extends to popular contexts. The term describes women who have gained the highest level of iconicity and visibility in politics, along with the highest degree of symbolic capital, which enables them to become legible to the collective citizenry as emblems of the nation itself, while being imagined and idealized as representatives of the national body and correlated with prevailing democratic ideals. In some instances, such significations have crystallized in the national imaginary for a brief period, but they also hold the potential to endure and to be reconstituted and sustained over time. Individual bodies of such women sometimes become emblems and symbolic representatives of the larger national body. They at times achieve salience in the political arena to the point that it even becomes possible to fantasize the face of such a woman as the face of nation. The diverse slate of candidates set forth by the Women on 20s movement provides prime examples of women who have made landmark contributions that have affected the nation so profoundly that all of them are thought worthy of representation once the currency is updated to include women in the future.[45]

As Benedict Anderson famously argued, the nation is an "imagined political community."[46] The idea of the nation has often been imagined as feminine and referred to with pronouns such as *her*, or adjectivally linked to the maternal. The feminine has been both romanticized and prioritized in embodying the nation as a formation, in keeping with typical representations of nationhood. This has been the norm in the United States even as women have been definitionally excluded from top leadership roles and primarily linked to the private sphere rather than the realm of public affairs. Such conventional national narratives that center women in this nation's definitions are typically premised on women's subjection rather than their empowerment. Postcolonial theory has raised questions about what is at stake in metaphors of the nation that link femininity to the land, which are premised on colonial and imperial perceptions of women as sites of conquest, subordination, and domination.[47]

In *Diana and Beyond: White Femininity, National Identity, and Contemporary Media Culture*, Raka Shome provides valuable critical insights on the salience of white femininity in authenticating national identity by examining the role of whiteness in the iconicity of Princess Diana of Wales and fueling the public fascination with her in national and global contexts, noting that women who are not white and Western and who are immigrant are unlikely to be idealized in the vein of the princess as a royal. Shome's study is indispensable for its sustained comparative critique of the role of white femininity in constructing national identity in the contemporary era in contexts such as

Britain and the United States. As she points out, "White femininity is a nationalized category that is always already imbricated in the production of various borders and boundaries—of gender, race, sexuality, class, globality—in the staging of a nation's sense of the modern."[48]

Shome is quite right in underscoring "the primacy of white womanhood in national scripts."[49] In advancing these claims, however, she fails to recognize black women's capacity to embody national identity in the United States on their own terms and in ways that do not simply mirror and reflect white women's subjectivity to account for the moments when women of color gain legibility at the national level, notwithstanding her study's significant critical contribution to areas such as feminist studies, transnational feminism, and whiteness studies. That is to say, Shome frames all "black female icons" who gain legibility at the national level, including Michelle Obama, as a manifestation of how "neoliberal logics of race today often articulate privileged black women through scripts of privileged white femininity."[50] Shome's reading reduces black women's iconic legibility in the national arena to the capacity to mimic behaviors, values, and aesthetics associated with white womanhood, which elides black women's specificity and casts them as appendages of whiteness delinked from larger, more complex histories and more nuanced and intricate cultural politics. The logic recalls the notion of "colonial mimicry" described by Homi Bhabha.[51] Moreover, it is a perspective that fails to consider the concerted ways in which black women have challenged and expanded exclusionary definitions of American subjectivity.

I find the reductive premise that only whiteness has the capacity to define the national body to be as limited as the presumption that black women are constrained to the space of the abjected other in the cultural imagination. This study rejects both sets of assumptions. My study departs from such logic in providing a sustained discussion of ways in which black women have repeatedly unsettled conventional significations of national identity in the United States and become legible within such national definitions *on their own terms*.

In acknowledging how constructions of the nation have been inherently raced and gendered with an emphasis on white femininity, it is also important to frame the prioritization of white womanhood in constituting national identity within larger dynamics of colonialism and imperialism in relation to idealizations of southern femininity in the U.S. national imaginary. I refer to the purist ideology of American identity and white femininity that is anchored in white supremacy and notions of black women's racial inferiority and otherness. In early Hollywood cinema, southern womanhood was also repeatedly invoked as a national ideal, as illustrated in the portrayal of Lillian Gish in *Birth of a Nation*. Significantly, this film frames the North and South as symbolic brothers through its primary male heroic figures, who were separated by the tragedy of the Civil War, along with their contestations over blacks, who had divided the union, a national family to which blacks did not belong and in which they had no place except one of inferiority. This narrative of white womanhood continues to be evident in contemporary cinematic scripts of white southern actresses such as Julia Roberts, Reese Witherspoon, and Jessica Simpson as "America's sweetheart."[52] Yet they are also tied to naturalized representations of southern femininity as abject and in relation to notions of the southern landscape. The U.S. South's historical racialist ideology of white supremacy typically exalted white southern womanhood as a symbol of the region's purity, premised on an essentialist and naturalized view of southern women as an extension of the region's landscape, in some cases drawing on the pastoral.[53]

Conventional notions of national femininity that conflate whiteness and womanhood have been premised on the debasement and subjection of black women through race, class, gender, and sexuality. Such narratives that foreground black women as nationally representative subjects have reconfigured and expanded conventional notions of the national body that prioritize whiteness and masculinity, or that at best imply that only white women can be legitimate national symbols. In the process, what I call *black national femininities* emerge and rupture prevailing white-centered notions of American identity, yielding a postwhite narrative of the national body and national femininity, creating an epistemology of national selfhood through a black and feminine lens, disrupting the conventional raced, classed, sexed, and gendered notions of the national body, embodying the black female subject as the quintessential national, hemispheric, and global subject.

Recurrent scripts of black female subjectivity in relation to the national body, including scripts of black women as representative subjects within the nation's prevailing discourses of national femininity, provide vital contexts and foundations for analyzing how the South has functioned as a primary backdrop for black women's repetitive significations in the U.S. public sphere. This is the backdrop against which it is necessary to consider how and why the region has been interpolated saliently and recurrently in the nationalization of black feminine subjects in the United States, who also frequently become global icons. The phenomenon I am describing is traceable from the twentieth century into the new millennium and has had a profound if seldom recognized influence in unsettling and critiquing the prevailing notions of national femininity in the United States, including notions of national family. Because black queer and trans women have been left out of these iconic narratives of black femininity, which have typically been premised on heterosexist motifs, including their prevailing tropes of family, these subjects reveal the limitations in these scripts and hold potential to fully radicalize and disrupt national narratives premised on whiteness and maleness.

In *On Racial Icons: Blackness and the Public Imagination*, Nicole Fleetwood examines "how we—as a broad American public—fixate on certain images of race and nation, specifically the black icon," explaining "the significance of the racial icon to public life."[54] She is invested in considering "public images that are normative to our understanding of race in the United States; these are images that have a commonsense meaning to them in terms of the national imaginary and a broad public's familiarity with them," and ways in which black bodies are visualized in processes of "narrating the nation."[55] Her work is significant for my purposes in affirming the agency of black subjects in narrating and representing the nation. It is subversive when black women, conventionally denied visibility and voice in the nation's public sphere, emerge as subjects in the political arena and act and frame themselves as nationally representative citizens. Discourses related to them provide a counternarrative to notions of black women's abjection and expand opportunities to advance civil rights and more expansive, inclusive, and visionary notions of freedom, democracy, and human rights. During the 1990s, cultural offerings from films like Jennie Livingston's *Paris Is Burning* (1990), which showcased black urban drag balls in Harlem, to the rise of RuPaul underscored the salience of black queer and trans women in constituting and expanding the iconicity of black femininity in the national arena through their performance practices. The contemporary public appeal of black lesbian women such as Robin Roberts and Wanda Sykes, along with trans women such as Janet Mock and Laverne Cox, affirms their influence in shaping the national narrative and complicates conventional representations of black womanhood. This is another reason that their status is essential to acknowledge in constituting black women's iconicity in the nation, along with black and queer women's invisibility within models of national femininity.

The foregrounding of platforms and policies advocating for children by national models of black femininity hold potential to restore intimacies shattered within slavery and help make them visible in the public arena. They challenge and provide a counternarrative to notions of "infantile citizenship" within the reactionary politics that Lauren Berlant discusses in *The Queen of America Goes to Washington City: Essays on Sex and Citizenship*.[56] The insights that she offers in this study, including her collaborative dialogue with Elizabeth Freeman on the Queer Nation political movement, also importantly shapes my perspective on envisioning black queer and trans women as subjects who hold potential to fully revolutionize articulations of American selfhood. Such critical contexts help clarify how productively and subversively the recurring motifs invoking the maternal, along with children and family, have mediated black women's public voices within civil rights and political discourses designed to redress the benign neglect and abuse of populations of children, including black youth, who have been and remain some of the most vulnerable and marginal citizens under the purview of the state. At the same time, they help distinguish such platforms from those within the dominant culture that weaponize narratives sacralizing childhood to reinforce and recast the heteronormativity within conventional national narratives and advance reactionary political agendas. Similarly, black queer and trans identities throw into relief limitations in foregrounding the feminine, including the maternal, in fashioning notions of national identity.

In general, my goal is not to offer a comprehensive or historical overview of all black women who conceivably affected national femininity over the past century. I also believe that it is important to raise questions about what is at stake in embodiments of national femininity through black female subjectivity that have materialized in the public sphere precisely during an era of neoliberalism, when multinational corporate conglomerates hold shares of economic power that rival those of conventional nation-states, and the United States, in the midst of globalization, no longer as singly signifies power within this geopolitics. How does national femininity manifest and remain relevant at all, even, at a time when the idea of the nation-state has been increasingly deterritorialized and destabilized, to the point of becoming an obsolete formation less relevant in shaping identity and mediating cultural flows and exchanges?

While the representations I examine in this study accord black female subjectivity more legibility and centrality and recurrently invoke black women in relation to notions of national motherhood beyond the realm of conventional stereotypes such as the mammy, it is noteworthy that in their varied articulations and manifestations, they are also consistently premised and centered on the black feminine body's hypervisibility and iconicity in the national arena. This phenomenon becomes more understandable when considering Karla FC Holloway's observation that within the nation's "body politic," "black women's bodies metaphorically represent the conflicted presence of gender and race within America's cultural history."⁵⁷ This work is grounded in and reflects my own intellectual investments and training in the fields of literary studies and cultural studies and aims to scrutinize the common ground within the discourses of these women on narratives that all of them have produced related to the maternal tacit in their own writing and speeches and also concomitantly in some of their most prominent constructions in cultural contexts.

Hemispheric Souths/Africana Souths

The new southern studies, an interdisciplinary critical movement, was initially defined by Houston A. Baker Jr. and Dana D. Nelson in 2001.⁵⁸ It challenges and unsettles the conventional approaches in southern studies, including binaries associated with the region, such as North and South, while expanding its archives for study and research in areas such as literature and culture. A cornerstone of the interdisciplinary field of the new southern studies, one of the research areas in which I have primarily worked, has been a move away from conventional geographies and temporalities for defining the South in the United States.⁵⁹

I believe that methods of the field provide a toolbox of perspectives that are all the more important, indispensable, and relevant to draw on to grapple with the region's historical legacies, along with ways in which reactionary southern agendas continue to influence the national political arena, including regressive policy agendas, and in some instances, help promote white supremacy and white nationalism. As the 2015 Charleston tragedy and its underlying causes of racism and hate reveal, the U.S. South will continue to be a salient point of reference in grappling with intersectional identities of African Americans and other members of the black diaspora, as well as a crucial terrain for advancing activist movements, from Black Lives Matter to #SayHerName, as we saw in the heroic protest of Bree Newsome. Indeed, not recognizing such vital connections risks reinscribing ideologies of the postracial and postblackness premised on colorblindness, while obscuring black intellectual and protest histories, including aspects of black radical thought that have informed such scholarship and political movements, rather than views of southern literature and history that romanticize and whitewash the region.

After the coronavirus pandemic that broke out in late 2019 and led to widespread infections and deaths around the globe, President Donald Trump tacitly invoked the ideology of states' rights in allowing U.S. governors to make decisions about approaches to the crisis rather than leveraging his authority to marshal federal emergency resources. The slowness of governors in the South to mandate the social distancing measures and lockdowns that could slow the spread of the virus and protect public health—along with premature plans to lift these measures to revive the economy even as the poor, African Americans, and other people of color experienced disproportionately high rates of infection and death—was also a clear and troubling manifestation of this ideology. These issues doubly illustrate why we can ill afford to deny the realness of southern identity and its connections to such struggles in this day and time or to dismiss identity concerns for minorities in the region. Reimagining southern identities as now obsolete or nonexistent fails to acknowledge such material conditions and is steeped in political escapism.

While Baker's legendary contributions in black studies and African American literary studies are well known, including ways in which he has helped to position African American literature more centrally within American literary studies, his pivotal contributions in areas such as southern literary studies are also significant. He has truly been a top beacon for numerous scholars, demonstrating possibilities for bridging areas such as black studies and southern studies, and African American literature and southern literature, a method that challenges conventional presumptions within the field, which marginalize and alienate black texts and black bodies (to echo Barbara Christian), while emphasizing the indispensability of African American literature and the black text specifically in southern literature and in southern studies more generally. In the process, Baker's intellectual project also broadened the space for critique and reflection in areas such as black southern literature and the black South. It built on interventions by John Oliver Killens and Jerry Ward.

I have valued and learned from the work of a new generation of scholars who study such South(s) from a critical and cultural standpoint, including Regina Bradley, Sharita Johnson, Jarvis McInnis, Julius Fleming Jr., Zandria Robinson, Delia Steverson, Maurice Hobson, and Brittney Cooper, along with the foundational contributions of scholars such as bell hooks, Trudier Harris, Thadious Davis, Hortense Spillers, Imani Perry, Farah Jasmine Griffin, Robin D. G. Kelley, and Tera Hunter, among others. Moreover, I have valued the work of scholars in the field, such as E. Patrick Johnson, Sharon Holland, and Zandria Robinson, who have stood at the forefront in advancing critical dialogues on black southerners and queerness.

In more recent years, studies of the Global South have emphasized political, social, and economic conditions linked to populations in the Southern Hemisphere, including African, Caribbean, Latin American, and Asian contexts. This critical work addresses the intensified flows of capital and culture in an era of globalization, eschews the prioritization of a nation-state such as the United States as a term of analysis, and grapples with the poverty of populations that are indigenous and predominantly located in the Southern Hemisphere, from Asia to Africa and the Americas, that have been inordinately affected by the West's hegemonic hoarding of wealth and resources. Comparative and interdisciplinary approaches and methodologies informed by areas such as postcolonial American studies and new world studies have enabled scholars in the new southern studies to take up the challenge that discourses on the Global South pose to move away from the essentialist borders that have conventionally circumscribed the South and North in the United States. At the same time, such critical approaches recognize the historical influence of these larger global geographies in constituting the U.S. South and examine continuities in development across these regions, making legible how the U.S. South's history of occupation in the United States in the years after the Civil War establishes the region as a postcolonial landscape. The U.S. South emerges within transnational and diasporic frameworks as just one conceivable Global South within a continuum of many others in the Americas, Africa, Asia, and Europe.

Dialogues on the Global South have also provided foundations for critical work on the hemispheric South, which acknowledges the influence of multiple Souths in shaping the Western Hemisphere while resisting colonialist and imperialist narratives premised on the singularity and ubiquity of the United States in defining this region. According to Carl Gutiérrez-Jones, "While the concept of the Hemispheric South suggests a move away from the nation-state as a primary unit of critical analysis, it also intends to foreground the manner in which imperial, colonial, and nationalist projects, along with predatory forms of capitalism, have shaped definitions of hemispheric 'Southernness' in terms of unique poverty (including constructions of indigeneity and the rural), wealth (including natural resources, beauty), and culture (including ideas of authenticity)."[60] Furthermore, Gutiérrez-Jones points out that this body of critical thought examines "the multiple realities, knowledge systems, migrations, and intellectual border crossings associated with 'southernness' in the Americas, especially as these dynamics contribute to articulations of the Americas as part of the 'Global South.'"[61] Discourses on the hemispheric South help us to recognize the magnitude of southern slavery's impact on modernity and to think about the effects of the plantation complex in the Western Hemisphere with more depth and complexity.

As Global South discourses have developed within the new southern studies, they have looked at the plantation as a context endemic to the materialist development and dispersal of the transatlantic slave system and foundational to how its labor economy has proliferated throughout the Western Hemisphere over several centuries. Global South discourses facilitate the comparative study of the plantation's dispersals in the U.S. South and throughout other sites in the Caribbean and Central and South America, along with the Canadian context. This work has also helped to expand the theoretical understanding of the influence of geography on identity, including the effects on race, gender, and sexuality formations. These dynamics have been understood far better in recent years as the region has been increasingly examined within transnational and diasporic frameworks as just one historical Global South within a dialectic of many others in the Americas, Africa, Asia, and Europe. The expansive plantation complex iterated across the Western Hemisphere within the temporalities and spatialities of modernity was concentrated on the landscapes of the U.S. South and was synonymously associated with the slave system and its various forms of labor, from forced work to the forced sexual reproduction of the subjected slave class.

As a term, the *plantation complex* literally refers to the physical environment, which consisted of areas from the main home to slave quarters, farmland, and animal pens, but as invoked in a critical sense, it also references the dominant labor infrastructure that was iterated for several centuries throughout the Western Hemisphere, and that emerged as the primary site within modernity for containing, disciplining, reproducing, abusing, and annihilating the black body.[62] The southern plantation was the primary site for perpetuating and replicating the system of American slavery, the driving force behind capitalism, colonialism, and imperialism in the nation during the antebellum era. The slave system of the U.S. South classified black women as subordinate as it scripted their children as illegitimate. The complex of plantation slavery that grounded the southern economy and the larger system of American capitalism is the backdrop against which these mechanisms unfolded.

The institution of slavery has also accorded the U.S. South a prominent role in engendering, articulating, and legally defining black women as raced, sexed, and gendered subjects.[63] Moreover, the U.S. South has had a long-standing role in shaping national identity, and it has, again, been instrumental in constructing notions of national femininity that have most typically exalted and prioritized white feminine subjectivity. These dialectics have played a role in processes of constructing black feminine icons in contexts such as the U.S. public sphere.

To be sure, the nationalization, and even in some instances globalization, of models of black femininity in relation to the U.S. South have been recurrent motifs that even the space and geography of the South Side of Chicago linked to Michelle Obama reflects and clarifies. One premise of this study is that the U.S. South continues, even in our time, to constitute a range of raced, classed, sexed, and gendered formations, including some of the prevailing conceptions and representations of national femininity in the cultural imagination. With the new southern studies' embrace of cultural studies, it challenges conventional geographic essentialisms about what counts as a relevant and appropriate object for study, an approach that limited the outlook of southern literature and southern studies as conventional fields. To the contrary, the new southern studies field has not prioritized factors such as a southern birthplace in its objects of study and has approached them with more openness. My examination of Chicagoan Michelle Obama by analyzing the South Side metaphors routinely related to her, as well as her family roots traceable to slavery on plantations in Georgia and South Carolina, epitomizes this approach in this study. Furthermore, I also draw on Jacqueline Jones's concept of *southern diasporas* as a term for framing black southern identities in the United States located far beyond the conventional sites situated below the Mason-Dixon Line in the national imagination, locating them in urban zones in light of histories such as the Great Migration.[64] Despite the popularity and currency of *black South*, I use the term *Africana South* as an alternative to acknowledge the diasporic cultural flows that constitute black southern identities.

On top of the new southern studies, this study is poised at the intersection of fields such as American and African American literary studies, black feminism and gender studies, black queer and trans studies, and black/Africana studies. In American literature and American studies, Cathy N. Davidson, Lauren Berlant, Priscilla Wald, Dana D. Nelson, Amy Kaplan, and Robyn Wiegman have produced brilliant studies of American selfhood, citizenship, and identity that have influenced and inspired me. From my days of graduate study at Duke University, discussions with Eve Kosofsky Sedgwick, along with reading her body of writings, profoundly shaped my understanding and knowledge of queer studies as a field and established foundations for my continuing study.

Similarly, my thinking on trans studies has been foundationally shaped by scholars such as Jack Halberstam, C. Riley Snorton, and Janet Mock.

Africana studies, an interdisciplinary (indeed, transdisciplinary) and comparative field that originated in my home department at Cornell University, has been increasingly embraced and universalized in departments across the nation. It has been adopted as a banner of identification for departments and programs to signal approaches to Africa and its diasporas that are grounded in geography and that are at once transnational, interdisciplinary, and comparative. In its conception and design, it facilitates critical inquiry and academic exchange throughout Africa and its transnational diasporas in the United States, the Caribbean, Central and South America, Europe, Asia, and Britain.[65]

Africana studies' complex and global circuits of investigation and critical engagement, like those in studies of the Global South, are a reminder of the centrality of geography in shaping identity and culture. The exciting education I have received in my home department in this critical discourse has reshaped my perspective as a thinker and theorist and deeply enriched this book while helping me to think toward new directions in Africana studies as a teaching and research field. Indeed, my study is energized by what I think of as the new Africana studies, which looks toward new *afro*futures and encompasses the innovative philosophical, theoretical, and pedagogical horizons toward which the field has been moving in recent years. Like this project's investments in black feminism, its investments in Africana studies recognize and affirm the value in linking academic work and forms of activism to help make a difference in the social and political world through community engagement.

Across four chapters, *Emancipation's Daughters* methodologically examines a diverse body of materials, including political speeches, art images, photographs, legal transcripts, national monuments and memorials, film and video, and literary works such as novels, poems, autobiographies, and biographies. The book is primarily grounded in literary and cultural studies. My training as a scholar in these areas primarily shapes the range of texts I explore, along with the archive of materials on which I draw and my methods of critical argumentation and investigation. Theoretically and critically, my study draws on areas such as transnational feminism, black feminism, black girlhood, childhood studies, black queer and trans studies, and more broadly, black and Africana studies, including Afrofuturism, and American studies. It is also grounded in southern studies, including the Global and hemispheric South.

Chapter 1, "Mary McLeod Bethune's 'Last Will and Testament' and Her National Legacy," revisits the role of Mary McLeod Bethune as a key black female model in the nation's public sphere, with organic linkages to the U.S. South, who purposefully organized and mediated a national and global black agenda during the Depression that provided vital foundations for civil and human rights activism later in the twentieth century, culminating in the publication of her "My Last Will and Testament," discussed in this chapter. Her "Last Will and Testiment" was premised on her status as a national mother in black America, which revised the matriarch. This chapter continues with an analysis of the Mary McLeod Bethune Memorial statue in Washington, DC, in Lincoln Park, sculpted by Robert Berks, a monument whose development was spearheaded for several decades by the National Council of Negro Women and its president Dorothy Height. The final section of this chapter draws on Senate and House hearings to examine contestations that emerged amid the struggle to establish the Mary McLeod Bethune Council House as a national historic site under the auspices of the National Park Service, to consider ways in which the congressional debates raised questions about Bethune's national significance and relevance to areas such as American and women's history. These dialogues boldly threw into relief contestations over national femininity, along with gross misapprehensions and lapses in cultural memory in the post–civil rights era about the import of Bethune's legacy.

In chapter 2, "From Rosa Parks's *Quiet Strength* to Memorializing a National Mother," I consider Rosa Parks, who emerged as a model of national femininity when her choice to remain seated on a bus in Montgomery played a central role in the crystallization of the civil rights movement, including its nationalization and globalization. I acknowledge the intersectionality of race, gender, and sexuality in constituting Parks as a model of national motherhood and emphasize the value in focusing on her voice and writings to examine the relationship she had with young people throughout her life, and her strategic uses of the mothering narrative that belie its reactionary appropriations in politics, as well as its dismissive critiques in some political and popular contexts. I examine Rosa Parks's *Quiet Strength* and *Dear Mrs. Parks: A Dialogue with Today's Youth* to consider how her dialogue with youth builds on her public construction as a symbolic mother. I go on to discuss how this metaphor was reinforced through the Afrofuturistic narratives that shape the Rosa Parks Children's Museum in Montgomery. I end this chapter by examining her postmortem mourning in the U.S. capital.

Chapter 3, "America's Chief Diplomat: The Politics of Condoleezza Rice from Autobiography to Art and Fashion," begins with a reading of the first installment of Rice's two-part memoir, *Extraordinary, Ordinary People: A Memoir of Family*, which reflects on her narrative of the tragic bombing at 16th Street Baptist Church, framing of her family as nationally representative, and the exclusion of blacks from notions of American democracy. I examine how Rice invoked such scripts in relation to foreign policy, including the war on terror, and their role in helping make her legible as a national leader and model of national femininity. I go on to look at representations of Rice in comedy in "Condi Comes to Harlem" skits by *Mad TV*, which draw on blaxploitation film techniques, science fiction, and Afrofuturism to revise and critique the public images of Rice that link her to Bush and the right wing by grounding her in Harlem as a geography and constructing her as a politically progressive and nationally representative black woman leader who primarily serves and advances the interests of black communities. I go on to examine representations that deconstruct her relation to iconicity and notions of national femininity in visual artworks by Terry Lloyd, Ayanah Moor, Luc Tuymans, Enrique Chagoya, and Amy Vangsgard. A brief dialogue on the role of fashion in shaping her iconicity concludes this chapter.

Chapter 4, "First Lady and 'Mom-in-Chief': The Voice and Vision of Michelle Obama in the Video *South Side Girl* and in *American Grown*," begins by exploring biographical scripts that invoke Michelle Obama in relation to plantation history and southern diasporas through narratives of the Great Migration. Furthermore, I consider Michelle Obama's recurrent self-descriptions in speeches in relation to the South Side of Chicago and, particularly, the video *South Side Girl*, which introduced her at the 2008 Democratic National Convention in Denver, Colorado. I argue that its raced and gendered geographic motifs unsettle masculinist constructions of this area and link it to a black woman's self-fashioning in the national arena, while staging her own African American family as a *representative* American family and constructing her as a representative American woman. Here, I also build on my readings of Bethune and Parks in earlier chapters to acknowledge that Michelle Obama's self-fashioning as "Mom-in-Chief" in relation to her daughters, Malia and Sasha, frames her as a mother figure in the nation and holds vital implications for the discourses on national femininity. I culminate this chapter with a discussion of the First Lady's first book, *American Grown: The Story of the White House Kitchen Garden and Gardens across America*, and an examination of her Let's

Move! project, focused on the nation's children, including her collaborative project with Beyoncé designed to mobilize young people into fitness.

The conclusion, "Beyoncé's South and the Birth of a 'Formation' Nation," briefly considers how the iconic Texas-born singer, whose career was launched in the popular female singing group Destiny's Child and who has gone on to achieve major success as a solo musical artist, actress, and entrepreneur, was further enshrined in the national arena as an icon through her romantic serenade of Barack and Michelle Obama with the Etta James classic song "At Last" during their first dance as president and First Lady. As Beyoncé has explained, this moment held a lot of symbolic import for her family given that her parents, Mathew Knowles and Tina Knowles, were born in the segregated South. This family story has been extended in her more recent projects, such as "Formation" and the album *Lemonade*, which invokes histories of slavery and oppression in the South. This study frames these cultural "texts" as important and relevant for registering the profound significance of the most salient and influential black woman's voice in the popular arena and its influence on contemporary political discourses in ways that build on Beyoncé's aforementioned collaboration with Michelle Obama through solidarity with movements from Black Lives Matter and #SayHerName to #TakeAKnee, movements whose messages have been amplified and mainstreamed all the more through the George Floyd protests. Through her national and global iconicity and increasing political visibility and influence, Beyoncé illustrates the role of popular culture in shaping national femininity. Analysis in Beyoncé studies, from Janet Mock's feminist insights about the superstar to reflections on Beyoncé's influence on black trans and queer women who promote her iconicity, also link her to some of the best possibilities for helping actualize more inclusive models of blackness and national femininity.

{ 1 }

Mary McLeod Bethune's "My Last Will and Testament" and Her National Legacy

> This African American woman from rural South Carolina developed into a leader who brought race and gender issues to the national agenda.... Her visibility, and her confident and dignified demeanor, contradicted notions of black inferiority. An important symbolic presence in national and international affairs, Bethune was one of the few members of her race and sex among the higher echelons of power and influence in the United States during the last decades of de jure segregation. She played a pivotal role in promoting and representing African American interests at the federal level and in establishing and enhancing black institutions. —AUDREY THOMAS MCCLUSKEY and ELAINE M. SMITH, *Mary McLeod Bethune: Building a Better World*

In Rex Barnett's 1996 short biographical film *Mary McLeod Bethune: The Spirit of a Champion*, the historian Francine King of DeKalb College (now Perimeter College at Georgia State University) describes Bethune as a woman born with "three strikes" against her: she was a woman, black, and poor in the segregated Reconstruction South; but she was never defeated by any of her disadvantages, which emphasizes the intersectionality of gender, race, and class in Bethune's formation. The film, which begins with a voice-over of Bethune stressing the importance of having faith in God and faith in oneself, establishes a linear timeline of her life, beginning with her birth on July 10, 1875, as the fifteenth of seventeen children born to poor, illiterate sharecroppers who were ex-slaves in South Carolina, to her death in Daytona Beach on May 18, 1955.[1]

Riché Richardson, *Mary McLeod Bethune: One of America's Greatest Sweethearts and the World's Best Leaders*, 2012–14. Photograph by Dave Burbank.

The film frames the famous story of Bethune accompanying her mother, a laundress, to the home of wealthy whites, being invited into their daughter's playhouse, and having a book taken from her by the child because of the perception that blacks could not read, as Bethune's early impetus to learn and to commit to education. This experience, which might be interpreted as a primal moment in Bethune's racial awakening, aligns with and revises motifs in African American literary history, such as "the trope of the talking book," which situates a failed primal encounter with reading as the catalyst for a black (and typically masculine slave) subject to begin the quest for literacy, which has also been linked inextricably to freedom.[2]

This film's narrative structure focuses on her birth in the years after slavery, links her to the continuing struggle for black freedom in the post-Emancipation era, and is useful to the extent that it describes the material conditions that shaped Bethune early in life, from economics to education, by acknowledging her experiences of picking cotton, making clear how education delivered her from a lifetime of fieldwork and opened the door to vast possibilities. Through a series of black and white photographs and videos, it visualizes the difficult work conditions for blacks within the southern agrarian economy in the years after slavery, along with horrors such as lynching. It pinpoints the geographic trajectory that Bethune followed early in life, beginning in 1882 with her experience as a small child of walking five miles there and back daily to attend school at Emma Jane Wilson's Maysville (the spellings of the school and town are different; there is no "e" in the spelling of the school) Educational and Industrial Institute in Mayesville, South Carolina; her subsequent enrollment for seven years at Scotia Seminary in Concord, North Carolina; and her journey on to Chicago, Illinois, on a scholarship she won to attend Moody Bible Institute, where she was the only black among more than a thousand students, and did volunteering on the city's South Side.[3]

The film then moves on to an overview of Bethune's earliest teaching experiences in the late 1890s, including appointments at Lucy Laney's Haines Normal and Industrial Institute in Augusta, Georgia; work at the Haines Institute in Atlanta; and jobs at Kindell Institute in Atlanta and the Presbyterian Mission school in Palatka, Florida, before opening the Daytona Educational and Industrial Training School for Girls. King points out that Bethune felt compelled to bring black women's plight to the forefront of public attention and focused on educating them to vanquish persisting stereotypes of black womanhood, such as being immoral, and in light of the belief that "if you educate a woman, you educate a generation." The film underscores that Bethune established her school in the "worst section" of the segregated city, where most blacks lived, because of her yearning to educate girls. Furthermore, the film makes clear that Bethune's early work in Daytona, such as lobbying wealthy white philanthropists for funding as she developed the school, including sewing machine company founder Thomas H. White and steel magnate Andrew Carnegie, was the foundation for cultivating alliances with powerful figures in national politics like President Franklin Delano Roosevelt.

These linkages illustrate how her experiences working as an educator in the U.S. South provided background that proved useful in her later work at the national level. The emphasis on these experiences for the first portion of the film, and an ending that emphasizes Bethune's return to Florida and a visual of her obituary in Daytona Beach, where she spent the final year of her life, embed a circular narrative that poignantly registers the U.S. South as the primary foundation for Bethune's later experiences and frames the region as her initial mission field, which helped season her for service at the national level. It compellingly illustrates how much her southern roots lay at the foundation in building her national legacy and in her development as a black woman who became a national leader. The story of Bethune's birth in the rural South and perseverance despite the poverty into which she was born is not the conventional individual American success story, akin to Horatio Alger narratives of "pulling oneself up by one's own bootstraps," but a testament to how much the nation gained through her tireless work as a black woman who embodied the motto of the black women's club movement, "Lifting as We Climb," by using her platform to advocate on behalf of black Americans and struggle to end their oppression.

In 1895, the death of Frederick Douglass, the best-known black abolitionist of the nineteenth century, marked the end of an era in which he had emerged as a representative black man and a reigning black leader in this nation, whom, as Paul Laurence Dunbar mused in poetry, "all the country heard" "with amaze," and who was dearly missed among black Americans, "For thy strong arm to guide the shivering bark."[4] Booker T. Washington was a former slave and founder of Tuskegee Institute who promoted the benefits of industrial education and who was favored by white philanthropists. W. E. B. Du Bois, the first African American to earn a doctorate from Harvard and a prolific scholar at Atlanta University, who eventually helped to establish the NAACP and edited its magazine, the *Crisis*, like Washington emerged as a primary black leader in the years after Douglass's passing. Bethune's central and profoundly significant role in African American national leadership has tended to be eclipsed by the emphasis on her black male contemporaries, such as Washington and Du Bois, whose philosophies on education and strategies for dealing with race issues famously conflicted with each other and got more national exposure and recognition than her visionary model of educational leadership in Florida.

Mary McLeod Bethune's establishment of the Daytona Educational and Industrial Training School for Girls in 1904 and Bethune-Cookman College in 1923; her leadership in the NACW and the National Council of Negro Women (NCNW), an organization that she also founded in 1935; and work as director of Negro Affairs within the National Youth Administration (NYA) established her reputation as one of the most persistent, hard-working, and effective ambassadors for black social and political advancement during the twentieth century.[5] Bethune used her influence, especially during the interwar years and the Great Depression, to help hold the government accountable for developing opportunities for African Americans in areas such as employment and education. Her status as a national leader in the African American context was fully consolidated through her friendships with President Franklin D. Roosevelt and his wife, First Lady Eleanor Roosevelt.

In the words of historian Joyce A. Hanson, "The Roosevelts and other government officials seriously considered Bethune's informed opinions."[6] Moreover, Bethune was a pivotal member of and the only woman on Roosevelt's famous Black Cabinet, or the Federal Council of Negro Affairs, a group that advised the president informally on public policy.[7] Paula Giddings aptly sums up Bethune's contribution and her profound national influence in *When and Where I Enter: The Impact of Black Women on Race and Sex in America*, noting that "the contributions of Mary McLeod Bethune in the Roosevelt era are undeniable. And her unflagging concern for Black women achieved an earlier goal: Because of her efforts, women were counted among the new groups with legitimate demands that had to be considered on the national agenda. As a result, Blacks, both men and women, were better prepared to go beyond 'separate but equal' to demand integration in the nation's mainstream, a demand that would be pressed as the nation entered upon a second world war."[8]

As co-editors of the collection of Bethune's writings *Building a Better World* (1999), Audrey Thomas McCluskey and Elaine M. Smith similarly acknowledge Bethune's significant and transformative influence:

> This African American woman from rural South Carolina developed into a leader who brought race and gender issues to the national agenda. Through her tireless activism, she challenged the popular assumptions of most white

Americans, who maligned and stigmatized black women as "immoral scourges." Her visibility, and her confident and dignified demeanor, contradicted notions of black inferiority. An important symbolic presence in national and international affairs, Bethune was one of the few members of her race and sex among the higher echelons of power and influence in the United States during the last decades of de jure segregation. She played a pivotal role in promoting and representing African American interests at the federal level and in establishing and enhancing black institutions. One national black women's organization expanded under her leadership, while another launched an international agenda, promoting dialogue among women of African descent, and seeking to maximize black women's political and economic clout.[9]

This assessment, like the film, acknowledges the path that Bethune journeyed in life from her birth in the rural South to her role as a leader and representative of black women at the national level. It highlights her agency in helping to unsettle the conventional stereotypical racist representations of black women through her self-fashioning in the public sphere and dignified and proud persona. It affirms the effect she had on black women's lives, specifically through her commitment to promoting black agendas at the national level and to using her platform to advance issues affecting black women. Furthermore, McCluskey and Smith acknowledge Bethune's status as a black woman national leader whose work and activism profoundly shaped the nation to the point that she became a symbol. Bethune was a vanguard leader in advancing the mission to make Washington, DC, a more democratic city, a mission that began with black women from the late nineteenth to the early twentieth century, a phenomenon examined by Treva Lindsey.[10]

Bethune's confrontation of conventional perceptions of black women by presenting a more empowering image of black womanhood was a central factor in her iconicity and in establishing foundations for her status as a model of national femininity in the African American cultural imagination, beginning during the Depression and continuing during her decades of public work, particularly once she became the only woman member of President Roosevelt's legendary Black Cabinet, assembled in 1935 to provide advice on policies related to the African American population, whose members referred to her as Ma Bethune. Her contributions set foundations for the esteem in which she has been held in the decades thereafter. They were the foundations of her cultural authority to speak to African Americans at large and to frame them as a family.

Bethune's "My Last Will and Testament," published in *Ebony* magazine in August 1955, cemented her legacy in leadership and established foundations for the national monuments later erected in her honor. The elegiac tone that inflects Barnett's film biopic from its beginning mirrors the mood that Bethune establishes in her final and perhaps most memorable piece of writing in the months before her death, framed to address an African American audience. In it, the weight of her mortality is palpable as she reflects on her legacy as a national leader and outlines "principles and policies" that she has cultivated through her "life's work" and that she aims to leave behind for blacks. Bethune presents this essay as a prelude to "my autobiography which will record my life-journey in detail, together with the innumerable side trips which have carried me abroad, into every corner of our country into homes both lowly and luxurious, and even into the White House to confer with Presidents."[11] But this essay was to be the final significant piece of writing that she ever published.

While Bethune wrote prolifically and produced a body of writings that included multiple speeches, essays, statements, and letters in areas related to education, women, politics, and autobiography, this piece produced at the end of her life is the best-known work by her and has been most central in sustaining her legacy.[12] It is a document that enshrined and immortalized Bethune as a national leader as it established foundations on which her legacy has continued to be reflected on and promoted. It cemented her reputation at this level more poignantly than any other piece of writing she ever produced, while establishing the groundwork for her lasting cultural influence. The essay is premised on Bethune's national iconicity as a black woman and would have been inconceivable without it.

I find it compelling because of its literariness in addressing African Americans as a collective to reflect on their struggle for equality and also as the final capstone of the journey toward literacy that she had begun early in life. This penultimate work is all the more important because discussions of Bethune's writing, including her autobiographical pieces, have primarily been limited to fields such as black women's history, and its valuable implications for African American literary history have not been adequately acknowledged. In this chapter, I reflect on this document in its configurations as a literary and cultural text. I am primarily interested in how saliently it challenges conventional black and patriarchal, male-centered leadership models and positions a woman such as Bethune speaking to black Americans, though such prominent platforms and high cultural capital were typically elusive for black queer women of the time, outside the world of popular culture and entertainment. Beginning with its title, the document draws on legal language. In constituting Bethune as a representative black subject in the African American context, it frames African Americans as a symbolic family while acknowledging the persisting exclusion of "the Negro" from the privileges of American democracy and underscores the importance of black youth to the project of black liberation, which accords with recurring strategies of black women's representations as national leaders.

I build on this analysis to consider the will's iteration and inscription of its content on the Mary McLeod Bethune Memorial, which visually and verbally draws on the performative dimensions of the original document and stages the main aspect of its core message related to young people in a public space in the nation's capital. Bethune's voice in the will and her visualization on the monument both reflect her leadership at the national level and the iconicity that she had attained in her lifetime, to the point of being regarded as a mother figure. While this script of Bethune, primarily circulated in the African American context, provided a radical counternarrative to stereotypes of black womanhood such as the mammy, its sacralizing of the maternal was no less premised on asexuality; she revises but does not fully unsettle the matriarch and was limited in sanctioning a heterosexist model of black family. I contrast my analysis in these two sections with a final one that draws on documents from House and Senate hearings held in 1982 and 1985 to examine the heated debates related to establishing the Bethune Council House as a national historic site and administering it under the auspices of the National Park Service (NPS), which threw into relief questions related to race, gender, and national identity, including Bethune's legitimacy as a representative American woman. This archive is significant not only because of the testimonies it offers related to Bethune's legacy, but also because it reveals the legal bureaucracy that the NCNW effectively navigated over a multiyear period in developing Council House as a national historic site and in struggling to secure federal support for the project, which built on earlier struggles to establish the Bethune monument. An examination of these earlier public monuments and tributes to Bethune is useful, too, at this point, considering the new statue in her honor scheduled to replace the statue of Confederate general Edmund Kirby Smith representing Florida in Statuary Hall in the U.S. Capitol.

"The Greatest of My Dreams"

In 1939, the concerted opposition of the Daughters of the American Revolution to the performance of the distinguished contralto Marian Anderson before a racially integrated audience at Constitution Hall illustrated the reach of Jim Crow to the nation's capital. Their protest was symptomatic of a purist, nativist, racially exclusive view of American identity premised on whiteness and the otherness of the black body within narratives of the nation's founding, including the racially exclusive fantasy of American family and notions of American selfhood, which they implied to be wholly incompatible with black women's subjectivity. The intervention that President Roosevelt and First Lady Eleanor Roosevelt made to address this situation by staging a national platform for Anderson to perform before a racially integrated audience at the Lincoln Memorial challenged such exclusionary scripts, was a gesture that bespoke new possibilities for blacks to achieve full citizenship during the first years of Bethune's work in Roosevelt's Black Cabinet, and was a step toward the modern movement for civil rights.

On May 17, 1954, the Supreme Court's ruling in *Brown v. Board of Education* legally ended segregation in public education and provided the most decisive challenge to the doctrine of Jim Crow, which had been institutionalized more than half a century earlier through the *Plessy v. Ferguson* decision in 1896. The "doll experiments" undertaken by psychologists Kenneth B. Clark and Mamie Clark, his wife, which revealed the detrimental consequences of segregated classrooms in undermining the self-esteem of black children, who consistently expressed a preference for white dolls and identified with and associated positive qualities with whiteness while associating negative qualities with the black dolls, played a vital role in influencing a decision that Thurgood Marshall, who was later appointed by Lyndon B. Johnson as the nation's first black Supreme Court justice, had helped shape. This landmark ruling posed the most assertive challenge to Jim Crow that Bethune witnessed in her lifetime and suggested that an end to racial oppression was possible.[13] This historical context makes it all the more noteworthy that Bethune's "My Last Will and Testament" reminds blacks of their responsibility to "our children" and emphasizes the vital role that black youth will play in the world in the future. Published just over a year after this landmark ruling, it positioned her as one of this movement's precursors and reinforced her status as a linchpin between the first generation of black Americans who had been born into freedom in the post-Emancipation South and witnessed the rise of Jim Crow and future generations of blacks who would continue the struggle against it after her death. In this compelling essay, she passes the torch to those who will remain behind to continue the fight for freedom. This document's publication at a time when the panic about communism remained acute was also significant for underscoring Bethune's deep commitment to American democracy, countering unfounded allegations against her and an attack on her public image by the House Committee on Un-American Activities.

The publication of Bethune's piece in *Ebony* magazine, whose audience was primarily African American, gave it a national platform and reinforced its development for a black readership. *Ebony* was founded by John H. Johnson in 1945 and had been circulating for nearly a decade by the time Bethune's piece was published. The magazine was developed on the heels of *Negro Digest*, the first periodical publication that Johnson had introduced, in 1942, which was designed in the vein of *Reader's Digest*, the compact American magazine that compiled and circulated condensed versions of stories from popular magazines for its audience. *Negro Digest*, however, featured stories related to African Americans and did not condense its features. Both enterprises were launched under the auspices of Johnson Publishing, which Johnson founded in Chicago in 1942, an enterprise that became the nation's largest African American publishing company and the most successful manifestation of the black press in the twentieth century. A few years later, in 1951, Johnson introduced *Jet*, a weekly digest also aimed primarily at a black readership.

Ebony's design and content recalled that of *Life* magazine, which was originally established in 1883 with an emphasis on humor and stories pitched to the American mainstream. In content, *Ebony* showcased cover stories related to black celebrities, athletes, and politicians and emphasized black achievement and success while featuring black businesses and black models in its advertising. One of Johnson's main goals was to challenge media norms, which tended to portray blacks in relation to crime, by featuring stories and advertisements emphasizing representations of blacks as successful, upwardly mobile people who, as he explains in his autobiography, *Succeeding against the Odds: The Autobiography of a Great American Businessman*, "also raised children and gave debutante balls and watched baseball and football games." "We wanted to show Negroes—we were Negroes then—and Whites the Negroes nobody knew."[14]

Johnson describes the first decade of *Ebony*'s publication as a "golden decade," during which breakthroughs to integrate the military and schools, as well as advancements in black voting rights, had made the idea of attaining full equality conceivable among many of his generation. In 1954, the year before Bethune's "My Last Will and Testament" appeared, a period of national recession had led to a drop-off in subscriptions to *Ebony* by 100,000, but the magazine continued to reign as the premier black publication. During that period, *Ebony* was the primary organ for black America, covering stories about African Americans that were often ignored in the mainstream press. At heart, Johnson Publishing was a family business run by Johnson and his wife, Eunice W. Johnson, whose publications were also heavily invested in promoting a positive image of the black family. In this sense, it was also an ideal forum in which to advance a narrative such as Bethune's that imagined blacks as a symbolic family in the nation.

In the post–World War II period, as wartime images of masses of American women working in factories supporting the war effort abroad were displaced by media emphasis on traditional white nuclear families, framing women primarily in relation to domesticity, representations largely excluded blacks or, at worst, idealized black women's work as maids and relegated them to the kitchen. *Ebony* provided Bethune with a prominent public platform that emphasized her leadership before a predominantly black audience. It vitally made up a black public sphere in the nation whose representations starkly contrasted with prevailing stereotypical images of black women.[15] Her essay challenged prevailing mainstream media scripts that excluded black families or portrayed them as being marginal to American life.

The background of Johnson as a black man born into poverty in the South, who became a self-made millionaire through his business enterprises, and who was consulted by presidents for decades because of his intimate knowledge of the black world gained through the production of his publications, mirrored aspects of Bethune's story. They had another connection that bound them more tightly than that. As a youth, John H. Johnson had worked for the NYA that Bethune headed and had gained training on its magazine. Johnson valued her and consulted her as an adviser. As he explains in his autobiography, "Mrs. Bethune, who was another one of the most unforgettable characters I've known, was short and black as polished ebony. She was not what the world considers beautiful, but she had so much soul force and authority that when she walked into a room all eyes were pulled to her, as if to a magnet. I was a graduate of her NYA program, and she considered me one of her boys. It was only natural for me to turn to her when the difficulties mounted."[16] Not only had Johnson been mentored by Bethune, but his life as a young man had also been concretely affected by one of the policies she supported at the national level, an opportunity that helped him and his family get off welfare, "a necessary first step that let us keep our hope and dignity until the private economy could provide alternatives."[17] His portrait speaks to the charisma for which Bethune was well known and widely admired. It is most serendipitous that he published her final essay and provided the public platform through which her voice as a black national leader was fully consolidated and through which she has since been immortalized.

Since the date of the piece's original publication, *Ebony* has reprinted it several times through the years. A look into the *Ebony* archives at its original printing in 1955 reveals editorial notes acknowledging that it was written "exclusively" for the magazine and falls within the "literary" genre, while promising to become "one of the great historical documents of our times."[18] Because Bethune passed away before its scheduled printing, it was published posthumously and simultaneously registers as a memorial tribute and retrospective on her life and achievements. The third-person subtitle, "As life draws to a close, black America's First Negro Lady prepared for her people a legacy of love," contrasts with the possessive noun and first-person voice of the main title and emphasizes Bethune's symbolic significance as a representative black woman in the nation. Furthermore, this framing recasts Bethune's references to herself in the third person. The invocation of the term First Lady posits her as the equivalent of the nation's First Lady, Eleanor Roosevelt, in the black cultural imaginary, and significantly, a photograph positioned alongside the subtitle, of Bethune and Roosevelt standing side by side, joining hands with the famed talk show host Ed Sullivan, further reinforces this analogy, which is grounded in Bethune's friendship with Roosevelt. The subtitle points to Bethune's ubiquity in the African American context as a representative woman and as the reigning leader. This narrative is iterated and revised across versions of the document that *Ebony* subsequently released in 1963, 1973, 1975, 1982, 1990, and 2002.

The language of the title recalls the Du Boisian "double consciousness" that blacks in the nation feel, being simultaneously African and American, and frames Bethune as the foremost woman leader in this nation within a nation.[19] More broadly, it symbolically scripts her in a way that acknowledges her renowned role as an intermediary between the nation's president and First Lady and the black community. Photographs that feature Bethune with figures such as First Lady Mamie Eisenhower iterate the narrative positing Bethune as a premier woman leadership model in the African American context and frame her as the most legible and influential black woman in the nation. Photograph captions that describe Bethune as a "Grand Old Lady" and that acknowledge her selection as "One of the 50 greatest women America has produced" reinforce this narrative of Bethune as an ideal national model of black femininity in the African American context as well as influencing the nation more broadly.

McCluskey has examined how strategically and consistently Bethune used the press, beginning with the unique platform that newspapers provided, to get her message across to both black and white audiences in a segregated society, along with the unique role that the black press played in projecting her voice and agendas at the national level. In describing her use of black newspapers, McCluskey notes, "Bethune seized that forum in an effort to present herself as the emblematic leader of black hope; to champion black progress, and to dislodge rampantly negative perceptions of black women and men in the American mind."[20] Such contexts are indispensable for thinking about the unique and exceptional platform for Bethune to speak provided by *Ebony*, which by that time had picked up the mission of "race vindication" that had inflected the work of black journalists, as V. P. Franklin and Bettye Collier-Thomas analyze in their history of black intellectualism and journalism.[21]

As Beverly C. Johnson-Miller has observed, Bethune's position as the only black person invited to participate in White House conferences on child welfare during the terms of presidents Calvin Coolidge and Herbert Hoover positioned her to shape dialogues related to youth, as did her role as the leader of the NYA Division of Negro Affairs, appointed by President Franklin D. Roosevelt, the most prominent national appointment of an African American woman.[22] According to Johnson-Miller, "Holding a key position in the New Deal's National Youth Administration, and serving as the director of the NYA Division of Negro Affairs, she successfully influenced national policies causing public attention and substantial funding of employment programs for black youth."[23] Similarly, McCluskey notes, "Beginning in 1936 her growing clout as director of the NYA in charge of distributing funds for education and jobs for blacks, also added to her national stature and role as race representative." McCluskey credits Bethune's work in the NYA with reinforcing her "national stature" and notes her "emblematic persona."[24] Perhaps more than any other aspect of her life's work, Bethune's role in the NYA underscored her investments in advancing the interests of young people at the national level and provided her the best opportunity to affect the lives of black youth in particular, notwithstanding the program's limitations.[25] In 1937, the White House conference "Problems of Negroes and Negro Youth," spearheaded by Bethune as an NYA leader, provided her with a national platform to advocate for issues related to children.

A year after the NYA conference convened to foreground issues related to black youth, Bethune led another major White House conference for the NCNW, for her concomitant agenda was devoted to empowering women, which she pursued not only through her sustained commitment to educating girls but also through her work in founding and leading the council. As McCluskey points out, this meeting actualized Bethune's goal of foregrounding black women at the national level and drew widespread media coverage. As Johnson-Miller points out, Bethune spent her fourteen years leading the NCNW advocating for African Americans with an emphasis on advancing the interests of women and improving their circumstances in the nation, noting the role of this unprecedented conference in engaging black women with the planning of social programs sponsored by the federal government. Like Bethune's founding of a school for girls and her ongoing commitment to education, her advocacy in these organizations during her prime years as a national leader highlights how much agendas related to women and children were her primary concern throughout her life. At the same time, these dimensions of Bethune's legacy are more familiar than the "hidden histories" of black queer women during the period, including civil rights and women's rights advocate Pauli Murray, who had authored *States' Laws on Race and Color* in 1950, and emerging writer and activist Lorraine Hansberry.

By the time Bethune wrote her "Last Will," she had long been separated from her husband, Albertus Bethune, who had passed away in 1918, leaving behind Mary and their son, Albert Sr., along with her adopted grandson, Albert Jr. As McCluskey notes, Bethune was "called the female Booker T. Washington, and enjoyed widespread popular support among the black masses, many of whom dubbed her 'Mother Bethune.'"[26] Of Bethune, McCluskey goes on to observe, "To her own race, she was a fount of black pride—a caring mother-figure who dispensed inspirational leadership that attracted wide coverage in a black press committed to ending racial segregation. These combined attributes incited recognition and acceptance on both sides of the color line and legitimized her role as race representative."[27] The maternal meanings related to Bethune in the African American cultural imaginary soundly negated and defied the racist mammy stereotype, an image that Bethune's dignified bearing contested as vigilantly as did her famous rebuff of the Auntie stereotype—when a white male Pullman car conductor (or elevator operator at the White House) used it to refer to her, she kindly asked him, "Now, which of my sister's sons are you?"²⁸ At the same time, her representation in this sense challenged emerging pathological images within urban sociology of black women as matriarchs who dominated black families, emasculated black men, and fomented poverty and crime in the lives of children. Contrarily, Bethune prided herself on claiming "pure African stock" and traced her mother to a lineage of royal African matriarchs. Yet even as the discourse on Bethune in the black public sphere affirmed the notion of fictive kin, it had inherent limitations, mainly according legibility to heterosexual models of mothering and family and refiguring the matriarch.

The reigning image and widespread embrace of Bethune as a mother figure in the African American context were a primary foundation on which she constituted African Americans as a symbolic family in her "My Last Will and Testament." In this document, Bethune marshals her status from her national platform to directly address the African American population as a collective. The view of her among many African Americans as a symbolic mother figure and the esteem with which she was held as a leader authorized her to speak at this level. Moreover, this status was the foundation on which she framed blacks as a family based on shared racial identity and oppressed status. Even the title implies that she is addressing a family with whom she shares a special and intimate relationship. It establishes intimacy and connection based on race and is premised on the notion that blacks are a nation within a nation through largely imagined connections.²⁹ Her implied audience is the blacks throughout the nation, whom she embraces as a distinct group within the national body; black populations in Africa and its diaspora are also a part of the community that she imagines in this document, along with humanity more broadly.

In the essay's title, Bethune invokes the "will" as the traditional legal document that outlines instructions for administering one's estate after death, including money, property, and personal belongings, a document that typically prioritizes and provides for one's closest family members, including one's children. The assets she leaves to black people once she is gone, however, are not the material or financial assets typically bequeathed in wills but more abstract provisions and wishes, beginning with love and hope. Whereas the contents of wills are typically kept private until a person's death, her original goal was to publish this document and share it widely with the public prior to passing away. It not only builds on her weekly columns published by the *Pittsburgh Courier* and the *Chicago Defender* but also recalls the famous fireside chats of President Roosevelt, delivered on the radio from 1933 to 1944, in which he addressed policy issues for a mass audience.

The reflective tone of the piece and the singular voice it establishes are heightened by the conditions under which Bethune produced it, as a leader who had retreated from prominent public life in the nation's capital and returned to her home in Daytona Beach to retire in a quieter, less fast-paced atmosphere, where she continued her work in relative solitude, albeit at a slower pace. The weight of her mortality is palpable as she feels her strength waning and as she assesses the impact of her life's work and legacy. Her recurring invocation of the word "work" across the document's first three paragraphs emphasizes what a priority work has been in her life and underscores it as a central aspect of what she has contributed and whose fruits have advanced the interests of her people. The will is one of the most visible indicators that this work continues in the present moment, even in the literal labor of the document's production. The document is autobiographical in tone, mentioning national and global contexts she has encountered in her life even as she points to her goal of writing an autobiography. That she mentions deeding her home for the purposes of establishing the Mary McLeod Bethune Foundation is another act, like the will itself, that anticipates her death and is designed to continue her work and carry on her legacy. It directly literalizes the legality of the bequest that the title anticipates.

Yet the document stresses that the wealth she might surrender is not in her limited material possessions as much as in the deeper lessons she has learned from the work throughout her life. As she muses, "Perhaps in them there is something of value. So, as my life draws to a close, I will pass them on to Negroes everywhere in the hope that an old woman's philosophy may give them inspiration."[30] This aspect of the narrative reinforces the notion of blacks as a national family. Bethune's invocation of the triumvirate of faith, hope, and love as attributes that she wishes to pass on draws on the New Testament, 1 Corinthians 13:13. In further mirroring this scripture by identifying love as the greatest commandment and placing it highest on her list, Bethune suggests that it holds potential to transform human relationships and the world itself by breaking down barriers to racial, religious, and transnational unity. Indeed, that *love* is the last word in this document underscores its significance all the more. Her narrative related to black racial empowerment and her constitution of this group as a family is reinforced in her definition of "the Negro" as a category defined primarily by its past slave experience and by her mention of a "new Negro" in the future no longer limited by racial subordination, echoing the title of Alain Locke's famous 1925 volume from the Harlem Renaissance of a modern black subject no longer defined by subservient roles within the southern slave system.[31] This dimension invoking Locke, who had passed away the year before, should further remind us of the silence, invisibility, and marginality surrounding black queerness and the distinct challenges and battles they fought while negotiating nonnormative sexual identities during the era of Jim Crow. In the document, the capitalization of all the attributes she is bequeathing emphasizes them and draws the focus of the audience to her remarks surrounding each point.

Bethune's framing of a collective black identity and her solidarity with its members is most assertive in her bequest of racial dignity: "I want Negroes to maintain their human dignity at all costs. We, as Negroes, must recognize that we are the custodians as well as the heirs of a great civilization. We have given something to the world as a race and for this we are proud and fully conscious of our place in the total picture of mankind's development."[32] This empowering view of blackness runs wholly counter to the narrative that excluded people of African descent from world history during the Enlightenment. Bethune also draws on the black sermonic tradition in framing herself as a voice for this collective.[33] Its ultimate framing in this treatise is global, highlighting its contribution to world history and exhorting all blacks not to lose sight of their humanity and important contributions to the world in a society that defines them primarily in terms of the color of their skin, invoking herself as an example of a woman who has taken pride in her color but not allowed it to define or limit her: "Despite many crushing burdens and handicaps, I have risen from the cotton fields of South Carolina to found a college, administer it during the years of growth, become a public servant in the government of our country and a leader of women."[34] In this narrative, Bethune frames her color as a source of empowerment and as an asset greater than wealth for enabling her to achieve more than a birth with white privilege might have incentivized. This assertion is also her basis for framing the plight of "American Negroes" in all the nation's regions in relation to problems affecting populations of color globally, while aspiring to live in harmony with the nation's white population.

Bethune's prioritization of agendas related to youth alongside women in much of her public work makes it unsurprising that her will culminates by underscoring the black population's collective "Responsibility to Our Young People." This is the point up to which all its other bequests build. Bethune suggests that "our children" are the most enthusiastic dreamers for a better future and will play the most decisive role in building that future. She stresses that it is incumbent on the black population to prioritize young people and, in doing so, suggests that they will advance the interests of blacks collectively because youth will shape and lead the world in the future. They are the possessors and inheritors of "the world around us."[35] She suggests that they are poised to pick up the mantle of leadership that she is in the act of passing on. She emphasizes that the hope for black people in the future lies with young people.

It is significant that she accentuates the importance of youth, recognizing the barriers that the majority of blacks continue to face in persisting deprivation, inadequate housing, poverty, and discrimination, challenging them to help bring about changes. She argues that it will be essential to move beyond outmoded ideas to help ensure that they achieve their greatest potential. Bethune explicitly links the black struggle to the long history since slavery in mentioning that "The Freedom Gates are half-ajar," emphasizing that full equality has yet to be achieved. She has witnessed the dark past as a woman born during Reconstruction who experienced the rise of Jim Crow, and she charges young people with paving the way to a brighter future in which blacks will experience full equality in the nation.

The document compellingly culminates her lifelong agenda of advancing the interests of children within the struggle for racial justice. While they are listed last in the structural schema of the document, she underscores that they are a priority and are the beacons for all African Americans. This organization also evokes biblical scriptures such as Isaiah 11:6, "a little child shall lead them," and Luke 13:13, "the last shall be first and the first shall be last." *Children* and *youth* function as interchangeable terms in the document. As the Barnett film points out, for Bethune, the drive to learn and lead began during childhood. In Bethune's "My Last Will and Testament," repetition of the phrase "the greatest of my dreams" for the Negro and mentioning her vision for black children in the future anticipate some of the themes evident in Dr. Martin Luther King Jr.'s famous "I Have a Dream" speech, delivered before the Lincoln Memorial in Washington, DC, on August 23, 1963, including his use of the dream metaphor and emphasis on his "four little children" being judged not "by the color of their skin, but by the content of their character." In this sense, Bethune was a forerunner in rhetorically invoking children in civil rights discourses in the nation's public sphere.

Bethune's will is a foundational work in the literature of civil rights, which lies in the continuum with King's "Letter from a Birmingham Jail." Bethune's invocation of "dreams" alludes to the notion of the American dream from which blacks have been alienated because of their race. In African American literary history, the poetic musings on dreams that Langston Hughes established in his 1951 poem "Harlem," in reflecting on notions of "dreams deferred," would have been a likely point of reference for Bethune, alongside works such as his poem "I, Too" (1926), which describes America as a family from which blacks are excluded, a dynamic that his speaker describes in a figurative sense through their relegation to the kitchen when company comes.[36]

Elaine Smith has offered what is arguably the most poignant and compelling analysis of "My Last Will and Testament" to date in reading its provisions against the backdrop of Bethune's biography to illustrate the relation of its nine bequests to Bethune's "richly textured life" in "Mary McLeod Bethune's 'Last Will and Testament': A Legacy for Race Vindication," which mentions Bethune's status as a "national heroine."[37] Smith describes the Black Cabinet, of which Bethune was a part in the Roosevelt administration, as the first significant black voice in national politics that had emerged since Reconstruction, an observation that positions Bethune as a vital linchpin between that era and the politics of the Great Depression.[38]

Smith goes on to observe, "Bethune's caretaker declaration for the young meant, in essence, nurturing youth. This constituted her single greatest imperative traversing all aspects of life."[39] Smith frames the passages on youth in this document as a manifestation and extension of the loving and maternal role that Bethune played among the young people she mentored as an educational leader. For my purposes, Smith's analysis is useful for attesting to the organic impact of Bethune's long-standing commitment to youth in education and in her public work, as well as to the point of prioritizing them as she weighed in on national policy agendas, as a basis for structuring her litany of bequests.

The document tacitly equates children with love as it enshrines Bethune's message in the public sphere for future generations. As a category, children represent the greatest of her dreams. In her affirmation of African Americans as a family in which she is a symbolic mother, Bethune emphasizes the importance of children to the triumph in the struggle against racism, as well as to the survival of African Americans in the future. She leaves youth with a challenge to help remedy the ills that impede black people. In it, she contests notions of African American otherness by placing them front and center in the struggle to actualize the nation's democratic ideals, which are blemished by the continuation of Jim Crow. Beyond the medium of print and several reprints in the decades after her essay's original publication, it is fascinating that this will's message was enacted, more saliently iterated, and permanently materialized for an even broader national audience, including future generations, through its circulation on the monument to Bethune in the nation's capital.

"Let Her Works Praise Her"

The bronze monument developed by the NCNW under the leadership of the organization's president, Dorothy Height, and unveiled in Washington's Lincoln Park before an audience of eighteen thousand people on July 10, 1974, Bethune's ninety-ninth birthday, was the first public monument ever dedicated in the nation's capital in honor of an African American and a woman (figure 1.1). The Mary McLeod Bethune Memorial statue was sculpted by Robert Berks, originally approved by Congress in 1959, and designed to mark the centenary of the Emancipation Proclamation, invoking her origins in the post-Emancipation era. In the end, the project cost four hundred thousand dollars and unfolded as a multiyear endeavor because of challenges related to fundraising.

Aspects of its composition, such as the bronze material, abstract features such as her ebony skin and pompadour hairstyle, and the upright posture of the figure recast personal qualities such as the dignity and pride for which she was known during her lifetime. The statue features Bethune standing in the dignified pose that typified her demeanor, gripping a walking cane in her right hand. After FDR died in 1945, former First Lady Eleanor Roosevelt sent to Bethune the president's monogrammed walking cane, which had been a gift from his uncle Theodore Roosevelt. Bethune had begun to collect walking canes years earlier, in 1927, on her first trip to Europe, where she began the practice of donning them as a fashion statement.[40] She treasured Roosevelt's walking cane and carried it with her for the rest of her life as a tribute to her long-standing friendship with the president and his wife.[41] The most powerful testament to how much Bethune cherished the president's walking cane and to how much it came to be associated with her identity is the cane's enshrinement in the Mary McLeod Bethune Memorial statue.[42]

That an image of President Roosevelt's cane is positioned physically supporting the body of Bethune on the statue suggests the levels to which he served as a resource for support by appointing her to high-profile positions at the national level, such as director of Negro Affairs in the NYA, even if some of his decisions and aspects of his policymaking that affected the African American population proved to be disappointing at times. President Roosevelt is known for giving ear as well as deep respect to her voice. The positioning of Roosevelt's walking cane in Bethune's hand inscribes on the monument her close alliance with him during her lifetime and suggests how definitional her association with him became to her reputation. At the same time, the weight

FIGURE 1.1 Robert Berks, Mary McLeod Bethune Memorial, Lincoln Park, Washington, DC. Photograph by Carol M. Highsmith.

of her hand on the walking cane speaks to the power of her influence on the president. Like the Mary McLeod Bethune Memorial's juxtaposition with the Freedman's Memorial, depicting President Lincoln and erected in 1876, this image of Bethune holding Roosevelt's walking cane inscribes and mirrors Bethune's association with Roosevelt as a U.S. president on the landscape at Lincoln Park, which is significantly located in the nation's capital. By extension, it pays tribute to her salience in the nation's public sphere, where she influenced a host of agendas related to African American politics, including policymaking. It also invites the public to meditate on her influence on a series of other U.S. presidents through her other prominent appointments, by Calvin Coolidge, Herbert Hoover, and Harry S. Truman.[43]

The figure of Bethune stands near two children, a girl and a boy, to whom she passes on her legacy, as emblematized by the scroll she holds in her left hand. The figures of Bethune and the children stand in a triangulated formation; the boy steps forward reaching for the scroll with both arms extended as the girl holds up her hands. Height explains in her memoir *Open Wide the*

Freedom Gates that Berks, who had won the design competition sponsored by NCNW, used a methodology that entailed visiting schools and doing hundreds of sketches of black children. While he produced a composite image of a boy, as the prototype for the girl he used Shari Belafonte, the daughter of the popular singer and activist Harry Belafonte, who was also known and admired for civil rights activism.⁴⁴

The monument, which is made of bronze with a concrete base, stands ten feet tall atop a six-foot base. A bronze plate in front of the statue and positioned at its base is inscribed with the words "Mary McLeod Bethune, 1875–1955, Let her works praise her."⁴⁵ It draws on Proverbs 31:31, relating Bethune to the ideal model of godly womanhood invoked in the scripture while associating her life's work with the achievement of a larger spiritual mission and purpose and her legacy with meaningful works in life. At the same time, it recollects Bethune's status as a woman of Christian faith.

Significantly, the words that run in a line on brass plaques around its pedestal are taken from Bethune's "My Last Will and Testament," which accentuates their continuing cultural influence and importance in sustaining her legacy.⁴⁶ A bronze plaque extending around the base spotlights each of the bequests that the will outlines: "I LEAVE YOU LOVE. I LEAVE YOU HOPE. I LEAVE YOU THE CHALLENGE OF DEVELOPING CONFIDENCE IN ONE ANOTHER. I LEAVE YOU A THIRST FOR EDUCATION. I LEAVE YOU A RESPECT FOR THE USE OF POWER. I LEAVE YOU FAITH. I LEAVE YOU RACIAL DIGNITY. I LEAVE YOU A DESIRE TO LIVE HARMONIOUSLY WITH YOUR FELLOW MEN. I LEAVE YOU FINALLY, A RESPONSIBILITY TO OUR YOUNG PEOPLE." Their capitalization reproduces the format of the original will, mirroring them on the monument. It includes Bethune's signature in cursive writing, which points to her authorship of the document, evokes her voice, and makes the iconicity from which the monument draws all the more visceral and dynamic. These words are positioned to almost fully embrace and nearly surround the figures on the pedestal. Their citation on the monument points to their centrality in defining her life's work and legacy.

Prior to the Bethune monument's erection, the landscape had to be lowered to ensure that it would not be taller than the Freedman's Memorial to Abraham Lincoln; the latter was turned away from a view of the Capitol so that it would face the monument featuring Bethune.⁴⁷ Lincoln Park, the largest park on Capitol Hill, is located east of the Capitol Building and was designed for public use. In 1867, when Congress named the park Lincoln Square, it became the first place named for the president after his assassination. Erected in 1876 and unveiled at a ceremony at which the speakers included Frederick Douglass, Freedman's Memorial was the first national memorial to the martyred president.[48]

The statue figures Lincoln reading the Emancipation Proclamation, which freed black slaves in the South and was delivered in 1863, during the Civil War, as he reaches his hand over a former slave, whose wrists are shackled with broken chains. The juxtaposition of an image of Bethune with a statue of Lincoln that emphasizes his role in the antislavery movement and his reputation as the Great Emancipator situates her legacy as a leader on the continuum with the struggles against slavery in the nineteenth century, as an African American leader born to ex-slaves during Reconstruction, who served as a primary advocate for African Americans in the national arena until the dawn of the civil rights movement in the twentieth century. The spatial distance between these monuments symbolically marks the time from slavery to freedom, as the two children depicted on the Bethune monument also hearken to the future.

The juxtaposition of the public monument honoring Bethune with a public monument that had been developed in the late nineteenth century, after the Civil War, as a tribute to President Lincoln frames her as a central agent in the long (and, as some scholars argue, *unfinished*) historical struggle for black emancipation in the United States. In embodying a woman such as Bethune as a black national leader in the public space of Lincoln Park, the monument unsettles the conventional marginalization of black women within narratives of African American liberation, which typically foreground black male subjectivity. Through the figure of Bethune, the monument frames discourses of Emancipation in relation to black women's subjectivity and cites her as a representative leader and black women as agents, which is significant given what Robyn Wiegman has described as black women's silencing and exclusion as raced and gendered subjects within emancipationist discourses.[49]

This monument to Lincoln has recently become the object of intense public scrutiny. In the midst of the protests that erupted after George Floyd's death at the hands of Minneapolis police officer Derrick Chauvin on May 25, 2020, and activists' demands for the removal of monuments around the nation dedicated to Confederate heroes and other racist figures in American history, Freedman's Memorial faced public criticism for its depiction of a slave kneeling subordinately beside the figure of Lincoln, and protesters attempted to tear it down. Recent calls for the removal of this statue echo long-standing concerns about this subservient image; the ex-slaves who financed the monument had no say in selecting the final design. District of Columbia representative Eleanor Holmes Norton, who has criticized this monument in the past, announced that she would introduce legislation to the House of Representatives urging its removal.⁵⁰

The geographic positioning of the monument on the nation's capital pays tribute to Bethune as a national figure while invoking the legacy of her work in the capital as president of the NCNW and as a figure in national politics. The monument's positioning in the capital links her legacy to the primary platform on which her influence unfolded. The permanent paean to Bethune in a public park in the capital city, which is geographically located south of the Mason Dixon Line, is all the more significant when considering the long-standing policies of segregating such spaces in the U.S. South and prohibiting African Americans from entering them. It hearkens to Bethune's trajectory of influence, which emerged in the rural South, reached the nation's capital, and eventually affected national and global affairs.⁵¹ The Mary McLeod Bethune Memorial emblematizes the central role of visual art in honoring and memorializing Bethune in the capital.

Dorothy Height, whose name also appears on the monument as the organization's president, documents the NCNW's process in developing it and its determination to "get Ma on the park." In *Open Wide the Freedom Gates*, Height acknowledges those who helped to conceive the project and lend support from its earliest stages. Her compelling and detailed firsthand chronicle documents the background of the monument, including how the idea originated and legislative hurdles that had to be cleared even before the NCNW undertook a multiyear fundraising campaign to make the monument materialize. Height, who led the NCNW for forty years, from 1957 to 1997, and was a champion of women's rights, civil rights, and gay rights, goes on to acknowledge the bill's signing into law by President Dwight Eisenhower, which was "the first joint resolution passed by the Eighty-second Congress, authorizing the NCNW to erect a memorial statue on public land in Washington, D.C."⁵² The perspective she offers is helpful for explaining the vision behind the monument and the role of the NCNW in drafting the original congressional resolution, further elaborating the logic of linking it to the tribute to President Lincoln, while framing it as a symbol for African American experience from the post-Emancipation period on to future generations. Furthermore, it acknowledges the role of a former slave in developing the tribute to Lincoln, which also depicts a slave marking the moment of Emancipation, as the representation of Bethune looks well beyond.

In the legal prioritization of family as a primary category of inheritance in the will as a legal document, it is significant that the inscription of phrases from Bethune's famous "My Last Will and Testament" around the base of the Mary McLeod Bethune monument, along with the children the monument features, construct African Americans as a symbolic family to whom she makes her bequest to promote the betterment of the large, diverse national family of Americans. The monument's portrait of Bethune builds on the symbolic capital invested in her as both a leader and a maternal figure in the African American context and further abstracts it at a national level. The two children who accompany the image of her on the pedestal reinforce this imaging of her as a leader and figurative mother, and they stand in for the collective body of young people whom she invokes in this document.

The law plays a constitutive role in shaping performative speech acts in the classic sense delineated by J. L. Austin and is concomitantly linked to the deconstruction of gender and sexual identity categories by Judith Butler in her classic theorization of performativity.[53] Bethune tropes the legality of the will in the title of "My Last Will and Testament" and in aspects of its content. Her repeated invocation of the phrase "I LEAVE" as she lists each of her nine bequests are readable as performative speech acts that confer these items to her posterity as she mentions them and affirms her agency in this process. Over time, its message has been iterated for newer publics every time the essay has been republished in *Ebony*, and it is permanently enshrined and nationally abstracted as writ in bronze on the monument's base.

Indeed, the Mary McLeod Bethune Memorial statue is also inherently performative in its dynamic enactment of the final bequest of the will, focused on youth, in staging the figure of Bethune holding a scroll, implicitly the will, as children, symbolizing the future, reach for it. It represents her in action instilling her message in young people, who will stand at the vanguard in the struggles for black liberation and equality in the United States. The statue draws primarily on this document in its composition and embodies its penultimate bequest, "A RESPONSIBILITY TO YOUNG PEOPLE," three-dimensionally, by staging the figure of Bethune modeling an illustration of this message, which also recollects her devotion to children in her life's work. The sculpture enacts a performance through the figures embodied on the pedestal. To explore its layered texts, including the extract from the will, the viewer must circumnavigate the monument to read its message, an aspect of its composition that further invites the viewer into a dynamic and thoughtful engagement and to view the three figures atop the pedestal from multiple angles, making the encounter with it inherently interactive.

David J. Getsy's essay "Acts of Stillness: Statues, Performativity, and Passive Resistance," which focuses its analysis on life-size and freestanding statues, argues that such statues are performative in their stillness and act on viewers through motionlessness. Getsy moves beyond conventional presuppositions that statues are simply passive and subordinate in relation to their viewers, critics, and sculptors. In his words, "Rather than see a lack of motility, I want to uphold the statue's refusal to move. Its immobility is an act—a performative act—that affects those who would approach it." "I propose that acknowledging statues' performativity and viewers' consequent desires to control it offer a means of better articulating a theory of the sculptural encounter in all of its variety. Our encounter with statues is always an encounter with other bodies that share our space, wait for us, and defiantly remain unresponsive. Consequently, a different way of characterizing the discourse of the statue is to see it as a history of its acts of passive resistance to the motile viewer or artist's attempts to assert control." As he points out, "The performativity of the act of stillness makes the statue—despite its monochromy, its immotility, its heaviness, its unresponsiveness—into something like a defiant agent."[54]

Furthermore, Getsy observes that the viewer's perceived power in motion as compared to the stillness of the monument obscures the latter's "critical passivity," or "enactment of passive resistance," which he describes by drawing on discourses of nonviolent resistance: "As we have learned from the history of nonviolent resistance as a tactic of civil disobedience, the refusal to move or to respond can be a powerful act that exposes the dispensation of power and the ethics of those who wield it."[55] When the Bethune statue was erected, it embodied the dimensions of nonviolent resistance philosophy in modern sculpture and linked them to civil rights discourses. By drawing on Barbara Johnson's discussion of muteness as a condition for idealizing the feminine in Western poetry to examine stillness in sculpture, Getsy provides rich critical foundations on which to think about Bethune's representation on the Mary McLeod Bethune Memorial. It is all the more subversive when considering how it resists and unsettles the subalternity intimately associated with the feminine body in this genre through the multilayered texts that it voices in relation to this figure in sculptural form.

Notably, Height's powerful testimony on July 2, 1982, before the U.S. Senate in the hearings concerning bill S. 2436, which proposed to designate the Mary McLeod Bethune Council House in Washington, DC, as a national historic site, also invokes the Mary McLeod Bethune monument and underscores Bethune's status as a representative African American, along with the leader's national and global significance for a diverse range of people:

Mary McLeod Bethune was chosen as the symbol because she was the undisputed person of this century who represented what all could agree upon was our contribution and we wanted that to be there, not only for the present but for future generations.

In that whole process there was a lot that we learned about Mrs. Bethune, but I think most of all we found that there was a coming together of people of every race, of every class, of every nationality with some from other parts of the world joining hands so that the Bethune Memorial in Lincoln Park became something which we were proud of.[56]

This pioneering project drew on Bethune's legacy of welcoming and bringing diverse people together through her leadership approach. It established groundwork for several later projects in the capital and beyond that have also been developed to honor Bethune, including the new national monument in Statuary Hall in the making.

As the Bethune legacy powerfully illustrates, the paternal and maternal motifs that have been foundational to conventional white-centered American national narratives have often been expanded, mirrored, and repeated with a distinct difference in the African American context. Yet they have remained limited because they have been preconditioned on (hetero)normative formulations of gender and sexuality. Visionary civil rights narratives within the modern civil rights movement that have invoked mothers, fathers, children, and family, including Bethune's, are distinct from citations of these categories within neoconservativism later in the twentieth century and into the new millennium. This latter movement's shameless and egregious appropriations of civil rights symbols, however, suggest the importance of ensuring that civil rights discourses vigilantly resist such reactionary mechanisms and formulate broader and far more inclusive definitions and advocacy agendas for family and children than ones that have typically been envisioned and sanctioned by the right wing. This is particularly vital given that right-wing rhetoric now serves as a springboard for mobilizing white supremacists and white nationalists; is routinely invoked in exclusionary scripts of American identity based on race, ethnicity, and sexuality; and is often weaponized in ways that undermine democracy and inclusive citizenship. Its reach has exponentially expanded under the leadership of Donald Trump in the contemporary political climate, fomenting misogynistic, antiblack, anti-immigrant, and antigay policies and propaganda.

Bethune and the Politics of Representing American Women

The efforts to memorialize Bethune's work and legacy began toward the end of her life with the establishment of the Mary McLeod Bethune Foundation. The main effort after the monument, the Bethune Council House, also serves as a primary repository for archives related to black women, first opened in 1979 and was officially established as a national historic site in 1982 by Public Law 97-329. Yet ironically, the very idea of Bethune as a representative figure of national womanhood was challenged during the 1985 congressional hearings held to amend the original act of October 15, 1982, which officially designated the Mary McLeod Bethune Council House as a national historic site. That is to say, some aspects of the dialogues related to questions regarding funding for this landmark institution in honor of Bethune were inflected by raced and gendered contestations of the highest order concerning the legitimacy of her status as a representative American and woman. It is noteworthy, for example, that some arguments questioning the institution's historical merit were premised on an implicit view of whiteness as being normative in constructing a universal and representative American identity, along with *woman* as a category, a binary framework that obscured sexuality altogether.

The initiative was partly spearheaded by the NCNW because the Bethune Council House was where Bethune both lived and worked during her years in the capital and lay in the continuum with these earlier projects to memorialize her. The public documents related to these hearings are important and worthy of revisiting analytically in their multilayered and multivocal textuality, with testimonies related to Bethune's national significance and public work, in part because they underscore her continuing significance. Because they were not widely discussed in the media, and they unfolded over a span of several years, the cultural implications of these historic hearings and the body of public records related to them have not been sufficiently recognized or examined. They are revealing not only for the attestations they provide related to her national contributions and continuing investments in youth as articulated in the "Last Will," but also because the dialogues on Bethune throw into relief reactionary resistances to black womanhood's embodiments of American national identity.

The contestations about Bethune's representativeness as an American woman that emerged during these hearings demonstrate how notions of national femininity have been tacitly defined by white subjectivity and have constituted essentialist and exclusionary definitions of nationality, gender, and race premised on heterosexuality. This aspect of the proceedings seems intensely ironic considering how Bethune disrupted and expanded prevailing notions of national femininity that marginalized and excluded black women in her lifetime through her striking record of public work and her legacy of representing the interests of black women on a national and global platform. It is also revealing to analyze how the strategies for framing Bethune within the rhetoric of the testimonies shifts and evolves over the course of the hearings, so that an emphasis on the national implications of her legacy and representativeness as an American woman is later substituted for a primary emphasis on her work on behalf of black women and children by advocates for the development of the Bethune Council House as a national historic site. During the hearings, the equally intriguing questions that emerged about the feasibility and appropriateness of publicly funding the museum in Bethune's honor were steeped in doubts by NPS representatives about her suitability as a persona for educating the general public about history.

The hearings related to the Bethune Council House were among the most salient national dialogues related to a black woman in the U.S. public sphere prior to the infamous Anita Hill–Clarence Thomas hearings before the Senate Judiciary Committee in 1991. They occurred at a moment of heightened debates in black and other feminist of color discourses over white-centered definitions of *woman* that obscured women of color. During the testimony, rationales about the importance of dedicating a national historic site in Bethune's honor on the nation's capital were weighed against the existing museum and archives at her home in Daytona Beach, Florida, which were argued to be too peripheral to highlight her national significance. Such arguments demonstrate the geographic contestations that emerged in constructing this national historic site, foreground dialectics of nation and region in Bethune's public construction, and illustrate the role of geographic location in shaping perceptions of national identity.[57]

Bethune emerges as a quintessential example in the twentieth century of how the U.S. South has inflected the nationalization and globalization of black and feminine subjects and grounded their iconic representation in the U.S. public sphere, a phenomenon I am tracing across the chapters of this study by studying signal examples from postslavery/Reconstruction to this new millennial era. Moreover, the salience of sites in this dialogue, such as Council House as an architecture, reflects the pronounced effects of space and geography in the African American context. The processes of monumentalizing and memorializing Bethune in the nation's capital hold weighty implications for the role of black female subjectivity in shaping discourses on national femininity, as well as registering the dynamic role that Bethune played in shaping discourses of national femininity during her lifetime and well beyond. The journey from establishing the Bethune Council House as a national historic site in 1982, and the legislative campaign to administer the institution under the NPS, which was finally achieved in 1994, was long and challenging. Studying key steps in this process is useful in light of what it reveals about discourses of nation, race, gender, and sexuality, as well as for what it can add to our understanding of Bethune's legacy. Dialogues on Bethune that unfolded during the hearings have added value in raising questions about the status of black women within areas such as black history, American history, and women's history, as well as adding to insights on her in areas from black feminism to law, including critical race feminism.

The Bethune Council House in Washington, DC, is an elegant three-story brick home replete with a raised basement, one-story bay window, and carriage house. It was built in 1876 in the Second Empire style and is located at 1318 Vermont Avenue. It was established as the headquarters for the NCNW in 1944 during Bethune's tenure as the organization's founding president and was a project that she spearheaded. Bethune resided there from 1943 until 1949, and it served as her base in the capital until she died in 1955. Dissatisfaction with the vision of the NACW, which had focused mainly on domestic concerns related to women instead of political affairs, along with the need that she perceived for a national organization to give more visibility and voice to black women's organizations in policy-related issues at the national level, drove Bethune to propose the development of the NCNW in 1935. As Joyce Hanson notes, "She envisioned her council as a vehicle for constructing a wider scope for African American women's organizations and promoting black women's participation within the new political climate created by the New Deal. During her tenure in the Roosevelt administration, Bethune attempted to expand black women's roles in the New Deal program, yet whenever she tried to get black women patronage positions, white administrators often wanted to know what organization she represented."[58]

The organization that Bethune envisioned promised to ground black women's activism during an era when interest groups were widespread, and she needed an organizational anchor as one of the nation's foremost black leaders.[59] Bethune suggested that the headquarters of the organization be located in Washington, DC. She soon secured the row house on Vermont Avenue and raised the five-hundred-dollar down payment for the residence from friends. With a generous donation of ten thousand dollars from Marshall Field, facilitated by First Lady Eleanor Roosevelt, Bethune paid off most of the balance on the fifteen-thousand-dollar property.

The project was endorsed on December 18, 1943, by the NCNW's board of directors, which included a regionally diverse cohort of twenty-four women. The council financed repairs and upgraded the facilities of the residence. Furnishing the rooms in the residence of the Council House was a collective effort. Businessman Abe Lichtman took responsibility for the front parlor and the board room, whose lavish mahogany conference tables and chairs were provided by Chicago congressman William L. Dawson. The remaining rooms were furnished by council members, including national sororities such as Alpha Kappa Alpha and Delta Sigma Theta, as well as individuals such as Emma Kelly, founder of the Daughter Elks. The Council House was dedicated October 12–15, 1944, in several ceremonies, including a service attended by distinguished guests, such as First Lady Eleanor Roosevelt. Flags from nations around the world were on display in a flag stand on the mantle, visible as guests entered the elaborate parlor.[60]

The Council House served multiple purposes, including as Bethune's office in Washington, DC, and as her primary residence in the capital for several years. Its primary purpose was for NCNW business, including committee meetings, as well as social engagements that the organization hosted. From its earliest years, publications such as the NCNW's newsletter *Telefact* were assembled and distributed from Council House. It was the site of an Open House in 1945 on the occasion of the fourth inauguration of President Roosevelt. Female visitors boarded frequently in the residence's uppermost room, which made it a refuge during an era when hotels were routinely segregated.

The successful collaboration of Dorothy Height, Dolphin Thompson, and Elise Austin with Ohio representative Frances Bolton in drafting the congressional resolution to establish a monument to Bethune in Lincoln Park set a precedent and served as a vital point of reference for efforts to establish national sites in tribute to Bethune in the Washington, DC, area. The initiative to honor Bethune by establishing Council House as a national historic site, spearheaded primarily by the NCNW, also had to clear major legislative hurdles to be implemented. On July 2, 1982, during the hearings related to the bill to designate the Mary McLeod Bethune Council House in Washington, DC, as a national historic site, and for other purposes, the statements on the floor recurrently emphasized Bethune's national significance as a leader. John W. Warner, a Virginia senator who presided over the hearing before the

Subcommittee on Public Lands and Reserved Water (of the Committee on Energy and Natural Resources), describes Bethune in his opening statement as "an example of spirit and hope upon which America was founded."[61] Similarly, Oregon senator Mark O. Hatfield describes Bethune as "the most influential black woman of her generation" and frames the Council House as "not only a very important segment of black history, but as it relates to the total history of this Nation, which is such a fundamental composite of many ethnic groups and I think over the years we have tended to neglect the vital part played by every facet of the history by the blacks."[62] Hatfield's commentary underscores Bethune's role as an international adviser on issues related to human rights and maps the Council House as a site visited not only by important figures in black history, from Charles Drew to Mary Church Terrell, but also by national and international figures such as Eleanor Roosevelt and William S. Tubman. Hatfield's implicit rationale is that the Council House merits recognition as a national historic site for its relevance to American history in and beyond the African American context, as well as to leaders of national and international significance who had visited the site at some point.

In 1970, the Afro-American Institute for Historic Preservation and Community Development began to survey the nation's land planning and noticed the paucity of national historic sites focused on African Americans. Because only three of fifteen hundred sites had been designed to highlight the role of African Americans in the nation's development, the organization began to work with the NPS to assess sites for possible development with the idea of incorporating them into the national park system.[63] As the final stages for installing the Mary McLeod Bethune Memorial were unfolding, the institute began a dialogue with the NCNW about the possibilities for spotlighting the Council House during the upcoming bicentennial celebration. The idea for the initiative to establish the Council House as a national historic site notably crystallized on the road to commemorating the nation's 1976 bicentennial, a point that Height mentions in her statement during the 1982 hearings.

Sue Bailey Thurmond, whose statement was presented by Bettye Collier-Thomas, the director of historic programs at the NCNW, maps the Council House as an epicenter for a range of civic and diplomatic projects during both the war and postwar eras.[64] Such comments reinforce and extend Hatfield's earlier framing of the Council House as a site regularly visited by numerous figures of national and international significance, framing it as an energetic scene where decisions were made frequently that had bearing on various states. They call to mind a vivid image of the Council House as the architectural locus in the capital from which Bethune journeyed to other parts of the nation as an ambassador for the NCNW and to help advance various national initiatives. If the White House is where governmental affairs unfolded in the capital and where many crucial national policy decisions related to the African American population were made, then the Bethune Council House lay in its shadows as an architecture where decisions with national relevance to blacks were also made. It anchored the spokes that reached out to black women's organizations in states across the nation and launched the trips to them. Furthermore, it even functioned as a veritable think tank for brainstorming and developing agendas related to black women. Thurmond's use of the word *beehive* evokes the Council House as a site trafficked by a host of dignitaries, as a building animated by constant activity, and as a symbolic home for black women in the nation, implicitly with Bethune as the queen bee.

The recurring commentaries during the 1982 hearings about Bethune's national and international significance, notwithstanding her legacy of prolific work and leadership legacy at the national level, reflect an understanding of the prevailing exclusion of African Americans, particularly African American women, from national narratives. Furthermore, they reflect awareness of the connection of this problematic to long-standing views of blacks as being inferior and perceptions of them as being irrelevant to world history. They reveal an awareness of tensions between her race and gender that her status as a black woman throws into relief given purist perceptions of American identity as being deracialized and detached from black subjectivity during a period when black feminism was challenging such politics of exclusion based on race, gender, and sexuality.

The cooperative agreement reserving the rights of the NCNW to help processes of preservation and interpretation at the Council House and that give the secretary of the interior, under the auspices of the NPS, access to public sections on the premises was initially acknowledged during these groundbreaking proceedings. The agreement made alterations contingent on mutual agreement and an annual report from the NCNW to enable oversight of activities and expenditures supported by governmental funding. As the cooperative agreement continued to develop in subsequent years, the NCNW also notably pledged to raise funding to supplement its proposed governmental support, demonstrating the self-help strategy that had been apparent during the years of work to bring the Mary McLeod Bethune Memorial project to fruition in Lincoln Park.

The NCNW had long been responsible for the perseverance of the Bethune Council House since its establishment in 1943 as the organization's national headquarters, a purpose the institution served until 1966. The building could not have ever survived over several decades and into the 1980s without the organization's sustained and ongoing fiscal support and commitment. The urging during the 1982 hearings that the organization seek out private donations to sustain the institution, as if this were some novel idea that the leaders had neglected to attempt up to the point of the hearings, underscored that the NPS had been entirely oblivious to the NCNW's history of ongoing and tireless work over several decades to sustain the institution, along with the NCNW's ongoing efforts to make the institution itself a private funding source. The NCNW simply sought to establish stability and continuity for the Bethune Council House in its public funding, maintenance, and administration, which the NPS was best designed to facilitate. At the same time, the proposed cooperative agreement provided a vehicle for the organization to continue to contribute financially to the livelihood of Council House.

The statement of Joseph Burstein, a lawyer at Fried, Frank, Harris, Shriver, and Kampelman, whose relationship with the NCNW was established through his past work with Housing and Urban Development, provides the most significant endorsement and rationale for the cooperative agreement during the course of the 1982 hearings. His testimony relates it to a Mississippi project funded by the Ford Foundation in which the NCNW participated, wherein an agreement was made to help residents gain equity in, and eventually ownership of, the homes they rented to highlight the organization's belief in financial self-help and principles such as cooperation and collaboration. He emphasizes that "the National Council as you have heard otherwise this morning is not looking for Government handouts. They are prepared not only on behalf of themselves but on behalf of the people they are trying to help to get the people to do so on the basis of helping themselves and providing a place of dignity for their families."[65] In his testimony, Burstein affirms the cooperative agreement as the best arrangement for operating the Council House in the future.

Moreover, his wording suggests his awareness of stereotypes of black codependency on the government, which were proliferating within reactionary Republican ideology, that cast young black single mothers as "welfare queens" who were lazy and unwilling to work, leeching off the government by relying on public assistance and exploiting the tax dollars of hard-working Americans. Yet the NCNW's sustained and autonomous work in developing the Council House for years, as well as the proposition to remain involved in the institution's financing to supplement its prospective federal funding, made the project a model self-help initiative spearheaded by black women during the first years of the Reagan era. In Burstein's statement, he also points out, "Black women's history, of course, is black history in this country," echoing the points that had already been made to emphasize the national significance of Bethune and national relevance of the Council House's archives related to black women's history.[66]

Ira J. Hutchinson, deputy director of the NPS, advocates in his statement for a study "to determine the national significance" to help the organization in making a recommendation on the Council House's eligibility for national historic site designation and points out that no such study had yet been conducted. He also acknowledges the body of scholarly material that addresses the issue in the wake of the prior hearing before the House. The presiding senator, John Warner, notes the presence of those in the audience who had literally devoted their lives to the study of Bethune and points out the work that had been accomplished in assessing her legacy during the bicentennial celebration. Hutchinson also expresses concern about committing federal involvement to a property not federally owned and hence reservations about the cooperative agreement and a preference for sole federal oversight of the Council House. In Hutchinson's words, "In this time of austerity and fiscal constraints, we are in a posture at this point and time where at best we would see in our relationships with owners of non-Federal property a limitation of funding basically to technical assistance and consultation and other activities in that area."[67] The insistence on a study was ironic considering that the NPS had refused to do one when the Council House was initially proposed as a national historic site.[68]

Dimensions of the hearings in both 1982 and 1985 are revealing for demonstrating how race and gender shape perceptions of the national body and for illustrating ways in which normative notions of American identity and the category *woman* have been routinely dissociated from black female subjectivity. These national dialogues are further significant and useful to study because they unfolded at a time when black feminists and other feminists of color were increasingly deconstructing essentialist scripts of the category woman as *white* and advocating for the recognition of terms of identity, such as race, class, and gender, as interlocking variables in shaping oppression. While the Council House was successfully established as a national historic site, such issues as Hutchinson voiced would resurface assertively in the 1985 hearings and reveal the lingering concerns that persisted within the administrative ranks of the NPS about the financial feasibility of continuing to provide federal funding for this museum, as well as questions about the historical significance and national representativeness of Bethune herself. Much of the testimony from advocates of the project seemed to anticipate these concerns and gross misapprehensions related to Bethune's national significance, even appearing designed to address them forthrightly.

The raced and gendered contestations related to Bethune's national significance and historical relevance fully erupted during the 1985 congressional hearings, chaired by Bill Vento, which addressed H.R. 1391, proposing the designation of the Mary McLeod Bethune Council House as a national historic site and for other uses. Mary Lou Grier, the deputy director of the NPS, went on the record opposing the measure. She acknowledged the original authorization of $200,000 annually to the council in grants and assistance, which included a proviso that the council contribute $100,000 in matching funds, and she itemized the disbursement of the funding to the council annually from the time that the original historic site was established in 1982 until 1985. Grier explains that the new bill was designed to amend the original 1982 legislation in two ways, including changing all references in the act from National Council of Negro Women to the Mary McLeod Bethune Archives and designating $200,000 annually to carry out the act, along with additional grants of $500,000 that would be matched by the museum in money or services. She then argues against H.R. 1391 primarily on the grounds that supporting the measure would go beyond the original intention to merely help establish the institution and would authorize the subvention of its operating needs indefinitely.

Her implication is that the original goals of the measure had been redefined and extended in the interim years since the historic site had been established in ways that well exceeded its original intent. In Grier's words, "As we understand the initial legislation, Mr. Chairman, it was to authorize funds to assist in the marking, interpretation, and restoration of the site which was designated as a national historic site in that legislation. We did not understand the intent of Congress to be that the act was a vehicle for funding the annual operating costs of the museum, and we believe those costs should be met from private sources. For that reason, we do not support an indefinite annual authorization of $200,000 or the $500,000 matching grant provision."[69] Despite the NCNW's initiative in providing the requisite matching funding annually and demonstrated commitment in following through in fulfilling this obligation, Grier suggests that the organization assume *full* responsibility for funding the operation and maintenance of the site dedicated to Bethune without the benefit of any further public financial support and underscores a private funding source as the best option.

At play here is fundamentally a question related to the role that the state should play in supporting an institution designated primarily to preserving the history and archives related to an African American woman, as well as the question of whether it has any responsibility at all. Grier's imposition of a rigid public/private binary is grounded in either/or logic that devalues the middle ground that the original bill's cooperative agreement had effectively achieved. The dichotomy implied in Grier's logic recasts the conventional ideology of "separate spheres," which primarily associates male subjectivity with "public" contexts while relegating female subjects to the "private" and domestic spaces.[70] The logic is all the more ironic considering Bethune's long-standing commitment to work in the nation's public sphere, not to mention how generously and tirelessly she worked throughout her life in raising funds, along with various organizations, to support education.

In the implied advocacy for a reliance on philanthropy, Grier in effect obscures how the appropriations committee had reduced the funding the year before, how much the Council House had already been sustained by private funding, and the challenge such a process might entail, particularly amid the economic downturn of the 1980s. In general, the drastic budget cuts of Ronald Reagan's presidential administration, which eliminated or severely reduced forms of public assistance that had been a lifeline to poor blacks and other minorities, registered for many as a sound reversal of Roosevelt's New Deal, which had offered so many hopes and possibilities to blacks in the 1930s. Furthermore, Grier's logic reflects the policymaking trajectory within right-wing political agendas, which favored corporate privatization and a retreat from any forms of government intervention (i.e., to discourage "big government"), that would increasingly be propagated within the discourse of neoconservatism. These factors also make it imperative to weigh her arguments in light of her Republican Party affiliation.

A native Texan, Mary Lou Grier's career in the Republican Party began in 1957 in the Bexar County Republican Party, of which she was vice chair from 1961 to 1965. Because of her pioneering achievements at the state level, in 1971, the Texas Federation of Republican Women named her as the Outstanding Republican Woman of Texas in 1971. In 1972, she served as a delegate to the Republican National Convention. Grier then served as deputy director and acting director of the Bureau of Outdoor Recreation in the Department of the

Interior from 1976 to 1977. She was also deputy director and acting director of the NPS from 1982 to 1986, an administrative term that aligned with the period during which the major congressional hearings related to the Bethune Council House unfolded at the national level.[71]

The strategic spatial juxtaposition of the Mary McLeod Bethune Memorial and Freedman's Memorial visualizes African Americans as a racial category through Bethune as a figure. In the public space of Lincoln Park, the monument to her stands as visual embodiment of black racial progress. She not only emerges as a representative black and female subject, but also as a representative American. As a precedent, this national monument and the significations attached to it are useful to recall when weighing how Grier's commentary tacitly dislodges Bethune as a representative of the national body because of her race and gender. Grier's opposition to increasing public funding for the Bethune museum as a historic site frames and in a sense veils larger concerns that surface as the hearings progress about whether history related to Bethune is truly relevant to the diverse body of American citizens who might conceivably visit a historic site, or universal in a sense that would merit such a substantial and sustained investment of public funding.

Significantly, the remarks of Ohio representative Mary Rose Oakar, immediately following Grier's testimony, begin by indicating that Oakar will submit a formal statement for the record and go on to emphasize the whitecenteredness of history books and how history has ignored black women's contributions. Oakar notes black women's contributions to a range of areas, highlighting Shirley Chisholm, Barbara Jordan, Harriet Tubman, and Rosa Parks.[72]

For Oakar, questions related to funding the museum in honor of Bethune become the backdrop for discussing the history of black women's marginal representation in Congress. Her comments situate Bethune's legacy as a black leader in the continuum with the first black woman elected to Congress, Shirley Chisholm, and to Chisholm's pioneering run for the presidency. Oakar's statement overviews the history of black women's leadership and radical activism, from slavery to the civil rights era, culminating in a mention of Rosa Parks, spotlighting black women who have made the most profound national impact.

Contrary to Grier's argument that the financial investment proposed in the revised bill is exorbitant and excessive, Oakar insists that the sum is relatively small. She makes the case for funding the Bethune museum and for its very existence by acknowledging it as an archive that will draw black women, and all women, along with their families, to the nation's capital. Oakar links the ignorance about black women's achievements to the lack of knowledge related to her own ethnic background as a person of Jewish descent. Furthermore, drawing on her experience as a community college teacher as the field of black studies emerged, Oakar mentions her observation of the routine exclusion of black women in black history as a further rationale for funding the museum and archiving and preserving black women's history. In her comments, Oakar posits Bethune as another model and representative black woman as she frames the Bethune museum as an exceptional institution for documenting the history of black women. The formal written statement reinforces and builds on the main points of this oral testimony. Oakar dialectically links the erasure of black women in U.S. history to the invisibility of women in American history and acknowledges the unique challenges in preserving research on black women.[73]

After Oakar's testimony during the hearings, Bill Vento, the chair, notes the overall congressional support for the museum as a historic site, and he presses Grier to explain the grounds on which she is opposing it: "Since we have demonstrated the strong support in Congress, . . . your testimony does not reflect that—that the Administration did support the initial measure in 1982. Here we have started something in terms of the Mary McLeod Bethune program, the legislation establishing it. Why the change [of] that support at this particular point? We seemed like we were on to something where there was a commonality of a goal. I'm sure that you don't disagree necessarily with the necessity of the archives. Why?"[74]

Grier mentions the Park Service's opposition to the 1982 bill based on questions about the museum's historical significance and argues that the standard procedure of exhaustive professional historical investigation when Congress designates a national historic site was not used in researching Bethune. Furthermore, she notes that the Park Service is recognizing black women's contributions within its Women's Rights National Historical Park, an institution "not specifically targeted in one case just to black women."[75] She mentions the dedication of Maggie Walker's home in Richmond, Virginia, by the NPS, and the exhaustive research into her background prior to authorizing the project as a case in point. Vento concludes that though the NPS had approved the site in 1982, Grier nevertheless seemed to be raising questions about the appropriateness of designating the museum as a historic site.

For Grier, Bethune's status as a black woman seems to be the primary factor that implicitly informs the sense that Bethune's legacy is too narrow to be representative for *all* Americans, including all women. Grier implies that the cultural memory related to Bethune is too distant or irrelevant for recollection, while obscuring and dismissing it during the hearings. In invoking women, Grier's logic associates the category primarily with a white feminine subjectivity implied to be normative and representative.

The urge for private funding for the museum articulated during the 1985 congressional hearings unfolded during the Reagan era, as federal fiscal retrenchments and cutbacks held dire consequences for the African American population. Indeed, while the council primarily consisted of middle-class black women, the raced and gendered logic of Grier's commentary and the staunch resistances she outlines in her platform opposing continued public funding for the Bethune museum and questioning Bethune's historical significance mirror and recast the public debate that the right wing was spearheading about welfare, dialogues that pathologized black women as single mothers and caricatured them.

The testimony of Bettye Collier-Thomas, the director of the Bethune Council House national historic site, adds valuable perspective to the congressional hearings by making a distinction between the "house museum" that Grier mentioned and the museum site dedicated to Bethune: "As a museum which does changing exhibitions and develops various educational materials and which utilizes manuscripts and artifacts to develop key themes in black women's history, the requirements for interpretation of the Bethune Council House are very different from those of a house-museum."[76] Collier-Thomas underscores that a professional and credentialed staff trained in research is necessary to hire at the site to fulfill its mission and its rigorous programming and exhibitions, which are unlike typical house-museums where displays remain static and do not require staffing at this level.

In her comments, Collier-Thomas also challenges Grier's claim that the Women's Rights National Historical Park adequately represents black women by explaining that this institution, despite its efforts to include black women, remains primarily focused on white women in American history:

> Also, Ms. Grier mentioned that they do black women's history as a part of their interpretation at other sites. She mentioned the National Women's Park. As a professional historian who has expertise in women's history, I am very familiar with the National Women's Park and indeed served as a consultant to that and the National Women's Hall of Fame when they were originally developing this. They do not do any in-depth interpretation on black women. They are dealing with, in particular, documentation on the

1848 Seneca Falls Women's Conference and suffrage, and they spotlight Elizabeth Katy [sic] Stanton, Lucy Stone, and the many other renowned figures who were part of that earlier movement.[77]

Collier-Thomas addresses the aspect of Grier's testimony that questions Bethune's historical significance by pointing out, "The Mary McLeod Bethune Council House, designated in 1982 by Congress as a national historic site, serves to interpret the life and legacy [of] one of the greatest Americans to ever live."[78] Finally, Collier-Thomas asserts that the development of the museum was also in keeping with Bethune's own vision and wishes for the Council House, that it would serve as a national site for archiving and preserving black women's history, built on Bethune's tireless work doing the same.

Lindy Boggs from Louisiana, during her testimony, comments, "I support this legislation because I believe the museum and archives are a valuable national resource and that the Council House and its history are a part of the fabric of our national heritage."[79] Moreover, Boggs emphasizes the glaring disparity between the $618.68 million in federal appropriations for the year to maintain national historic sites and the mere $2 million spent to maintain the eight black historic sites, which constituted less than 5 percent of the nation's nearly two hundred historic sites. This sobering observation makes Grier's concerns about continuing funding of the Bethune Council House seem petty, unfounded, and hypocritical. The acknowledgment of these facts and figures, like the testimony about the paucity of national historic sites devoted to commemorating black history, mentioned during the Senate hearings in 1982, throws into relief the persisting devaluation, marginalization, and exclusion of black people on national agendas. It speaks to their negligible and even pitiable share in the federal funding of such public institutions, and the unapologetic designation of the lion's share of such funding to support projects in keeping with the history related to the dominant white culture, notwithstanding the contributions of black taxpayers and other minorities. This reluctance to invest in the development of national historic sites related to black history mirrored, for example, the underfunding of predominantly black schools during the post–civil rights era.

Grier's stated opposition to designating the Bethune Council House as a national historic site emerged as a referendum on Bethune's credibility as a representative American and woman precisely because of her identification as an African American and black woman and the lack of universalism perceived in both categories, belying Bethune's veritable iconicity and prolific historical contributions and those related to the Council House itself. The ideological dislodging of Bethune from notions of U.S. national identity in Grier's rhetoric invokes commonplace ideologies of difference and otherness in relation to black women.[80] Grier's questioning of Bethune's representativeness as an American was also intensely ironic in light of how Bethune had been targeted, beginning in 1943, by the House Un-American Activities Committee and accused of being a communist. This charge, however baseless, also resurfaced in the early 1950s, during the McCarthy era, when Bethune was denied a public speech before the board of education in Englewood, New Jersey, because of the accusation that she had communist affiliations.[81] In effect, Grier's logic obscures and attempts to displace Bethune's genuine role in shaping and even transforming notions of national femininity through her ubiquitous presence in the U.S. public sphere for several decades and her influence in the capital, from the era of the Great Depression until the time of her death. Yet Bethune's "My Last Will and Testament" affirms her view of her own legacy as being simultaneously national and global and acknowledges the potential of African Americans as a collective to transform and better the entire nation.

H.R. 5084, which authorized the NPS to gain proprietorship over the Mary Bethune Council House national historic site, under the auspices of the secretary of the interior, passed in the House of Representatives by a voice vote on July 30, 1990; was addressed by a subcommittee hearing on September 20, 1990; and was endorsed without amendment at the business meeting of the Senate Committee on Energy and Natural Resources on September 26, 1990. The accompanying report, submitted by J. Bennett Johnson Jr., begins with a background section that names Bethune as "a distinguished African American educator, political activist and leader who devoted her life to championing the causes of African American women."[82] H.R. 5084 stipulates that the property be managed by the NPS under the supervision of an advisory group with fifteen members, which would include various organizations affiliated with the Council House. It authorized cooperative agreements with private organizations to do interpretive work and administer archives. The language here primarily highlights Bethune's contributions to black women's history without acknowledging her broader contributions to U.S. history, in effect deviating from the narrative about Bethune that prior hearings in 1982 and 1985 had established.[83]

Despite the endorsement of H.R. 5084 by the two major legislative branches of government, the statement from Denis Calvin, NPS associate director for planning and development, opposed the measure. As Calvin's statement avers,

"Mr. Chairman, we oppose the enactment of H.R. 5084 and request that you defer action on this bill until the National Park Service completes a Suitability-Feasibility study to analyze alternatives for addressing several issues related to the Council House site."[84] For the NPS, even at this point, as was the case in 1982, the primary reservation about taking on supervision of the Bethune Council House continued to be the lack of a study, which it was then working to complete. As Calvin's report indicated, further concerns related to how much H.R. 5084 promised to expand the archives of the Council House, along with its scope: "H.R. 5084 significantly expands the existing scope of the Council House and the archives: Under H.R. 5084 the site would preserve and interpret the life and work of Mary McLeod Bethune, the history, lives and contributions of African-American women, and the struggle for civil rights in the United States. This expanded scope could significantly affect the operation, operating budget of the Council House, and the archives."[85] The suggestion at this point is that the implementation of the legislation be suspended until the completion of the typically requisite suitability-feasibility study.

Here, the contestations are not as ostensibly ideological as they were in Grier's testimony, which in effect questioned Bethune's historical relevance to the larger public as an African American woman. At this juncture, the lack of the study's completion notably continues to serve as the main rationale for NPS's hesitation to take on the management of the Council House. The Congressional Budget Office had projected that federal expenditures for enacting the legislation would be $1 million initially and $0.8 million annually thereafter for maintenance and operations. While the feasibility of federally financing the maintenance of the institution annually is not the major point of contestation here, as it had been in 1985, other concerns had to do with the implications of expanding the archive for the available budget. Yet it is intriguing that the two major reservations about pursuing the project, which were originally related to the absence of the study and questions of financial feasibility, when all is said and done here, fundamentally remained the same. Notwithstanding the Council House's establishment as a national historic site in 1982, it is sobering that almost a decade later, it had failed to be embraced fully as a project for supervision by the NPS, the national organization primarily responsible for managing such facilities. Inevitably, the persistence of this line of argumentation throws into relief continuing resistances to Bethune's status as a nationally representative black woman in the sense that the broad scope and range of the Council House archives devoted to her legacy of public work effectively demonstrated she was.

Subsequently, civil rights leader John R. Lewis from Georgia presented H.R. 609 in the House of Representatives on January 29, 1991, with the goal of authorizing the NPS to acquire and manage the Mary McLeod Bethune Council House national historic site, and for other purposes; the Interior and Insular Affairs Committee referred it for passage with several amendments. On March 7, 1991, the Subcommittee on National Parks and Public Lands held a hearing on H.R. 690; the amended bill was reported to the full committee on March 21, 1991, and passed on April 24 that year. According to the report summarizing the final round of debates, the background comments on Bethune began with an emphasis on her southern roots and linkages to the legacy of slavery.[86] Furthermore, they also emphasize her connections to the Roosevelts and work in support of civil rights.[87] In overviewing the activities of what was now called the Bethune Museum and Archives, the background comments primarily stress the significance of her work for black women and the relevance of the archives to black women's history. The bill was referred to the Senate, and after more modifications, it passed on October 24, 1991, and became public law on December 11.

The committee recommended donation of the National Archives for Black Women's History in light of past federal funding, a proposition that also held critical financial implications for the NCNW, given the organization's long-standing initiative to help provide administrative support for the Bethune Council House and its primary role in carrying on the museum's work. The 1991 act ended the cooperative agreement established on October 15, 1982, instead authorizing the NPS exclusively, because of its expertise, to supervise the management and administration of the site, along with its interpretation and preservation. Nonetheless, it allows the secretary of the interior the option of establishing cooperative agreements with nonprofit organizations to support the processes of interpretation and preservation, as well as to administer the archives. As this long journey culminates, the linkages of Bethune to the Roosevelts and her rural southern background are among the primary lenses through which she is made legible during this historic series of public hearings.

The discourses related to Bethune have not only unsettled white-centered notions of national femininity but have also helped decenter whiteness within notions of American identity. Public monuments from the Mary McLeod Bethune Memorial to the Bethune Council House in the nation's capital reinforce the significations of national femininity associated with her and in effect extend them, so that memorializing and enshrining Bethune in the nation's capitol has also helped to expand the definition of national femininity.

It is most significant and ironic that legal debates related to Bethune provided one of the most decisive challenges to exclusionary narratives of American identity, including notions of American womanhood, during the late twentieth century. The very contestations about her universality that emerged demonstrate persisting resistances to black women as representational models of womanhood in the nation. Aspects of the battle continue.

"The Long and Brutal Fight"

If mother-and-child motifs mediated Bethune's accessibility to advance causes related to women and children, such a platform was possibly more complicated for Pauli Murray to access because of her transness. Murray was also engaged more ambivalently and cautiously by the NAACP than leaders like Bethune, a 1935 recipient of the Spingarn Medal, for failing to conform to its protocols and standards for respectability in several instances. A cofounder of the National Organization for Women (NOW), Murray eventually left the organization because it adhered to a narrow, white-centered definition of *woman* in the sense that shadowed these hearings.

At the time these hearings were unfolding, during the 1980s, the reactionary discourses of "colorblindness" and "reverse discrimination," primarily designed to unsettle the gains of the civil rights era, expanded exponentially and have been serviceable in helping to propagate deracialized narratives of American identity, as white subjectivity stands in as its primary deracialized and unmarked signifier. This problematic has only become more pervasive in the contemporary millennial political climate, where notions of the "postracial" and "postblackness" have gained rhetorical currency. The successful establishment of Council House as a national historic site and its eventual administration under the auspices of the NPS easily stands to obscure the formidable hurdles that had to be cleared to actualize such remarkable milestones, along with some of the initial and obviously ideological resistances to funding this project federally. The debate itself valuably adds to our understanding of how politics of race, class, gender, and sexuality ideologically played out in the political realm within the emergent neoconservative era of the 1980s. The Bethune Council House was finally purchased by the NPS in 1994.

Contestations resurfaced in 2014, however, over the decision to relocate the National Archives for Black Women's History (NABWH), which had been housed on the site, to the Museum Resource Center (MRC) in Landover, Maryland. Bettye Collier-Thomas issued a press release urging that the order to shut down the collection at Council House be rescinded, that the Federal Advisory Commission ordered by Congress be reintroduced, and that budgetary funds appropriated by Congress be restored, along with a plan to purchase additional property that would facilitate expanding the collection.[88] Moreover, she included a sample letter and urged the public to contact Sally Jewell, secretary of the Department of the Interior, and Jonathan Jarvis, director of the NPS, to register their concern about the decision. Peniel Joseph describes Collier-Thomas's framing of these recent concerns within the "long and brutal fight . . . that led to the congressional designation of Mary McLeod Bethune's last residence on the nation's capital as National Historic Site."[89] In the February 22, 2014, edition of the *Washington Post*, Colbert I. King discusses the implications of the move proposed by the NPS in a piece entitled "Dishonoring Bethune's Legacy," while acknowledging the irony of announcing the plan during Black History Month: "In a letter to supporters of the Bethune site, Timothy Jenkins, the former vice chairman of the original Bethune Museum and Archives Board, calls the park service's decision a 'travesty' that 'must not stand.'"[90]

The NPS issued a statement designed to address "inaccurate" information, and emphasized that a 2013 review by the museum program found that "the carriage house does not meet the basic museum collection storage requirements" outlined in their handbook, a conclusion that an additional inspection of the site on January 10, 2014, had confirmed. The statement contradicted the claims of Council House supporters, who noted that the 108th Congress did not enact a bill introduced to expand Council House by purchasing the property adjacent to it, and that in the wake of a 2007 NPS appraisal of the adjacent property valuing it at $2 million, legislative proposals to allocate $2 million to purchase it were submitted but not approved by either the 111th Congress or the 112th in 2010. The NPS statement explained that the materials would once again be made available to the public once the three-week process of the move was completed. It pointed out that the collection would be available digitally at the Mary McLeod Bethune Council House National Historic Site, which would remain open to the public, and that Council House advisory commission would be restored.

The public dialogues and debates that have resurged in recent times suggest that the long-standing concerns about the Bethune Council House have not disappeared; that on some levels, the genuine investments of the NPS in the legacy of Bethune and in black women in the United States continue to be questioned; and that the future of the archives at Bethune Council House, even in this day and time, remains uncertain and continues to be hotly contested. These newer debates are particularly crucial to consider given the elisions of black women's historical relevance and postures of indifference to their subject category in the national context, both linked to NPS officials during the 1980s, along with their seeming devaluation of Bethune's legacy. When considering the routine exclusion by tourist agencies of the Mary McLeod Bethune Council House and the Mary McLeod Bethune Memorial in Lincoln Park on tours of the capital, the relocation of the collection to a suburban location makes it even less likely the public will be able to readily access the primary public tributes to Bethune and to be led to reflect on the vital contributions she made to this nation's history. Furthermore, the relocation of the collection to suburban Maryland, a site mainly accessible by bus, obscures the symbolic and political significance of locating the materials in the nation's capital. The new debates also build on previous arguments advanced by Timothy Jenkins, who emphasized the importance of locating the memorial to Bethune in the nation's capital to honor her national legacy.[91]

The Bethune memorial was a prototype and forerunner of various other civil rights monuments that have been erected to black national leaders in public parks and museums, while establishing groundwork for all its successors in much the same sense that Bethune helped to establish foundations for the modern civil rights movement. Significantly, the lynching of fourteen-year-old Chicago teen Emmett Till while visiting his relatives in Money, Mississippi, in the weeks after Bethune's death horrifically dramatized the vulnerability of black children in the struggle against racism and their transformative influence on the civil rights struggle. After Bethune's "Last Will," the choice to publish an image of Till's mutilated body in repose in Johnson Publishing's weekly *Jet* magazine helped fully ignite the modern movement for civil rights. Bethune's essay established groundwork for themes that emerged in later speeches and writing associated with the civil rights movement, but it also deserves recognition and study as a literary work. I value it for study in terms of its formal structure and thematic content, which culminates with a pronounced reiteration of the youth-related agenda that inflected the heart of Bethune's public work. An examination of its performative dimensions not only heightens the understanding of the legalese invoked in its scripting but also provides frameworks for thinking through its continuing circulation in published form, as well as its embodiments in the form of a public artwork like the Mary McLeod Bethune Memorial statue. The voice of Bethune that resonates in this document was both exceptional and ubiquitous at a time when few black women in politics had a similar platform. Bethune's piece, because of its publication in *Ebony* and her high profile as a leader, garnered an audience far broader than what was accessible to black women writers at the time of its publication, and this reflective piece holds significant implications in juxtaposition with the reigning genre of protest literature that proliferated at the time.

In 1989, *Ebony* highlighted her among the "50 Most Important Figures in Black U.S. History" and in 1999 included her among the "100 Most Fascinating Black Women of the 20th Century," revisiting her legacy on the cusp of a new millennium for a new generation.[92] The decline of *Ebony* in recent years makes the "Last Will" and other parts of its vast archive all the more important to study and treasure. With Bethune's birth in the years after slavery and her death in 1955, she has often been described as a leader who served as the linchpin between Reconstruction and the civil rights movement. Just a few months after Bethune's death, Rosa Parks made history by refusing to give up her seat on a public bus in Montgomery, Alabama.

Parks's choice catalyzed an international freedom movement for civil and human rights and, in effect, led to her emergence as an international icon. In many ways, during the latter half of the twentieth century, her work continued the project of civil rights activism that Bethune's had begun. While in Bethune's case, the maternal motif, which had been more legible in black communities, was more distant in national memory in the mainstream by the time of these hearings, through Rosa Parks, it was more thoroughly nationalized and even globalized in relation to black womanhood during her lifetime and consolidated further in the wake of her death. Like Bethune, Parks is useful for examining invocations of mothers and children in the work of black women political leaders, along with the limitations of such scripts. In general, the legacies of Bethune and Parks are useful to consider comparatively to the extent that they provide an epistemology on how the U.S. South has helped to constitute iconic models of black femininity that have also in effect unsettled and helped to revise and expand the prevailing discourse of national femininity in the United States. The fruitfulness in comparative approaches to black women's history in examining eras from slavery to freedom is one factor that suggests the utility of considering the legacies of Bethune and Parks side by side, and emphasizing their fascinating and seldom acknowledged interconnections.

{ 2 }

From Rosa Parks's *Quiet Strength* to Memorializing a National Mother

> As time has gone by, people have made my place in the history of the civil-rights movement bigger and bigger. They call me the Mother of the Civil Rights Movement and the Patron Saint of the Civil Rights Movement. I have more honorary degrees and plaques and awards than I can count, and I appreciate and cherish every single one of them. Interviewers still only want to talk about that one evening in 1955 when I refused to give up my seat on the bus. Organizations still want to give me awards for that one act more than thirty years ago. I am happy to go wherever I am invited and to accept whatever honors are given me. I understand that I am a symbol. But I have never gotten used to being a "public person." —ROSA PARKS, *Rosa Parks: My Story*

> Almost instantly, Parks became the most famous African American woman in America. —JOYCE HANSON, *Rosa Parks: A Biography*

Rosa Parks's body as famously visualized in the now iconic black and white mug shot photo (figure 2.1), taken as repression escalated against the Montgomery bus boycott and more than eighty of its participants valiantly identified themselves for arrest and photographing at the courthouse in February 1956, is often mistakenly thought to have been taken immediately after her arrest on the bus that fateful evening in Montgomery, Alabama, on December 1, 1955. Contextualizing Parks's photo as one among those of numerous community activists taken during this mass arrest frames the Montgomery bus boycott as

FIGURE 2.1 Rosa Parks's iconic arrest photo, February 21, 1956.

Riché Richardson, *Rosa Parks, Whose "No" in 1955 Launched the Montgomery Bus Boycott and Was Heard around the World*, 2006–12. Dedicated to Georgette Norman. Photograph © Mickey Welsh—USA TODAY NETWORK.

a collective movement while resisting the typical narratives that idealize her as a lone heroine who chose to remain seated on the bus. This photo is also instructive and revealing for purposes of reflecting on that evening, in showing her dressed in a suit, hat, and glasses, with a pinned-up braided hairstyle, replete with a flower pin, which bore all the conventional gendered and sexed significations of a "lady," and highlighted gender and sexuality alongside race as factors that had made her legible on the bus as a public space.

Civil rights supporter Virginia Durr's account of the evening of the arrest notably emphasizes Parks's appearance and demeanor: "She was an exceedingly fine-looking woman and very neatly dressed and such a lady in every way—so genteel and so extremely well-mannered and quiet."[1] Because black women were invisible within the category *lady*, in addition to humiliating Parks based on her race, it was defeminizing that she, along with all other black women targeted by this routine degradation and abuse, was expected by law to give up her seat to a white man on a public bus. Such hostility was steeped in the systematized ungendering of black bodies, a phenomenon Hortense Spillers links to the violence against blackness during antebellum slavery. Within public spaces of the Jim Crow era, codes of respectability as signaled through their fashioning elicited white anger and abuse and made African Americans more vulnerable in some instances.[2] The white male passenger; the bus driver, James Blake; and the two police officers who were called to the scene had no social obligation to respect Parks. As Felicia McGhee has pointed out, "The city gave bus drivers the responsibility to maintain segregation on the buses."[3] White men most often denied such time-honored social courtesies to black women, who were expected to know their "place" and stay in it. Such courtesies were a residual trace of the romanticized raced, classed, and gendered ideology of the "southern lady" from the antebellum era, who was defined as white in the southern cultural imaginary.

When Parks refused to give up her seat on the Montgomery bus that fateful evening in 1955, she risked life and limb in resisting the authority of at least four white men in a southern public space. In a later interview, Blake obviously remained unrepentant for the actions he took against Parks on the bus that evening: "I wasn't trying to do anything to that Parks woman except do my job. She was in violation of the city codes, so what was I supposed to do? That damn bus was full and she wouldn't move back. I had my orders."[4] His desubjectifying and dismissive reference to her as "that Parks woman" mirrored the forms of sexed and gendered degradation that shadowed the original encounter and parallels his reference to her that night on the bus as "that one."[5]

The ways in which Parks confronted racism through her courageous choice to remain seated sometimes obscure the levels on which she also in effect confronted sexism that fateful December evening. According to Parks biographer Douglas Brinkley, who draws on Parks's reflections, Blake directed most of his hostility and verbal tirades at black women with slurs such as "bitch" and "coon."[6] Such epithets are inflected by a host of raced, sexed, and gendered pathologies and stereotypes. Long-standing ideologies of black female sexuality, traceable back to slavery (again, a system that Spillers has notably argued "ungendered" black men and women), inflected the flagrant disregard for Parks on the bus given her status as a black feminine subject and a southern climate in which black women were frequently abused not only verbally but also physically and sexually.[7]

Such sexual abuse was horrifically evident in the case of Recy Taylor, a black woman who was brutally gang raped by a group of six white men, including a serviceman in the U.S. Army, in Abbeville, Alabama, in 1944. Parks had investigated this case as secretary of the NAACP in Montgomery, Alabama. Personal writings discovered in recent years possibly refer to Rosa Parks's own painful memory of nearly being raped in 1931 by a white male neighbor for whom she was working.[8] Alabama State University professor Jo Ann Gibson Robinson, who became the leader of the Women's Political Council in Montgomery and laid the groundwork for the city's famed bus boycott in the wake of Parks's arrest, observed that black women were especial targets for degradation on public buses and acknowledged the irony in Parks being expected to give up her seat to a man.[9]

In the words of Danielle McGuire, who examines the routinized black female abuse of the Jim Crow South, "Only by understanding the long and relatively hidden history of sexualized violence in Montgomery, Alabama, and African Americans' efforts to protect black womanhood, can we see that the Montgomery bus boycott was more than a movement for civil rights. It was also a movement for dignity, respect, and bodily integrity."[10] An approach that considers the interplay of gender and sexuality with race is useful, too, because white masculinity also profoundly shaped the encounter on the bus. The body was writ large, and race, gender, and sexuality were relevant to the situation on the bus, not only because it primarily counterposed Parks with four subjects who were white and male, but also because of what it meant as Parks stood under the gaze of a white man who had routinely made his disparaging estimation of black women evident. A perspective focused on Parks's intersectionality allows us to recognize the implications of Parks's heroic activism for later second-wave feminism and can help situate her as an important precursor, adding valuably to the understanding of how Rosa Parks sustained a lifetime of political engagement, as Jeanne Theoharis has emphasized in her compelling political biography of Parks.[11] In addition to these issues, Theoharis acknowledges Parks's disappointment and concern about how some black women also used their sexuality, including tactics such as flirting with rude and abusive police officers, to benefit themselves.[12]

The intersectionality of race, gender, and sexuality increasingly acknowledged in studies of Parks is a crucial lens through which to analyze her encounter on the bus and the larger political movement that emerged in its wake, in part because black women were its primary architects. Prior to Parks's arrest in Montgomery, the local NAACP had envisioned a woman as being the most ideal plaintiff against the bus system because a woman would evoke more sympathy.[13] Two black teen girls, Claudette Colvin and Mary Louise Williams, had played a central role in confronting the bus system when they were arrested in the months prior to Parks.[14] Significantly, the flier circulated to announce the Montgomery bus boycott in the wake of Parks's arrest, a movement that was primarily driven by the black women who made up the Women's Political Council under the leadership of Robinson, who reproduced 52,500 copies of it with a mimeograph machine, underscored the mistreatment of black women on the buses. Aurelia Browder and Susie MacDonald were other black women who had resisted segregation on the buses in the months before Parks and, alongside Colvin and Williams, served as plaintiffs in the 1956 case, *Browder v. Gayle*, that attorney Fred Gray filed to challenge such laws.

Rosa Parks's vulnerability as a raced *and* gendered subject and sexual being has typically been obscured in light of her universalization as a "mother," and this title's attendant desexualization. As the first epigraph of this chapter reveals, however, Rosa Parks embraced her iconic image as a symbolic mother, despite her reservations about it and the mythologies that inflect it, and used it strategically in her public outreach to inspire others, including children, whom she frequently centered in her writing and activism. We cannot neglect or dismiss the mother motifs related to Parks because they are equally steeped in race, sexuality, and gender and are tacit in all her primary cultural representations invoking children, which are less linked to romanticizing her in relation to past civil rights history than to articulating her in relation to a more visionary future. Because of the contradictions and ambivalences that riddle the mother motif, it remains the most understudied aspect of Parks's identity and public construction as a woman. Her best-known published writings center youth and link them to possibilities for actualizing a better future. Children are intimately and recurrently connected to Parks not only in her own writing but also in her primary economies of representation in cultural and political contexts.

Black women leaders have strategically and consistently staged the trope of the mother in the nation's public sphere within their speeches and writing discourses, as they have claimed voice, agency, and authority therein, and in the process, they have posed a challenge to white-centered national symbolism, which has alienated black women based on race and gender. Moreover, it would be limiting to simply dismiss such representations as apolitical, or to conflate or confuse them with pathologies of the black maternal body, such as the mammy and the matriarch, while failing to recognize levels on which they are subversive and work to unsettle and confront stereotypes of black womanhood steeped in pathologies of black maternity. Indeed, the representations figuring Parks as a mother within civil rights discourses, though coterminous, were the obverse of the scripts of black women as matriarchs circulated in popular culture and later authorized at the state level by Senator Daniel Patrick Moynihan in his infamous treatise on the Negro family.[15]

In Parks's long-standing honored designation as the mother of the civil rights movement, the maternal metaphor shaped this script to the point that she was coined as a Black Madonna in the years after her arrest in 1955. Indeed, a Montgomery city councilman, Luther Oliver, dubbed her Saint Rosa.[16] The metaphor has been foundational in constituting Parks as a "national mother" in the cultural imagination. The first epigraph to this chapter from Parks's autobiography attests to her awareness, tolerance, and acceptance of this maternal narrative and to the ways in which it even virtually enacted a deification of her. Indeed, the metaphor of Parks as the movement's mother in a symbolic and representative sense has complemented the movement's recurrent narratives invoking children, which reached their rhetorical height in Martin Luther King Jr.'s "I Have a Dream" speech during the March on Washington for Jobs and Freedom in 1963.[17]

At the same time, it is crucial to recognize ways in which tropes of mothers, children, and family obscure the legibility of black queer subjects who have been alien and other within conventional definitions of such categories. While this historic event extended Parks's national visibility, she and other women civil rights activists, with the exception of figures such as famed gospel singer Mahalia Jackson, were absent from its program. This marginality mirrored the silencing on civil rights platforms of figures such as the black gay activist Bayard

Rustin, notwithstanding his advocacy with A. Philip Randolph for a march on Washington in 1941, protesting discrimination against blacks in employment; his role in organizing the Freedom Rides and the aforementioned historic march; and his cofounding of the Southern Christian Leadership Conference (SCLC). As the legacy of Pauli Murray reveals, there remains a need for more nuanced and inclusive narratives of civil rights history that throw into relief contributions of black queer and trans women, along with those of leaders such as Rustin, to accord legibility to the queer role in shaping civil rights history. In 1987, Rustin passed away weeks before the National March on Washington for Lesbian and Gay Rights on the National Mall, at which the AIDS Memorial Quilt was first displayed.

My engagement of Rosa Parks grounded in methods of literary and cultural studies prioritizes her voice and writings, as well as cultural tributes to her, and considers the complexity with which race, gender, and sexuality are useful for reflecting on her profound influence on national femininity in the United States, through her fashioning as a national mother since the civil rights era against the backdrop of her global iconicity, despite black and feminine subjects' sexual subjection, prevailing exclusion, and illegibility within U.S. femininity's definition. Rosa Parks's national and global iconicity as a civil rights movement heroine began to crystallize in the months after her arrest and further consolidated during the post–civil rights era, as the movement itself was widely studied, memorialized, and celebrated within a range of institutions established in dedication to its history and memory. Her status as a woman who was never a literal birth or adoptive mother to a child has made her imaginable as a mythic and universal mother in civil rights discourses and facilitated her abstraction as a nurturer of an infinite variety of causes in the global context related to freedom and human rights.

Newer scholarly studies of Rosa Parks have rightly redressed the longstanding relegation of discussion about Parks's life and legacy to books designed for young readers and children, along with studies that fail to examine her life with depth and critical rigor. Concomitantly, they critique the ways in which such conventional dialogues have obscured her agency as an activist by propagating the myth of Rosa Parks as a woman who remained seated on the bus because she was tired and describing her as a quiet woman, a staple narrative in the mythic portrait of her as a national heroine and mother. Yet it is important not to throw the baby out with the bathwater. We should weigh the emphasis that Rosa Parks placed on her scripts as a national mother and on young people, not only in her legacy of activism and community work, but also in the body of books she produced collaboratively and published, including *Quiet Strength: The Faith, the Hope, and the Heart of a Woman Who Changed a Nation* (1994), *Dear Mrs. Parks: A Dialogue with Today's Youth* (1997), and *Rosa Parks: My Story* (1992), to ponder why she consistently aimed her work at juvenile audiences. The publication of these works extended her public voice, introduced her legacy to newer generations, and built on her mission to make a difference in the lives of youth. In an effort to recenter Parks's voice and remedy her limited representations in children's books, Rosalyn Cooperman, Melina Patterson, and Jess Rigelhaupt underscore the importance of reconsidering Parks's biography, including works by McGuire and Theoharis, but fail to take Parks's *own* words into consideration, as well as the importance and centrality of her platform related to young people within her discourse.[18] Taking a closer look at her written work is also essential because in studying her legacy, too little attention has been paid to how she represented herself and told her own story.

The black feminist critical lens through which I examine her work draws on the black feminist field's embrace of personal testimony as a resource for theorizing and informs my investments in recognizing and prioritizing her voice from my disciplinary standpoint as a literary scholar. It is a voice that in her autobiography *Rosa Parks: My Story*, which she wrote with author and scholar Jim Haskins, chronicles the activism in which she had engaged in the years leading up to the fateful encounter on the bus with James Blake in 1955, a background that was part of the process of her radicalization.[19] These contours of her autobiography reveal her emerging political consciousness and commitment to activism since the 1930s. While the contemporary retellings and elaborations of her story are tremendously valuable from a scholarly standpoint, it is crucial to acknowledge that this narrative was also to some degree evident in her autobiographical self-portrait, so as not to reductively correlate such accounts with newer biographies and histories focused on her life.

As a literary scholar, I find it important to reflect on how Rosa Parks wrote about her own activism to accord more legibility to her distinct voice, because doing so further unsettles the myth of "quiet strength" frequently associated with her leadership, throwing into relief how decisively she challenged it herself.[20] I continue this chapter by examining Rosa Parks's *Quiet Strength*, along with *Dear Mrs. Parks*, which were both written with her lawyer Gregory Reed. Her published books are fascinating because of their status as collaborative writings developed through interviews and strategies of documentation in oral history, and yet they affirm her voice and agency as a woman, which have been obscured all too frequently. They have been virtually ignored in literary studies. Examining these works comparatively and through a lens that recognizes and prioritizes the voice of Rosa Parks also highlights their implications for discourses of oral history and her autobiography. Furthermore, when thinking of them in relation to scholarly initiatives, such as the SIS Oral History Project at Spelman College, established by Gloria Wade-Gayles, critical work in black feminism designed to focus on the stories and wisdom of black women elders, we can also recognize their value as significant writings produced by a black senior woman in the late twentieth century.[21]

I go on to discuss the Cleveland Avenue Time Machine, the central installation at the Rosa Parks Children's Museum at Troy University in Montgomery. Added to the Rosa Parks Museum in 2006, the wing centers children and, in its conception and design, is premised on the mother motif so frequently related to Parks. It challenges white-centered scripts of American identity in casting her as a representative national figure and centers black women's voices and legacies in narratives of black liberation struggle. The futuristic bus installation is relevant for my purposes because it echoes major themes that inflect her writings related to freedom and challenging children to help eliminate injustice and create a better world in the future. It is valuable to draw on for its dialogism with themes in her writings related to freedom and the universality in her message, which counter scripts that consign civil rights legacies to the past. The installation draws a national and global audience of thousands of tourists annually within one of the foremost institutions established as a tribute to her national legacy in civil rights.

I end this chapter by examining the imaging of Parks as a national mother during her mourning on the nation's Capitol Rotunda in 2005, which culminated long-standing representations of Parks as the mother of the civil rights movement and provides the most profoundly salient illustration of her influence in shaping national femininity. At one level, it is important to view such public commemorations of Parks with skepticism and to critique them because the state has routinely appropriated the legacies of radical figures and framed them as national heroes without redressing the political concerns such figures championed, mechanisms that are inherently reactionary and typically designed to mute rather than enable the messages of radical and insurgent leaders and movements. While motifs highlighting Parks as a mother unsettle stereotypical and pathological scripts associated with the black maternal body, they have been limited by their linkages to typical symbolic feminizations within prevailing patriarchal national narratives. As postcolonial insights reveal, these narratives routinely romanticize women in relation to landscapes and subordinate women's leadership, revealing the role of gender in constituting nationalisms, which, as work in queer studies has illustrated, is intimately linked to sexuality.[22] At the same time, such public honorifics are valuable for redressing the long-standing erasures of blackness in narratives of American identity. In this sense, such tributes should not be devalued, because they have been hard won within the ongoing struggle for black inclusion in American democracy.

Rosa Parks's Message for the World's Young People

The script of Rosa Parks as a civil rights mother and the recurring framing of Montgomery's NAACP leader E. D. Nixon as its father were symbiotic terms that, when juxtaposed with narratives invoking the movement's children, portrayed the national movement as a family. The influential social science scholarship of the period, most notably Gunnar Myrdal's *An American Dilemma: The Negro Problem and Modern Democracy* (1944), had emphasized black otherness.[23] The epistemology of black family within civil rights discourses countered scripts of blackness as pathological and alien to notions of American identity by implying that its ideals related to freedom were quintessential for achieving democracy. The stereotype of black mothers as matriarchs was a primary site on which pathologies of black family as dysfunctional and deviant were propagated in the era after World War II, in contradistinction to normative nuclear families in the white American mainstream.

Lorraine Hansberry's acclaimed play *A Raisin in the Sun*, which opened on Broadway in 1959, confronts and unsettles this ideology's linkages to notions of black family dysfunction at the same time it immortalizes the matriarch's strength through the character Lena Younger. The development of this subversive portrait by a black queer woman has only been clear retrospectively, in the wake of newer research on the author, including Imani Perry's groundbreaking biography.[24] During the period in which the ideology of the matriarch was disseminated and mainstreamed, which was coterminous with the launching of the modern civil rights movement, citations of Parks as a mother figure within civil rights discourses were a script of black womanhood that did not draw symbolic power from the black matriarch. Parks's diminutive body and the quiet demeanor associated with her also unraveled this staple construction of black womanhood that the media popularized and social science legitimized, premised on the myth of the strong black woman, which reached its height when Daniel Patrick Moynihan famously released *The Negro Family: The Case for National Action* in 1965. Yet emerging citations of Parks as a mother within civil rights discourses belied the threats that were made to her and her family after the incident on the bus, her firing from her job as a seamstress at Montgomery Fair, the subsequent challenges she faced in finding work, and the eventual decision to leave Montgomery and resettle in Detroit.

Just as the rhetoric of Parks as a mother, along with the symbolic family evoked within civil rights discourses, provided an alternative script to the pathological narratives about black womanhood in mainstream social science in the postwar era, it stood apart from the popular romanticized narratives of black family within the black nationalist rhetoric of the black liberation movement, which portrayed black men as kings heading a symbolic family premised on a romantic African past, as famously illustrated by Eldridge Cleaver in *Soul on Ice*.[25] In the wake of the black power movement of this period, black women leaders produced autobiographies that confronted the marginalization and devaluation of black women's leadership, along with persisting sexism, within the black liberation movement. For example, the research of Margo V. Perkins primarily focuses on autobiographies by women activists such as Angela Davis, Assata Shakur, and Elaine Brown and frames their work in relation to autobiographical writing produced throughout the long history of black resistance writing and struggle since Emancipation. Angela Ards has also contributed valuable critical insights on black feminist autobiographies by black women activists produced since *Brown v. Board*. Such work holds critical implications for Parks's writing, shaped by her experiences during the civil rights era.[26] Writings related to Parks's political activism and thought are crucial to situate not only within the black radical tradition alongside such women leaders, but also within epistemologies of Pan-Africanism.[27]

Parks's writings, including her autobiographical books and other materials, provide insights into her political vision and should be valued for the contribution they make to black intellectual history, along with African American literary history. Black feminist scholar Joanne M. Braxton, a pioneering critic in studies of black women's autobiography, who developed one of its earliest critical histories and who has linked this genre of writing by black women in the late twentieth century to the black women's literary renaissance of the era, broadens its definition to include materials such as images, reminiscences, memoirs, diaries, and journals, acknowledging the intertexuality of black women's autobiographical writings. She provides indispensable critical contexts for examining the epistolary formats in which Parks framed some of her most poignant writings and for examining their linkages to the work of a precursor such as Mary McLeod Bethune.[28] Furthermore, Braxton's observation that "Black women's autobiography is . . . an occasion for viewing the individual in relation to those others with whom she shares emotional, philosophical, and spiritual affinities, as well as political realities" is also helpful for thinking about how civil rights, faith, values, and a commitment to eliminating racism and injustice bridged the legacies of these black women leaders.[29] A close analysis of Parks's writings reveals how they instate her within a spectrum of civil rights leaders, from Mary McLeod Bethune to Martin Luther King Jr., and establish intertextuality with the most famous messages that these leaders shared with national audiences, while building on, mirroring, and broadening their core themes related to youth, strategies that pay tribute to other iconic black national civil rights leaders while amplifying her message.

Recent work on Parks, such as Sheila McCauley Keys and Eddie B. Allen Jr.'s *Our Auntie Rosa: The Family of Rosa Parks Remembers Her Life and Lessons*, reveals that Parks's closest family, including her nieces and nephews, were among the young people whom she most profoundly influenced and who saw her up close in a way that the public rarely experienced.[30] The book provides a pastiche of testimonies from them about her influence in their lives and lessons they learned from her. Mary Frances Whitt, who was mentored by Parks in the NAACP's Youth Council and became a university professor at Alabama State University, has discussed Parks's indelible influence on her life in interviews and essays. She was a friend and federated club sister of my mother's, and this influence was always clear in the reflections she shared with me in several conversations we had about her relationship with Parks, along with her writings related to Parks's mentoring in her life.[31] Parks's loving and generous influence as a mentor of children as documented in testimonies by those whom she knew best and loved most are indispensable for the personal and dynamic portrait of her life that they offer, along with another perspective on her voice.

Parks's writings are primarily scripted for a young audience and extend her concern and mentoring to children everywhere. Just as the experiences of black children have been increasingly centered in studies of slavery, it will also be increasingly important to recognize their role in shaping civil rights history. Such insights are all the more vital when considering that the tragic deaths of youth such as Emmett Till in Money, Mississippi, in 1955 and Addie

Mae Collins, Cynthia Wesley, Carole Robertson, and Denise McNair in the bombing at 16th Street Baptist Church mobilized the movement at key junctures. Such tragic histories informed Parks's continuing investments in prioritizing children in her political and cultural agendas. Parks also recurrently engaged them as a primary audience for her books and incorporated their voices into the written narratives she developed, which are an indispensable resource because they are a primary site on which she articulated and circulated her political message. The backdrop of black children's historical stereotyping within American material and popular culture also throws into relief the revolutionary implications in Parks's centering of children within her early activism and her continuing prioritization of them in her public work and writing.

The biography of Parks that frames *Quiet Strength*, written in collaboration with Gregory J. Reed and edited by Elaine Steele, notes that Parks is "nationally recognized as the mother of the modern-day civil rights movement in America," and that her refusal to give up her seat "changed America and redirected the course of history."[32] It is explicit in acknowledging her as a symbol of freedom for the world. This signals Parks's personal investments in her public image as a mother figure in civil rights history and as a national symbol. That it frames her book also underscores her agency in helping to shape this image and compellingly illustrates her strategic use of it as an activist.

In representing herself as a mother figure in the nation, highlighting children, tying them to the future, and acknowledging them as a primary audience for this book, aspects of Parks's message recall that of Mary McLeod Bethune's "My Last Will and Testament." Such continuities make these texts useful to compare on some levels. Like the "Last Will," *Quiet Strength* similarly singles out terms and uses anecdotes from Parks's life to reflect on them, terms that include *fear, defiance, injustice, pain, character, role models, faith, values, quiet strength, determination, youth,* and *the future*. Parks frames each of the book's short chapters with a biblical scripture, which similarly grounds it in the black sermonic tradition while also invoking call-and-response narrative techniques. Like Bethune, she positions children at the center, stresses their agency as activists, posits them as the hope for the future, and challenges them to carry on the civil rights struggle.

The cover art for the book features a photograph of Parks against the backdrop of two little girls and a little boy, visually signaling its thematic investments. Significantly, the first phrase of the volume, "As a child," foregrounds Parks's reflections on her own childhood, when she learned early on to live by faith in God and to not be afraid of racial terrorists. The latter lesson she learned from her grandfather, whom she often sat beside on the porch at night as he vigilantly watched out for Ku Klux Klan members, shotgun on hand in case his family was ever threatened. Parks foregrounds this experience early in life as one that taught her not to be fearful of white racism and that prepared her for the encounter with Blake on the bus that fateful December evening. The themes that unfold across the book intersect with those that run across the paragraphs of Bethune's famous letter, despite the difference in genres. Parks traces her beliefs in Christian faith to the Bible instruction she received in her family as a child and describes her investments in freedom as God ordained. She links the title chapter of the book, "Quiet Strength," scripturally to Isaiah 30:15—"In quietness and in confidence shall be your strength"—to helping children in need, and to the impetus for her continuing work.

Similarly, Parks begins the second chapter, "Defiance," by discussing the optimism that change would come in the wake of *Brown v. Board of Education*, describing the apprehensive expression of "a little child" whom she saw with his mother being taken to an integrated school, a child who was reluctant to go, as an illustration of the hostility that some whites continued to show blacks in schools despite this landmark ruling by the nation's highest court. *Brown v. Board of Education*, which aimed to integrate public schools, established the import and centrality of children within the modern civil rights movement, a movement that this monumental case heralded.

For Parks, the children at the vanguard of the movement who integrated predominantly white schools demonstrated the resolve that was critical for all blacks to embody in the face of a segregationist mindset. She suggests that it also affected her resistance on the bus that night. Notably, in her reflections, she mentions the "police powers" of bus drivers and acknowledges how unsettling it felt for her as a woman to be asked to give up her seat for a man, which also registers the role of gender, and her subject positioning as a black woman in particular, in shaping her response during this encounter: "It did not seem proper, particularly for a woman to give up her seat to a man."[33] In sharing this reflection, Parks speaks to how gender and sexuality shaped the encounter and critiques the exclusion of black women from the social respect accorded white women in the South.

The third chapter, "Injustice," reinforces her narrative thread related to children by incorporating dialogue about a program Parks initiated called Pathways to Freedom, designed to teach history to young people under the auspices of the Rosa and Raymond Parks Institute for Self-Development, which she established with Elaine Steele, who serves as the organization's executive director, in 1987 in Detroit, Michigan, as a community organization to design programs for young people. Indeed, like Whitt, Parks began to mentor Steele as a youth when they met in 1965 while working as seamstresses at a factory; they remained close thereafter, and Steele ultimately became her caretaker. Pathways to Freedom operated for five weeks during the summer, and focused on teaching lessons related to the Underground Railroad and the civil rights movement. It also taught students lessons about life. Five years earlier, Parks had also offered reflections on the organization in her autobiography, which mentions the organization's mission of helping to educate young people and teach skills that will help them in life.[34] This work reflects and builds on Parks's life history in Montgomery working with and mentoring students in the NAACP Youth Council, including Whitt, who had famously stood outside the courthouse after the hearing that followed Parks's arrest and chanted, "They've messed with the wrong one now," and who found inspiration in Parks's example throughout her life.[35]

Parks's chapter titled "Pain" further foregrounds the youth-related themes that suffuse the book through her reflections on a young black man named Joseph Skipper, who broke into her home in 1994 and robbed her when she was eighty-one, hitting her violently several times and bruising her in the process, an attack on her as a senior woman that led to her move to a high-rise apartment and that underscored the crisis of crime and violence perpetrated by youth in black communities. For her, the incident was symptomatic of a lack of respect for elders among some contemporary young people. Her response to the incident emblematizes her continued commitment to principles of nonviolent resistance and Christian love and forgiveness, including the gospel principle of turning the other cheek.

She draws on the incident to emphasize the importance of persevering and remaining hopeful in the face of suffering, evoking the freedom song "We Shall Overcome," the main anthem of the civil rights movement: "I pray for this young man and the conditions in our country that have made him this way. I urge people not to read too much into the attack. I regret that some people, regardless of race, are in such a mental state that they would want to harm an older person. Young people need to be taught to respect and care for their elders. Despite the violence and crime in our society, we should not let fear overwhelm us. We must remain strong. We must not give up hope; we can overcome."[36] It was also unsettling because it subjected her to a form of violence she had never experienced in her life, even while coming of age and living in the violent Jim Crow South. As she put it, "I had never been hit in that manner in my life."[37] Such abuse was all the more hurtful to experience at the hands of a black youth, a group for whom she had primarily advocated throughout her lifetime in her community work as a leader and an activist.

Parks's two final chapters of the book, which are framed by the Joel 1:3 scripture "Tell it to your children, and let your children tell it to their children, and their children to the next generation," fully synthesize her message, focused on young people and looking toward a future to which they pave the way. "I am motivated and inspired by young people and children. My eyes light up whenever children come around. They are our future. If the changes we began in the civil rights movement are going to continue, they will be the ones who have to do it."[38] Here the resonance of Parks's message to youth at the end of the twentieth century with Bethune's from nearly half a century earlier is even more evident. Like Bethune's "Last Will and Testament," it relates children to the future and poses a challenge to them to help bring about change and continue the effort to eradicate racism. Like Bethune, Parks stresses how important it is for young people to remember the struggles of their ancestors. She is very precise in outlining seven key areas on which to focus in supporting them.

Her message, aimed at empowering young people in black communities, suggests that good, effective, and engaged mentorship and leadership are vital in their lives. She suggests that adults set the example by being positive role models. She stresses the importance of encouraging young people to cultivate love and respect for their elders and for one another. In her estimation, teaching youth lessons in core subjects, as well as providing them with a biblical foundation, is another channel through which to instill values. She suggests that adults have a responsibility not only to work hard but also to teach youth the values of hard work and working together. She stresses the importance of teaching youth how to do collective work and to do so in peace, along with the importance of encouraging and supporting them to give back to their communities by doing service. Parks pitches this core section of her message to African American youth, a group whom she suggests most urgently needs the sage wisdom and guidance she offers. She culminates her chapter, however, with a message to young people "of any race," stressing the importance of hard work and encouraging them to make the country a better place.[39] Her urge to young people to avoid drugs and alcohol notably relates such substances to bondage and the loss of freedom in a sense that transcends definitions established within black liberation struggle from the eras of slavery and Jim Crow, emphasizing their relation to all humans achieving well-being. What she wishes for them she suggests would improve the lives of youth everywhere.

If Bethune's famous letter anticipated the "I Have a Dream" speech of Martin Luther King, then *Quiet Strength* ends by building on it in outlining Parks's vision for children everywhere:

> My message to the world is that we must come together and live as one. There is only one world; and yet we, as a people, have treated the world as if it were divided. We cannot allow the gains we have made to erode. Although we have a long way to go, I do believe that we can achieve Dr. King's dream of a better world.
>
> From time to time I catch glimpses of that world. I can see a world where children do not learn hatred in their homes. I can see a world where mothers and fathers have the last and most important word.
>
> I can see a world in which one respects the rights of one's neighbors. I can see a world in which all adults protect the innocence of children. I can see a world in which people do not call each other names based on skin color. I can see a world in which people of all races and all religions work together to improve the quality of life for everyone.
>
> I can see this world because it exists today in small pockets of this country and in a small pocket of every person's heart. If we look to God and work together—not only here but everywhere—then others will see this world too and help to make it a reality.[40]

Parks explicitly draws on King's dream in outlining her vision here. King's "I Have a Dream" speech at the March on Washington, which drew more than 250,000 people from across the country to the nation's capital on August 28, 1963, was grounded in a list of ten demands designed to achieve civil rights legislation that would ensure equal access to public facilities, jobs, education, and voting; establish a national minimum wage; expand job training opportunities; desegregate schools, jobs, and housing; and promote fair labor practices. King's charismatic speech, which followed up a selection by the famed gospel singer Mahalia Jackson and remarks from the president of the American Jewish Congress, Rabbi Joachim Prinz, was the climax of the march.

Parks, like other black women leaders, had been excluded from the male-centered program for the March on Washington; she was not given the prerogative to speak to its agenda and was asked to participate by walking alongside the wives of civil rights leaders. Even more troublingly, her autobiography describes her removal from the front row of the Selma-to-Montgomery march of 1965 multiple times.[41] It is important to relate Parks's comments in her book to this historic speech, which is the most famous oration of the modern civil rights movement, which was catalyzed by her choice to remain seated. She links her own voice, which is often reductively related to the myth of "quiet strength," to the booming charisma and authority associated with King, while challenging the logic of a movement that had typically prioritized the voices of black male leaders. As Cooperman, Patterson, and Rigelhaupt point out, "The traditional narrative presents a biased picture of the Civil Rights Movement. It marginalizes the contributions of women, reflects a broader pattern of pedagogy that relegates women's participation to the sidelines of politics and history, and offers an overly narrow view of how substantive social and political change occurs."[42]

Parks claims authority as a woman and affirms her status as a leader to address youth in a collective sense in this book, which centralizes her own voice as a black woman leader within civil rights discourses, which have conventionally marginalized black women's contributions and prioritized masculine leadership. The *I* that she recurrently invokes places her voice front and center in this narrative and helps to establish intimacy with her audience. That she directs her message to a global audience rests on her symbolic capital as a leader and is grounded in the transnational achievements of the freedom movement she catalyzed. Her repeated use of the phrase "I can see" lends poetic resonance to the vision she describes and, like the speech it builds on, links it to the conventionally masculinist black sermonic tradition. Each point she mentions is grounded in her renown and in her vision as a national leader with political capital who has made an international impact. Parks's riff on the final portion of the "I Have a Dream" speech is significant, too, because it, like her own, advocates for change to help better the lives of children.

Dear Mrs. Parks shares common ground with *Quiet Strength* in framing Parks as the mother of the movement and as a national symbol. More broadly, both books primarily direct Parks's message toward a young audience, which they frame as universal and global. Furthermore, both books mention the goals of the Rosa and Raymond Parks Institute for Self-Development to promote peace and justice globally. In voicing their message to children, the books draw on Parks's role and voice as a national leader to send a message to children around the world. In keeping with the collaborative strategies of developing her books, Parks's lawyer Gregory Reed collaborated with her on *Dear Mrs. Parks*, which was published when she was eighty-three and, like

Quiet Strength, is pitched primarily to address a young audience and shares themes with this precursor. A preface, a foreword by Reed, and a commentary by Steele frame the book.

Like Reed's reference to Parks as Mother Rosa, the preface highlights Parks's status as a symbol and the view of her as a mother: "In the years since her arrest, Rosa Parks has been recognized throughout America as the mother of the modern-day Civil Rights movement. For children and adults, Mrs. Parks is a role model for courage, an example of dignity and determination. She is a symbol of freedom for the world."[43] These dimensions of the book acknowledge that Parks embraced her role as a mother. Steele's commentary similarly speaks to Parks's symbolic influence by acknowledging her kind treatment of all people, and the impression of her love for "all humanity" left on everyone whom she encounters, framing Parks's book as "a gift to the young people of the world," which points to the universality of her message and inclusive vision that embraces all youth. Parks reinforces this message in her response to the second letter, when asked whether she has children: "No, I don't have any children born from me, but I consider all children as mine," and describes Steele as her closest friend, who is like a daughter.[44]

Dear Mrs. Parks ends with an updated version of the remarks that ended Parks's previous book, extending and building on the elements she believes will be essential to help create a better world. In this new version, she explicitly addresses the need to end acts of violence. At one level, this shift likely reflected Parks's long-standing investments in eliminating violence in the world, particularly violence based on the color of one's skin. Even more personally, it may have reflected Parks's experience being robbed by Joseph Skipper. That she ends this book with the same powerful statement that ended the previous one reinforces and iterates her message all the more. Invoking such a ubiquitous speech in African American cultural history reinforces the dialogism of her writing, reflects the intertextuality of these two books, and underscores the value in reading and studying them comparatively.

One of the main public tributes that emerged after her death is premised on the running themes across her writings, invoking Parks as a mother, framing the freedom struggle in which she was an activist as universal, and challenging children to help bring about change in the world in the future. The writings by Parks are valuable to juxtapose with an analysis of the primary cultural institution established in the South in her honor, which as a space builds on core themes related to children and futurity that her books repeatedly mention. Bridget R. Cooks and Susan E. Cohen are among contemporary art historians who have analyzed the challenges of depicting and exhibiting black images in the post–civil rights/black power era and discussed the racial politics of museums as institutions, while critiquing the persisting Eurocentrism of the art establishment.[45] While they focus on cultural dynamics in New York City in relation to Harlem, their critique holds important implications for southern cultural institutions, suggesting that the extent to which a preeminent museum focused on Rosa Parks in Montgomery was visionary and groundbreaking. Its close proximity to the new Legacy Museum and National Memorial for Peace and Justice, a project of Bryan Stevenson's Equal Justice Initiative, bridges dialogues about civil rights and Jim Crow and traumas of slavery and lynching, expanding contexts for exploring her life and legacy.

The Rosa Parks Children's Museum and the Cleveland Avenue Time Machine

Two high-profile controversies reflecting contestations over Rosa Parks's legacy have emerged in African American popular culture in music and film. In 1998, the rap group OutKast, along with its production company LaFace Records, was sued by Rosa Parks for the song "Rosa Parks," included on the 1998 album *Aquemini*. Parks, who was represented by Reed, argued that the song appropriated her name and also included vulgarity in its lyrics. Similarly, the 2002 comedy film *Barbershop*, directed by Tim Story, garnered controversy because it stages a heated debate about Parks between two of its characters, Calvin Palmer Jr. (Ice Cube) and Eddie (Cedric the Entertainer).

In this scene, Palmer, who is sitting in a barber chair eating, remarks, "You've got to give it up to Rosa Parks because they was deep, they was on the front lines in the 1960s." Eddie responds, "Who the hell is Rosa Parks?" He goes on to assert,

> Man, she was tired. That's what you do when you're tired. You sit your ass down. Rosa Parks ain't do nothing but sit her black ass down. . . . I'm gon' give her her just due because what she did, her act, led to the movement and everything, but she damn sure ain't special. No. It was a whole lot of black folks sat down on buses and they got thrown in jail. And they did it way before Rosa Parks did. The only difference between them and her was that she was secretary of the NAACP and she knowed Martin Luther King and they got a lot of publicity. That's all.

This dialogue in the barbershop reflects distinct dynamics that Melissa Harris-Perry relates to black grassroots and community contexts in her study *Barbershops, Bibles, and BET: Everyday Talk and Black Political Thought*. She points out, "Ordinary spaces of everyday talk among African Americans serve as forums for dialogue that contribute both to the development of individual ideological dispositions and to the revisions of ideologies across time." Harris-Perry goes on to note, "Churches, political organizations, news outlets, fraternal clubs, mutual aid societies, barbershops, juke joints, and labor unions that constitute the black counterpublic are internally contested spaces. Identities of gender, class, color, sexuality and privilege crosscut the terrain of a racially homogeneous public sphere."[46]

If Eddie's comments attempt to acknowledge Parks's several precursors, who had been arrested in Montgomery, and to remedy their relative invisibility in narratives of civil rights history, this character's purposefully iconoclastic and irreverent comments are also grounded in the widespread and misleading myth that being "tired" that evening on the bus was the primary factor that led Parks to remain seated. This portrayal of Parks also seems reductive and suspect in light of the film's primary investments in endorsing black conservatism through Palmer's admiration of the entrepreneur Stedman Graham. Furthermore, Eddie's comments, which are inflected by profanity and the use of the word *black* as an epithet, are ironic as voiced by a young black male at the beginning of the twenty-first century (while costumed on screen portraying a black male senior) in recasting forms of disrespect, devaluation, and humiliation to which Parks was subjected by the white bus driver James Blake in the Jim Crow South, a man known for routinely insulting black women.

This scene also seems ironic given the status of Parks's husband, Raymond Parks, as a barber. Indeed, director Julie Dash's 2002 made-for-television movie *The Rosa Parks Story* depicts the character portraying Parks's husband, Raymond (Peter Francis James), criticizing the NAACP while working in a barbershop because of his disapproval of its strategies for dealing with the case of the Scottsboro Boys. As he works, he asserts, "The NAACP just a bunch of scared old men who blow hot and cold." While the films were released in the same year, *The Rosa Parks Story* reached a far more limited audience than the blockbuster hit *Barbershop*.

These episodes as witnessed in popular culture in recent years have been shaped by factors such as generational tensions and political sensibilities mediated by hip-hop. Provocatively, Melba Joyce Boyd argues that OutKast's invocation of Rosa Parks's name reflected "a huge generation gap looming between the consciousness of the civil rights era of the 1950s and 1960s and the onslaught of commercialism and materialism that now impacts and directs the culture of contemporary youth, who see themselves as outcast and believe in 'getting' paid."[47] In attempting to resist the prevailing public impulses of revering Parks as enacted in her life as well as posthumously, they obscure the national and global effects of her legacy. At the same time, the scene in *Barbershop* is symptomatic of film's emergence as a primary site for closely meditating on Rosa Parks at the dawn of the new millennium.

While constituted from black and masculine subject positions, such dismissive popular representations of Parks risk replaying the sexist and misogynistic narrative of Parks produced by Blake, which insistently misnamed and misread her as a black woman subject and minimized and dismissed the significance of the encounter on the bus. Premised on the script of her as a relic from the past disconnected from newer generations, they obscure Rosa Parks's ongoing legacy of public service and outreach and continuing commitment to engaging young people within her activist work. This spin on Parks in *Barbershop* shares common ground with narratives in mainstream cinema of the post–civil rights era, such as *Mississippi Burning* (1989) and *A Time to Kill* (1996), that have linked corruption to traditional civil rights leaders while discrediting them. Such assessments of Parks in popular culture are particularly interesting to revisit when examining her dynamic and consistent engagements with youth in her writings, and as a prelude for discussing the Rosa Parks Children's Museum, an institution that augments and mirrors her investments in young people in her writings and public outreach and links her to black futurity, while challenging narratives of her legacy and the larger civil rights movement struggle as being disengaged from contemporary black struggle. This museum is vital to study in part for how much it reckons with and builds on the themes of futurity that saturate Rosa Parks's repertoire, to the point of linking her discourse to Afrofuturism. This is a concept frequently related to OutKast by critics, including pioneering OutKast scholars such as Regina Bradley, which helps throw into relief some common ground between them not evident if Parks and the civil rights movement are reduced to the past and Afrofuturism to youth and hip-hop.

In one of my previously published essays on Parks, I examine the time and space motifs that run through *The Rosa Parks Story*, including the recurring flashbacks to Parks's childhood that ground it.[48] The Cleveland Avenue Time Machine also meditates on Parks's legacy by prioritizing the subject position of children, the audience for which it is primarily developed. In this installation, a robot displaces the logic of race and gender premised on a black/white binary, which structured the original encounter with Blake on the bus, by reconstituting and remembering Parks through fantasies of space and time travel. During the Cold War, the space race was catalyzed after the Russian launching of Sputnik into orbit in 1957 and gained salience in the U.S. national imaginary after President John F. Kennedy's announcement several years later of the ambitious plan for Americans to land a man on the moon by the end of the 1960s, a period that coincided with the final phases of the civil rights era and its major legislative hallmarks, such as the Civil Rights Act of 1964 and the Voting Rights Act of 1965. The story of Katherine Johnson's role as one of the black women hired by the National Aeronautics and Space Administration (NASA) for her mathematical genius as a "human computer" to do computations to help launch the first American, astronaut John Glenn, into orbit, is among those told in the 2016 book *Hidden Figures*, by Margot Lee Shetterly, as well as on screen in the 2017 film by the same name. The book and film pay tribute to the black unsung heroines whose contributions helped to enable space travel. The long-standing invisibility, marginality, and exclusion of blacks within narratives related to the space age, coupled with the national fascination with space travel evident by the civil rights era, make it intriguing that space travel is invoked imaginatively in this public tribute to Parks and that it centers blackness in relation to notions of space-time travel, literally linking race and space, themes I also examine critically through the lens of Afrofuturism.

Just as Parks's writings recurrently invoke her encounter with Blake on the bus, the Cleveland Avenue Time Machine is a landmark museum installation grounded in the literary genre of science fiction, which it draws on to link Parks to the long history of black struggle for freedom from slavery and Jim Crow. The installation draws on narratives of Parks as a mother of the civil rights movement and mobilizes her national iconicity, linking her to national femininity, which had been sutured all the more in the wake of her death in the preceding months, by reconfiguring and reimagining her as an emblem of freedom movements past, present, and future and throughout the vast universe the bus navigates. The first national institution established in the months after Parks's death invoked her long-standing citations as mother of the civil rights movement through its framing for an audience of children. With the driver as the only passenger on the bus, which welcomes its passengers in place of Parks, the installation frames children as the central agents in the imaginative and futuristic space of the bus and challenges them as the bearers of her legacy to help bring about a better future. The installation relates black subjects historically linked to the experience of slavery and Jim Crow in the past to unlimited movement and possibilities for freedom in the future.

In 2000, Troy University's Rosa Parks Library and Museum in Montgomery, Alabama, emerged as the nation's second major institution designed to honor the life, work, and legacy of Rosa Parks and the history of the Montgomery bus boycott. It opened to the public on December 1, 2000, in a ceremony that featured Parks as the guest of honor. Georgette Norman, who had established and worked for years in the Alabama African American Arts Alliance, was appointed as the founding director. The 55,000-square-foot building, on the site of the former Empire Theater, where Parks's famous arrest occurred, is a landmark institution and national tourist attraction, which now includes a children's wing. On top of its outstanding installations, the Rosa Parks Library and Museum's extensive databases on Rosa Parks, the Montgomery bus boycott, and various legal cases that emerged during the civil rights era also make it an unsurpassed institution for researching and learning about the life and legacy of Rosa Parks.[49] Just as we have witnessed a profusion of documentaries, dramatic films, and scholarly studies examining the history of the civil rights movement, the Rosa Parks Library and Museum in Montgomery is one of the primary institutions in the nation that has been established in recent years to explore those legacies. It is an institution established to promote knowledge about Rosa Parks, just as the King Center in Atlanta, Georgia, has been a central site for teaching about the life and legacy of Dr. Martin Luther King Jr. Significantly, the Rosa Parks Museum is one of the most prominent and elaborate tributes dedicated to a woman of the civil rights movement.

The Rosa Parks Library and Museum's exhibitions stand at the cutting edge in incorporating digital media and technology. Here, temporality and spatiality are the primary lenses for engaging Parks as a persona, along with Montgomery bus boycott history. The tour in the main museum stages a visceral encounter with civil rights history for tourists during its multiple phases. The centrality of video in mediating and facilitating the tour in the main exhibition at the museum is useful to acknowledge here because it establishes foundations for the even more extensive and elaborate uses of technology in the concept and design of the Children's Museum and draws on Parks's national and global iconicity. The location of the museum in the shadow of the state capitol building evokes the memory of this architecture as a symbol of how the state worked to legally disenfranchise the black population, which was routinely targeted by forms of violence and terror to which the state turned a blind eye.

The situation of the museum near the state capitol building frames Parks as an indispensable aspect of cultural memory in Alabama and in the United States more broadly. The mapping of Parks's famous trip down Dexter Avenue at sites marked along the path to the museum is paralleled within the museum by repeated video re-creations of the events, a dialectical, intersecting, and overlaid narrative that encourages engaged and heightened reflections on her encounter in 1955, while demarcating the progress from that fateful evening to the present day. In thinking of what its performativity means, it is crucial here, too, to register the allusion to the crossroads in both the museum's location and the ongoing engagements with histories and futures at this site. That is to say, the physical location of the museum at the scene of her arrest, at the intersection of Lee and Montgomery Streets, borrows and recasts the blues motif of the crossroads, alluding to Robert Johnson's description in the 1936 song "Cross Road Blues," which discusses the struggle to get a ride at the intersection and the desperation to get home before nightfall in a place where lynching was rampant. Legend has also popularly associated the crossroads with the myth of Johnson selling his soul to gain extraordinary musical gifts. While black masculine figures have conventionally been positioned at the center within blues aesthetics, Rosa Parks stood at the center of a similar story in 1955 and changed the world through her belief in Christian love, nonviolent forms of resistance, and unremitting faith in God.

The 1999 poetry collection *On the Bus with Rosa Parks*, by Rita Dove, who served as U.S. Poet Laureate from 1993 to 1995, culminates in a section titled "On the Bus with Rosa Parks," which features a series of ten poems dedicated to Parks. Dove's narrative foregrounding of her daughter's voice in the title situates a child's subject position front and center in the poetic tribute to Parks, which centers and prioritizes the citizens whom Parks prioritized within her political agendas. Dove's poems devoted to Parks are inflected by invocations of technologies associated with cinema, including the camera flash, flashbulbs, and video. This imagery in Dove's tribute anticipates how technology, spatiality, and temporality converge in the space of this museum.[50]

The Cleveland Avenue Time Machine is the centerpiece of the children's wing at the Rosa Parks Library and Museum, which opened in 2006. In March 2009, the installation won a TEA Award for Outstanding Achievement in the category Exhibition on a Limited Budget (from what was once the Themed Entertainment Association) at the fourteenth annual Thea Awards Ceremony, held at the Disneyland Hotel in Anaheim, California. The installation was a collective design effort by Eisterhold Associates of Kansas City,

Missouri; Jan Bochenek of Virginia; Ben Lawless of Maryland; Peter Vogt of Washington, DC; and Hadley Exhibits of New York, which conceptualized its primary features, including special lighting, a seven-projector video, audio and fog video, and digital dimensions. The large bus installation most viscerally climaxes the museum's emphasis on temporal themes and uses of video and digital media.

The bus is painted green, gold, and beige to resemble the one on which Parks was arrested in 1955. Yet several features accord it a futuristic aura: the larger size and rectangular shape; the larger than average bus seats; the wider aisle; and the robot driver, Mr. Rivets, poised over a dashboard with gadgets resembling those on spaceships in science fiction films. As a space, the bus evokes the past through its color scheme, as its design and features evoke an image of the futuristic.

The bus is framed through its naming and appearance as a time machine. The installation of the giant bus is a space designed to look larger than life from the perspective of a child and to provide a more imaginative tour to engage the history of the Montgomery bus boycott. The bus is "parked" in a large open warehouse-like display space, framed by black metal posts, connected to a host of wires and steam pumps one might see in an industrial factory. It must be boarded by walking down a long L-shaped ramp lined with metal rails that lead up to its entrance. Once a passenger is seated, Mr. Rivets starts the engine, and the bus uses a host of special effects, such as vibrations, flashing lights, steam, and sound, to create the sensation of motion, features that draw in the senses and create the illusion that the bus itself *is* a machine. An overhead video screen on the bus becomes the focal point as a video narrated by actress Tonea Stewart emerges, a parallel to the feature that begins the tour in the main museum.[51] The main exhibition casts its tourists as pedestrians and ushers them on a walk through the exhibit, movement that alludes to the day-to-day material conditions and practices that enabled the Montgomery bus boycott, but alternatively stages an imaginative ride at the Children's Museum.

Time travel in the sense popularized through science fiction surfaces as the central motif in the video, as the tourist goes back in time 150 years, an imaginative journey into the past signaled by the physical vibrations of the bus. The naming of this bus installation invokes the H. G. Wells novel *The Time Machine*, which popularized the concept of time travel and expanded the possibilities for imagining the phenomenon, given this novel's publication in 1895, the year before the *Plessy v. Ferguson* decision was issued by the

Supreme Court sanctioning the "separate but equal" doctrine segregating public facilities, including forms of public transportation. Navigating the trip forward in time emerges as the main purpose of Mr. Rivets. On the Cleveland Avenue Time Machine, which conserves original coloration but otherwise fully reimagines and redesigns the No. 2857 GM on which Parks was arrested, the robotic Mr. Rivets manifests qualities associated with the cyborg and anticipates a posthuman subject, even as his status as a male bus driver might seem to conserve the conventional logic of gender. He is also marked as postracial, but in a sense that lays bare rather than attempts to repress the social consequences of racism as is typically the case with this ideology. In effect, Mr. Rivets replaces James Blake in his role as the navigator for a diverse generation of passengers and realigns the significations of race, gender, and sexuality that had been related to Parks in 1955. Rethinking and reimagining the driver of the bus in terms of gender and sexuality would have dislodged all the more the patriarchy that has typically shadowed both white southern racism and civil rights activism. Mr. Rivets facilitates their encounter with the past as he sits poised to transport them to a world of new possibilities in the twenty-first century and beyond. The videos that unfold on screens positioned outside the bus windows create the sense that one is surrounded by and traveling through history as Parks's story is narrated.

To acknowledge the origins of the term Jim Crow, which eventually emerged as a euphemism for segregation, Mr. Rivets goes back to Cincinnati, Ohio, in 1828, when stage entertainer Thomas "Daddy" Rice donned the burnt-cork mask of minstrelsy and did the song and dance routine called "Jump Jim Crow." Stewart explains that minstrelsy propagated an image of blacks as foolish, which reinforced a desire for segregation. The video displays a host of caricatures of blackness that were circulated in U.S. material culture and linked to notions of black inferiority. The year 1857 is the next major time period to which the bus travels. The video's most compelling feature at this juncture is a skit highlighting local actors portraying the family of Dred Scott, which facilitates its discussion of his famous legal case, protesting the exclusion of blacks from citizenship rights; acknowledges discrimination against blacks in the North; and explains "how Scott became the most famous black person in America" at that time. The video's next phase of time travel stages an imaginary conversation between Harriet Tubman and Henry "Box" Brown given Tubman's numerous trips to the South to free black slaves once she escaped to freedom via the Underground Railroad, and the story of how Brown famously boxed and shipped himself to freedom.

The year 1892, in New Orleans, Louisiana, emerges as another signal juncture on the journey, pinpointing an early challenge to Jim Crow on public transportation in the case of Homer Plessy. The time machine's next major stop occurs in 1955, when the narrator raises the question, "How much has changed?" and acknowledges, "Not enough, I'm afraid, by this time." At this point, actors once again dress in period clothes to evoke the period of the Montgomery bus boycott and Parks's heroic choice to remain seated, a story that Stewart punctuates by intoning, "Something happened that changed America on that bus that evening," registering Parks's indelible influence on the nation.[52] The performance and theatricality embedded in these videos mirror the historical reenactments of the bus encounter and Montgomery bus boycott staged in the museum's main exhibits.

If a video is initially mobilized as a medium for thinking about the history related to the Montgomery bus boycott on the main tour, including Rosa Parks's pivotal encounter on the bus, the video highlighted in the Children's Museum is equally invested in launching its young audience on an imaginative journey. It reveals ways in which blacks have challenged and resisted racism in signal moments since the antebellum era and hearkens to the future by drawing on images associated with the space age. Nomenclature for the Children's Museum in Montgomery, by tacitly citing Parks as a symbolic mother, further consolidated the prevailing narratives linking Rosa Parks to national femininity in the United States, narratives that had been increasingly mainstreamed and embraced in the post–civil rights era. If the mother metaphor is tacit in the Children's Museum's naming, however, the museum effectively recasts it by eschewing its typical romanticization within civil rights history, while detaching it from its typical national and global moorings and associating it with notions of futurity as much as with the past. The naming is also significant for alluding to the famous Children's March in Birmingham, Alabama, in 1963. Moreover, the young audiences toward whom the institution pitches this tour can be thought of as an extension of the youth mentored by Parks during her lifetime, a group whom the recurrent maternal metaphors associated with her also played a vital role in constituting.

Forced movements and migration that attended modernity, and that were intricately linked to slavery, are replaced on this time machine by imagining a world with travel as voluntary and the removal of all limitations on time and space. It ruptures the containment and marginalizing negotiations with which black subjects have been associated in the schema of modernity since slavery by creating a futuristic space in which all human subjects are free from mental and physical constraints, with the entire universe at their disposal, and in which alternative and more inclusive historical narratives of the past flow freely. In this space, the hope and potential looking toward the year 2055 is an indispensable complement for thinking back on the historic events of 1955. While the ship, given its materialist linkages to the African slave trade, has recurrently functioned as a symbol of slavery and the oppression of African diasporic subjects in the Western world, the bus emerges in this installation as the primary symbol that encompasses post–civil rights struggles against Jim Crow and the journey on to new horizons.[53]

While the civil rights movement and the legacies of its most prominent leaders continue to be widely celebrated in the African American context, questions related to its continuing relevance persist, as we see in the aforementioned scene in the film *Barbershop*. The movement has been relegated frequently to the past and viewed as being detached from the urgent political needs of the contemporary African American context. At worst, the movement, with its integrationist goals and nonviolent strategies, and during a time of widespread retrenchment against legislative, political, and social breakthroughs achieved in the civil rights movement, has been imagined as primarily nostalgic and trapped in a bygone era, linked to forms of resistance that have no use or relevance in the present. Moreover, the emergence of the type of iconic and charismatic leadership that sustained it seems less conceivable and desirable in communities where local mobilization at the grassroots level is perceived to be more effective, feasible, and conducive to social and political advancement than mass movements led by a central nationally prominent leader.

The representation of Parks within this dynamic installation is not designed to reaffirm or reinstate this leadership paradigm, as quintessentially embodied by King. Yet the Cleveland Avenue Time Machine challenges narratives of the civil rights era as passé, beginning in its accompanying video, by making Rosa Parks a reigning emblem in the long-standing African American struggles against segregation of public facilities, while signifying her as a harbinger of African American futurity. The bus serves as a symbol of the future as its movement also prompts its tourists and passengers, with Mr. Rivets as navigator, to reflect on the past. The installation registers the axis of temporal nodes from past to present and constitutes a vision that dislodges Parks from romantic and nostalgic narratives of civil rights history, framing her as a prominent revolutionary and as a woman who made a national difference in ending segregation, but whose significance is global and universal.

The trajectory of time travel staged in this installation is primarily backward. The Cleveland Avenue Time Machine creates an interactive and intersubjective engagement with the past, as signaled by its visual colorization, along with features such as the video and the animated sound and light effects it creates to simulate movement backward in time. Yet the main movement suggested is travel forward. The dynamic installation mobilizes these features to ground the bus boycott in a transcendent narrative of movement and time that signals the future, exceeding earthly dimensions and temporalities by drawing heavily on science fiction, a genre in which black and female subjects have remained largely invisible and marginal as characters and topics of interest, with the exception of writers such as Octavia Butler. Moreover, the accompanying video's narrative emphasizes Rosa Parks as a black feminine subject, along with a range of black female precursors who challenged segregation in public transportation, and unsettles conventional male-focused chronicles of African American history, as well as individual narratives focused on her. Movement simulation, sound effects, and visual aesthetics inscribe Rosa Parks as a figure within a futuristic aesthetics that serves as a paean to the digital era in which this exhibition was constructed. Rosa Parks is simultaneously synonymous with the past, present, and future in this installation.

The installation constructs a broad timeline-based narrative of the civil rights movement as diverse and inclusive and accords it a periodization that exceeds its typical temporal parameters, linked to the 1950s and 1960s, so that it spans the antebellum era up to the twenty-first century. The dynamic installation in effect dislodges civil rights history, including the Montgomery bus boycott, from the notions of stasis to which it has been linked at times in the national imagination, along with aspects of African American and diasporic consciousness. This approach is particularly significant when considering the diverse audience of children and adolescents to whom this aspect of the exhibition is primarily pitched. It is aimed at a new generation of youth born in the postmillennium, who sometimes lack knowledge about civil rights history and internalize the myth of its obsolescence; who will stand at the forefront in rethinking and retelling this history to future generations, growing up in a digital age; and who often learn most effectively though technology and multimedia.

The representations linking Parks to notions of journeying across time showcased in this installation are also classifiable as Afrofuturistic. Moreover, in historicizing and remembering the Montgomery bus boycott and monumentalizing Rosa Parks as a civil rights leader via video, while drawing centrally on features derived from technology and science fiction, the Cleveland Avenue Time Machine installation poignantly actualizes a visual and aural aesthetics in keeping with Afrofuturism. Afrofuturism is a critical and cultural discourse in areas such as literature and art that draws on areas such as fantasy, magical realism, speculative fiction and science fiction to engage the past and present in relation to the lives of minorities, including people of African descent, while decentering Western-centered frames of reference. Mark Dery, author of the seminal essay "Black to the Future," introduced the term in 1993. It has been further advanced and developed critically by scholars such as Alondra Nelson, who established an Afrofuturism listserv in 1998 and edited a special 2002 issue of the journal *Social Text* on the topic.[54]

Nelson points out that the listserv emerged in part because dialogues about blacks and technology proved limiting in their vacillation between a focus on the utopian fantasy of technology in eliminating race and an emphasis on the rhetoric of a digital divide, an issue that has been brilliantly theorized by scholars such as Anna Everett.[55] As Nelson argues, "The racialized digital divide narrative that circulates in the public sphere and the bodiless, color-blind mythotopias of cybertheory and commercial advertising have become the unacknowledged frames of reference for understanding race in the digital age. In these frameworks, the technologically enabled future is by its very nature unmoored from the past and from people of color."[56] Enlightenment philosophy, and most notably the perspectives of G. W. F. Hegel, famously excluded Africans in the schema of world history and posited them as being out of time, a framing that denied their humanity, marked them as inferior, and helped to rationalize their enslavement and subjection. Afrofuturism, along with queer and gay and lesbian studies, has played a primary role in shaping discourses on temporality in African and African diasporic thought, as it provides a counternarrative to conventional narratives that have marginalized and excluded blacks from notions of time in Western thought, in keeping with Hegelian racialist premises, which the Time Machine effectively confronts and unsettles.[57] Yet despite the liberatory narrative portended by the Time Machine, new technologies have limits and are potentially oppressive for minority populations. Ruha Benjamin's *Race after Technology: Abolitionist Tools for the New Jim Code* reveals limitations in newer and emerging technologies that perpetuate inequality and sustain long-standing racial hierarchies and divisions.[58]

Birmingham, Alabama, musician Sun Ra, who later migrated to Chicago and founded a band known as the Arkestra in the 1950s, stood at the forefront in developing an Afrofuturist discourse in music through forms of synthesis that drew saliently on images of Africa, space, and science fiction in costuming, sound, and visual aesthetics. While his groundbreaking innovations in jazz and experiences in cities such as Chicago, New York, and Philadelphia typically link his Afrofuturist musical production to urban contexts, Sun Ra's foundational musical training and performances in clubs in Birmingham during the bitter years of the Jim Crow era shaped the staging strategies and visual aesthetics that emerged later in his career. (Black power discourses are similarly urbanized and routinely delinked from their Black Belt roots in rural Alabama and Mississippi.) Sun Ra and his Arkestra challenged stereotypes of the South as backward and trapped in time. These contours also organically link the origins of Afrofuturism to Alabama and the U.S. South and make it all the more compelling to draw on in thinking about an installation such as the Cleveland Avenue Time Machine in Montgomery and the legacy of Rosa Parks.[59]

The installation frames Parks's choice to remain seated on the bus as the outgrowth of a longer history of movement for freedom that continues to unfold, a movement that her transcendent legacy continues to influence. At the same time, this framing challenges the perception of her choice to remain seated as an individual act of heroism by emphasizing the boycott that it catalyzed as a collective and interdependent community initiative. The installation enacts and stages the messages running through Parks's dialogic books, directed at young readers, affirming their potential to help catalyze change in the world, just as she did, framing them as the hope of the future, staging a visceral, dynamic, and interactive encounter with her legacy.

Established as a paean to her status as a symbolic mother in the nation, the Rosa Parks Children's Museum is designed to help spread the message that mattered to her most, and the Afrofuturistic digital Time Machine to emphasize its timelessness and universality. Like her books, the museum, in its conception and design, primarily addresses a young audience and challenges narratives of the civil rights movement as being passé by linking its message to young people in the twenty-first century, who are charged with carrying forth its work into the future. In it, Parks as a black woman is unfettered by the venomous ideological scripts of black womanhood propagated by James Blake, and the museum embodies the triumph of this subject position into a national ideal as one of its universal emblems of freedom and democracy. If her image failed to dislodge conventional media myths of black mothers as mammies and matriarchs, which were enshrined in the national imaginary by the time of her arrest, she staged one of the most visible and subversive alternatives to them during the civil rights era and well beyond, literally for the rest of her life, as the iconic mother of the civil rights movement, notwithstanding the inherent limitations in this symbolism. Parks's legibility as a symbolic mother in the nation, however, was immortalized and most saliently evident in the public sphere during the moment of collective mourning for her in the nation's capital in 2005, which profoundly registered her cultural influence.

Rosa Parks's National Body

Rosa Parks's iconicity as a heroine and symbolic mother figure in the United States was reinforced and more thoroughly nationalized through her prominent public honors during the 1990s, under Clinton's presidential administration, when she received the Medal of Honor (1994) and the Congressional Gold Medal of Freedom (1999). I end this chapter by reflecting on how the memorial commemorations of Rosa Parks in 2005 in the wake of her death articulated her as a reigning emblem of the national body and reinforced her status as a symbolic mother in the national imagination, immortalizing her as a premier emblem of national femininity. Her status as a model of national femininity was further reinforced when she lay in repose in the nation's capital in 2005. How do we understand and analyze the memorial's relationship to valued African American cultural practices? What does it mean that while funeral rituals remain among the most segregated practices in the United States, and African American mourning rituals have remained relatively obscure in the U.S. mainstream, aspects of Rosa Parks's memorials showcased these traditions at a national level and for a racially and culturally diverse citizenry?

Parks's final repose in the Capitol—in a space reserved primarily for U.S. presidents—also culminated a revolutionary life in a way that reinforced her subversive resistance on the bus in 1955. While the verb *sitting* is invoked most frequently as a descriptor for the action in her heroic choice, the verb *lying* notably emerges as the primary signifier to describe her repose at the Capitol Rotunda, in a space not typically linked to black or feminine subjects, and to punctuate the ending of her revolutionary life. If her decision to be arrested on a Montgomery city bus in 1955 catalyzed the Montgomery bus boycott, launched an international movement for civil rights, and became a defining moment in her life, after her death on October 24, 2005, nearly fifty years later, Rosa Parks also made history when her body lay in repose in Washington,

DC, in the Capitol Rotunda, where mainly white men had been honored in U.S. history. In the nation's history, this honor has typically been reserved for military officers, elected officials, and U.S. presidents, among them Abraham Lincoln, John F. Kennedy, and Ronald Reagan. Parks's death thus was yet another revolutionary moment in her history: a black woman lying in honor was an unprecedented event. The ritual of her public mourning in effect integrated the space not only by race, given her status as the second African American ever honored there, but also by gender in light of her status as the very first woman so honored.[60] Race and gender were as relevant as they had been on the bus that night in 1955.

U.S. Representative John Conyers of Michigan, for whom she worked as a secretary and receptionist in his congressional office in Detroit from 1965 until her retirement in 1988, spearheaded the effort to secure permission to accord Parks the distinction of lying in honor, which was granted by Senate Concurrent Resolution 61 on October 29, 2005.[61] The two-day public viewing of Parks at the Capitol Rotunda on October 30 and October 31 began with a brief congressional ceremony, during which President George W. Bush placed a wreath at her casket, the Morgan State University Choir sang the "Battle Hymn of the Republic," and Senate chaplain Barry C. Black remarked that Parks's courage "ignited a movement that aroused our national conscience" and served as an example of the "power of fateful, small acts."[62] The long line to enter the rotunda extended for several blocks.[63] From senior citizens to parents with small children, an estimated thirty thousand people, some of whom were tearful, filed by quietly for hours to view the casket. The casket was flanked by a military honor guard at both ends while on display. Many had traveled long distances to be a part of this historic and unprecedented moment in the nation's capital and to pay tribute to Parks.

The national map traversed by Parks's body in death culminated and heightened the motifs of movement that have long been associated with her through her symbolic significations in relation to the bus as a grounded space. Her mappings in relation to regional, national, and global contexts reached their apex in her memorializing in multiple cities in the wake of her death and demonstrated the centrality of geography in constituting her iconicity from national to local sites. The memorial services and public viewings held for Parks in three cities, including Montgomery, Alabama; Detroit, Michigan; and Washington, DC, spanned five days, yielded an outpouring of public support and magnified the deep respect and adoration for Parks felt throughout the nation and around the world. Her family and friends attended all of them, and to facilitate the extensive traveling during this period, her casket and family members and friends were transported to the various sites on an airplane that was volunteered by Southwest Airlines.

In death, the traversal of her body across these multiple geographies reflected the national significance of Parks as a leader in the civil rights movement and her personal history as a woman who was born in Pine Level, Alabama, migrated to Detroit, and transformed the nation and world. Reportedly, when initially airborne and transporting Parks's body from the events in Montgomery to the events in the capital, Louis Freeman, the nation's first black chief pilot, and the copilot, also an African American, circled the city and tipped the left wing of the plane while bearing Parks's body away from her hometown, never to return, signaling her final farewell.[64] This moving moment affirmed her historic moorings in the city of Montgomery and the larger state of Alabama, notwithstanding her move to Michigan, which aligned her with the phenomenon of the Great Migration of African Americans from southern states to the urban North, and her final home and resting place in Detroit. At the same time, the multiple memorial ceremonies delink Parks's legacy from just one geographic location and point to her widespread cultural significance. Moreover, all her public tributes mapped Parks's journey from the segregated bus to the Capitol Rotunda and framed it in a continuum with her activist legacy, and within long-standing struggles for attaining African American legibility and recognition in the nation's public sphere.

Through the participation of a singer such as Aretha Franklin, the honor guard that carried her casket, and the black gold-trimmed horse-drawn carriage in a processional to the cemetery, aspects of Parks's Detroit ceremony, the culminating memorial in the monumental multicity homegoing for Rosa Parks, recalled aspects of the regal funeral for Annie Johnson famously featured in the 1959 film version of *Imitation of Life*.[65] This film features gospel singer Mahalia Jackson singing the African American spiritual "Soon I Will Be Done" and a public ceremony and parade replete with bands and a horse-drawn carriage, a glorious homegoing that Johnson had described in detail to her employer Lora Meredith and dreamed of having once passing on. Yet the horse-drawn carriage originally designated as the vehicle for making Parks's final journey to Detroit's Woodlawn Cemetery did not complete it. After the seven-hour service, and with daylight waning, a white antique hearse picked up the processional after just a block, completing the seven-mile journey to the cemetery for Parks's interment in the mausoleum alongside her mother, Leona MacCaulay, and her husband, Raymond Parks.[66]

In Karla FC Holloway's study *Passed On: African American Mourning Stories*, she describes how the "ornate funeral" that the character Annie outlined in *Imitation of Life* "provoked the teary-eyed bonding of a generation of mothers and daughters," acknowledging through a reading of the film audience's reactions the inspiration that these scenes provided for black women. Holloway points out that the film led some, inspired by Annie, to "write out their own funeral instructions" to shape their ceremonies, a practice spanning back to the nineteenth century.[67] Holloway notes the importance of a "symbolically rich display," or a "special" funeral, for people in the African American context who lacked public acclaim. Drawing on the work of C. Eric Lincoln, she notes that by the late twentieth century, the trend toward "cremation and minimalist funerals" had not affected the widespread belief in the African American context that homegoings, regardless of one's status, are important.[68] Rosa Parks's service resonated profoundly with such elaborate African American funerary practices and put aspects of such rituals on display at the national level. It drew a multiracial public into its ceremonial aspects at every level, and critical terrain provided by Sharon Holland in *Raising the Dead: Readings of Death and (Black) Subjectivity* underscores the importance of nuancing these confluences.[69] Parks's Detroit ceremony recollected the visual aesthetics of African American postmortem photography featured in James Van Der Zee's classic *Harlem Book of the Dead*, which capture a diverse range of elaborate African American mourning rituals and funeral practices, including those of celebrities, such as the young actress Florence Mills, that had occurred early in the twentieth century and were largely invisible, unknown, and marginal in the segregated culture of the American mainstream.[70]

Precisely for these reasons, and despite valuing and admiring Theoharis's work to throw into relief the complexity of Rosa Parks's political background in her brilliant and groundbreaking biography, I resist Theoharis's description of Parks's 2005 ceremonies as a "national spectacle" and "public spectacle."[71] Such words belie the significance and dignity of the event, along with its deeper cultural significance. Similarly, in a later chapter, she suggests that the "fanciness" of the funeral for Parks ran counter to her political legacy of activism and investments in grassroots struggles. However, some aspects of the memorial Theoharis describes as excessive or "fancy"—a word that has incidentally also been condescendingly and snidely invoked at times to trivialize African American dress and demeanor, deemed as being too uppity—might be more productively interpreted as a manifestation of long-standing black cultural practices and mourning rituals in African American cultural history and memory. Drawing on Holloway's analysis, which suggests the value of black feminist epistemologies when scrutinizing African American mourning rituals and burial practices, I want to emphasize the importance of relating the pageantry of Parks's public ceremonies to cultural contexts and practices that reflect long-standing traditions grounded in the African American context, including forms of expressivity and performance distinctly associated with black female subjectivity.[72]

At the same time, I share Theoharis's larger concerns and frustrations about the uses, abuses, and appropriations of Parks's activist legacy in the wake of her death. The discourses related to Rosa Parks have become a salient metaphor at the national level and have been increasingly serviceable in the millennial era for articulating investments in freedom, social justice, and human rights struggles among liberal as well as conservative political leaders, whose policies to enable and protect such values have nevertheless frequently conflicted. In some instances, contemporary invocations of Rosa Parks have tacitly served as a unifying force across political party lines and as a site on which to establish common political ground. At times, invocations of her name have demarcated stark divisions, as witnessed when White House adviser Stephen Moore compared the predominantly white right-wing protesters and supporters of President Donald Trump to Parks after they staged armed demonstrations at state buildings in cities across the United States in defiance of mandatory social distancing guidelines designed to protect public health in the wake of the 2020 coronavirus pandemic. Such citations of Parks revealed a grossly superficial understanding of black protest movements. Just as Parks faced the threat of state violence at the hands of multiple white men on the night of her arrest, white and masculine figures associated with state authority—public officials such as liberal U.S. president Bill Clinton and conservative U.S. president George W. Bush—have paradoxically played a major role in publicly honoring her legacy even as they have advanced policy agendas inimical to African American community interests. These new narratives as developed in the post–civil rights era thoroughly revise and displace the facade that Parks encountered in the menacing white masculine figures who represented state power on the bus that fateful evening. It is also important to raise questions about what is at stake in invoking Rosa Parks to mediate a redemptive portrait of southern white masculinity through U.S. presidents such as Bush and Clinton and to offset narratives in civil rights history of white masculine villainy and abjection.[73] Similarly, how do we grapple with the misguided appropriations of her legacy in the era of Trump?

Parks's ubiquity in the African American context and broader national imaginary constituted her as a mother figure worthy of respect on par with statesmen, including presidents, in a sense that is not simply reducible to being merely a passive symbol. Indeed, the long-standing struggles to memorialize and monumentalize blacks in the capital and in the Capitol building made Parks's postmortem national honors revolutionary and subversive in those geographic and architectural spaces, in which blacks have been conventionally cast as alien and other, alongside all the major honors accorded to Parks by presidents during her lifetime and her strategic uses of public celebrations to advance political goals. I am intrigued by what can happen with a view of Rosa Parks's multiple memorial services that situates them in relation to the long history of struggles for memorializing and making black subjects legible as citizens and as reflections of the national body, spanning back to Bethune. In this sense, the services, and particularly the one in the nation's capital, become less divorceable from Parks's activist political history and register as being continuous with it, and even as an extension of it.

This brings me to my main points related to Parks's subversive status as a national mother. The period of mourning Parks's body on the Capitol Rotunda in 2005 enshrined her status as a reigning symbol of national femininity and as a symbolic mother in the nation. Her figuring as a symbolic mother momentarily united the nation within a raced, sexed, and gendered discourse, scripting Parks as a maternal figure, and composing a narrative of Americans as a diverse national family. Parks's funeral before the world and the enshrining of her body on the Capitol Rotunda recollected the civil rights movement within national memory and memorialized her before an audience of international proportions. During this time of mourning, Parks was figured as the quintessential emblem of the national body on the Capitol. Parks emerged as a site of mourning and recollection related to the civil rights movement across sites from Montgomery to Detroit, with the nation's capital as the focal point on the map of the national celebration of her life.

In a figurative sense, she became synonymous with notions of national femininity in the United States in the wake of her loss. Her public memorials in recent years have thoroughly reinforced and extended the maternal metaphor that has inflected her long-standing honored designation as the mother of the civil rights movement and further underscored it in the cultural imagination. This raced, sexed, and gendered script of Parks initially emerged in the African American context during the civil rights era, was eventually nationalized and globalized, and accords with narratives of the nation *as* feminine and scripts that associate it with the feminine body and the maternal, representations that postcolonial scholarship has intimately linked to constructions of national identity. Such formulations linking the nation to notions of the feminine and maternal are problematic and limited to the extent that they romanticize femininity and link it to the earth and land. At the same time, they reveal the depth of her influence on the American consciousness and open the door to possibilities for representing more diverse and representative race, ethnic, gender, and sexual identities within scripts of national selfhood, including black queer and trans women.

The long-standing effort to erect a statue to Bethune in the nation's capital discussed in the previous chapter reminds us of the importance of not devaluing or dismissing memorials and monuments in the national context to African Americans, who have long been illegible, invisible, and marginal in U.S. history. It reminds us that such forms of public recognition have been the outgrowth of intense struggle, have been hard won, and should by no means be taken for granted. The Washington, DC, National Cathedral's 2012 dedication of a stone carving in honor of Parks in its section on human rights, which also includes tributes to figures such as former First Lady Eleanor Roosevelt and the 2013 postage stamp in honor of Parks's one hundredth birthday, along with the monument in Statuary Hall at the Capitol, the first life-size statue featuring an African American, are achievements and breakthroughs that would have been unthinkable even a generation ago, underscoring her historical significance and reflecting her national iconicity.[74] In 2018, the toy manufacturer Mattel released a Barbie doll in honor of Parks.

In 2005, the national commemoration of Rosa Parks in the wake of her death held profound meaning and significance for many in the African American cultural context, at levels that conceivably ran counter to the reactions of a national mainstream that might easily meet time-honored African American mourning rituals with irreverence, mockery, mystification, and even outright dismissal. In my own research over several years, I have been far more interested in examining how aspects of Rosa Parks's lying in honor on the Capitol Rotunda as the first woman and second African American at some levels punctuates and extends her lifetime of activism, making additional interventions related to race, class, gender, and sexuality. To divorce Parks's public honors from her activism obscures ways in which grassroots activists and politicians advocated for and helped to enable such honors for Parks.

In the weeks after her death, and to acknowledge the fiftieth anniversary of the Montgomery bus boycott on December 1, 2005, President George W. Bush introduced House Resolution 4145, supporting the placement of a statue of Parks in the national Statuary Hall in Washington, DC.[75] This tribute, which permits the erection of monuments honoring two figures in each state, makes Parks the first African American woman honored in the Capitol's marbled gallery, and the third Alabamian (in addition to the legendary visually and hearing-impaired educator Helen Keller and Confederate general and U.S. congressman Joe Wheeler) to be honored in this fashion. Hence, this moment represents another crucial link in the chain of breakthroughs related to Parks based on race and gender, which becomes all the more significant if we recall the long history of struggle to garner honor and respect for blacks through monuments in the nation's capital. It becomes all the more significant in light of debates related to Confederate monuments since the Charleston tragedy in 2015, which have in some cases led to their removal. In Bush's comments, he invokes Parks as an example for all Americans. He links her to the nation's founding fathers and frames her as a central agent in actualizing the nation's founding ideals. His comments are also significant to the extent that they link the fate of all Americans to African Americans.

Yet such inclusive gestures will be limited as long as there is a failure to recognize, rethink, and fully reform patriarchal and capitalist abuses underlying the nation's founding ideals, which were paradoxically rooted in slavery, along with race, class, gender, and sexual violence and subjection, which sanctioned colonialism and imperialism, and which failed to live up to promises of democracy, freedom, and equality. Just as the postmortem body of Parks broke ground as the first woman to ever lie in state in the nation's capital, the statue depicting her is the first life-size statue of an African American woman ever included in Statuary Hall, which also includes a bust of Martin Luther King Jr., installed in 1986, and a bust of Sojourner Truth, installed in 2009. A statue of Bethune is currently in development.[76] Such honors will become more inclusive when no longer premised on a gender binary and limited to normative sexual identity categories.

Such shifts will yield more inclusive and complex national stories that reflect a more nuanced portrait of black liberation and civil rights histories, while according legibility to a broader spectrum of freedom fighters, from Bayard Rustin to Pauli Murray, whose contributions have gone unsung. They hold the potential to inspire new and emerging leaders in the black queer and trans communities. Still, the reality is that it may be possible to fully empower such othered categories only when the nation-state, which has routinely authorized and reproduced oppressive models of sexuality and carried out violence against the body based on sexuality to consolidate its power, is fully reimagined or becomes obsolete. Similarly, it is mandatory to broaden notions of national family, while moving beyond narrow policymaking agendas that primarily invest social support systems and benefits in protecting, providing, and advocating for a citizenry whose legibility is narrowly premised on conventional heteronormative models of family, marriage, and childbearing. Such policy agendas undermine the rights of subjects from queer and trans to heterosexual and single, sustaining forms of social and political inequality and alienation, and appropriating or limiting the subversive potential of queer activist movements, as some scholarship in queer studies has pointed out.[77]

In 2009, sculptor and master artist Eugene Daub and his partner, Rob Firmin, serving as project manager and primary historical researcher, joined the competition with 150 other artists for the commission from the National Endowment for the Arts and the Artist of the Capitol to create the Parks monument.[78] The nine-foot bronze statue, which weighs six hundred pounds, depicts Parks with her hands crossed in her lap. It stands on a black granite pedestal that weighs 2,100 pounds. The statue shows Parks on the day she was arrested. She wears a hat, glasses, a coat, and oxford shoes and holds her purse handle with her body positioned to the right, with a straight back and head. It aims to convey dignity and the "quiet strength" that have typically been claimed as a defining characteristic of her philosophy and demeanor.[79] The statue was developed in Daub's studio in San Pedro, cast in a Hawthorne foundry, and sent to the East Coast for storage in a warehouse until its public unveiling, though no images of it were circulated, and its design was kept secret, along with the names of the artists who created it.[80] According to Daub, the team aimed to portray Parks's sitting position as heroic and to highlight the agency and national significance in the action that her choice represented. At the same time, they chose not to depict her on a bus seat over concern that such a depiction "would trivialize things" and take the focus from her.[81] The artists also self-consciously aimed to portray Parks's image emanating from a rock, to underscore solidity. The choice is also compelling, given the trajectory of analysis that I am pursuing, for the levels on which it alludes to the presidential images on Mount Rushmore and further amplifies her status as a national mother and symbol. As the next chapter explains, invoking such national monuments has also been serviceable in moments for critiquing reactionary politics of iconic national leaders such as Condoleezza Rice.

Riché Richardson, *Condoleezza Rice: From Birmingham to the White House*, 2011–12. Photograph by Dave Burbank.

America's Chief Diplomat

The Politics of Condoleezza Rice from Autobiography to Art and Fashion

We must remain patient. Our own history should remind us that the union of democratic principle and practice is always a work in progress. When the Founding Fathers said "We the People," they did not mean me. My ancestors were considered three-fifths of a person. Knowing the difficulties of America's own history, we should always be humble in singing freedom's praises. But America's voice should never waver in speaking out on the side of people seeking freedom. —CONDOLEEZZA RICE, remarks to the Chicago Council on Foreign Relations, October 8, 2003

I represent the United States. And the United States has had to do some really difficult things. And not everything is popular that the United States has done. But I look at how many people still want to come to America, that this is the place that everybody wants to study, particularly in graduate school or in college. I look at the popularity of American culture, some of it good, some of it bad. And I think America is widely admired. Some of our policies are not very popular and not very well liked, but I think you can't base how you use the influence of the United States on whether a decision is going to be popular. —CONDOLEEZZA RICE, *Essence* magazine, May 25, 2006

The slow response of the Federal Emergency Management Agency (FEMA) in providing relief in the wake of Hurricane Katrina, an ecological and environmental disaster in August 2005, which devastated the nation's Gulf Coast region and New Orleans, Louisiana, resulting in high casualties when the levee system failed and the city flooded, led to widespread criticism of President George W. Bush and members of his administration.[1] Bush's administration was criticized for failing to provide faster governmental relief to the population in the city that was predominantly black and poor, lacked the resources to evacuate before the hurricane hit, and had been stranded without food and water for several days in various locations, including the Superdome, where thousands had sought shelter. In the days thereafter, as Bush and Michael Brown, the director of FEMA, were being attacked widely for slowness and inefficiency in responding to the crisis, *Gawker* reported in a sensational feature that Secretary of State Condoleezza Rice was spotted shopping at Salvatore Ferragamo, an exclusive designer boutique on Fifth Avenue, where she spent several thousands of dollars on shoes. According to *Gawker*, as Rice shopped for Ferragamos in New York that fateful day, another customer confronted her, exclaiming angrily, "How dare you shop for shoes while thousands are dying and homeless!"[2] Allegedly, the customer was removed from the store by security.[3]

Rice has denied that this incident with an irate fellow Ferragamo shoe customer ever happened. Whether or not it happened, this story about Rice shopping in an exclusive boutique as poor blacks in New Orleans suffered circulated widely, to the point of becoming a veritable urban legend, epitomizing a view of Rice as being apathetic about the plight of blacks in the United States.[4] Spike Lee's documentary *When the Levees Broke* reinforces this representation of Rice in its interview with scholar Michael Eric Dyson, who comments, "While people were drowning in New Orleans, she was going up and down Madison Avenue buying Ferragamo shoes. Then she went to see Spamalot!"

The report about Rice's shopping at an exclusive shoe boutique while the levees broke reinforced the public perception of the Bush administration as elitist and indifferent to the acute suffering of the predominantly black population in New Orleans. Famously, the rapper Kanye West remarked, "George W. Bush doesn't care anything about black people," before a nationally televised concert sponsored by the Red Cross to raise funds to help the victims, which aired on NBC.[5] It also reinforced the association of Rice with policy agendas of white conservative Republicans perceived as being oppressive and detrimental to the economic, political, and social well-being of black communities and the public perception of Rice as being indifferent to black interests, notwithstanding Rice's identity as a black woman and upbringing amid the racism and violence of the segregated U.S. South. Her biographers have highlighted her southern background, which she has also discussed recurrently in her writings and interviews.

Rice explained her trip to New York to see the play, shop, and attend the U.S. Open as a much-needed vacation after visiting forty-six countries over a period of nine months. Moreover, as the nation's secretary of state, a role that, unlike her previous post as national security adviser, was not related to domestic matters, she perceived Hurricane Katrina as beyond the scope of her charge. She cut her trip short and returned to Washington to help address the international response to the situation, traveled to Alabama because of her origins in the state and the impact of the hurricane there, and spearheaded outreach to Bruce Gordon, a leader of the NAACP.

An interview with *Essence* magazine, the premier organ pitched primarily to the nation's black women, on May 25, 2006, registers the magnitude and import of Rice's role in politics, as well as its mutual race and gender implications, as "one of the most powerful women in America" and as "the top official—black official" in the Bush administration, acknowledging concomitant expectations of her to address matters concerning the black population. She explains that the aftermath of Hurricane Katrina was when she first fully grasped and understood her perception as a national leader by many black Americans, who expected her to weigh in on national affairs concerning the population because of her public profile and platform: "I guess—sure, I've never felt that—even though my responsibility is foreign policy, I realize that I'm the highest ranking African American in the government. I realize that I have a close personal relationship with the President. And so yeah, I feel responsible for helping on those issues, too."[6] Similarly, in 2011, Rice acknowledges this moment of realization in her 2011 memoir, *No Higher Honor: A Memoir of My Years in Washington*, the sequel to *Extraordinary, Ordinary People: A Memoir of Family*: "[I] sat there kicking myself for having been so tone-deaf. I wasn't just the Secretary of State with responsibility for foreign affairs; I was the highest-ranking black in the administration and a key adviser to the president. What had I been thinking?" She went on to comment, "I'm still mad at myself for only belatedly understanding my role and responsibilities in the crisis."[7]

The moment simultaneously registered Rice's positioning as the nation's most powerful woman and African American leader and threw questions into relief related to her racial solidarity with black community interests. Rice was perceived to be indifferent to the suffering of black and low-income minority communities during Hurricane Katrina in what was described as the worst ecological and environmental disaster in the nation's history, which reinforced perceptions of her complicity with the policy agendas of the neoconservative Bush administration, widely perceived to be inimical to black communities, sometimes to the point of being linked to antiblackness. Notions of color-blindness had increasingly inflected neoconservative thought in the post–civil rights era, fueled by a backlash against civil rights within a political climate that routinely downplayed the significance of race and denied the continuing repercussions of racism. This moment that put national and global attention on the predominantly black and poor population of New Orleans, however, was revealing for Rice in providing an epistemology on the relevance of her African American racial and cultural identities in shaping expectations among blacks for her as a leader working on matters related to domestic and national affairs. It was a moment of reckoning in which she was forced to grapple with her influence and legibility as the nation's most powerful and prominent black national leader and as a representative black woman, who was expected to use her voice, platform, and power to add perspectives and insights to public dialogues that affected the nation's black citizenry.

As the most prominent black woman in the national arena, who was initially silent in the wake of this national crisis, the appropriation of her raced, classed, sexed, and gendered body and its serviceability for the advancement of reactionary and controversial domestic and foreign policy agendas mirrored and extended ways in which black feminine bodies become hyperembodied, highly visible, and nationally abstracted while simultaneously remaining rigidly contained and voiceless. Rice's intersectional race, class, gender, and sexual identities have grounded her status as a national icon inasmuch as they constituted her as one of the foremost emblems of national femininity to emerge in the first decade of the twenty-first century. The vociferous criticism of her in the post-Katrina moment both reflected and responded to her high level of visibility and national iconicity, including among many in black communities who viewed her as a "race traitor" because of the neoconservative policy agendas she played a key role in advancing as a member of Bush's cabinet. This iconicity consolidated even as Rice viewed her status as a national leader ambivalently, and her role in sanctioning the war on terror in the wake of the tragedy of September 11, including the Iraq War, garnered widespread public distrust and criticism.

Rice's role as national security adviser in the Bush administration focused on domestic issues and played a pivotal role in her nationalization as a public figure, just as her role as secretary of state accorded her unprecedented power and influence as a black woman in the international arena. Significantly, *Forbes* magazine named her the most powerful woman in the world in both 2004 and 2005. Even as national security adviser, Rice's profound influence on U.S. foreign policy was patently evident in her salience in helping to provide rationalizations for the Iraq War in the wake of the September 11 tragedy. Rice famously invoked the history of blacks in the South by comparing the pressure to withdraw U.S. troops from the war in Iraq to northerners advocating for the end of the Civil War before slaves had been freed: "Absolutely. Because it's difficult, it doesn't mean that, first of all, it won't work out. I think it will. I'm sure there are people who thought that it was a mistake to fight the Civil War to its end and to insist that the emancipation of slaves would hold. I know there were people who said why don't we get out of this now, take a peace with the South, but leave the South with slaves?"[8]

While Rice was a child of the South and viscerally linked to its civil rights history, there was an irony in bringing up its antebellum past given that she was part of the group whose rights were frequently compromised by its racial politics. In the post-civil rights era, the neoconservative movement mainstreamed the notorious southern strategy, designed to dismantle legislative gains, such as the Civil Rights Act of 1964 and the Voting Rights Act of 1965. Rather than address persisting racism, it routinely prioritized agendas that were designed to undermine affirmative action and to propagate reverse discrimination claims by whites, who contended that they were disadvantaged and discriminated against within employment and educational systems that used "quotas" based on race to increase the number of minorities within institutions. Rice gained a political voice and platform in the national mainstream in the new millennium amid a neoconservative backlash against civil rights that appropriated civil rights discourses to advance reactionary agendas. Paradoxically, Rice gained symbolic capital from invoking civil rights legacies, which have saliently mediated her claims to moral authority in the public sphere, along with her rise as a black model of national femininity in the new millennium.

Rice emerged as the most ubiquitous and legible black woman in national politics and consolidated her power against the backdrop of a climate in which black women's voices had been marginalized by Republicans and Democrats alike. This climate suggests that by the end of the twentieth century, the space for black women leaders in the political arena was severely limited as the ideology of neoconservatism gained traction during the post–civil rights era. Pondering the conditions within the political climate that yielded Rice as a national leader is important for recognizing the anomaly that she was, within a space that severely limited the participation of black women and that had established a pattern of maligning, ridiculing, and pathologizing through a barrage of negative media anyone who even got close to entering its top echelons of power.[9] James D. King and James W. Riddlesperger Jr. remind us in "Diversity and Presidential Cabinet Appointments" that Rice, Hillary Clinton, Colin Powell, and Madeleine Albright are among the handful of leaders who have diversified the inner cabinets of presidents by representing race and gender categories other than white men, who have historically held such positions.[10]

If Rice was embraced as a top leader within the cabinet of George W. Bush as a Republican presidential leader, there were clear limitations to the unprecedented power she wielded in the national arena as a black woman. If we consider Nicholas Boushee's analysis of the concerted Republican Party efforts in recent years to expand beyond its conventional base of white voters, drawing in more ethnic minorities as new messengers within a diversifying electorate to increase odds for success, then Rice registers as a harbinger of this turn at the dawn of the new millennium.[11] The articulation and sanctioning of Rice as a national leader and symbol by the Republican establishment in the new millennium was paradoxically premised on her complicity with race-neutral narratives, which repressed civil rights agendas or rearticulated and appropriated them in relation to reactionary policies in the political mainstream. It relied on gross and superficial appropriations of civil rights history to advance agendas in which the needs and concerns of black citizens were subordinated to prioritize the advancement of race-neutral, colorblind policies that seemed designed to reverse the gains of the civil rights movement. Though Rice emerged as a leader and one of the prominent emblems of the national body and national femininity, her embodiment and articulation of national femininity was paradoxically premised on an ideology of the postracial. Isabelle Vagnoux has noted that the careers of leaders such as Madeleine Albright, Hillary Clinton, and Rice obscure the persisting challenges to women being elected to high-ranking positions.[12]

In recent years, the stories of Rice joining the formerly segregated Shoal Creek Golf Club in Birmingham, Alabama, in 2009, and in 2012, making history by being one of the first two women inducted into the formerly segregated Augusta National Golf Club in Georgia, the home of the annual Masters championship, adds to her record of groundbreaking achievements and points to her continuing efforts to challenge the specter of southern segregation in her adult life.[13] Because of the more sustained space for reflection that Rice's memoir provides, it is a valuable text to draw on for thinking about her public leadership and relationship to the national body and for tracing the conditions of her emergence as a model of national femininity back to her history in the segregated South. I begin this chapter with a discussion of the first volume of Rice's monumental memoir, *Extraordinary, Ordinary People*, to examine the deliberation with which she has attempted to help shape and redefine notions of the national body and citizenry in the United States, which profoundly registers her voice in meditations on notions of national selfhood.[14] It builds on the recurring narratives within her public speeches and interviews, which have centered family by invoking the Rice clan as a representative American family and recollecting the values and struggles of her paternal ancestors, as well as by emphasizing children in references to the bombing of the 16th Street Baptist Church, which claimed the lives of Denise McNair, Addie Mae Collins, Cynthia Wesley, and Carole Robertson, to advance policy related to the war on terror.

As a scholar of African American literature, I also value this work because it contributes to the subgenre within African American literary history of serial autobiography. This subgenre was inaugurated in slave narrative writing in the late eighteenth century and reached epic proportions in the multivolume autobiographical masterpiece produced over a span of more than thirty years by Maya Angelou. Rice's autobiography is another prime illustration of how profoundly and consistently black women in politics have produced literature primarily concentrated in the genres of memoir and autobiography, which have often failed to gain legibility or garner critical interest and notice from literary scholars.

I build on this literary analysis by examining signal representations of Rice in the realm of culture that draw on her national iconicity, an approach that reflects my concomitant critical investments in cultural studies. I consider *Mad TV*'s "Condi Comes to Harlem" comedy skits, which draw on blaxploitation cinema motifs to critique, reconstruct, and redefine Rice's relationship to the Bush administration. These works imaginatively invoke temporalities from slavery to the 1970s and spaces from Harlem to the White House to critique Rice's influence on the political arena and her relationship to President Bush, along with neoconservative ideologies. They are useful for my purposes for the extent that they are premised on her status as an emblem of the national body and notions of national family, as well as centering blackness in framing her as a model of national femininity. They script her as a national symbol and deconstruct her iconicity, linking her to the black liberation movement, framing her as a primary advocate for black community interests, mediated by her queer interlocutor. Simultaneously, they critique her serviceability in consolidating repressive neoconservatism, along with highly conventional scripts of national selfhood, unsettling the authority of neoconservative ideology in shaping the national narrative and notions of American patriotism. In turn, they illustrate the limitations in fashioning the black female body as a liberatory symbol or subversive site in revising conventional national narratives grounded in a discourse of reaction and premised on the alienation and subordination of black subjects within the national body, obscuring the potential of black queer and trans subjects to expand and diversify American democracy.

A prolific body of interviews and photographs that circulated for over a decade in print newspapers, magazines, on television, and on the internet has shaped Rice's emergence as a visual icon in national and global contexts. Her popular representations have recurrently invoked her iconicity in staging visual representations provocatively premised on recurrent narratives of Rice as a race traitor, while critiquing her neoconservative politics. The final section of this chapter furthers my investigation of cultural works by examining art by Terry Lloyd, Ayanah Moor, Luc Tuymans, Enrique Chagoya, and Amy Vangsgard to consider ways in which they variously respond to and deconstruct Rice's iconic force by emphasizing race, class, gender, and sexuality in imaging her as a black woman in the public sphere and critiquing her relationship to whiteness, including white patriarchy and notions of southern paternalism.[15] The visual art representations of Rice that I examine in this chapter have been produced in the United States as well as in transnational contexts, from Great Britain to Mexico, and all share commonalities in registering and citing her national and global iconicity. I conclude by examining fashion's role in shaping Rice's iconicity.

America's "Birth Defect"

In "Long Time: Long Lost Daughters and the New 'New South,'" Hortense Spillers methodologically foregrounds a detailed reading of autobiographical and biographical volumes related to African American Supreme Court justice Clarence Thomas to illustrate the retrograde policies reflecting a temporality that on the front end would have conceivably led him to oppose the *Brown v. Board of Education* decision in 1954, which ended segregation of public schools. She argues that his ascendance to the nation's highest court in 1991 foreclosed the civil rights era and assaulted the legacy established by his predecessor, Thurgood Marshall, in effect ending the long span of the 1960s.[16] Thomas's birth in poverty in Pin Point, Georgia, and his upbringing by a grandfather who instilled values in him such as hard work were widely cited to demonstrate his rootedness in black communities in the months preceding his confirmation to the Supreme Court. Like Thomas's infamous claim that he was the victim of a "high-tech lynching" during the weeks of hearings before the Senate Judiciary Committee related to law professor Anita Hill's allegations of sexual harassment, such stories about his southern background linked him to notions of black authenticity.

Similarly, trauma narratives related to civil rights history and black southerners during the era of Jim Crow, specifically the loss of the four girls when Rice was a child coming of age in Birmingham, have been instrumental in legitimizing and authenticating Rice as an African American who understands racism and discrimination, notwithstanding her right-wing political alliances. The stories framing Rice as the daughter of a Presbyterian minister in Birmingham who stressed the value of education have been appropriated and promoted by the right wing to create essentialist and romanticized scripts, linking black subjects to conventional narratives of success and uplift that define the conventional national narrative and obscure or downplay the reality of racism. In addition to reinforcing her linkages to conservative ideology in the national mainstream, *Extraordinary, Ordinary People* reinforces and further enshrines Rice within discourses of black conservatism, because autobiography and memoir are primary genres in which such reactionary ideologies about blackness have been historically elaborated, circulated, and promoted.[17]

The invocation of a southern background to invoke strong values and tradition is a central device in instating conservative African American leaders at the national level, such as Thomas and Rice, whose policies have been controversial and associated with retrenchments against civil rights in the nation and human rights in the international arena, respectively. Louis Prisock uses the autobiography of former national Republican Party chairman Herman Cain as a lens to explore themes within the literature of black conservatism and to suggest how the critiques that typically portray black conservatives as what Sumo Cho describes as "racial mascots" in effect obscure the larger work of this group in upholding notions of American exceptionalism and global superiority.[18] These critical reflections by Prisock centered on Cain, who also grew up in the Deep South, also hold implications for Rice's memoir.

Rice's memoir not only accords with the classic bildungsroman but also builds on the body of coming-of-age stories in the Jim Crow South, a genre that was heralded by Maya Angelou's *I Know Why the Caged Bird Sings* (1970) and includes signal works such as Ann Moody's *Coming of Age in Mississippi* (1968). In more recent years, autobiographies by black feminist critics, from bell hooks's *Bone Black: Memories of Girlhood* (1997) to Trudier Harris's *Summer Snow: Reflections of a Black Daughter from the South* (2007), have provided revealing insights on subject formation for black girls in the South. Beyond the account of the unrest in Birmingham, Alabama, during the civil rights era at the foundation of Angela Davis's famous 1972 autobiography, produced during the black liberation era in the wake of her imprisonment and trial, Rice's story is valuable for providing what is perhaps the most gripping and detailed account of what it meant to come of age in a time during which the city gained notoriety to the point of being referred to as Bombingham because of the bombings that white supremacists frequently carried out to terrorize black communities. In the post–civil rights era, this body of autobiographical work by black southern women has valuably informed black feminist epistemologies related to the repercussions of race and gender oppression on black women and girls who grew up in the Jim Crow South and their reflections on its lingering traumas.

Such writings provide valuable perspective for childhood studies and hold critical implications for the growing body of scholarly work in black girlhood studies, particularly by scholars such as Robin Bernstein, Wilma King, Stacey Patton, and Nazera Sadiq Wright, who are among the authors who have increasingly investigated the effects of racism on black children, including black girls.[19] Such critical epistemologies are also an indispensable foundation for reflecting on Rice's account in *Extraordinary, Ordinary People* of growing up in her middle-class family in segregated Birmingham and the childhood experiences that have continued to influence her perspective as an adult woman, including her political outlook and view of the nation and the world. More to the point, critical insights from studies of black childhood and girlhood are helpful for thinking about Rice's reflections, which affirm the continuing influence of slavery in shaping the nation, as well as about how the mourning story related to the four girls who died in the bombing at 16th Street mediated

Rice's nationalization as a leader and shaped her policy outlook on the war on terror as an international leader.

Images of Addie Mae Collins, Carole Robertson, Cynthia Wesley, and Denise McNair circulated worldwide in the wake of the bombing and further nationalized and globalized the civil rights movement during the 1960s. The images of the girls became iconic transnationally and emerged as a site of national mourning in ways that linked the girls to notions of national selfhood. Rice originally rose to national prominence through her keynote speech at the Republican National Convention in Philadelphia, Pennsylvania, in 2000, in which she focused on her paternal ancestors by incorporating anecdotes related to her grandfather's quest for education in the postslavery South and her father's shift to the Republican Party when Democrats refused to allow him to register to vote during the era of segregation. Yet invocations of the female-centered narrative of the iconic four girls seared in the national imagination have played the primary role in linking Rice to civil rights history and in mediating her scripts in the U.S. public sphere, including her emergence as a leader in the national arena and her relationship to national femininity. In speeches and interviews, Rice repeatedly invoked the tragic losses of the four girls, one of the most salient and familiar national scripts of black femininity that emerged during the civil rights era, in reflecting on her childhood before her audiences, and she mobilized it to advance the war on terror in contexts such as Iraq and Afghanistan.

For example, in keeping with Rice's recurring invocations of civil rights in discussions of the war on terror, in a speech to the Mississippi College School of Law in May 2003, she acknowledges the exclusion of blacks within the nation's founding ideals and frames the civil rights movement as the catalyst for the birth of a new and more inclusive nation. She goes on to analogize the tragic church bombing that took the lives of the four girls in Birmingham with terror in the Middle East.[20] In these moments, Rice both draws on and reinforces the recurring scripts that linked the girls to notions of American identity at the time of the bombing. At the same time, in linking slavery and the erasure of blacks to the nation's failure to achieve its founding ideals and the civil rights movement to the nation's rebirth, Rice reframes the national narrative to centralize black subjects in its origin and definition.

Nonetheless, such comparisons have been critiqued and resisted by Rice's critics. In reflecting on Rice's invocation of civil rights history to justify the Iraq War in an interview with Katie Couric, journalist Eugene Robinson frames Rice's analogy as a "retrospective reinvention" that "left me wondering whether I was hearing polished sophistry or a case of total denial."[21] Robinson, who mentions his own upbringing in the South as the Jim Crow era ended and critiques Rice's failure to acknowledge that the terror against blacks during that period was typically state sponsored, suggests that she posits a false equivalence between the Klan bombing of the church and contemporary jihadists. More broadly, his critique suggests the limitations in Rice's positing of the movement against terror in the global arena as a continuation of the modern civil and human rights movement.[22] Her analogy obscures continuing black traumas in the South, including residual traces of the political and social climate that led to the bombing.

Not only did references to the girls' deaths regularly inflect Rice's speeches and interviews during her years in the Bush administration, but they are also foundational in her memoir. In the first installment of Rice's two-part memoir *Extraordinary, Ordinary People*, an image of Rice's friend Denise McNair, the youngest of the victims, being conferred a kindergarten diploma by Rice's father, John Rice, encapsulates their shared histories and memories and links Rice to this horrific tragedy in a visceral way as a child growing up in segregated Birmingham. That Denise's father, Chris McNair, a professional photographer, took the photo of his daughter being conferred the diploma by Rice's father points to their mutuality as "daddy's girls" and to the McNairs as another model black family like the Rices in the city. Rice's memoir indexes the foundational role of the southern landscape, including the horrific bombing at the 16th Street Baptist Church, in structuring her consciousness and shaping her identity.

Rice's reflections on the tragic losses of the girls at the 16th Street Baptist Church simultaneously conform to conventional and even reactionary narratives of civil rights history in popular and literary contexts that mainly associate the problem of racism with the past. As Valerie Smith points out, contemporary literature and films often present a narrative of the civil rights movement suggesting that "through shared sacrifice and exemplary action, the movement triumphed over white supremacy and delivered the nation from its past injustices into a brighter future of freedom, equality and opportunity," a narrative that presents its martyrs sentimentally, implies racism to be a bygone phenomenon, and reinforces the notion of America as a land of opportunity.[23] Smith notes that "the martyred Sunday School girls have come to symbolize the innocence and moral rectitude of southern black communities under siege" and argues that Spike Lee's 1997 HBO documentary *4 Little Girls*, by using strategies such as featuring family members and friends of the girls who continued to be affected by their losses and presenting a more dynamic and complex story of the girls' lives, "dislodges the 'four little girls' from their symbolic status as a collective icon."[24]

Lee's film both builds on and reinforces the iconicity of photographic images of the girls, images whose circulation worldwide helped to nationalize and globalize the civil rights movement during the 1960s. The girls became iconic at a national level in the wake of the tragic bombing. These images illustrate a key instance when black and southern feminine bodies have become iconic and circulated transnationally in constituting this nation's sense of selfhood, including discourses of loss and mourning, in relation to the civil rights movement. The Lee documentary extends these abstracted significations by casting the children as angels within its visual iconography, with their pictures underneath, all atop a banner that reads, "The story of four young girls who paid the price for the nation's ignorance."

Rice's reflections on this tragedy have typically been framed within the discourse of American patriotism and conservative politics and in relation to her endorsement of the fight against terrorism in the global arena. Her invocations of the bombing at the 16th Street Baptist Church have also continually played a key role in scripting her in relation to discourses of national femininity, by drawing on the tragic losses of these iconic young girls and her experience of racism and segregation in Birmingham to underscore how her achievements have given her optimism about the American dream, notwithstanding the painful struggles that she both witnessed and experienced growing up in Birmingham. This story was an established aspect of the national narrative and had a lingering presence in national memory.

Citing it and noting her connections to the girls mediated Rice's entry into national politics and made her legible and relatable in relation to civil rights histories in the South. It helped to moor emerging scripts of Rice as a national leader once she entered the public sphere as national security adviser and gained increasing iconicity in the media. The press conferences Rice staged, which typically featured her standing behind a podium near an American flag, recast and mirrored the backgrounds typically used by presidents and featured her as a key representative and spokesperson within Bush's presidential cabinet, framing her as a spokesperson for him and as an extension of his authority. She was the most visible and vocal woman in national politics and a reigning national leader, authority that made her a constant presence in the media, conditioned her national iconicity, and articulated her in relation to national femininity. Speaking of the children in dialogues about the urgency of the war on terror reinforced the long-standing global reach and power of this story, acknowledged its continuing significance, and made linkages between the violent history of the U.S. South and newer forms of terrorism.

At the same time, Rice's narratives about this tragedy in effect obscure the role that some conservative whites in the U.S. South have played in endorsing right-wing policies related to the war on terror because of anxieties about Islam and the Middle East, whites who, unlike her, typically do not prioritize this tragic history related to the four little black girls, register it as a lingering trauma in the sense that accords with Rice's experience of it, or acknowledge the South's racist and violent past in thinking about the urgency of the war on terror. Rice's narratives about this tragedy obscure the ways in which the right wing has typically repressed and disavowed the U.S. South's violent history and racism. Furthermore, the levels on which Rice was exposed to this tragic bombing in her youth have made it unsettling and ironic for some of her critics that in the battle against terrorism, she has been identified with war policies that perpetuate violence against civilian communities and that have resulted in more than three hundred thousand civilian casualties in Iraq and Afghanistan, including thousands of women and children.

Another image from Rice's childhood that she includes in *Extraordinary, Ordinary People* holds important implications in anticipating her eventual emergence as a national and global black female public figure. The photo shows her as a little girl standing in front of the White House in Washington, DC, during a family vacation to the city when she was nine. She wears a dress and holds a book, with one foot positioned slightly forward. Marcus Mambry's biography of Rice, *Twice as Good: Condoleezza Rice and Her Path to Power*, features this photo as a cover shot to suggest a progression in the path that Rice walked from this moment early in life on to numerous career achievements and her eventual historic appointments as a black woman in Bush's presidential cabinets, as national security adviser and secretary of state.[25] This photo is intriguing for its bold representation of Rice during the era of segregation, in relation to the White House, one of the nation's most prominent and famous architectural symbols. Her pose resists, defies, and assertively revises conventional scripts of blacks as being excluded and alienated from notions of national belonging and definitions of the national body.

This image set the stage for Rice's iconicity and her work in the West Wing of the White House later in life. It established foundations for her recurrent representations as an emblem of the national body. If the journey began in her distant past with this childhood pilgrimage to the White House with her parents, it culminated with her friendship with President George W. Bush and appointment to cabinet-level positions in his presidential administrations. In the process, Rice emerged in the first years of the twenty-first century as a premier emblem within recurrent narratives highlighting the black feminine body in relation to the White House and the Capitol as symbolic architectural spaces while being abstracted as an emblem of the national body and as a model of national femininity.

Rice's formative childhood years in Birmingham, Alabama, during the civil rights era; her family's move when she was thirteen to Denver, Colorado, when her father was offered a job at the University of Denver, and her years of matriculation in the city as a student; her graduate work at Notre Dame in South Bend, Indiana; her eventual relocation to Palo Alto, California, to assume a professorship at Stanford; and her decade of work in Washington, DC, are all factors that link her subject formation to a range of geographic contexts and circuits of migration within the United States. They situate her amid newer waves within the long continuum of black movement in the United States, historically known as the Great Migration. Indeed, several chapters in Rice's *Extraordinary, Ordinary People*, such as "Tuscaloosa," "Denver Again," "Leaving the South Behind," "D.C. Again," and "Back in California" explicitly invoke geographic points across the national map that she has traversed throughout her life. Rice's scholarly studies of the Soviet Union and work in the Pentagon during the presidency of George H. W. Bush were the earliest gateway through which she began to travel and circulate internationally as her academic career began. Her eventual appointments as national security adviser and secretary of state by George W. Bush increased her movements around the globe exponentially and are the basis of her emergence as a global icon. It is significant that a chapter title mentions leaving the South "behind," which implies that the region is an aspect of her past. Yet the region has continued to play a dynamic role in shaping her subjectivity, as well as the public discourses related to her, including her own interviews and speeches.

The numerous biographies of Rice chronicle the foundational influence of her upbringing by her doting mother, Angelena Rice, and close relationship to her father, John Rice, in establishing foundations for her success and emergence as a leader in the global arena. It is noteworthy that scripts of Rice alternatively emphasize the passion and commitment in their parenting, stress her close relationship with them, and frame her as a model daughter in place of the narratives that have recurrently framed black women national leaders in relation to maternal motifs. Just as family has served as a salient lens through which Rice has presented her story in speeches and interviews, *Extraordinary, Ordinary People* narrates her personal story *as* a family story, as signaled in the title, and frames her success as an outgrowth of conscientious parenting, the values of her extended family, and a resilient community. Rice grounds and centers her story in her linkages to a patrilineal heritage spanning back to itinerant minister and educator John Wesley Rice Sr. on her father's side and the insurgent and hard-working miner Albert Robinson Ray III on her mother's. Narratives that foreground Rice's parentage have inflected scripts of Rice's family as a representative American family in the public sphere and in her writings. Beginning with this memoir's title, Rice frames her African American family of origin as being a unique and yet typical and highly representative American family that embodies values related to perseverance because of its roots in the segregated South. Concomitantly, she frames the black population collectively as being definitional and foundational to notions of the national family.

Just as *Extraordinary, Ordinary People* draws on Rice's story of the girls at the 16th Street Baptist Church in part to advance neoconservative foreign policy agendas, it also meditates on the social problem of racism and invokes blacks in relation to the prevailing notions of national family while revealing her investments in conventional patriotic and nativist scripts of the national narrative in the United States. The memoir includes numerous anecdotes and stories that draw on her experiences and those of others in her family to reflect on race and racism and, in keeping with her comments in multiple interviews and speeches, frames slavery as America's "birth defect."[26] This personifying metaphor for the nation, which is also tacit in the phrasing of the first epigraph from Rice that frames this chapter, notably unfolds against a backdrop of reflections related to her own family, situates blacks and whites within a symbolic national family and shared history, and points to their long-standing interracial sexual intermixture at the same time that it speaks to how slavery was systemically institutionalized during the colonial era and shadowed the nation's emergence as a republic in the late eighteenth century, when notions of citizenship and democracy were originally formulated.

Rice's image of a baby conceived and birthed with a defect to embody the nation alludes to conventional raced and gendered birth metaphors of nationhood that have circulated in American literary and cinematic history. In a symbolic sense, Rice invokes the reigning right-wing discourses that Lauren

Berlant has linked to an excessively intimate public sphere in the United States constituted through the phenomenon of "infantile citizenship." As Berlant argues, "In the process of collapsing the political and the personal into a world of public intimacy, a nation made for adult citizens has been replaced by one imagined to be for fetuses and children."[27] Berlant goes on to describe "a strong and enduring belief that the best of U.S. national subjectivity can be read in its childlike manifestations and in a polity that organizes its public sphere around a commitment to making a world that could sustain an idealized infant citizen."[28] The national iconicity of the four girls that coalesced in the wake of the bombing is the obverse of scripts of infantile citizenship fetishized by reactionaries.

Even as Rice's metaphor of an infantile abnormality emphasizes the nation's failure to live up to its cherished ideals, its continuing limitations, and the inherent flaws that shadowed its rise as a republic, her interpretation of the nation's history is premised on conventional notions of American exceptionalism, purity, and innocence. Prisock relates such logic to complicity with American exceptionalism and argues that it reinforces white supremacy, pointing out that "because America's history is so closely intertwined with its 'original sin' (slavery), making the black-white conflict the defining racial conflict in the nation, to have the descendants of slaves validating America's heralded traditions while putting the nation's reprehensible treatment of their group behind them symbolizes to the right a closure of the nation's ignominious racial history, thus truly validating America's greatness."[29]

This section of Rice's memoir illustrates the deliberation with which she has attempted to help shape and redefine notions of the U.S. national body and citizenry and profoundly registers her voice in meditations on notions of national selfhood. By implication, if unwittingly, she also marks disabled bodies as marginal and undesirable within the nation's normative citizenry. Moreover, Rice's acknowledgment of her preference to use the term *black* over the hyphenated African-American, by aiming to unsettle conflations of black experience in the United States with the nation's immigrant narratives, reinscribes the hegemonic signification of African Americans in relation to the category *black* and is steeped in a nativist, U.S.-centered definition of the category *black* dislodged from the larger African diaspora.[30] It reveals how her definition of blackness has been developed against the backdrop of historical debates related to race, nationality, and ethnicity, as well as contemporary discourses on immigration and transnationality.[31] By narrowly defining the term as a referent for African American subjects, her exclusionary formulation of blackness holds even direr implications when recognizing its elaboration during a historical moment when the nation's increasingly reactionary immigration policies were routinely targeting black immigrants alongside Middle Easterners and Mexicans through heightened surveillance and racial profiling. Ultimately, though Rice's framing of blackness as central in defining the nation is subversive and provides valuable critical reflection on notions of national identity, her perspective is limited and mirrors prevailing themes in conservative autobiographies premised on American exceptionalism.

The essays in *Between Woman and Nation: Nationalisms, Transnational Feminisms, and the State*, edited by Caren Kaplan, Norma Alarcón, and Minoo Moallem, foreground study of the influence of gender, particularly women, in shaping the nation-state, including nationalisms, while expanding the terrain of study within transnational feminism to Latin America and the Middle East. Their study provides a reminder that the salience of the feminine in framing national identity holds potential to both subvert and reinscribe the power of hegemonic states, including forces of colonialism and imperialism.[32] Such insights are also indispensable for reflecting on Rice's centrality in the early 2000s in advancing the foreign policy of the Bush administration in nations where women continue to face subjection and remain vulnerable to state forces from within, as well as to the ravages of U.S. policy agendas. The accessibility and serviceability of women in constructing national narratives routinely linked to fundamentalisms and abuses carried out at the state level is no less true in the United States than in the contexts examined in this landmark critical anthology. Even as the power that Rice wielded in national and global contexts as a black woman was unprecedented, such geopolitical dynamics remind us of what was at stake in her iconicity and empowerment, and they complicated her representational politics.

More to the point, the authority and value in models of national femininity in the United States are compromised when mobilized to buffet imperialism and colonialism. In some cases, such national iconicity and visibility paradoxically serve as a signpost of women's continuing subjection and lack of power by showing the limitations in women leaders who nevertheless remain beholden to patriarchal political agendas. In the new millennium, the familiar narrative of the girls victimized by the bombing in Birmingham mediated Rice's emergence as a national leader alongside citations of her family as a model and representative black family that maintained continuing faith in American democracy, notwithstanding its imperfections, and persevered. Her emergence as a model of national femininity was paradoxically reinforced and consolidated by her prominent role in advancing the war on terror. Still, her iconic femininity was less linked to her subjectivity and agency as a woman leader, or even to agendas designed to advance the interests of women globally, than to authorizing and rationalizing foreign policies that advanced militarism on behalf of the Bush administration. In the section that follows, I discuss the profuse cultural representations that register Rice's status as a powerful leader. They stage bold fantasies and incorporate queer motifs that marshal her authority and iconic femininity on behalf of black communities and realign her political identity as a black woman to redress the benign neglect of black populations in the United States, a domestic issue that reached its height after Hurricane Katrina. In the process, they portray her as a revolutionary with more agency and autonomy in foreign policy.

Condi Comes to Harlem

In April 2011, Rice made a cameo appearance on the NBC sitcom *30 Rock*, in which she poses as a woman who once dated Jack Donaghy (Alec Baldwin). She is asked to help him because his new wife has been kidnapped in North Korea, a scenario with a provocative subtext of interracial romance that alludes to Rice's challenging diplomatic engagements with North Korea as secretary of state. In the episode, her character also challenges him to a duel, with her on piano and jazz flute. In Francesca T. Royster's essay "Condi, Cleopatra, and the Performance of Celebrity," she argues that such representations are steeped in rumors and fantasies about romance between Bush and Rice and draw on Rice's iconicity. In depicting Jack as being reliant on her expertise, Royster points to how the episode throws into relief the marginality that Rice experienced as a woman within Bush's male-dominated cabinet. Royster relates such popular representations premised on rumors about Rice's private life and relation to powerful men, which play up "her specularity as a beautiful black woman" instead of engaging her political work, to the myth of Cleopatra.[33] She frames them as "sources of distraction," relating Rice to celebrity and anxieties about her political power, representations that deflect from serious dialogues about her role in the nation's foreign policy, including sanctioning torture.[34] William L. D'Ambruoso offers a revealing reading of how policies and limitations on torture establish norms that paradoxically escalate torture practices by political leaders who rationalize circumventing those strictures for the greater good.³⁵

Rice's representations in comedy draw on race, class, gender, and sexuality and are inflected by anxieties about her racial identification, her relationship with President Bush, and her role in international politics, including her work in helping to constitute the war on terror. Rice has been recurrently embodied, abstracted, and rendered as a character for performance when parodied in contemporary television comedy. Royster's reading of the representation of Rice on *30 Rock*, which fantasizes Rice in relation to white masculine lovers in ways that emphasize aesthetics and belie her power, obscures popular comedy representations that ground her in black specificity, while linking her to both power and agency, such as in *Mad TV*'s "Condi Comes to Harlem" skits. Given Rice's black identity and widespread social concerns about the consequences of conservative policies on African Americans, it is also not surprising that some of Rice's most assertive critiques have been staged in African American comedy.

Black comedians, from Redd Foxx, Flip Wilson, Richard Pryor, Eddie Murphy, and Whoopi Goldberg to newer contemporary performers such as Wanda Sykes, Steve Harvey, Chris Rock, and Dave Chappelle have routinely incorporated political topics in their comedy routines. As Mel Watkins notes in his important history of black comedy, *On the Real Side: Laughing, Lying, and Signifying—The Underground Tradition of African-American Humor that Transformed American Culture, from Slavery to Richard Pryor*, African American comedy has made a vital if typically overlooked contribution in shaping American humor.³⁶ Richard Pryor was one of the first black comedians whose shows attracted diverse audiences and enabled him to achieve crossover success in the post–civil rights era, akin to that associated with pop musicians. As a performer, his comedy helped to break down color barriers and boldly confronted controversial topics related to race and politics. In more recent years, comedian Dave Chappelle offers some of the most compelling confrontations of race as a topic in comedy. As John H. Jackson argues in his study *Racial Paranoia: The Unintended Consequences of Political Correctness*, the provocative content of Chappelle's work, given its recurrent engagements of race, is valuable for thinking through social anxieties related to race and racism.³⁷

Chappelle famously lampooned Rice on *Chappelle's Show* during a 2004 segment called "The Racial Draft." "The Racial Draft" is broadcast live by several commentators before a spirited audience, whose members are separated into racial and ethnic categories, such as blacks, whites, Latinos, Asians, and Jews, and whose atmosphere recalls that of a sporting event, such as the annual drafts of the National Basketball Association and National Football League (NFL), an institution of which Rice is, incidentally, a longtime fan and supporter. While *Chappelle's Show* frames this skit within the broadcasting style associated with sporting events, it ironically alludes to the commodification and trading of black bodies on the auction block during antebellum slavery and links this dehumanizing and humiliating practice to a range of contemporary ethnic and racial categories. As K. A. Wisniewski notes in his edited volume on Chappelle's comedy, "The Racial Draft" ranks among skits that illustrate "the powers and problems surrounding stereotypes."[38]

In this suspenseful and excited atmosphere, Chappelle uses comedy as a medium to draw attention to anxieties and concerns in the African American context about the political alignment of Colin Powell and Rice with the Republican right wing. By voluntarily trading her over to the "whites" to complement their request for Powell, Chappelle marks Rice as expendable and undesirable within the African American context and as the quintessential "race traitor." The logic here reinscribes notions of black authenticity, in this case based on the perception that black leaders who are Republican and conservative are not truly black and, in a symbolic sense, are identified with whiteness. The right-wing affiliation of Powell and Rice is the basis for their rejection by the black race. While Rice is correlated to Powell, the implication is that both are inimical to African Americans because of their mutual alignment with neoconservative politics and work in Bush's presidential administration.

Comedy's energetic and frequently profane linguistic economies and visual staging, which so frequently prioritize the voice and narrative authority of the singular performer, make it fascinating to weigh within the vector of performance studies, which engages critical theories of performativity, even though the field has not prioritized comedy. For example, performativity discourses shape the arbitrary ascriptions of different racial categories to subjects on the spot within this skit, which is premised on the notion that race is changeable and decidable by verbal pronunciation and decree. The aforementioned public performances also make performativity discourses highly relevant to Rice. At bottom, the Chappelle skit is premised on a view of race as being performative and socially constructed, on *black* and *white* as binary categories, and on passing as a phenomenon that enables movement within and across them.

Like Chappelle's "Racial Draft," the series of skits entitled "Condi Comes to Harlem" on *Mad TV*, a television series rooted in Harvey Kurtzman's satirical *Mad* magazine, resonates with the history of black comedy and draws on film as a genre. The title of these skits alludes to Chester Himes's 1964 novel *Cotton Comes to Harlem* and the 1970 blaxploitation film based on it, directed by Ossie Davis. The *Mad TV* comedians portray Rice by drawing on the conventions of blaxploitation and the personas portrayed by prominent black actresses who became its best-known action heroines, including Tamara Dobson in *Cleopatra Jones* (1973) and Pam Grier in *Foxy Brown* (1974). In this sense, they allude to the profuse Cleopatra motifs that Royster suggests have been linked to Rice in popular contexts.

A segment of one of these videos begins with a view of the White House's facade, with Rice, who is wearing a conservative pinstripe suit, receiving an urgent message on her futuristic televisual wristwatch indicating that she is needed in Harlem. The camera cuts to an image of Rice wearing a 1970s-style bright orange jumpsuit to evoke the fashion of the decade during which the blaxploitation genre first gained popularity and to undercut the prim, conservative dress style with which she has been associated.

This radicalized version of Rice is riding a motorcycle into Harlem, a place posited within the narrative logic of these short skits as the symbolic locus of blackness and as a primary counterpoint to the White House, which they make synonymous with white subjectivity. She discovers from an effeminate black male informant known as Knee-Hi, who tells her in a dramatic voice with exaggerated animation that blacks are "glowing" after entering a Korean grocery store. She discovers that its owner has built a nuclear missile site in the middle of Harlem and brags about "outsmarting you dum dums in Washington by building a nuclear missile in Harlem." Rice does karate moves to conquer "two gigantic Korean men" and disarms the missile, whose use is appropriative and ironic here given the association of the martial arts with Asian male subjectivity. The motorcycle also masculinizes her image in the skit.

The skit, which also seems designed to critique growing patterns of gentrification in Harlem, culminates with the promise of a romantic encounter as she walks off with a seductive black man named Duke and asserts that her work in Washington can be put on hold. In this instance, the skit invokes Rice's struggles as secretary of state with North Korea and its nuclear threat. Yet it is vital to raise questions about what is at stake in Rice's reclamation in black communities when it is premised on Asian and black queer stereotypes and an uncritical endorsement of her foreign policy agendas.

Similarly, another skit in this vein features Rice being interrupted in her official job in Washington as she is beeped on her watch by Knee-Hi, who reports that Big Whitey has forced all black people in Harlem to drink his "crazy juice," which is grape flavored. The "crazy juice" invoked here alludes to the mass murder that occurred in Guyana in 1978, when the minister Jim Jones forced more than nine hundred of his predominantly African American followers in Jonestown to drink Flavor Aid poisoned with cyanide. Rice drives into Harlem in a long seventies-style red convertible, confronts Big Whitey, and physically vanquishes two of his accomplices with deft karate moves. In the end, she assertively takes the initiative and joins Duke for what promises to be a romantic encounter, proclaiming that "the president can wait."

The queer subject who summons her to come in and rescue the black community throws the masculine bravado associated with the Rice characters in these skits into relief. The skits draw on retro style and futuristic technologies in portraying Rice as a heroine with superhuman superhero qualities. They enact a fantasy wherein Rice is devoted to remedying the plight of the African American community and dropping her work at the state level to go to its rescue. Unlike Chappelle's "Racial Draft," which exiles and eliminates Rice as an African American, the "Condi Comes to Harlem" skits reinvent Rice as a quintessential embodiment of black subjectivity who identifies with and works primarily in the interests of black communities. In this sense, they unsettle pervasive perceptions of Rice as being detached from black communities.[39]

Both of the "Condi Comes to Harlem" skits that I examine here attempt to unsettle narratives that portray Rice as a "race traitor," identified with whiteness, and as a devoted and loyal friend of George W. Bush by drawing on blaxploitation motifs and Harlem as a setting to construct an image of her as a woman who is "down home" and identified with black communities. Reconstructions of Condoleezza Rice in these skits, which draw on retro blaxploitation film aesthetics primarily linked to urban and northern contexts, to the 1970s, and to her geographic reframing in Harlem, unsettle her conventional southern moorings and link her to an alternative geography and period. This genre rescripts Rice as a radical and insurgent black woman leader.

The skits signal a shift in her political consciousness at a visual level through her style and geographic setting, though *Condi* (and by extension, tacitly *rice*) notably replaces, displaces, and substitutes for the word *cotton* in the title of the skits, whose original point of reference dealt with the incursion and intrusion of a product linked to southern plantation economies on the urban landscape. It is useful to draw on critical epistemologies of the Global South in southern studies that unsettle conventional North/South binaries, geographies, and temporalities in defining the U.S. South, and that invoke Malcolm X's speech that famously located the region anywhere below the

Canadian border, to ponder the realignment of Rice with an urban northern geography in her characterization.[40] At the same time, the status of the urban northern area of Harlem as the site of her radicalization and politicization accords with long-standing essentialist historical conflations of the black radical subject primarily with urban contexts.[41] Action and agency reside in the dynamic environment of Harlem, and the U.S. capital is represented as a static, distant place. Indeed, these skits posit Harlem as the nation's capital in a symbolic sense, mirroring and nationally abstracting the scripts of Harlem as the "home" for blacks that emerged in the African diaspora during the Harlem Renaissance.

Sexuality centrally disrupts Rice's relationship to Bush in these skits, which portray him as being "jilted" by her. She puts work demands on the back-burner for a romantic tryst with a physically attractive black man to whom she is romantically attracted, alluding to her well-known fascination with football players. These implied trysts disrupt Rice's reputed closeness to the president, map her outside the space of the White House as a workspace, and present black and white masculinities in competition, with black masculinity triumphing in the implied contest for Rice's heart and allegiance. As the action in the latter skit begins, queer masculinity is ideologically mobilized to emphasize the physical strength and assertiveness of the Rice character and to ascribe her heroic qualities of popular blaxploitation heroines. Reinventing Rice within this conventional heteronormative black coupling obscures the queer performativity inflecting her characterization, as well as the potential of black gay men and black queer and trans women to shape a more democratic and inclusive model of black community. Knee-Hi's marginal representation also obscures the dynamic and complex historical contours of black queer communities in Harlem, including its legendary drag ball contexts, which have been at the forefront in reimagining black subjectivity and challenging conventional scripts of family and democracy.[42] The skit ends with an emphasis on her sexuality, as a seductive, strong, and hypermasculine black male woos her away. Tacit, too, in the company that Rice opts to keep with black men are black nationalist narratives from the 1960s that routinely constructed white men as economically and politically powerful while being sexually effeminate and impotent.

What happens next in both skits is left to the imagination, as they conclude with Rice putting play above work and associate an air of mystery with her. The skits enliven and animate Rice with a style and sexuality that undercut her constructions as prudish and reserved. At the same time, they unsettle fantasies of Rice in relation to powerful white men like Bush, along with images such as the one depicted on *30 Rock*, by emphasizing black men as her primary social companions and objects of her sexual desire. The skits imply that their Rice is the *real* one, not the reserved, prim persona in the public sphere. They unsettle Rice's link to the conservative political establishment by reconstructing her as the adventurous Condi persona and reclaim and embrace her within black communities.

The bold no-nonsense Condi in Harlem is the obverse of the staid Condi in Washington. The skits imply the latter to be an inauthentic facade. They are grounded in a binary that constructs black communities as dynamic, lively, and vibrant, and whiteness, as linked to Bush and sites such as the capital, as static. The skits disrupt an overdetermined friendship connection between Rice and Bush, who is significantly imagined as absent as a figure and is never fully embodied, in contrast to Rice's hyperembodied persona. The skits construct superhero-like Condi as a woman who harbors more power than the state-based and typically male-centered authority associated with the president in Washington. They frame Harlem, not Washington, as the nation's political epicenter. As much as they draw on the past by foregrounding blaxploitation, the futuristic technologies in the skit that facilitate Rice's updates via a digital watch and that enable her instant movements from Washington to Harlem, as well as her radical transformations in appearance, posit her as an ultimate mobile subject on a national and global stage, to parallel her physical agility and superhuman, cyborg-like fighting ability, which makes her so invincible. "Condi Comes to Harlem" presents Rice within the aesthetics of Afrofuturism, which unsettles conventional Western, Eurocentric logic in combining elements from science fiction and speculative fiction, fantasy, and historical fiction to rethink the past and envision alternative futures.

By according the character Condi authority that supersedes and circumvents the power of the state as embodied in the president (a figure who is notably absent from their action), "Condi Comes to Harlem" skits challenge the conventional conflation of state power with white masculinity, including presidential authority, along with their typical disjunction from black femininity, appropriating its power and authority for a black female subject. The depiction of the character Condi on sojourns to Harlem from the nation's capital abstracts and hyperbolizes her body and voice to underscore her autonomy and independence from the president as a figure and portrays her as a black revolutionary. She functions as the de facto president, and as the site for reinventing American identity in a way that accords legibility to and embraces black bodies, viewed as expendable within conventional scripts of the national body premised on black alienation.

By scripting Condi as a public official who keeps Harlem on the top of her agenda, with the priority of getting there and serving the population's urgent needs, the skits fantasize the United States as a nation in the new millennium that prioritizes rather than denies the citizenship rights of black subjects, who were excluded in the original formulations of citizenship as the republic emerged in the late eighteenth century. Rice emerges as the consummate leader at a local level, whose power is tacitly sanctioned by the state. Interestingly, the fantasy here mirrors Rice's arguments in her speeches and writings about the centrality of black struggles in advancing the nation toward a truer, more inclusive sense of democracy and definition of American identity. In this context, she emerges as an idealized, respected, and beloved leader. This portrait is far removed from the heartless, abusive, and despicable despot envisioned in Carlos Fuentes's apocalyptic, futuristic novel *La Silla del Águila* (2002). Rice's ability to go out and literally kick butt on the street backs up her mettle behind the podium in Washington, a provocative depiction that also mildly alludes to and critiques her suspected complicity in enhanced interrogation techniques such as torture.

Chappelle's "Racial Draft" implies Rice's politics to be extreme enough to be beyond redemption and recategorizes her into a white subjectivity suggested to be more befitting of her neoconservative ideological beliefs. While his strategy is to alienate her from the category black, the "Condi Comes to Harlem" skits stage a critique of Rice's neoconservative politics by linking her to narratives of black uplift and empowerment. "Condi Comes to Harlem" skits provide an alternative script of Rice by positing her as the quintessential symbol of the national body and linking it intimately to black subjectivity. African Americans emerge as the central national subjects, and Rice emerges as the most valued and reliable leader in the nation. As a woman, her superhero-like strength empowers her to gain a level of leadership, authority, and control that trumps the president, whose position is merely nominal.

The Condi character is a lens through which these skits envision Rice as the ideal model of national femininity as black and feminine, appropriating and redirecting the power and authority associated with the president as a white and masculine figure to address the specific needs of African American communities. In the world that these skits imagine, the plight of urban blacks, as represented in Harlem, is highest and most urgent on the list of the nation's priorities. The skits posit an assertive counternarrative to what happened in

New Orleans in 2005 after Hurricane Katrina, as African Americans suffered from benign governmental neglect and were initially labeled as refugees instead of being recognized as citizens in the media. Instead of drawing on slavery to reflect on Rice as evidenced in Chappelle's skit, "Condi Comes to Harlem" skits focus on the 1970s to envision an *Afro*futuristic, radical version of Rice fully freed from the encumbrances of the white political masculine elite and directing her energy and agency toward advancing the interests of black communities. The skits imply that progress in the United States is contingent on black inclusion and advancement within the social order. They draw nostalgically on the 1970s, a time prior to the rise of neoconservatism in the political arena and prior to the Reagan era, when drugs and crime escalated exponentially in black communities, to fantasize a more democratic America and a better future for blacks, and by extension, for all Americans.

The depiction of Rice with supernatural, superhuman power, with the ability to travel across time and space, counters comedy scripts that objectify Rice or downplay her strength, agency, and power as a woman. The portrayal lies in the continuum with Marvel's Black Panther superhero character. Masculine power, whether black or white, is sidelined to fully showcase the Rice character's strength and, if anything, is trivialized through its linkage to bodily objectification and possibilities for romance. That Harlem is Rice's home base, as well as the nation's, frames this black community as a family, invoking notions of national family, as well as centering and prioritizing blackness in definitions of American identity. The intimate relationship of Rice to this black community and the usage of her voice and national political platform on its behalf to ensure that it shares in American democracy recall the vision of Mary McLeod Bethune. The skits interestingly align with the logic in her memoir that frames blacks as central agents in the long struggle for citizenship and democracy in the nation, repositioning black subjectivity as central in defining America, while situating her as a central agent in fighting against forces that terrorize and threaten to destroy black communities. Rice's reflections linking the recognition of the full humanity of blacks during the civil rights era to breakthroughs in American democracy not actualized at the time of the nation's founding, when slavery existed, well suggest her values along these lines, even as she initially failed to recognize or embrace any responsibilities as a black leader after Hurricane Katrina.

The skits hold up a mirror to her iconicity and ubiquity as a black woman national leader during the first decade of the twenty-first century. In them, the mapping of 1970s visual aesthetics onto Rice as a millennial leader conflates and reconstructs these temporalities, another queer dimension of the skits. Such techniques seem designed to remind us that while in the wake of the civil rights movement, such power for a black woman was only imaginable in the fantasy world of blaxploitation film, it had become a reality for Rice as the world's most powerful woman leader and visible representative of the United States. In the fantasy that these skits stage, Rice emerges as a foremost emblem of national femininity. Yet the crucial difference for her is a point belied in her representations in these skits.

She was different from her predecessors in being positioned and framed to speak on behalf of everyone, not primarily for marginalized African Americans, who had been denied civil and human rights, as had been the case with her predecessors, who emerged as emblems of national femininity in politics. Her emergence as a model of national femininity was premised not on having changed the world, as was the case for Rosa Parks, but on her status as a world leader and one of its foremost diplomats, who had ascended to the top echelons of power in the nation. In the cultural arena, Rice's representations in visual art, like those in comedy, have been premised on her iconicity and status as a model of national femininity. Yet their critiques of her power have been far more direct and assertive.

Rice and Reaction in Visual Art

Amiri Baraka's controversial poem "Somebody Blew Up America," which ponders the tragedy of September 11, 2001, has been the most striking and controversial poetic response to Rice to date.[43] Nas critiques Rice in his 2004 song "American Way."[44] These pieces by Baraka and Nas invoke slavery and represent Rice as a race traitor, a motif that has been associated with her repeatedly in the national arena, and particularly in the black public sphere.[45] Such perspectives are rooted in a black arts sensibility, which is not surprising when considering this movement's grounding in poetry and spoken word and Baraka's status as one of its founding theologians and Nas's investments in storytelling and lyricism in his rap artistry. Such representations of Rice are noteworthy not only for how they relate her to black stereotypes, which were critiqued in visual art related to the black arts movement, but also for resonating with the body of contemporary creative works in visual art, emerging in diverse ethnic contexts, that consistently read her in relation to slavery and depict her as a race traitor while scrutinizing her relationship with George W. Bush.

While poetry was the literary genre that mainly fueled the black arts movement, the movement was also saliently advanced by the visual arts. In light of the civil rights and black power movements, which were bringing about radical social transformations for blacks during the 1960s, the black arts movement was an epoch during which items featuring black stereotypes in American material culture, alongside ubiquitous advertising trademarks, would emerge as objects of intense scrutiny. The Aunt Jemima from advertising was the most salient image in black liberation art that confronted these stereotypes.[46] Jeff Donaldson's *Aunt Jemima and the Pillsbury Dough Boy* (1963–64), Joe Overstreet's *The New Jemima* (1964), John Onye Lockard's *No More* (1967), Murray DePillars's *Aunt Jemima* (1968), and Betye Saar's *The Liberation of Aunt Jemima* (1972), are among the signal works of this period that transformed Aunt Jemima into a black militant. The same is true of a later piece by Faith Ringgold, *Who's Afraid of Aunt Jemima?* (1983). Through varying strategies, they recuperate the "sassy" and assertive qualities that were historically associated with the mammy, which tended to be muted in Aunt Jemima, and recast them as black militancy.

Though the philosophy of the black arts movement stressing that art should be politically useful was primarily oriented toward literature, it was also discernible in the visual arts, in this revisionist work concerning such black stereotypes. The seeming goal was to make images of black servility serviceable to the black revolution. Art of this era sent the message that if a type ordinarily so accommodating to white interests as Aunt Jemima could be reclaimed, redeemed, and drafted for participation in the black liberation struggle, then the movement had to be effective, pervasive, and infectious. In addition to suggesting to blacks their own potential to become revolutionaries, the art also suggested to whites that blacks were not going to tolerate social and political disenfranchisement any longer.

Rice's iconicity in politics in the new millennium decisively departs from such national brands in advertising premised on notions of national abjection and paradoxically epitomizes possibilities for the black feminine subject to help expand and redefine national narratives of black women, conventionally premised on whiteness, toward a definition that envisions national femininity in relation to blackness. Rice's images as a powerful black woman in the political arena are the obverse of this stereotype steeped in notions of black women's voicelessness, hyperembodiment, and specularity. Her alignment with the policies of the Bush establishment, however, fed narratives of her as being politically reactionary and regressive. For some, such postures recollect the political positions of sellouts linked to these stereotypical images, which is why references to them inflect some of the art representations of her.

The revisionist portraits of Aunt Jemima make assertive political statements in challenging stereotypes of black womanhood enshrined within advertising through Aunt Jemima as a national brand. Some of the contemporary art depicting Rice during the first decade of the new millennium resonates with this subversive body of visual art by drawing on her national iconicity in the political arena to critique her association with reactionary policy agendas and the war on terror, while linking her to the Uncle Tom stereotype frequently invoked to critique black leaders as sellouts and race traitors in relation to their own communities. These works acknowledge Rice's salience in contemporary debates related to race, including definitions of blackness and the meaning of black authenticity. This racial discourse on Rice is particularly significant when considering contemporary characterizations of the United States as postracial and postblack, which escalated exponentially in the wake of the election of Barack Obama as the nation's first black president in 2008, and obscure the continuing social repercussions of racism in this nation, while perpetuating the ideology of the United States as a colorblind society.

In recent years, critiques of Rice have been staged in the visual arts in media ranging from oil painting and drawing to digital art and large-scale wall installation. Works on Rice have been produced by artists in national contexts from Mexico to Great Britain, reflecting her status as a global icon. While art and politics have been conventionally perceived as mutually exclusive areas, and notions of authenticity and form in art premised on a detachment from political concerns, all the works I am considering here that engage Rice thematically foreground her political alliances. They use the technique of juxtaposing her image with President George W. Bush or other presidential figures and incorporate texts and images that align her with state power, authority, and even violence. As is the case in Baraka's poem, a hermeneutics invoking slavery has been amazingly consistent and recurrent in reading, thinking about, and imagining Rice within the realm of visual art. Almost all of these works incorporate design elements to emphasize her salience as an embodiment of black femininity in the nation's public sphere, at the same time registering and drawing on her symbolic capital as a model of national femininity. They draw on her iconicity to critique her alignments with reactionary neoconservative ideology and to highlight her complicity with abusive U.S. foreign policy in the form of the war on terror. In the process, they play up the irony of wedding a black feminine body to abuses that have typically been associated with white patriarchal men.

FIGURE 3.1 Terry Lloyd, *Uncle Tom's Condi Rice*, 2006.

In a 2006 digital art piece, *Uncle Tom's Condi Rice* (figure 3.1), artist Terry Lloyd visually relates Rice to the Uncle Tom stereotype, an image that accords with her representation in the poetry of Baraka and verbal art of the rapper Nas. The piece puns on her last name and alludes to advertising trademarks, such as Uncle Ben's rice, in its banner—"Perfect Every Time"—by including as a logo a round cameo portrait featuring an image of Rice wearing her famous flip hairstyle and gold earrings. At this level, this piece reflects the recurrent citation of Rice in relation to food in popular culture, as evidenced in the reference to Rice as a "chocolate lady" in the 2006 film *Borat*, and comedian Loni Love's joke that Rice's name "sounds like a side dish of Kentucky Fried Chicken" on *Comedy Central Presents* in 2007.[47]

A banner with the phrase "Prevaricates Every Time" cuts across it. Phrases on the box such as "Enabling Loss Globally," "Trusted by Despots Everywhere," "Recant in 5 Minutes," "Working for the Man Brand," and "100% refined Ingreedience" associate Rice with a lack of integrity and suggest her to be complicit with oppressive and hegemonic policies in the global context.

Recall that "the man" was a slang term that became popular in black nationalist movements of the 1960s as a reference to the power and authority of the white patriarchy in the United States. In invoking this term in its textual economy, Lloyd's piece suggests Rice's alienation from black communities and her failure to advance or support their interests. Moreover, it implies her to be beholden to the contemporary white masculine and patriarchal political establishment as a worker in the presidential cabinet of George W. Bush.

At the same time that these works of art invoke her relationship to Bush and to repressive foreign policy agendas, they give salience to her national iconicity by linking her to one of the most famous advertising trademarks in U.S. history. Uncle Ben, like Aunt Jemima, has been one of the best known and most prominent advertising trademarks highlighting a black image and has frequently been associated with stereotypical and degrading representations of blacks circulating in U.S. material culture, a visual economy to which this art piece also alludes. The appropriation of Rice's raced and gendered body and its serviceability for the advancement of reactionary and controversial foreign policy agendas against minority populations in the global arena mirrors and extends ways in which black feminine bodies become hyperembodied, highly visible, and nationally abstracted while remaining rigidly contained and voiceless.

Such advertising images have been intimately linked to nostalgia about slavery and the plantation South and have inherently queer roots, which lie at the foundation of their race and gender mutability and are patently evident in this cross-gendered figuring of Rice as an Uncle Tom. By invoking them and positioning Rice on a background whose facade resembles the boxes on which they were primarily circulated, this image suggests that despite her prominence in the national arena and the national iconicity that she has attained, her role more closely mirrors and mimics that of conventional black stereotypes, even if her body does not accord with the Aunt Jemima stereotype in a visual sense and enters the public gaze under radically different conditions and meanings from those attached to black women's images in the commercial marketplace. The shadow of the Aunt Jemima trademark is inescapable as a prelude to her articulation and commodification as a national model of femininity, given its ubiquity and hyperembodiment in advertising from the late nineteenth century in making black womanhood legible within the national imaginary, as other representational models of black womanhood largely remained invisible. The use of the term *brand* here calls to mind products that are advertised and circulate as commodities for purchase and consumption, suggesting that Rice has fully internalized and consumed the ideology of "the man." The word *brand* also seems to figuratively cast Rice as a slave when considering the routine branding of slaves' bodies during the antebellum era.

More to the point, it seems to link her, even, to the history of black overseers who routinely carried out abuses against other black slaves. Rice, like other crops such as cotton, tobacco, and sugarcane, was among the chief agricultural products resulting from intensive physical field labor primarily among slaves in the U.S. South. In the contemporary era, rice is a staple consumer item across some Latin American, African, and Asian nations in the Global South. The added irony is that Rice's last name mirrors and echoes the name of this staple crop of plantation slave economies. Lloyd's art piece links her to the abuses and labor exploits associated with this product. This work accords with the litany of creative representations heralded by Amiri Baraka that invoke the history of slavery to meditate on Rice's alignment with contemporary neoconservative political agendas and as a strategy for dramatizing their oppressive, regressive character.

By foregrounding a portrait-like image of her, the piece cites the iconicity that Rice developed in international contexts during her two terms of work in the presidential administration of George W. Bush. The portrait of Rice depicts her with a stern look on her face and hovers over a ship in movement across water, an image that most literally alludes to the Chevron oil tanker once named for Rice, the *Condoleezza Rice* (a naming undone once she joined the Bush campaign); her board membership in this corporation; and Chevron's alignment with an oppressive political regime to sustain its drilling exploits in Nigeria for profit. This ship also invokes both military vessels and slave ships and associates Rice with oppressive ravages of modernity such as colonialism, imperialism, and capitalist greed. The piece visually foregrounds modern technologies that have been used to destroy and contain black bodies, such as the gun and the ship, even as it is produced and staged digitally itself and therefore grounded in one of the most innovative media for contemporary visual art production and circulation in the global arena.

The face is much lighter than the neck on the image, a technique that presents her face as a mask and associates her with superficiality, duplicity, and deception. This veneer of Rice in "whiteface" implies a coveting of whiteness, and even racial passing, while paradoxically associating her with the visual aesthetics and racist ideologies of blackface minstrelsy. That rice as an agricultural product is literally whitened in its processing makes the double meaning of this term in the piece all the more significant. This work is also a powerful basis on which to analyze and deconstruct notions of the postblack and postracial that have increasingly inflected contemporary art discourses, particularly given representations related to Rice, race, and questions of black authenticity.

Venezuelan president Hugo Chávez's remark about secretary of state and former First Lady Hillary Clinton—"To me, she's like Condoleezza Rice, a blond Condoleezza"—while aiming to associate Clinton with the reactionary policies reminiscent of Rice's, is a statement based in the hemispheric South, which accords with the representation of Rice in Fuentes's aforementioned novel and that attempts to capture her influence on Latin America by suggesting that Clinton as secretary of state mirrored and extended abuses in the global arena associated with Rice while previously in the position. Chávez's comment also in effect links Rice to the narratives of racial masquerade, betrayal, and passing cited by Lloyd.[48]

These associations are even more explicit and direct in Ayanah Moor's digital print and wall drawing *Never Ignorant Getting Goals* (2005). This piece (figure 3.2) draws on a newspaper feature documenting the celebration of Bush's appointment of Rice as secretary of state, a happy moment that both registers her national iconicity in her positioning against the backdrop of an American flag and draws attention to the dire consequences of their policies in the international arena. It indicts her for her alliance with abusive white masculine authority and power and symbolically masculinizes her inasmuch as she is whitened in Lloyd's piece.

The artist invokes hip-hop and portrays Bush and Rice as "thugs," juxtaposed with images of them wearing formal suits in the news photograph that serves as the focal point of the installation, alongside newsprint that announces the official appointment. It is most significant, too, that the piece unsettles the typical associations of black masculinity with the thug to link it to a white man such as Bush and a black woman like Rice. Because of the ostensible formal attire, the converse of the casual sportswear and street identification associated with the "thug" as a figure, the image suggests that this sensibility is manifested internally in Rice and Bush, rather than externally, in their tactic of sanctioning enhanced interrogation techniques in implementing the war on terror. Again, as in Lloyd's piece, the emphasis in the image is on Rice's complicity with abusive foreign policy agendas.

Moor's incorporation of text in this art piece draws on a strategy in conceptual art quintessentially identified with artists such as Glenn Ligon. This large-scale work of visual art even recalls techniques associated with the revolutionary

FIGURE 3.2 Ayanah Moor, *Never Ignorant Getting Goals*, 2005.

impulse in modern art by muralists such as Diego Rivera, who was known for his epic public art installations, a genre that is profoundly ironic to invoke when considering Rice's association with counterrevolutionary and reactionary policy agendas. Furthermore, in size and scale, this piece by Moor is reminiscent of Kara Walker's monumental wall-size silhouette tableaus, which often feature grotesque and graphic images of abuses of slavery within the Old South's plantation system, sometimes by juxtaposing the bodies of white masters and black slaves, including children, engaged in sexual acts. In this piece, as in Walker's tableaus, black and white are the dominant color scheme.

Here, the black and white of the newsprint and the photographs symbolize the racial categories connected to Rice and Bush. By highlighting the image of Bush kissing Rice, Moor sexualizes and eroticizes their collaboration and invokes interracial sexual desire. Moor's image uses a different strategy from Lloyd's in acknowledging the specter of slavery by alluding to the conventional sexual relationship between white masters and black women slaves. Even more specifically, it alludes to the affair of Sally Hemings and Thomas Jefferson, though Bush's kiss of Rice is staged in a public context and captured in the news—a central medium for broadcasting and circulating information—not in a private setting. Through these thematics, Moor stages a portrait that links a black feminine figure to the presidential and portrays a fantasy of Rice and Bush's relationship that is overtly sexual. The banner of bold capital letters going across the wall, which reads, "Getting Goals Accomplished," parallels Lloyd's tag with the words "Prevaricates Every Time." It makes the intimate juxtaposition of these figures all the more provocative, for the word "accomplished" covers them, suggesting their (potentially romantic) intimacy and that their shared goals may not be related only to policymaking.

Moor's image also provocatively suggests, through the centralization and salience of their bodies in the intimacy of the kiss, the possibility of another kind of affair in a private context. Such perceptions were fed when Rice famously slipped up at a 2004 dinner in Washington, DC, sponsored by the city's *New York Times* bureau chief Phillip Taubman and his wife, Felicity Barringer, and said of George W. Bush, "as I was telling my husb—," before stopping herself from saying the word "husband" and correcting herself: "As I was telling President Bush."[49] The national arena is the context in which Bush and Rice are primarily partnered, and the piece registers Rice's status as an icon of national femininity through the patriotic symbolism that it associates with her. Yet the text also emphasizes their impact on foreign and global affairs.

Belgian artist Luc Tuymans's *The Secretary of State* (2005), which is now housed in the Museum of Modern Art, is an oil painting that accords with Lloyd's and Moor's works in drawing on Rice's iconic photographic images in its composition (figure 3.3). The piece presents Rice as a commanding figure with strong features, including eyes that serve as a focal point and a gaze resolutely into the distance, highlighting her vision in a more abstract sense. The painting, Like Lloyd's, features Rice wearing all the accents associated with her image as iconic, including gold earrings and the flip hairstyle. The arched eyebrows and dark lipstick emphasize her traditional and conservative style, even as the lips resemble the color of blood and allude to the casualties of the war on terror. The partial and fragmented image of her face, which is cut off at top and bottom, seems to position her behind a symbolic veil and as a woman hidden, an image of her body that is provocative given her role in the international arena working primarily on policies related to the Middle East, where Muslim women are often figured by the West as being oppressed by patriarchal mandates and traditions such as veiling. In this sense, the image can be interpreted to suggest that Rice has a lot in common with the women whom her policy agendas are aimed to help "free" in that she, too, is in some ways covered, obscured, and dominated by men. At this level, the painting points to this

FIGURE 3.3 Luc Tuymans, *The Secretary of State*, 2005. Courtesy Luc Tuymans.

situation by depicting Rice as hyperembodied and voiceless, notwithstanding her position as the "most powerful woman in the world" as secretary of state.

This image also, as some art critics have noted, features Rice in a pose associated with the faces of U.S. presidents on Mount Rushmore—which features George Washington, Thomas Jefferson, Theodore Roosevelt, and Abraham Lincoln—representing her in relation to the landscape and as an extension of it.[50] In Tuymans's image, Rice's implicit association with Mount Rushmore, one of the nation's most popular tourist attractions, relates Rice to the most highly revered models of leadership in the nation's history, links her to greatness, and situates her in relation to the reigning presidential figures in U.S. history. In this sense, it figures her in relation to one of the most prominent national symbols and draws on her iconicity to instate her as a premier model of national femininity, even as it suggests that she reinforces rather than revises the nation's prevailing national narratives and underscores the limitations in her political vision. The association may not be entirely accidental or coincidental when considering that Rice's press secretary has admitted that once Rice became secretary of state, many photographs of her were staged behind a podium with a seal in press conferences to link her to power and authority ordinarily attached to the president.[51] Despite her famous resistances and hesitations to run for public office, Rice has frequently been idealized as a potential presidential candidate in the Republican Party.

Tuymans was inspired to develop this piece by the comment of a close friend who had served as minister of foreign affairs in their country. According to Tuymans, this friend who knew very little about Rice had described her on reading an article about her upcoming visit to the nation, and as she began her work within the Bush administration, by saying, "She is very intelligent, and she is not unpretty." In the artist's view, this statement was sexist and reduced her to an object. Such comments echo Libyan leader Muammar Gaddafi's fascination with Rice. He had remarked, "Leezza, Leezza, Leezza. . . . I love her very much. I admire her, and I'm proud of her, because she's a black woman of African origin" on Al-Jazeera television in 2007. When his Tripoli compound was raided in August 2011, Gaddafi's cherished album of glossy photographs featuring images of Rice was uncovered.[52] Tuymans's aim in developing the painting was to foreground the paradox related to Rice's attractive and desirable body and the destructive and despicable policies that she endorsed or helped to develop in her work with Bush.

That Tuymans's native country is historically linked to colonial exploits in the African Congo may also inflect his critique of a contemporary national official in his home country in constructing an image of Rice, whose color, fashion accessories, facial expression, and scale make a critical statement on the impact of the U.S. government's military on nations in the Middle East, such as Iraq and Afghanistan, and newer forms of colonialism. As in Moor's piece, white masculine interracial desire for the black feminine body linked to histories of slavery, colonialism, and imperialism emerges as a subtext in this work and primarily surfaces through the story underpinning its composition instead of registering at a visual level. It imagines Rice as a prominent model of national femininity. At the same time, it acknowledges the transnational reach of her feminine iconicity and demonstrates how artists in a range of global contexts have deconstructed and critiqued the controversial foreign policy agendas with which she has been associated.

Mexican artist Enrique Chagoya is another international visual artist who has produced images that critique Rice's relationship to problematic U.S. policy agendas. His 2004 charcoal and pastel work on canvas, *Untitled (Snow White and the Seven Dwarfs)*, features the cabinet members of George W. Bush dressed as characters in the fairy tale *Snow White* (figure 3.4). For example, the piece depicts Colin Powell as Doc, and Rice as Snow White, a representation that also, like Lloyd's image, associates Rice with whiteness and a lack of black authenticity and portrays her as a race traitor in the vein of the Uncle Tom. The invocation of the fairy tale as a genre links these political figures to infantile rather than adult behavior and decision making. The invocation of Snow White in relation to the diminutive dwarfs also points to her ubiquity and salience on the national and global political stage.

Similarly, *Poor George #3 (After P. G.)* (2004) is a provocative image by Chagoya that portrays Rice being held, doll-like, by George W. Bush, who is portrayed as a ventriloquist, to imply how much she has been controlled and manipulated by him, as well as toyed with, and has served as a mouthpiece for his problematic policies (figure 3.5). Significantly, they are positioned in front of an old-fashioned camera, which suggests the framing, multiplication, and circulation of this dynamic involving an infantilized Rice and Bush. Here Rice is dressed in a red and white ensemble that makes her resemble a little girl sitting on her daddy's lap. The drawing features Bush wearing a red tie, the same color in her dress, perhaps to symbolize blood and the losses associated with the war on terror and the Iraq War, which his administration spearheaded. It is also significant that this piece and other pen and ink drawings in this series by Chagoya revise drawings by Philip Guston, from the latter's early 1970s *Poor Richard* series satirizing President Richard Nixon, including one depicting Nixon holding a black doll for a photo op. These allusions allow Chagoya to critique a longer history of right-wing politics, spanning back to the end of the civil rights era and the rise of the neoconservative movement. We can also draw on them to recognize levels on which this political climate advanced neoconservative agendas into the new millennium and established foundations for current policies connected to anti-immigration and antiblackness in the Trump administration.

Like Tuymans's, this piece uses red in cosmetic makeup to metaphorically invoke blood. The image presents Bush as Rice's symbolic white father, who has, by implication, usurped the place of John Rice, her real one. The image associates power with Bush as a figure and casts her as pliable, subordinate, childlike, and dollish in relation to him, staging a fantasy of their relationship implying that the authority in her office as secretary of state is an illusion. She is positioned on his arm as a puppet would be, suggesting that she is manipulated and controlled by him. This representation recalls digital artist Amy Vangsgard's depiction of Rice (figure 3.6), in the form of a clay art sculpture, as a marionette wearing a suit and holding a book on Iraq, which associates Rice with egregious foreign policies and postures of racial accommodation, as well as evoking the grotesque and caricatured black collectibles that were circulated in U.S. material culture, described by Patricia A. Turner as "contemptible collectibles."[53]

FIGURE 3.4 Enrique Chagoya, *Untitled (Snow White and the Seven Dwarfs)*, 2004. Courtesy Enrique Chagoya.

FIGURE 3.5 Enrique Chagoya, *Poor George #3 (After P. G.)*, 2004. Courtesy Enrique Chagoya.

FIGURE 3.6 Amy Vangsgard, *Politician Clipart #12206*, n.d. Courtesy Clipart of LLC.

Chagoya's image of Bush is not only fatherly but also fundamentally paternalistic. Paternalism subtended and rationalized the antebellum plantation economy and structured its race, class, and gender hierarchies. When considering slavery's afterlives and rearticulations from Jim Crow to the present, residual traces of this concept of paternalism associated with southern culture are indispensable for analyzing Rice's relationship as a black woman with an elite wealthy white family in the South like the Bushes, who are often described as a "political dynasty." Rice was descended from a family whose ties with the Republican Party went as far back as her grandfather, and she had previously worked in the George H. W. Bush administration. These linkages point to the southern landscape as a relevant context for thinking about representations of Rice that have emerged in visual art and popular culture in the global arena. Her global paths of travel as a black woman during her years as secretary of state inflect the creative discourses related to her that have emerged in various transnational contexts in the growing body of work on Rice in art and popular culture.

In slavery, paternalism premised on a view of slaves as being childlike and intellectually inferior was fundamental to mythologizations of slave masters in the antebellum myth of the Old South. Slave masters were imagined as being generous and benevolent to their slaves, who in turn were devoted servants who understood and remained in their "place." Chagoya's *Poor George #3* stages a powerful visualization of a white masculine typology that emerged during slavery. It is a useful and relevant site on which to ponder the benevolence of a wealthy and primarily white and masculine right-wing establishment, including a southern political dynasty such as the Bushes, based in Texas, in investing in Rice's career and facilitating her advancement in the political arena. It follows that we can also draw on this image of Rice as childlike for pondering her devotion and complicity in advancing right-wing political agendas.[54] Such a reading properly situates Bush and Rice against the backdrop of the plantation complex, which structured the geographies of the Western Hemisphere, while framing their policies in the Global and hemispheric South as an outgrowth of governing systems of slavery, colonialism, and imperialism.

Rice's representations in the visual arts are schematized to critique her engagements in foreign policy. These representations emphasize her femininity, fashioning, and accessories, such as her elegant hairstyle and jewelry, to imply her conventional qualities and to highlight an external beauty that starkly contrasts with the ugly consequences of her policies. The hard and stern look on the faces of figurations of Rice in the work of Lloyd, Tuymans, and Chagoya all allude to questions about her character and conscience that have emerged among her critics. Her style, including the impeccable and staid veneer for which she is well known, serves as a primary device in these artworks to emphasize her conservative image and to visualize her as a reactionary. The use of the visual serves as a means of giving testimony to atrocities that have not been emphasized in the media as much as the veneer of Rice's charming and attractive persona has. These pieces all centralize and deconstruct Rice as an icon in the national and global arenas and present her as hyperembodied paradoxically to suggest her subordination and manipulation within the neoconservative establishment. Unlike the "distractions" that comedy highlights in depicting Rice, which, as Royster suggests, have tended to deflect direct criticisms of policy agendas to which she has been linked, her critiques in visual art have been unremitting. The art featuring Rice builds on the graphic, violent, and troubling images in media reports that dramatize the consequences, including casualties, of Bush's war on terror, which it associates ironically with forms of state-sanctioned terrorism and deploys the visual to highlight critiques of Rice and her linkages to state power.

The idealized fantasy of Rice rooted in black urban community staged in comedy differs starkly from the biting realism depicted in art images of her, which link her to repressive foreign policy agendas steeped in legacies of colonialism and imperialism. As Carole Boyce-Davies points out from her perspective in black feminism and transnational feminism, black Americans produced by histories of slavery and Jim Crow and subjected to persisting racism are routinely complicit with the nation's military in helping to carry out U.S. policy agendas that play out abusively against populations in the African diaspora.[55] These artists are less invested in celebrating than in castigating her iconic force. Rice is not represented as an enlightened, visionary, or insurgent model of black identity but is conversely linked to politically regressive and oppressive political agendas. They register ways in which Rice's association with state power has been linked to war and violence in the global arena. They recurrently relate her to an abusive foreign policy and suggest that she fails to help the United States become a better or more perfect union, contradicting her own reading that centers black subjects as agents in shaping American democracy in her speeches and memoir. While Rice embodies a model of blackness that unsettles and disrupts conventional race and gender stereotypes of the past, such visual images that associate her with white patriarchy suggest that her agency and representational space as a black woman remain limited.

These works suggest that even as a black woman working in the presidential administration and categorized as the most powerful in the world,

Rice leaves narrow definitions of American citizenship unexamined and undisturbed and does not offer a visionary or empowering alternative through her reactionary leadership model. Instead, they emphasize her uses as a black woman and token presence within Bush's administration to camouflage the egregiousness of U.S. foreign policy agendas through her high visibility and iconicity, which fails to disrupt or even challenge the neoconservative establishment, to the point of sanctioning and reinforcing all the regressive notions of American selfhood in which it continues to remain invested, while invoking her iconicity steeped in her salience as a model of national womanhood and emblem of American patriotism. While Bush's administration prided itself on "spreading freedom" in the Middle East, all these artworks suggest that the model of national femininity that Rice represents not only undermines freedom and democracy but also helped to frame the United States as a repressive, reactionary, and oligarchic force in foreign affairs. Fashion provides a final context and subtext vital for its role in helping to consolidate Rice's iconic force and legibility as a model of national femininity.

Commanding Clothes

In the introduction of a 2015 guest-edited issue of *NKA: A Journal of Contemporary Art* entitled "Black Fashion: Art, Pleasure, Politics," Noliwe Rooks remarks, "Fashion matters. It provides and pulls tight the threads of identity that tell others how to locate one within a culture, in relationship to a society, or inside the realms of one's imaginings."[56] She goes on to observe, "The significance and meaning of fashion are nowhere more visible than in how it manifests and functions at the site of the collision between identity and race in the African diaspora. There, black fashion has identified and continues to identify wearers as part of political, cultural, and social groups or movements."[57] This critical project affirms the intimate linkage between fashion and art as well as the profound role that fashion plays in Africa and in its diasporas in scripting race and signaling political investments. Her insights can also help us understand how and why fashion played a key role in conditioning Rice's iconicity and mediating her rise as a model of national femininity in the new millennium.

The fashion subtexts related to Rice are important to throw into relief for the important role that they have played in consolidating her national and global iconicity as a woman leader, a dimension that has been the subject of substantial commentary in the media. Like visual art, fashion played a primary role in shaping discourses of race, gender, and sexuality related to her. Pearls, designer shoes such as Ferragamos, and St. John knit suits were signature fashion pieces in Condoleezza Rice's elegantly stylized public appearances on national and global stages, including events such as President Bush's periodic State of the Union addresses. Rice received substantial attention in the fashion world, including listing on *Vanity Fair*'s International Best Dressed List in 2006, alongside figures such as Oprah Winfrey, Kate Moss, and Prince William, and has been lauded for being "immaculately groomed." Some in the fashion industry credited her with helping to resurrect the flip hairstyle. In a 2005 interview, Rice was asked by conservative Fox television host Sean Hannity if she had an idea that she would become a "fashion trendsetter."[58] Her clothing ensembles, in their varying forms and combinations, have tended to be plain, dark, demure, and understated, but in their own way, and for their own purposes, have often commanded attention and made statements.

In a 2008 article in the *Guardian*, "This Is the Age of Power Pearls—And No One Exploits Their Potency Better than Condie Rice," Germaine Greer describes the significance of Rice's regular wearing of white pearls. According to Greer,

> Condie is the consummate power-dresser. Every pant suit—whether by St John, Armani or Versace, in black, navy or charcoal grey—is immaculate, no matter how long she has been crouched memorizing briefs as she is whirled by plane from one end of the earth to another. She is said to work out at 4am each morning; certainly the belly is flat and the stride purposeful, no matter how long she has been cooped up in a plane. Her hair is regularly beaten into submission. Right now she is sporting a ringer for the Michelle Obama bob, which itself is a version of the Jackie Onassis big hair flick. Occasionally, Condie lets herself be seen in knee-high, high-heeled jackboots, to the unspeakable excitement of the armies of lackeys that follow her about. She wears dark lipstick, highlighting the expressiveness of her eyes and the occasional dazzle of her smile. Otherwise her subfusc is relieved only by the milky radiance of her power pearls.[59]

As a fashion accessory, pearls align Rice with an image classically and even quintessentially associated with traditional American elite women, including the white southern model of femininity most legible to the politically conservative establishment of white male leaders with whom she has primarily worked, presidents who are Texas natives such as George Herbert Walker

Bush and his son George W. Bush. In her public appearances, Rice has strategically used pearls to adapt and embody the image associated with the southern "steel magnolia" in her public forms of dress and stylization. The steel magnolia type manifests the traditional trappings of southern femininity on the outside, including beauty, and may wear items such as pearls, suits, and dresses but is fundamentally defined by qualities such as strength and toughness at their core. That she was adorned with pearls as a signature accessory in media interviews and statements about the Iraq War helped lend credibility to war policies that she advocated and to accord them legitimacy.

Even as Greer registers the performative aspects of Rice's gender identity, that she devalues trans women and victims of rape makes it crucial to critique the essentialist narrative of femininity that her description of Rice ultimately enshrines, and to more broadly ponder how much Rice's reification in the national imaginary reconsolidates narrow and exclusionary definitions of womanhood. That Greer draws on the rhetoric of 1990s power feminism and emphasizes the uses of lipstick and hairstyling in the case of Rice's gender fashioning, which Greer famously minimized and dismissed as being superficial when embraced to aestheticize trans women such as Caitlyn Jenner in the wake of Jenner's selection by *Glamour* magazine as a "Woman of the Year" in 2015, suggests the conceptual and theoretical limitations in feminist discourses that obscure diverse and multifaceted feminine formations and sanction conventional definitions of the category *woman* premised on binary and heterosexist formulations of femininity. Such blind spots that read Rice's fashioning on the surface and draw on it to link her to essentialist notions of femininity obscure visual and cultural representations that look beyond this veneer to examine what is at stake in her alignments with a white patriarchal political establishment, while failing to recognize and reflect on more complicated race, sex, and gender discourses, as we see in works from Terry Lloyd's art to *Mad TV*'s "Condi Comes to Harlem," that describe how appropriations of masculine imagery reinforced her power.

One moment in particular during which Rice flouted the typical decorum and respectability politics associated with her fashioning in the political arena stands out and bears noting. Significantly, one instance of Rice's self-fashioning in the global arena strategically borrowed from visual codes associated with the dominatrix, an alternative feminine type whose sheer evocation serves as a valuable and telling counterpoint to the genteel feminine aesthetics that inflect some of Rice's most familiar visual representations. In February 2005, Rice's wearing of all black, including a short skirt, a long gold-buttoned military-style coat, and knee-high high-heeled boots to the Wiesbaden Army Airfield held great symbolic significance. The sleek black ensemble, at a visual level, made an assertive statement and established a no-nonsense mindset before an all-male military audience. The outfit associated her with power and reinforced her authority as a woman while occupying the historically masculine leadership role of secretary of state. Robin Givhan's article in the *Washington Post*, "Condoleezza Rice's Commanding Style," observes that the look projected a combination of sex and power to the point of evoking the dominatrix.[60]

This figure is associated with sadomasochism, perversion, the appropriation of forms of control and domination associated with masculinity, and the use of sex and force to subordinate and subdue men and put them in positions of submission. The dominatrix is an inherently paradoxical figure in the sense that she is feminine yet dominant and powerful. In the most literal sense, she is often depicted dressed in tight and skimpy black leather ensembles such as body suits, shoes or boots with steep high heels, and props such as whips. It is provocative that Rice evoked some elements of the edgy attire associated with this figure, such as the sleekly tailored black suit with the coat and skirt and the black high-heeled boots, to project an image of authority before an audience of military men.

The appropriation of this stark black image becomes all the more significant if we consider factors such as race, gender, and sexuality. That is to say, Rice's status as a black woman leader makes her assertive and symbolic use of this imagery before an audience of predominantly white and male military men all the more subversive. In its ostensible evocation of sexuality and power, the ensemble belied the reserved and desexualized image as a "black lady" that has typically been associated with Rice in the public sphere of politics.[61]

Givhan points out that in this ensemble, "Rice boldly eschewed the typical fare chosen by powerful American women on the world stage. She was not wearing a bland suit with a loose-fitting skirt and short boxy jacket with a pair of sensible pumps. She did not cloak her power in photogenic hues, a feminine brooch and a non-threatening aesthetic. Rice looked as though she was prepared to talk tough, knock heads and do a freeze-frame 'Matrix' jump kick if necessary. Who wouldn't give her ensemble a double take—all the while hoping not to rub her the wrong way?"[62] Givhan concludes by pointing out that "Rice's appearance at Wiesbaden—a military base with all its attendant images of machismo, strength, and power—was striking because she walked out draped in a banner of authority, power, and toughness. She was not hiding behind matronliness, androgyny, or the stereotype of the steel magnolia. Rice brought her full self to the world stage—and that included her sexuality. It was not overt or inappropriate. If it was distracting, it is only because it is so rare."[63] Givhan suggests that the outfit makes Rice appear more dynamic, powerful, and larger than life because it links her to qualities typically associated with masculine heroes in action films.

In Givhan's estimation, this edgy outfit lends Rice authority because it walks the fine line of connoting strength while remaining distinctly feminine, and yet not too stereotypically or overtly so. Givhan explicitly articulates a point about Rice that few of her critics notice: her ability to both emblematize and subvert conventions and codes associated with the feminine in politics by using fashion. Yet at the same time, it is limited in eliding the subversive potential of androgyny. In some ways, in this moment, Rice mirrored the fashion ingenuity, attitude, and boldness associated with her imaginative superhero persona in the "Condi Comes to Harlem" skits. In general, for me, such intensely performative moments are critically fascinating and most useful for thinking about queer epistemologies in relation to Rice.

Drawing on imagery connected to the dominatrix for body fashioning takes on a very different and more problematic meaning, however, when one considers the white male-dominated, neoconservative establishment and power structure in the United States that she represents in the international context. The implications of making her body legible as a woman on its behalf by drawing on such provocative sexual imagery at a male-centered military base need to be considered in light of the historical serviceability and subjection of the captive black feminine body within a white patriarchal structure, which arguably used it prosthetically in this moment, and the attendant raced and sexed power relations. Furthermore, evoking such an image purposefully flouts the high-profile controversies involving the sexual harassment of women that have been associated with the military in recent years. Such uses of fashion by Rice have served as a device to reinforce her authority and link her to patriarchal power and have by extension helped to advance policies related to war in the global arena.

That Rice's suiting in styles ranging from the classic southern lady to a bold dominatrix, to the point of engaging in forms of political showmanship, garnered high-profile media attention and helped her gain legibility and power is just one valuable lens through which we should recognize her complex negotiation of race, gender, class, and sexuality within a global context as a black woman. Just months after this trip to Germany, the politics of her fashioning and stylization became much more complicated after she was famously said to have shopped for shoes at the New York boutique in the aftermath of Hurricane Katrina.

The cultural texts that I have examined in comedy and art all code fashion, from the retro clothing and color and design of blaxploitation to classic designer suits in reflecting on Rice's national and global leadership. By emphasizing her adoption of Harlem as a space and advocacy on behalf of black communities, the former genre imaginatively scripts Rice in relation to maternal political narratives of black women that have recurred in politics, and that are epitomized in the examples of Bethune and Parks, suggesting that one does not have to be a literal mother to be linked to this narrative of the black feminine. Rice's writings also retool this maternal narrative by alternatively emphasizing parentage and ancestry. While in the post–civil rights era, the conventional model of black femininity that characterizes Rice's fashioning is exceptional in light of the political power that she wielded, she also emerged as the prototypically reactionary black woman national leader and icon during the new millennium.

If she challenged the conventional white-centered models of national femininity through the unprecedented power that she had attained in the global arena, in contrast to the prolific scripts of marginalized black women leaders that consolidated during the post–civil rights era, she failed to produce a radical black feminine model that posed an alternative to Eurocentric ones, unlike predecessors such as Bethune and Parks. Although Nadia Brown emphasizes the legislative level, her discussion of the importance of examining differences among black women in the political realm and acknowledging black women in all of their diversity provides some helpful critical contexts in political science for thinking about such differences among black women leaders.[64] Despite what may have been good intentions, Rice's recurring rhetorical citations of civil rights discourses such as the tragedy at 16th Street obscured its dimensions related to the South's domestic terrorism and were a far cry from the radical messages linked to earlier black women leaders. This may have been because Rice's citations of civil rights were framed within reactionary right-wing ideology rather than organically within freedom movements, which historically constituted the most empowering and visionary scripts of black femininity. A consideration of Michelle Obama in the next and final chapter, who shares common ground with Rice in staging scripts of her black family as nationally representative and is useful to read in comparison, will help us reflect on black women's constructions in the post-Emancipation era as national models of femininity in contexts from politics to popular culture in the new millennium.

Riché Richardson, *The Magnificent Michelle Obama, Our First Lady: "Strength and Honor Are Her Clothing" (Proverbs 31:25)*, 2009. Photograph by Dave Burbank.

First Lady and "Mom-in-Chief"

The Voice and Vision of Michelle Obama in the Video South Side Girl *and in* American Grown

Nothing had changed about her in who she was and what she stood for. True, the White House was not the upstairs tiny apartment where we grew up, and Pennsylvania Avenue in the District of Columbia was a far cry from Euclid Avenue on the Southside of Chicago. But one thing clearly had remained the same in the two settings and that was the importance of family. Our country needed children in the White House, a reminder of why we strive and need to strive for the next generation coming up behind us. —CRAIG ROBINSON, *A Game of Character: A Family Journey from Chicago's Southside to the Ivy League and Beyond*

So Michelle Obama isn't cut from the Dolley Madison or Laura Bush cloth, and this isn't Camelot. Maybe the predecessor whom we will most often be reminded of is Eleanor Roosevelt. Tireless in her dedication to human rights, Roosevelt was a First Lady with no peer. She was an early U.S. delegate to the United Nations. She drove through the night to the very heart of Ku Klux Klan country to attend a civil rights rally. And, of course, Eleanor served the nation, as Mrs. Obama will, in times of economic hardship. If Eleanor Roosevelt was a grandmother of the women's movement, Mrs. Obama is a daughter of it. —ANDRÉ LEON TALLEY, *Vogue*

Michelle Obama's birth and upbringing in Chicago, Illinois, on the city's predominantly black and working-class South Side was recurrently cited during Barack Obama's first presidential campaign, which was launched on February 10, 2007, in Springfield, Illinois. As she initially gained salience in the national arena, a purpose of such scripts seemed to be to portray her as an African American woman who could identify with the lives and circumstances of ordinary, everyday working people. After Barack Obama's historic election as the nation's first black president in 2008 and reelection in 2012, references to the South Side continued to shape Michelle Obama's public representation and self-fashioning as the nation's First Lady, which culminated in Richard Tanne's 2016 romance about the first couple, *Southside with You*.

In *Michelle: A Biography*, after mentioning the nexus of migrations for Michelle Obama's family, the Robinsons, in Georgetown, South Carolina, Liza Mundy points to the complex geographic circuits in the South and North that have shaped Michelle Obama:

> Ultimately a half million African Americans would move from the South to Chicago, swelling the city's black population from 2 to 27 percent in 2000. The South Side would be where the majority would settle, though an African American section would grow up on the west side as well, and those two populations would expand toward each other and meet, making an L that forms one of the country's largest contiguous African American populations. Much of the world outside Chicago would assume the South Side was poor and black and criminal. In fact, the South Side has, for much of its history, been economically diverse and culturally vibrant.[1]

Mundy goes on to point out the continuities and discontinuities that link Michelle Obama to a southern background:

> It's true that Michelle Obama's experience was different from an earlier generation of African Americans who grew up in the 1940s and 1950s in the segregated South. But it is still a classic narrative, the one that came after that. More urban, more modern. Rather than being explicitly shut out or regularly and unapologetically discriminated against, during her lifetime Michelle Obama was granted admission to privileged quarters that only recently had become open and that were still uneasy about her presence, or, at best, unprepared. She has lived and worked in a series of transitional landscapes. One way to understand Michelle Obama is as a person who has lived much of her life on contested terrain.[2]

Indeed, it is significant that references to her ancestors who migrated to Chicago from the South, and who have roots in South Carolina and Georgia that are traceable back to slavery, have consistently complemented and counterbalanced her profile as urban and working class. The former references have also played an equally if not more meaningful role in framing Michelle Obama by race and class while linking her to a rural and southern background, references that similarly draw on geography.[3]

In a March 31, 2009, editorial, "On Lady Obama," the *Root* columnist Stanley Crouch draws on blues motifs and emphasizes the importance of geography in having shaped the First Lady's identity by pointing to the fundamental role of the "South" within an urban geography in constructing her, along with its complex dispersals and refractions across regions, which speaks to her transcendent appeal in the nation. As he remarks, "Perhaps what makes Michelle Obama so truly extraordinary is how ordinary she seems simply because the first lady reminds us of all those remarkable women from the South sides of so, so many places, north and south, east and west. If it was called for, they knew how to *bring* it. If we lacked morale, they knew how to serve it on a hot plate that wouldn't burn but didn't fail to inspire. When you saw them coming you knew the heart and the brain of the world were within communicative range."[4]

Repetitive citations of Michelle Obama as a girl born and raised on the predominantly black South Side of Chicago feminized the typically masculinized metaphors of the South Side as spatiality that have conventionally been resonant in contexts such as black blues culture.[5] In centrally mediating and enshrining her articulation in the U.S. public sphere as a representative woman, they yield a radically alternative and even revolutionary script of national femininity as black and female, as they simultaneously constitute her family—a black family—as a representative national family in the United States. If we recognize the multiplicity of South-related contexts and temporalities within which she is cited and in her moves through "transitional landscapes" and "contested terrain," we can recognize the First Lady as a reigning emblem and byproduct of black southern and global modernity.

In this sense, the recurrent references to the term *South Side* in Michelle Obama's public profile, particularly as they unfold alongside references to the roots of her family in plantation slavery, might be interpreted in the broadest sense as a linguistic register of the U.S. South's unruly and dispersed geographies and temporalities, along with its infinite mutability and inherently migratory, transnational dimensions. Even her spearheading of the planting of a vegetable garden at the White House to promote healthier eating in the nation, notably on the South Lawn, further connects the First Lady to the South as a signifier, but in a sense wholly different from the agriculture cultivated and harvested by blacks on the grounds of the White House in the context of antebellum slavery, within Western modernity's plantation complex of hemispheric proportions.

Chicago is a midwestern, multiethnic city that emerged as a prominent trading epicenter, whose earliest settler was Jean Baptiste Pointe du Sable, a free Haitian immigrant whose background links the city's history to African and Caribbean diasporas. Notwithstanding her primary background in urban Chicago, the complex geographic migrations associated with Michelle Obama's family history point to the usefulness of a regional epistemology that draws on the Africana South as an interpretive lens for analyzing her. This framework builds on global and hemispheric South discourses to recognize how Africa and its diasporas imprint black identities in the Americas, acknowledging their hemispheric and transnational dimensions, dislodging them from static and conventional southernist binary North-South regional epistemologies, while registering how, in the urban North, the inherent migratory aspects embedded in black identities articulate and manifest cultural practices primarily associated with black southerners. Citations of Michelle Obama's connection to the south area of the city of Chicago emphasize her intimacy with the closest example of a South in the city, and by extension, link her to what Jacqueline Jones describes as "Southern diasporas" in the urban North that sustained family and cultural traditions brought up from the South during the Great Migration.[6] This rhetoric emphasizes the U.S. South as a migratory, fragmented, dispersed, diverse, and highly unstable concept within the nation. At the same time, a critical recognition of the region's inherent transnationality detaches the U.S. South from its narrow and conventional spatial borders and temporalities, mapping it in relation to what Jafari Sinclaire Allen describes as "black queer diasporas."[7]

The earliest concerted efforts to examine Michelle Obama's background, which uncovered linkages in her family history tied to plantation slavery in the South, were related to Barack Obama's run for the presidency.[8] In 2008, his campaign team initially hired genealogists to excavate Michelle Obama's family history on the campaign trail. The only public mention of this background occurred in Barack Obama's March 2008 speech during the primaries, "A More Perfect Union," delivered at the National Constitution Center in Philadelphia, Pennsylvania, in which he describes himself as a person "married to a black American who carries within her the blood of slaves and slave owners."[9] Barack Obama's presidential campaign hired genealogists at the University of South Florida in Tampa to research Michelle Obama's family background, and the result was a 120-page report that has been mostly kept confidential.

More detailed information about Michelle Obama's family background related to slavery appeared on December 1, 2008, in a *Chicago Tribune* piece, "Michelle Obama's Family Tree Has Roots in a Carolina Slave Plantation," by Dahleen Glanton and Stacy St. Clair. The essay traces Michelle Obama's ancestral background to Jim Robinson, her great-great-grandfather, and focuses on his history as a slave on the Friendfield Plantation, owned by Frances Withers in Georgetown, South Carolina. The article mentions that Robinson was born a slave circa 1850 and, after the Civil War, became a sharecropper and lived with his wife, Louise, and children in the former slave quarters once slavery ended. Though little is known about Robinson's life and experiences on the plantation during the antebellum era, he worked in the rice fields on the riverfront after the Civil War. The article identifies five of the cabins that remain on the site now as remnants of what once were three parallel rows of slave cabins, which were visible on a map from the early 1870s on Slave Street at a time when Robinson still lived there.[10]

Further inroads into documenting Michelle Obama's family history were highlighted the following year by reporters at another major national newspaper. An October 8, 2009, *New York Times* article by Rachel L. Swarns and Jodi Kantor, "In First Lady's Roots, a Complex Path from Slavery," examines the linkages of the ancestry of Michelle Obama to the history of slavery on her maternal side. Through investigating various archival materials such as a marriage license, a will from the nineteenth century, photos, and oral histories of senior women, the preliminary research of a genealogist named Megan Smolenyak, in collaboration with the *New York Times*, uncovers information about a ten-year-old slave girl named Melvinia. In documents from the South Carolina estate of her owner, David Patterson, she is listed as the "Negro girl Melvinia."[11] The research has revealed that she was given to his daughter Christianne and her husband, Henry Shields, and that she was sent to Georgia after Patterson's death. Melvinia gave birth to Dolphus T. Shields, her first child, at age fifteen, a child fathered by a white man whose identity is not conclusively known, though DNA tests have suggested Charles Marion Shields, the oldest son in the Shields family, as the most likely possibility.

The research identifies this unknown white male ancestor and Melvinia as the great-great-great-grandparents of First Lady Michelle Obama. It reveals that Melvinia was illiterate, and that she did work that may have entailed planting and harvesting wheat, corn, sweet potatoes, and cotton, or caring for "3 horses, 5 cows, 17 pigs, and 20 sheep."[12] This information, including the work conditions that Melvinia may have conceivably encountered as a slave in Georgia during the antebellum era, inextricably ties Michelle Obama's ancestry to the traumatic history of plantation slavery experienced by blacks in the United States as it links her genetically to forms of racial intermixture and hybridity typically discussed in relation to her husband in light of his parents' interracial marriage and his mixed-race identity. It situates Michelle Obama as a premier linchpin for connecting the nation's first black family in the White House to the history of American slavery, given that her husband's mother was white, and his father was of African ancestry. As Kenneth T. Walsh notes in *Family of Freedom: Presidents and African Americans in the White House*, "a fascinating part of her personal narrative was that it was Michelle, not Barack, whose ancestors were slaves. Barack's mother was a white woman, Ann Dunham, from Kansas, and his father was a black man, Barack Obama Sr., from Kenya, and he was not descended from anyone who had been in bondage.... So she had much more of a personal connection to America's bitter racial history than her husband did."[13]

Swarns builds on Smolenyak's compelling research with the *New York Times* and explores both the paternal and maternal roots of Michelle Obama, including her ancestral history rooted in slavery and the story of the young slave girl Melvinia, in the landmark study *American Tapestry: The Story of the Black, White, and Multiracial Ancestors of Michelle Obama*.[14] This study, with its exhaustive and comprehensive look at Michelle Obama's family history, provides the most authoritative and detailed examination of the contours of her vast genealogy and is organized across chapters that alternate between dialogues on her paternal and maternal ancestors. Thematically, across its three major sections, it addresses the experiences of her family within the broader historical contexts of slavery, the Great Migration, and Jim Crow. While it begins by exploring the experiences of her paternal great-grandparents, Phoebe Moten and James Preston, as they united and settled in the urban North in Chicago, it is structured around a timeline that builds up to an examination of Melvinia's background in slavery, coming full circle from its briefer exploration of her story in the introduction to the dialogues related to her that ground the book's final chapters. In Swarns's words, "The First Lady is the descendant of both Irish immigrants who nurtured their dreams in a new land and of African Americans who triumphed over servitude and segregation. Michelle

LeVaughn Robinson Obama is the inheritor of our nation's complex, often unspoken lineage."[15]

Swarns draws on this multiracial family lineage to frame the First Lady as a quintessential embodiment of the nation's inherent racial diversity and hybridity, challenging purist narratives of the nation as white, which are steeped in taboos, anxieties, and legalized prohibitions against interracial sexual relations, and that repress the routine interracial sexual intermingling that has occurred across its history, beginning during slavery. The First Lady's history outlined in this study frames her family within its long history as an exemplar of the inherently racially hybridized model of American family that has been foundational in the nation's development. Like the multiracial family of Sally Hemings and Thomas Jefferson, birthed in plantation slavery at Monticello, the story of the young slave girl Melvinia and her son's white father at the foundation of First Lady Michelle Obama's family demonstrates a national heritage that is fundamentally interracial while challenging the purist beliefs and myths of American history that repress truths and realities related to black and white racial and sexual intermixture. At the same time, such stories inextricably frame black women as foremothers and tie American history to slavery, including the reality of plantation slavery in the U.S. South and its assault on the black maternal body.

In Clifton Ellis and Rebecca Ginsburg's introduction to a landmark edited volume, *Cabin, Quarter, Plantation: Architecture and Landscape of North American Slavery*, the architects underscore that a consideration of slavery is indispensable to understanding "the built landscape" in North America.[16] After Barack Obama's inauguration as president in 2009 and the family's move into the White House, the narrative about Michelle Obama's kinship to slaves helped to highlight the significance and irony of a black family living in the White House, built with the labor of slaves and historically staffed by black servants but never envisioned as a home for blacks given black exclusion from notions of citizenship and democracy in the United States. That slaves played such a vital role in constructing the White House is symptomatic of the central role that they also played in building the United States as a nation. In the study *The Black History of the White House*, historian Clarence Lusane discusses the role of black labor in constructing the nation's capital and links this work to the history of slave labor instrumental in constructing early cities in the United States, particularly in the South.[17] Even the executive order issued by President Theodore Roosevelt in 1901 that officially changed the name of the building from the Executive Mansion to the White House, David Leslie

Hancock provocatively argues, reflected the reactionary racial climate of the period and symbolically affirmed whites as the quintessential and superior Americans.[18]

When considering the slave labor that went into its construction, its historical reliance on a predominantly black servant class to function, its construction in a Georgian building style characteristic of the architecture of the wealthiest and most lavish southern plantation homes, and its location in a region geographically categorized as southern, the White House epitomized the nation's plantation complex of slavery, which was iterated across geographies throughout the Western Hemisphere. This monumental architecture on the nation's capital materially emerged and long functioned through a slave labor force, even as it served as a primary site, alongside the nation's Capitol, from which agendas of U.S. imperialism and colonialism were advanced globally. Though it has not typically been legible in this respect, when we frame the White House as prominent plantation architecture on the American landscape, and take into account Michelle Obama's historical linkages to slave cabins on a plantation in South Carolina and her role in the White House as First Lady, her story emerges as a lens through which to ponder more tangibly how inextricably the labor of black slavery has been linked to this nation's historical development. These historical contexts are an important backdrop against which to examine her remapping of the White House as an architecture and a landscape by incorporating and cultivating a garden on the grounds designed to promote nutrition, a choice that is inherently subversive and oppositional given her positioning as a black and female First Lady and the White House's legacy of slavery.

In this nation, the interior design, decor, staff organization, and supervision of the White House, especially in the East Wing (as opposed to the West Wing, where presidential power resides), have been conventionally duties of the First Lady.[19] The emergence of Michelle Obama at the forefront of the nation's public sphere has unsettled the deeply entrenched raced and gendered narratives in the nation of the First Lady as white. Equally significant, Michelle Obama's public role as First Lady destabilizes conventional narratives of blackness associated with subjection and subordination in relation to the White House and makes the role of First Lady synonymous with a black woman for the first time in history. As First Lady and as a black woman living in the White House, Michelle Obama, described by *Essence* as "the world's most visible African American woman," emerged as the most salient and quintessential black feminine figure in both constructing and representing notions of national femininity. As Michael Jeffries has reminded us, "Michelle Obama's standing as the predominant symbol of American womanhood is constantly modulated by the metalanguage of race."[20]

Regional epistemologies that emphasize the U.S. South are also indispensable for studying her in light of how recurrently both conservative and liberal media have invoked the reactionary literary, cultural, and ideological heritage of the region in representing her in the nation's public sphere. The fluidity and flexibility of the South as a signifier in her public construction make her a compelling and, I believe, indispensable topic for southern studies, including epistemologies on the hemispheric and Global South. The new southern studies, along with methodologies that draw on the Global South paradigm as articulated in relation to a range of global geographies, have reinforced comparative interfaces in black/Africana and diaspora studies. Yet discourses on diaspora within thought about the global, including studies of the Global South, have remained relatively peripheral, just as black and Africana studies have remained marginal areas of interest in southern studies.

The topic of Michelle Obama becomes all the more crucial for expanding and bridging dialogues in these areas in the new millennium when considering the complex significations and meanings of the South in her nationalization and globalization as an iconic public figure and in scripts of her family background and cultural history. From the recurrent references to connections in her family background to plantation slavery in South Carolina and Georgia to invocations of the South Side as an area in Chicago where she was raised, the concept of the South has been a central trope in constructing narratives of Michelle Obama in relation to race, class, gender, sexuality, and geographies from the urban North to the rural South, whose diasporas constitute her subjectivity. Furthermore, her status on the world stage underscores the indispensability of interpretive frameworks of black feminism and transnational feminism in my analysis.

Just as previous chapters have considered how figures such as Mary McLeod Bethune and Rosa Parks help to unsettle and expand conventional scripts of national femininity through significations as national mothers attached to them, in ways that have linked them to the concept of national family and platforms centering children, Michelle Obama has built on and expanded scripts of black womanhood in relation to this ideal in her primary self-representation as "mom-in-chief" within her husband's presidential establishment, given her priorities related to raising her daughters, Malia and Sasha, and political platforms prioritizing children in spearheading the Let's

Move! campaign developed to help fight childhood obesity. To be sure, the moniker has been interpreted by some feminists as regressive and reactionary given the levels on which it sanctions and prioritizes the domestic, maternal role traditionally associated with womanhood, which some critics also linked to the Obama administration's strategy to portray a softer side of Michelle Obama as First Lady to offset linkages of her to the "angry black woman" stereotype in the media, beginning on the campaign trail.

This moniker is more complicated than such dismissive readings suggest. In effect, mom-in-chief counters Michelle Obama's infamous labeling as her husband's "baby mama" by neoconservatives on Fox News in June 2008, a crude appropriation of a popular urban slang term used by black men to refer to the mothers of their children to whom they are not married, and that was loosely invoked by reactionaries on this television network to link the Obamas to pathological narratives of black poverty, womanhood, and family. It is a poignant moment that illustrates how, in the new millennium, *baby mama* has been mobilized as an epithet at the national level by reactionary politicians to pathologize black mothers in the continuum with previous ideological images, such as the mammy, matriarch, and proverbial welfare queen. Furthermore, the moniker *mom-in-chief* wittily signified and riffed on the masculinized and militarized role of the president as commander-in-chief by implying her role to be an equally important and valid complement to her husband's position, framing any familial and domestic responsibilities that she carries in the White House as a form of political leadership within her broader repertoire of responsibilities as First Lady in the East Wing. The maternal role through which she opted to primarily frame herself as First Lady, from her positioning in this area of the nation's White House, also holds crucial implications for the typical domestic roles and responsibilities of mothers throughout the nation, affirming her agency as a woman and a leader. Nancy Green's introduction as her human embodiment at the World's Columbian Exposition in Chicago in 1893, during the early years of the Aunt Jemima logo, a racial stereotype of black womanhood and ubiquitous national brand in American advertising, steeped in the mammy myth of the antebellum era, was radically counterposed in Michelle Obama, whose emergence in Chicago in the first decade of the twenty-first century as an iconic emblem of the nation was based on her role as First Lady. To be sure, the maternal model that she presented in her self-naming as mom-in-chief was a far cry from mammy in invoking the primacy of her relationship to her daughters, Malia and Sasha, and her advocacy for all mothers and children in this nation. It was worlds apart from mammy's obsequious investment in nurturing white babies and children.

In this chapter, I analyze the video *South Side Girls*, which first introduced Michelle Obama to a national audience at the Democratic National Convention (DNC) in Denver, Colorado, in 2008. I explore its framing of her family of origin, the Robinsons, as a representative national family and its emergent narrative of her as a quintessential model of national femininity, which is significant for placing blackness front and center in scripts within which black subjects have typically been marginalized or altogether excluded. Such scripts anticipated the public dialogues on Michelle Obama that surfaced in ensuing months, focused on her family roots linked to the South and the history of slavery, which have recurrently framed her family story as an emblematic African American story that also epitomizes the biracial character of the nation birthed in slavery, whose elaboration by Condoleezza Rice I discuss in the previous chapter. Concomitantly, within the vast body of visual materials related to Obama, including her public speeches, I revisit the speech that followed up this video, which reinforced the narrative of both the Robinsons and Obamas as model and representative American families and highlighted Michelle Obama's role as a mother, further countering ideological scripts of black maternity that had been invoked in relation to her on the campaign trail and anticipating her emphasis on children within her national platform and her intimate linkages to narratives relating her to motherhood and family. At the same time, in this speech, I acknowledge the limitations in premising her authorization to speak to a national audience on a heteronormative family model by invoking her roles as a sister, daughter, wife, and mother. Such cultural logics were limited where they exclude those subjects, from single women without children to black queer and trans women in this nation, whose lived realities do not conform to such traditional relational models, obscuring their legibility and legitimacy as citizens.

I go on to examine major writings by Michelle Obama that have articulated her primary political investments in advocating for children, beginning with her March 22, 2010, cover feature article in *Newsweek*, "Feed Your Children Well: My Fight against Childhood Obesity," which discusses the Let's Move! campaign.[21] I build on this discussion by examining her first book, *American Grown*, published in 2012, which further advances her national platform related to childhood obesity.[22] I conclude by examining her collaboration with the singer Beyoncé on this national campaign against childhood obesity to promote exercise through music and dance, which also centralized images of black women and girls in this campaign. In "'First Lady but Second Fiddle' or the Rise and Rejection of the Political Couple in the White House: 1933–Today," Pierre-Marie Loizeau observes, "The experience First Ladies have acquired through the years has set precedence and enhanced women's credibility on the political stage, though their power and influence remain limited given their contingency on marriage."[23] The political power of Michelle Obama is undeniable and was evident in polls in which she consistently outranked her husband in popularity, ongoing pressures that she has faced to run for president, and policy initiatives that she has spearheaded to fight childhood obesity. The ascendance of Michelle Obama to the role of First Lady posed a direct challenge to the dominant and deeply entrenched raced and gendered ideological narratives of femininity, motherhood, and beauty as being intrinsically white. Michelle Obama's status as the nation's first black First Lady not only further challenged the conventional notions of national femininity in the United States by inextricably linking it to black female subjectivity, but was also exceptional and groundbreaking in expanding and abstracting black women's influence in constituting national femininity to the status of First Lady. In her critically acclaimed 2018 bestselling memoir *Becoming*, Michelle Obama reveals that she was keenly aware of black women's complicated positioning in relation to national femininity in reflecting on how her status as the nation's first black First Lady othered her, made her vulnerable to racial stereotypes, and made her "worried that many Americans wouldn't see themselves reflected in me, or they wouldn't relate to my journey."[24] At the same time, her acknowledgment of the loss of privacy that becoming "a walking, talking symbol of the nation" entailed also acknowledges the challenges in negotiating her iconicity, but given her historic role, also provides the most compelling firsthand testament in history of black women's potential to embody national femininity.[25]

From the Michelle Obama Backlash at the *Daily Kos* to *South Side Girl*

The symbolic significance of the First Lady and her role in the White House in the national imagination has been imprinted by the prevailing white-centered elite and middle-class-oriented ideology of domesticity and femininity that crystallized during the nineteenth century in the United States.[26] As a black woman, Michelle Obama has expanded the definition of who the First Lady is, can, and should be. She also poses challenges to conventional conceptualizations of womanhood, femininity, marriage, motherhood, and beauty in the national mainstream. Her renunciation of her professional work to focus on her husband's campaign, mothering her girls, and public duties associated with this role, which linked her to the domestic space of the White House, in amplifying her platform and voice, enshrined her as a national leader and, in the process, challenged conventional feminist thinking about marriage and family. At the same time, criticism that she faced from mainstream feminists ran counter to the nuanced readings of her personal choices among black feminists, who acknowledged how they were shaped by her positioning on the basis of race, gender, and sexuality, readings that underscore the indispensability of black feminist theory for pondering Michelle Obama.

Citations of the U.S. South have been implicit and explicit in formulating raced (including racist) ideological narratives about Michelle Obama in both liberal and conservative political contexts, alongside uses of the South in narratives of authenticity and selfhood in her public construction since her emergence in the national arena during the presidential campaign. The expansive and egregious economy of visual and rhetorical narratives that have circulated about Michelle Obama in the public sphere bears the imprint and carries the heavy weight of southern history, including the residue of institutional racism linked to its systems of slavery and Jim Crow. While this kind of visual imagery and verbal propaganda was mainly leveled at President Barack Obama, much of it has routinely singled out Michelle Obama and lies in a continuum with stereotypical and racist images of the black body that have circulated in advertising and U.S. material culture since the late nineteenth century. Repeatedly, the bodies of the Obamas were accessible to forms of caricaturing and ridicule in the contemporary political arena in ways that seem to go well beyond conventional political satire and to cross the line into the realm of racist representation. Such contexts are essential for interpreting this political propaganda, particularly given the ideological continuities linking them to neonativist movements such as the Tea Party and the Birthers, which were also steeped in purist, nativist notions of American national identity that implicitly and explicitly constituted the most desirable American citizens as white, and concomitantly yielded scripts of American selfhood that alienated ethnic minorities, including blacks, within this nation's long history. They heralded the resurgence of white supremacy and white nationalism in the nation's contemporary political arena under the presidential leadership of Donald Trump.

Given the liberal political agenda of the Obamas and a political climate so profoundly imprinted by a southern ideological heritage, it was ironic but still not surprising that one of the most infamous images evoking the concept of the South in relation to Michelle Obama emerged in a liberal context. The blog the *Daily Kos* spurred outcry during the summer months of the 2008 presidential campaign when, to critique reactionary right-wing attacks on then-senator Barack Obama as a presidential candidate, it visually depicted his wife Michelle Obama wearing a sultry red backless evening dress that was torn as if it had been ripped off, while she is tied to a tree by a group of white Ku Klux Klansmen in a vivid colorful cartoon illustration whose title recalls historical romance: *Fear Mongering and Race-Baiting: Our New! Hi Tech! Southern Strategy (To Burn the Middle Class), Sponsored by the David Duke Fan Club* (figure 4.1).[27] The imaging evokes the Jezebel, a foundational stereotype of black womanhood that Patricia Hill Collins traces back to the antebellum era and that, as Tamura Lomax shows, also inflects representations of black women in the black church and black popular culture.[28] Four Klansmen dressed in white robes are visible in the illustration, and the hand of another, whose face is unseen, is visible holding a branding iron against her back, where the dress has been torn and as the flesh is irradiated by the light of the heat and fire and begins to sear. Their robes feature symbols such as the American flag and the Republican Party elephant. The words "Sponsored by the David Duke Fan Club" are visible in the lower right corner, and in the lower left corner, "One Citizen" is credited with creating the photoplay for the image. The *Daily Kos* illustration recasts forms of white nativism that have taken root in the new millennium and played a role in shaping raced and gendered responses to the Obamas in the contemporary public sphere, even as some of the older forms were resuscitated. It ultimately reinscribes the racial logic associated with the notorious southern strategy of the right wing, establishing foundations for the politics of "racial resentment" through which Jonathan Knuckey and Myung-hee Kim argue she was often evaluated as First Lady.[29]

I analyzed this illustration at length in a 2009 essay.[30] I mention it here briefly as one of the most salient illustrations of the reactionary South's impact in shaping racialist scripts of Michelle Obama in the nation's political arena, and a text to which the South-centered epistemologies propagated in her husband's political campaign signal the obverse in providing a narrative of gender and race that centers blackness in its script of American identity. In depicting reactionary narratives related to blackness under the guise of progressivism in the new millennium, this troubling image registers the South's

FIGURE 4.1 One Citizen, *Fear Mongering and Race-Baiting: Our New! Hi Tech! Southern Strategy (To Burn the Middle Class)*, Sponsored by the David Duke Fan Club, 2008.

lingering influence on the national political culture. It recollects the traumatizing "southern horrors" elaborated by Ida B. Wells, which linger in black historical and cultural memory, by visualizing the extremist violence and abuse of the black body in the South in the national imaginary. In hindsight, this image in the *Daily Kos* seems further ironic in light of the actual outcome in the election, which unsettled and sidelined the typical stronghold of the southern strategy in national politics.

The southern strategy, as riffed in the title of the *Daily Kos* image of Michelle Obama, emerged in the wake of the civil rights movement and shifted the political alignment across southern states to the Republican Party, invoking states' rights and engaging in race-baiting as a primary strategy for mobilizing white voters to ensure electoral victories for Republicans in the South, while marginalizing and disenfranchising black voters, who were overwhelmingly associated with the Democratic Party. In the 2008 presidential election, Democratic electoral vote victories for Obama in such conventionally Republican states as North Carolina, Virginia, and Florida were said by some political scientists to have ruptured the historical conservative voting patterns in the "solid South" and the long-standing southern strategy political agenda.[31] Even this breakthrough and moment of optimism did not fully anticipate the chronically divisive partisan strategies that shadowed Obama's presidency as a result of concerted Republican Party opposition to his policies, particularly in southern states, and Republican posturing as the "party of no." Such maneuverings escalated all the more in the wake of Donald Trump's election in 2016.

Another story that emerged on the Obama presidential campaign trail was equally embedded in southern history and revealed how southern racism from her roommate's mother shadowed Michelle Obama's rooming situation as a newly arrived freshman student at Princeton. Beyond the epistemologies of slavery in relation to which she has been represented in the media, it is a signal narrative that relates Michelle Obama to traces of Jim Crow legacies by illustrating an attempt to pathologize her as a young woman because of her family's origins on Chicago's South Side. In an April 13, 2008, *Atlanta Journal and Constitution* story by Brian Feagans, "Georgian Recalls Rooming with Michelle Obama," Alice Brown, the mother of a new Princeton student, Catherine Donnelly, confesses, "I was horrified" on learning that her daughter had been assigned a black roommate. Brown confronted the campus housing office and demanded to get her daughter's room changed when hearing that she had been housed with a young black woman from the South Side of Chicago, informing them, "We weren't used to living with black people—Catherine is from the South."[32]

According to the piece, Donnelly's "mother and grandmother filled her head with racist stereotypes, portraying African-Americans as prone to crime, uneducated and, at times, people to be feared." Similarly, the article notes that Brown had also been "raised to think that way." As it reports, "Her grandfather, a sheriff in the North Carolina mountains, bragged about running black visitors out of the county before nightfall. And Brown's parents held on to the n-word like a family heirloom."[33] In Donnelly's comments, she describes her amazement on seeing her former roommate, then Michelle Robinson, on television as the wife of a Democratic candidate running for the presidency and to hear of her outstanding achievements. She looks back to their time as roommates at Princeton and expresses regret about her family's racist reaction back then to this young black woman from Chicago.

On the day that Brown's daughter moved into the dormitory room, Brown's very phrasing in speaking to Princeton's housing office about her disapproval of the black roommate that her daughter had been assigned reflects a separatist view of the U.S. South as being synonymous with white subjectivity, logic that consigns blacks in the region to irrelevance and invisibility. Similarly, Brown's comments reveal deeply ingrained stereotypes of blackness, as well as of spaces identified with black culture, such as Chicago's South Side. That the effort to move her daughter was urgent and frantic is evident in the article's description of the overnight calling marathon in which Donnelly engaged with her own mother and a family friend to find a contact at the university who might facilitate a room change: "Donnelly called her mother, who in turn phoned the friend who had traveled with her to Princeton all those years ago. The friends had stayed up that night calling everyone they knew with a connection to the university, hoping to get Catherine moved. 'We thought this is so ironic,' Brown says. '[Obama] could be the first lady, and here we wanted to get my child out of her influence.'"[34]

It is much to Donnelly's and her mother's credit that, after all these years, they chose to come forward and be honest about the thinking in which they had been mired back then that pathologized black girls and families, and that their views about race relations have since become more enlightened. The story provides a concrete and sobering illustration of the continuing influence of segregationist logic in the early 1980s and confirms its far-reaching influence. In this case, southern racism bitterly surfaced over the prospect of a young white southern woman sharing living space and having social contact with a black woman from a working-class background in a campus dormitory. Its tentacles were evident in the attempt to alter housing arrangements at Princeton, an Ivy League university in the Northeast, a move that attempted to replicate in a northern context the racial separation associated with the South throughout its segregated history.[35] The episode poignantly illustrates the inhospitable and hostile climate for blacks and other minorities that was evident on some campuses in the post–civil rights era and that persists even now.

The reactionary and racist scripts of Obama that invoked the South make it all the more significant and subversive that South-related motifs subtended her fashioning as a raced and gendered subject in making her legible before the national body. Recurring references to her as a "South Side girl" in her introduction via video and in her speech at the DNC in Denver in 2008 were mobilized in portraying her family as nationally representative during the campaign while establishing foundations for her embodiment as an emblem of national femininity as First Lady. That this event introduced Obama to the nation through a biographic video and a speech in which she claimed central stage and a voice before a national audience for the first time makes it particularly useful to analyze through methods from literary and cultural studies.

The South Side is an area of Chicago predominantly black and working class and has been historically associated with industries in the city such as meat packing and steel mills. From the 1920s, the Great Migration from the rural South to destinations in Chicago fueled the expansion of the black demography in this area.[36] By the mid-twentieth century, Chicago's South Side emerged as the scene of a major artistic renaissance in areas such as literature and painting, alongside innovations in music such as jazz and blues. This area helped to give rise to an area called Bronzeville, along with its Black Belt. It increasingly became associated with crime and violence, including drugs and gangs, after World War II. The famous 1940 Supreme Court case *Hansberry v. Lee*, which involved the family of the writer Lorraine Hansberry, had addressed racially segregated housing politics in the Washington Park area on the South Side, and as blacks moved in, many of the immigrants who had resided there moved out, a pattern of *white flight* mirrored in Brown's effort to relocate her daughter on the Princeton campus.

Marcia Chatelain's 2015 study *South Side Girls: Growing Up in the Great Migration* is a pioneering contribution to historical studies of the Great Migration and black girlhood in foregrounding the voices and experiences of black girls in the early twentieth century up to the postwar period in contexts from social organizations to families who lived on the South Side of Chicago. Chatelain acknowledges Michelle Obama as a premier contemporary emblem of this subject position. While the episode concerning Michelle Obama's freshman roommate at Princeton is loaded with the more pejorative connotations that have been attached to the South Side of Chicago in the cultural imagination, the first Obama presidential campaign framed Michelle Obama's roots in this area of the city as an empowering asset and anticipated the complex narrative of black girlhood on Chicago's South Side that Chatelain presents in this scholarly study, beginning with *South Side Girl*, a short biographical video narrated by Marian Robinson, Michelle Obama's mother, to introduce her to a national audience on August 25, 2008, the second night of the DNC in Denver, Colorado.[37]

The video, which is six and a half minutes long, begins by slowly flashing a photograph of Robinson and her daughter, Michelle, as a small child, with close-up facial shots of them on a screen against a black backdrop, an image that emphasizes their close mother-daughter relationship. Describing her as "my baby," Robinson gives her daughter's birth date, January 17, 1964, a narrative that stresses Robinson's maternal connection and establishes the biographical orientation of the video. The title of the video pops up on the black backdrop and replaces this photograph.

Various photographs highlight images of Michelle Obama's brother, Craig; their father, Fraser C. Robinson III; and the apartment on the South Side of Chicago where the Robinson family lived and she grew up, along with an image of the water plant where her father worked. Interview commentary by Barack Obama and Craig Robinson describes Fraser Robinson, emphasizes Michelle Obama's closeness to her father, and links her to his values related to work, compassion, and community. In Barack Obama's words, Fraser Robinson was a "kind-hearted man who thought everybody should be treated with respect," qualities that Obama also sees in his wife. In her narration, Marian Robinson emphasizes Michelle Obama's lifelong commitment to serving the South Side by describing how much she and her husband believed in education and urged their children to return to serve their community after college. In Robinson's words, "All those years ago, we taught her to serve her community and that's what she came back and did."

The video incorporates cross-cutting as a technique to tell the story of how Michelle and Barack Obama met and went out on their first date. A black and white photo from this period featuring each of them is also included in this cross-cut sequence. The camera alternates between shots of Barack Obama, framed on the right side of the screen, while sitting at home in the formal dining room, and Michelle Obama, framed on the left side of the screen, against the backdrop of what also appears to be a home setting. One of Michelle Obama's law school mentors, Harvard law professor Charles Ogletree, reinforces Robinson's remarks by highlighting Michelle Obama's commitment to serving the South Side of Chicago.

South Side Girl emphasizes that work in a law firm was not right for Michelle Obama because of her passionate commitment to community service. A medley of voices of people who have collaborated with Michelle Obama or worked with her on her former jobs and witnessed firsthand her continuing commitments to outreach to young people and public service, along with her ability to motivate others, including Yvonne Davila from Mayor Richard Daley's office and Travis Rejman and Jobi Petersen Gates from Public Allies, offers testimonies about Michelle Obama's work ethic. In Craig Robinson's 2010 basketball-themed memoir, *A Game of Character: A Family Journey from Chicago's Southside to the Ivy League and Beyond*, which builds on and reinforces his introduction of his sister at this historic event, he offers comments that accord with such colleague portraits in emphasizing that "Whatever the competition was, if I was good at it, nine times out of ten, Michelle LaVaughn Robinson was better. She could do just about everything and anything at the level of mastery without appearing to have to try. And yet she coupled talent with a ferocious work ethic."[38]

South Side Girl describes Michelle Obama's creation of a community service center at the University of Chicago, further emphasizing her outreach in her community in Chicago. Toward the end, one photo highlighted in the video features Michelle Obama standing against the backdrop of an American flag. Marian Robinson comments, "Michelle has been like a mom to so many people over the years," as the video explains how Michelle Obama, like many other women, has faced the typical challenges in negotiating her roles as a worker and a mother. Her comments also emphasize Obama's strengths as a mother to her daughters, Malia and Sasha. In effect, her mother's comments begin to consolidate the portrait of Michelle Obama as a national mother and establish foundations to frame her in relation to notions of national femininity.

Robinson goes on to say, "I hope America gets to know the girl we raised and the woman she became" and describes her daughter as "the most remarkable person I know." Visually, the video highlights several photographs of the Robinson family as a foursome, featuring Craig and Michelle as children with their parents, along with photographs of Michelle Obama, her daughters, and the girls' grandmother Marian Robinson, emphasizing their bonds as females across three generations. The narrative in the film fundamentally describes Michelle Obama as a "daddy's girl" who shares her father's values about family, education, compassion, problem solving, and community outreach, qualities that she wishes to share with the American people. *South Side Girl* culminates with a visibly larger shot of the same photo of Robinson and her daughter, Michelle, that introduces the video, which thus unfolds as a circular narrative and ends where it begins.

The video frames Michelle Obama in relation to her roles as a daughter, sister, wife, and mother. "South Side" recurs as a sound bite in this video, just as the words "came back" are repeated by her mother and others in describing Michelle Obama's devoted relationship to the area and return home to work there after college. It is notable that an early photo features the Robinsons' apartment. Numerous biographical profiles of Michelle Obama, particularly those invested in tracking her journey to the White House, have not only acknowledged her upbringing on the South Side but have also mentioned the spatial constraints in the small apartment in which she grew up, where space was so limited that the living room had to be divided by a separator and made into improvised bedrooms for her and her brother, conditions referenced by the *Daily Kos* in the article accompanying this image. The video links Michelle Obama with a stable and solid family background and depicts her through its narratives, visual interviews, and photographs as the product of a two-parent home, the kind that mirrors the structure of what is typically imagined as normative for the American family.

Images of the Robinsons as an African American family whose archive of vintage photos indicates their deep roots in the United States also visually offset anxieties in some sectors about Barack Obama as the product of a white mother and a Kenyan father, along with his degree of black authenticity, given his mixed-race background. Similarly, the photo featuring Michelle Obama in front of the American flag is a visual testament to her patriotism and offsets her depiction as anti-American, which stemmed from the controversial comments she had famously made on February 18, 2009, about being proud of her country for the first time in her adult life.[39] This video narrative presents Michelle Obama as a model woman and unsettles the typical pathologies linked to the South Side of Chicago by describing it as a place where stable, loving black families exist who are capable of raising successful children like Craig and Michelle. Similarly, it reveals the existence of devoted black mothers such as Marian Robinson, in effect further decoupling the South Side from pathology and foregrounding an African American woman who was a stay-at-home mother raising her children with a hard-working husband in a nuclear family.

The 2006 book of essays *The Audacity of Hope: Thoughts on Reclaiming the American Dream* is just one of the numerous public contexts in which Barack Obama has acknowledged his awe over how much Michelle Obama's traditional nuclear family model, while African American, reminded him of iconic family models that have been immortalized in 1950s television shows such as *Leave It to Beaver*, which are now remembered nostalgically.[40] Similarly, Craig Robinson's several references in *Game of Character* to his family as the "Southside Family Robinson" riffs on the popular and beloved castaway family in Johann David Wyss's classic 1812 novel, *The Swiss Family Robinson*, by invoking the distinct experiences and perspectives that have influenced their lives on the city's South Side, encoding his family in relation to familiar adventure narratives of family that are known and beloved in literature, and reconsolidating its linkages to the motif of the South Side in the public consciousness.

The video's invocation of the word *girl* echoes the term *home girl* and frames Michelle Obama as the byproduct of a stable family as much as it constructs an image of her as down-to-earth and in touch with everyday people as a woman, as her father had been as a man. Furthermore, the mention of her as a "girl" highlights light and youthful images and offsets media images of her as an "angry black woman" and a revolutionary. This revolutionary image was epitomized in the now infamous satirical cartoon of her on the July 21, 2008, cover of the *New Yorker*, in which she wears combat boots and a bullet strap, an afro à la Angela Davis's iconic hairstyle during the 1970s, and totes an AK-47, portrayed as the stereotypical black nationalist revolutionary. In the image, she bumps fists with her husband, who is garbed in the white robe and sandals of a traditional Muslim. They are flanked by a portrait over the mantle featuring the infamous al-Qaeda leader Osama bin Laden.[41]

The *South Side Girl* video positions Fraser Robinson, her father, who is a black man, as the primary source of the values that have influenced Michelle Obama in raising her daughters and on which she hopes to draw in working with the American people. In narrating the video, Marian Robinson frames her daughter as a quintessential mother not only to her daughters, but also in contexts such as mentoring relations with co-workers and in the community. The video highlights as its centerpiece a narrative about the committed and continuing work of Michelle Obama on the South Side of Chicago to outline a model of what her public outreach would look like as First Lady, framing her community work in the area as an inspiration and example for all Americans, as much as it presents the Robinsons as a family deeply committed to service.

The emphasis on her birth and upbringing in a family that lived on the South Side of Chicago and had long been committed to public service in this area, supported by the labor of a hard-working father, is a portal to the larger narrative that links her family background to the history of the Great Migration and plantation slavery in the U.S. South. Historically, black southern migrants helped swell the population of the Chicago South Side and shape its black culture. At the convention, this narrative of Michelle Obama was instrumental in signifying her family of origin—the Robinsons—as a *representative* American family and demonstrates how America is fundamentally "one nation," in effect aligning them with the overarching theme of that evening's program at the convention. This is a narrative that the story of her cross-racial heritage rooted in slavery would further ground and reinforce in the coming months.

Michelle Obama's speech at the convention the night that *South Side Girl* premiered, a moment that allows us to analyze the manifestations of her public voice as she addressed the nation for the first time, echoes the video in primarily framing the South Side as her place of origin. A passage toward the beginning of this speech, before she comes to the main content of her message, includes a range of parallel sentences in which she describes herself in relation to her various roles in the context of her own family as a sister, wife, mother, and daughter, an introduction that closely parallels the visual narrative in *South Side Girl*.

> I come here tonight as a sister, blessed with a brother who is my mentor, my protector, and my lifelong friend.
>
> I come here as a wife who loves my husband and believes he will be an extraordinary president.
>
> I come here as a mom whose girls are the heart of my heart and the center of my world—they're the first thing I think about when I wake up in the morning, and the last thing I think about when I go to bed at night. Their future—and all our children's future—is my stake in this election.
>
> And I come here as a daughter—raised on the South Side of Chicago by a father who was a blue collar city worker, and a mother who stayed at home with my brother and me. My mother's love has always been a sustaining force for our family, and one of my greatest joys is seeing her integrity, her compassion, and her intelligence reflected in my own daughters.[42]

Michelle Obama highlights these various roles to stress her commonality with other Americans, roles that authorize her to speak in the public sphere about the range of issues she cares about and that also affect their lives, while also linking children in and beyond her family to the nation's fate and future. "I come here" is a recurring phrase, which evokes the "I come" that punctuates the ending of every verse of the classic Christian hymn by Charlotte Elliott, "Just as I Am"(1835): "Oh Lamb of God I come, I come." It is a phrasing that emphasizes her individualism, initiative, and sincerity in addressing her audience, as well as her presence. Moreover, the repetitive *I*'s that inflect these phrases as the speech begins underscore her status as a subject apart from the iconic public persona embodied in her husband, as a politician who should be reckoned with on her own terms, in light of her distinct personal identity and background, while establishing her voice in the nation's public sphere. When we consider that she might have substituted the word "speak" for "come," its use becomes all the more significant, for it stresses her humility and, at a performative level, suggests the primacy of action over speech in her mind.

The phrase *I come* also establishes the rhythm and pattern of repetition that emerges later on in the speech in the several places, where Michelle Obama overviews her husband's mission and the significance of his contributions, including his work on the South Side: "It's what he did all those years ago, on the streets of Chicago, setting up job training to get people back to work and afterschool programs to keep kids safe—working block by block to help people lift up their families." The repetition of the phrase "It's what" throws these contributions into bold relief and makes them more memorable. In general, the simple and straightforward sentences that punctuate this speech also convey Michelle Obama as a straight talker and as the kind of person with whom average Americans, many of whom are working class and come from families structured like her own, can identify, as does the urban, working-class geography of the South Side, which she cites at its outset, seem designed to do. The video pinpoints and frames Michelle Obama primarily in relation to place.

The recurrent references to the South Side as a sound bite in describing Michelle Obama in the national arena link her to the *local* and saliently emphasize the profound effect of space alongside gender in constructing her identity, as much as they suggest the significance of geography in constructing African American and African diasporic identity. At the same time, it asserts her legitimacy as a representative American woman despite the social and cultural particularity associated with Chicago's South Side, unsettling the conventional disarticulations of blackness from notions of universality and representations of national identity, which have typically been linked to white normativity, along with stereotypes of the area. It anticipated and heralded a broader space for coming to voice in the public sphere than had been possible before for categories that have been marginal and excluded. At the same time, authorizing herself to speak to the American public primarily through the narrow, heterosexist, and nuclear family kinship networks that she outlines (i.e., sister, wife, mother, daughter) risked alienating and silencing a host of citizens in the nation, from single, childless women to LGBTQ communities.

In the national arena, the recurring narratives that make the area synonymous with who she is have in effect made Michelle Obama a reigning symbol of the South Side of Chicago, as they have positioned her as one of the nation's foremost ambassadors for the area alongside her husband. At the same time, the term mediated her framing as a representative American woman on the national stage and introduced her as a premier model of national femininity.

At a rhetorical level, this speech, more than any prior one, established her alignments with the values of the U.S. mainstream and universal identification with it as a woman, increasing her legibility, legitimacy, and force as a national feminine icon. It has organically shaped the dominant narratives related to her as a wife and mother and served as a foundation for scripts of Michelle Obama that have been developed as First Lady.

As First Lady, the official narratives about Michelle Obama and her public work, such as her profile on the website of the White House, also highlighted her origins on the South Side of Chicago.[43] In numerous interviews, she frequently emphasized her roots on the South Side to emphasize the barriers she surmounted and to suggest that her achievements are possible for other girls and women. For instance, in an October 2011 interview in *Essence*, she remarks, "My story to young people around this country and around the world is, Don't look at me as the First Lady first; look at me as Michelle Obama, a girl who grew up on the South Side of Chicago. Because I was there, and this is attainable."[44] Talk show host Oprah Winfrey, who has maintained a long-standing television and media production base in Chicago, has linked Michelle Obama's perception of the White House as the "people's house" and effort to make it more open and accessible to the public to the deep sense of family, community, and connectedness with everyday people that the First Lady gained through an upbringing on the South Side.[45] Similarly, André Leon Talley has described the First Lady by remarking that "no doubt this attitude owes a lot to the sense of community she drank in as she grew up in a modest house on the South side of Chicago, where her parents carved a bedroom out of the living room for her and her brother, Craig Robinson, to share."[46] Such interviews have only reinforced the salient emphasis on the South Side that the video *South Side Girl* and her "One Nation" speech established, pointing to the significance of space in constructing her identity as a woman.

In making her debut before a national audience at the DNC in 2008, Michelle Obama's reflections are similarly patronymic in underscoring the influence of her father on her values and in emphasizing her linkage to a South in the United States, if only in a symbolic sense through Chicago's South Side, an area that mirrors the U.S. South in being frequently linked to poverty and struggle in the African American experience. The linkages of Michelle Obama to the South Side in describing her home and family origins parallel and replay all the conventional metaphors that signify the region of the South as a home for African Americans in the United States. That historically, plantation slavery was based in the South and the vast majority of slaves were imported through the region, has also shaped the view of the region as the primary linkage to Africa for blacks in the United States and constituted its associations with notions of black authenticity and black selfhood. The history of the slave experience in the South has linked the region inextricably to black subjectivity in the United States and constituted a narrative of the region as a symbolic black home in this nation. In the African American context, invoking southern roots has frequently served as a strategy for signaling a solid grounding in values related to family, religion, tradition, and hard work. Numerous black politicians positioned on the political spectrum from liberal to conservative have invoked a southern background for self-representation in the national arena.

As is the case with Condoleezza Rice, such patronymic references to the South in constructing Michelle Obama are limited to the extent that they are grounded in associations of the South with notions of African American authenticity and rhetorically function as a device for associating African Americans with mainstream American values. Such invocations of the South as a region in the public sphere of politics reveal its continuing ideological serviceability in national and global contexts for shaping notions of identity in American and African American contexts, including models of black femininity. At the same time, Michelle Obama's scripts are subversive and even revolutionary in challenging stereotypes of black womanhood, including pathologies of the black maternal body, unsettling such ideologies through her self-proclaimed title as mom-in-chief, emerging as a national model of American selfhood in her role as First Lady, while constituting the Obamas as a representative American family. Still, it is important to recognize the weighty limitations in such representations. In examining this historic speech, it is crucial to ask what is at stake in preconditioning the authorization to come to voice and serve as a representative citizen on the ability to invoke highly conventional models of family and affective kinships rooted in a traditional marriage and nuclear family model, along with fixed notions of home. The limits become clear and are starkly thrown into relief given the implications for black queer and trans subjects, frequently shadowed by alienation from the family intimacies highlighted within her narratives, and alienated from home, sometimes to the point of homelessness, circumstances that concomitantly condition their invisibility, along with exclusion from American citizenship and democracy. It is just as important to recognize the reactionary dimensions of the Obama administration when discussing Michelle Obama. Eric Cheyfitz's insights suggest the importance of counterbalancing her profound cultural significance with a recognition of the Obama administration's support of neoliberal policies that advanced militarization and corporate interests.[47]

"Feed Your Children Well"

The routine abuses of blacks as laborers in the predominantly agrarian economy of southern plantation slavery and their continuing economic exploitation after Emancipation within the region's rural sharecropping economy, in which black families were sometimes victimized by racial violence, terror, brutality, intimidation, and lynching to help ensure their continued subjection within this abusive system, constituted black cultural memories that link trauma to farming, despite the limited opportunities that it created for black land acquisition and accessibility to food. During the late nineteenth and twentieth centuries, the federal Homestead Acts overwhelmingly privileged whites and helped to institutionalize the long-standing systematized inequities in the farming industry, which have limited the access of blacks and other minorities to land. While the government made resources available to blacks to enable their participation in agriculture, they were systematically marginalized and disenfranchised within this economy. Black farmers have been disadvantaged through discriminatory federal practices that have limited their equal access to governmental loans and to adequate compensation for farmers in the wake of disasters. Policies of the U.S. Department of Agriculture (USDA) that have primarily benefited white farmers led black farmers to the historic class action suit against the agency in the 1999 *Pigford v. Glickman* case, which challenged their discriminatory practices in allocating loans and assistance. The 2012 Farm Bill was proposed to address persisting inequities in farming.[48]

Blacks have remained marginalized within the growing national food movement, a health and nutrition movement that has primarily focused on outreach to white, educated, elite and middle-class consumers, as manifested from Food Network and Cooking Channel television networks to local farmers' markets. Increasingly, the food justice movement has addressed issues such as persisting food deserts in urban areas, shorn of grocery stores that sell fresh fruits and vegetables and that are instead occupied by convenience stores selling junk foods that lack nutritional value, issues clarified by Rashad Shabazz in *Spatializing Blackness: Architectures of Confinement and Black Masculinity in Chicago*.[49] More efforts are also now being made by black grassroots activists to engage black communities in farming and to redress their alienation from this industry in light of internalized messages that dissociate them from farming and reinforce public perceptions primarily linking the practice to whiteness and rurality and blackness to urban contexts.

Within this growing movement, black women scholars and activists have increasingly established their voices in public dialogues related to food in the effort to promote nutritious eating, including practices such as vegetarianism and veganism. For example, Amie Breeze Harper does public outreach to promote literacy related to vegan diets, including ones for groups ranging from pregnant women to babies and children, to raise critical awareness related to veganism and the politics of race, class, gender, and sexuality. Her signal critical volume, *Sistah Vegan: Black Female Vegans Speak on Food, Identity, Health, and Society*, brings together an ensemble of critical voices and makes a meaningful contribution through its analytical focus on vegan food practices, race, and black female subjectivity.[50] She relates critical race studies, including a critical study of whiteness, to cultural geography and vegan food practices typically linked to white subjectivity, logic that even prevails within the context of the progressive social movement and that unsettles the conventional perceptions of veganism as being inclusive. Her ideas for veganism in the food practices of black mothers and children, including her outlining of strategies for vegan-centered pregnancies and childrearing, which draw on her life and work as a mother, contribute to black feminist discourses and hold crucial implications for areas such as black women's health. They are particularly interesting in relation to national agendas on children's nutrition that have been developed by Michelle Obama.

Michelle Obama's Let's Move! campaign, the signature initiative designed to fight childhood obesity that she introduced as First Lady, reflects the long-standing investments of black women political leaders in prioritizing agendas related to children. The campaign also reflects the visceral understanding of the challenges that families can face in making healthy eating choices that she gained through her experiences as a mother raising two daughters, Malia and Sasha. Yet it is important to frame this public health campaign as an outgrowth and extension of Obama's professional work at the University of Chicago Medical Center, as vice president for community and external affairs, where her job had entailed diversity and community relations, as well as helping establish the South Side Health Collaborative to find care for patients without sufficient support. Indeed, studying this work helps us to recognize how her agendas as First Lady built on her professional work in health administration. Writings by the First Lady, along with interviews, speeches, and videos, were a primary tool for circulating information about this campaign and publicly promoting it.

On March 22, 2010, Obama published an article in *Newsweek* as part of a cover story, "Feed Your Children Well." The title recollects and seems to play on the title and lyric content of a 1970 country folk song by Crosby, Stills, and Nash, "Teach Your Children," which includes the line "Teach your children well."[51] In the piece, which complements Obama's public outreach to promote the campaign, she pitches her message primarily to parents, schools, and communities to redress the chronic apathy about obesity. It positions her as the foremost advocate for the nation's children on this issue because "Kids don't impact policy," even as one of her goals is to help children make healthier choices related to food and exercise.

Obama links this epidemic to lifestyle changes in recent years that have minimized the exercise and recess time for students in schools, along with conveniences such as cars and buses that cut down their walking time, while the current norm is for them to spend many sedentary hours with TVs, videogames, and the internet as their parents spend more time working, have less time for family meals, and often allow them to eat fast food for convenience. As the article begins, its repetition of the word *we've* throughout the first paragraph accords the piece an oral quality and establishes intimacy with her audience to acknowledge what most people hear and know within their shared collective understanding of the issue of childhood obesity, including statistics, its effects, and the health and economic risks related to it. The stated goal is to give parents more "tools" to encourage "manageable changes" and to promote more nutritious menus and more physical activity in schools.[52]

Her goal in pursuing the initiative designed to promote the health and well-being of children is to help them live long, successful, and productive lives that will allow them to see their grandchildren grow up, and possibly their great-grandchildren. The First Lady's core message in this piece links children to the future, a theme that situates it in the continuum with the platforms of black women civil rights leaders such as Bethune and Parks. The World Health Organization's release of an October 2017 report indicating that rates of obesity in children and teens are now ten times higher than they were forty years ago further confirms the urgency of the initiative that Obama spearheaded during her years as First Lady, suggests the epidemic proportions of the problem, and reveals its continuing consequences and global reach.[53] Julie Hirschfeld Davis's claim that Michelle Obama "spent years in the White House staying away from politics" until finally using her platform to campaign against Donald

Trump in 2016 belies Obama's continuing commitment to making a difference through causes that she championed such as Let's Move![54]

Black women's occupations as cooks within plantation households and as laborers during slavery linked them to food preparation. Within the mythology of antebellum plantation ideology, their intimate relationship to food was related to their nurturing capacity. The mammy stereotype was telling in its serviceability as an emblem of black women's roles as caretakers for children of the master class, on the one hand, and of their work as cooks on the other. Doris Witt has critically examined how the essentialist linkage of black women's bodies to food, including this stereotype's manifestations in Aunt Jemima as an advertising trademark, is rooted in the exploitation of black women's bodies during slavery and examined how such stereotypes of black women's bodies have been serviceable in acculturating a range racial and ethnic identities in this nation since the late nineteenth century.[55]

As Toni Tipton-Martin points out in *The Jemima Code: Two Centuries of African American Cookbooks*, a study that chronicles black women's production of cookbooks spanning two centuries, as far back as the era of antebellum slavery, the ubiquitous and reductive Aunt Jemima stereotype rooted in the mammy, which has been associated with a natural and instinctive cooking aptitude, has routinely obscured black women's profound historical role in shaping cuisine in the nation, including its southern varieties.[56] Situating Michelle Obama's first book, *American Grown: The Story of the White House Kitchen Garden and Gardens across America*, in relation to this vast body of cookbooks helps us recognize how it builds on this culinary archive and throws into relief its subversion of conventional raced, sexed, and gendered ideologies, including the Aunt Jemima figure, that essentially relate black women to food. Obama's positioning as a wife and mother whose experiences with addressing the nutritional needs and protecting the health and well-being of her own children help to inspire and catalyze her national agenda related to the nation's children collectively, the obverse of the stereotypical hyperembodied, voiceless, and asexual mammies who nurture white children while neglecting their own. In "Michelle Obama, Mom-in-Chief: The Racialized Rhetorical Contexts of Maternity," Sara Hayden suggests the importance of recognizing the multiple levels on which "maternal performances" were scripted in relation to Obama, ranging from intensive mothering associated with whiteness to other mothering practices, which Patricia Hill Collins has associated with women in black communities, underscoring how they worked to challenge stereotypes of black women such as the mammy and the matriarch.[57] Significantly,

Hayden notes how Obama related her policy initiatives in terms of her concern for the nation's children and was in part inspired to launch Let's Move! because of a physician's concern about her daughter's weight.[58]

As Stephanie Houston Grey makes clear in "Contesting the Fat Citizen: Michelle Obama and the Body Politics of *The Biggest Loser*," Obama's advocacy platform threw heated contestations into relief surrounding questions of the national body: "The iconic status of the First Lady's body, particularly her capacity to represent a synecdoche for the national body, brought her into conflict with the visual politics of US citizens' complex relationship with food and body size."[59] By contributing to this dialogue and advocating for the nation's children from her standpoint as First Lady, she occupied one of the most powerful and visible political platforms ever held by a black woman in history. It framed her as an empowered emblem of black womanhood and as a representative voice for mothers in the nation. Her role as First Lady is the site on which she emerges as a premier model of national femininity and national motherhood in the twenty-first century. In this sense, she transcended the national abjection associated with commodified images of black femininity, such as the mammy, despite lingering raced, sexed, and gendered stereotypes.

Obama's *American Grown* amplifies the message of her *Newsweek* essay by offering a book-length dialogue on her major project as First Lady, designed to address childhood obesity by promoting healthier eating, including reflections on establishing and nurturing a White House kitchen garden and its relation to her launching of the Let's Move! initiative. Significantly, in addition to her husband and daughter, and all who have taught about how food affects health, she dedicates this book in part to "our nation's children, who deserve to grow up healthy and strong and have every chance to pursue their dreams." Michelle Obama begins this book with reflections on her experiences as a child growing up on the South Side of Chicago, where her father had worked on a vegetable truck as a youth and where her mother's family had a plot in the nearby victory garden, community gardens that proliferated in Chicago during the World War II era.

In chronicling this all but forgotten history of times gone by, and recollecting an era in which children were expected to eat their vegetables, the book assumes a more didactic tone. She recalls growing up in a home in which she had daily family meals that incorporated fruits and vegetables, as well as the experience of recess at school and playing outside at home. They serve as background for thinking about the contemporary era, in which parents face far more frenzied daily schedules and demands, recess is not the norm in schools, children do not play outside as frequently because of safety concerns, and videogames have become a popular pastime for them.

Michelle Obama frames this initiative in relation to the long history of planting gardens on White House grounds, from the days of early presidents such as John Adams and Thomas Jefferson. The location of the garden on the South Lawn of the White House punctuates the litany of South metaphors that paved Michelle Obama's journey to the White House on the campaign trail. Against the backdrop of the historical lineage of Michelle Obama rooted in plantation slavery, along with the historical role of slaves in building the White House and serving as some of its earliest laborers, the garden project she orchestrates on its landscape as the nation's first black First Lady is subversive and oppositional in centralizing a black woman subject linked to these painful histories, in redesigning and repurposing portions of the White House's geographic terrain for an agricultural project to promote the health and well-being of all the nation's children. The weight of this past is evident when Obama remarks that during the groundbreaking ceremony for the garden with a group of fifth graders, she had "scooped up layers of history."[60]

According to the First Lady, she wrote the book with the goal of starting a national conversation about the childhood obesity crisis and to offer concrete strategies for addressing it. The garden was planted on the first day of spring, within the first two months of her arrival at the White House, and is linked to her concerns about childhood obesity, the issue about which she advocated for the most comprehensive and sustained period while her husband was in office. The personal narrative acknowledges the rarity of gardening on the South Side of Chicago and, as did her "South Side Girl" speech at the DNC in 2008, links her to nurturing parents and frames the South Side as a site of cultural dynamism, where her core values were instilled, including her understanding of the effects of fresh fruits and vegetables on nutrition. As Joanne M. Braxton has noted, black women's autobiographical writings are evident in contexts such as letters and journals, which suggests the value in analyzing such textual layers as manifestations of this genre.[61] Obama's hope is to tell the story of how the White House kitchen garden, along with many others, have begun "to grow a healthier nation."[62]

A key metaphor that emerges in her reflections suggests that the potential of every seed planted in gardens to become extraordinary is akin to that of every child. Michelle Obama emphasizes that just as the White House is "the people's house," the White House kitchen garden is "the people's garden," which reveals her investments in underlining the openness of the nation's most visible national and symbolic architecture and geography as being inherently democratic, welcoming, and inclusive of all members of the nation's diverse citizenry. She clarifies the project's educative purpose for children in promoting their knowledge about nutrition by providing hands-on work in gardening and sharing meals, but she also explains the social outreach function of the garden through contributions to food pantries for the homeless. In Terre Ryan's discussion of *American Grown*, she observes, "When speaking of public health, Obama typically speaks as National Mom, an advocate for the well-being of American children, and as Everymom, a busy mother who understands how the challenges of managing work and family obligations sometimes play out on the kitchen table."[63] She observes that this posture as a National Mom emphasizing family and children allowed Obama to build on her past work as a professional in public health, without appearing to challenge the traditional strictures placed on the First Lady. Ryan's analysis, which argues that Obama combined Republican postures of motherhood with what Nina Eliasoph describes as "public Momism," terminology that some mothers use to address activist concerns in public sphere rhetoric, reveals Obama's strategic organization of the book. She emphasizes its heterogeneity, in using gardening as a foundation for engaging the political concerns further along in the book, but in a way that would not be off-putting or overly didactic, so that it is "an activist text that does not look like one" and a text that is "nonthreatening because these arguments are strategically placed among disarming photos, recipes and brief stories."[64]

While Obama is the primary author whose narrative voice grounds and runs through it from beginning to end, the book's investments in fostering a democratic and inclusive vision of the White House and the nation more broadly are mirrored in its dialogism, from highlighting the White House kitchen garden as a collaborative effort and quoting from various members of its team to incorporating short essays throughout the book about model community gardens across the nation. The book's sections, arranged into headings invoking the four seasons, beginning with spring, point to the rhythms and cycles of planting and harvesting.

At the same time, like the South Side motifs, they mirror motifs in African American literary history, recollecting the structure of classic novels in African American literature, such as Nobel laureate Toni Morrison's *The Bluest Eye*, which was groundbreaking in telling the story from the perspective of a black girl and foregrounding black girls' and women's subject positions in its strategies of characterization and prioritization of their narrative voices.

American Grown echoes this classic novel's organization around seasons and motifs invoking nature, beginning with the opening line mentioning the marigolds that failed to bloom and the thematic emphasis on family. The Obama family embodies a healthy model of black family and its greatest possibilities, as opposed to the dysfunctional and abusive model of the Breedloves, which has been so typically stereotyped and pathologized as a byproduct of poverty and American racism. While Hayden acknowledges the limitations in Obama's focus on family that the First Lady consistently emphasized, she argues that "Obama's familial rhetoric circulated through a multifaceted set of contexts and mothering rhetorics" and does not "restrict women (and others) to a limited form of citizenship," emphasizing that we need to recognize "the complicated, messy and mulilayered contexts within which Obama's rhetoric circulated and participated."[65] We can draw on the insights of Cheyfitz to throw into relief how her policy initiative against obesity obscures obesity's linkages to inequality. Its limitations and contradictions become evident when recognizing the failings of the Obama administration to design concrete policies that address the issue of poverty, or even acknowledge it openly in political dialogues.[66]

American Grown's recipes provide its audience with concrete ideas for making dishes that incorporate vegetables and fruits cultivated in the garden and lend the book a pastiche quality. This quality reinforced the work at the level of policy that Obama was working to achieve at the national level, beginning with her advocacy for the inaugural task force on childhood obesity. Her signature achievement as First Lady and the primary policy initiative that Obama spearheaded was revamping the nation's school lunch program, and effecting the passage of the Healthy, Hunger-Free Kids Act in 2010, which mandated stricter regulations on vending machines and the choices available in school lunches. The backlash came mainly from panicked food producers, the School Nutrition Association, farm states concerned about losing money, and Republicans who framed it as a manifestation of excessive government intrusion. Its lasting effects have been more whole grain foods, along with fruits and vegetables; food assistance for mothers and children in poverty; and more transparency about nutritional content in food labeling.[67]

The foundations for the collaborative and dialogic aspects of Obama's Let's Move! campaign, designed to promote the project, were importantly anticipated and heralded by the 2011 song and video "Move Your Body," by Beyoncé, the iconic singer from Houston, who, by the time of its release, had increasingly become known as the world's greatest entertainer.[68] She initially became famous as the lead singer of the female singing group Destiny's Child. Her serenade of the Obamas at the historic 2009 inauguration expanded foundations for her friendship with the First Lady, a relationship that the media has acknowledged periodically. The moment heralded Beyoncé's increasing engagement with national political issues in a way that has only become more assertive, influential, and pronounced over the past decade, as evidenced in her more recent projects such as *Lemonade*. Significantly, Beyoncé was the foremost celebrity advocate for the Let's Move! campaign, and her release of "Move Your Body," a remix of the tune "Get Me Bodied," from her 2006 album, helped popularize it. The content of the video showcased the singer leading a routine amid an energetic group of youth dancing in a cafeteria setting and was designed to encourage healthful food choices and exercise.

The performance recollects the dynamism and precise choreography of her music videos. At the same time, it echoes the infectious empowerment anthems that have been a cornerstone of her artistry since her days in Destiny's Child and have recurrently been pitched at girls and women throughout her career. "Run the World (Girls)," a song released the same year as "Move Your Body," is a paean to girls throughout the global context, reflecting Beyoncé's emerging feminist sensibility and anticipating the "Bey feminism" that she has increasingly popularized though her brand, which has been contrasted with conventional models of black feminism for simultaneously embracing marriage, motherhood, and sexuality. This integrative perspective resonates with Riché Daniel-Barnes's critical work, which challenges disarticulations of black womanhood from marriage and family in studies that center whiteness by examining middle- and upper-class black women who are stay-at-home moms and their strategies for juggling competing demands in ways that simultaneously moor them in relation to serving black communities and belie conventional nuclear family trends in the United States, while providing counternarratives to earlier generations of black women who described marriage as oppressive. Such cultural frameworks are indispensable for thinking about Michelle Obama's invocations of marriage, motherhood, and family as sources of her empowerment as a woman.

A diverse group of boys and girls is featured in "Move Your Body," underscoring Let's Move! as a rallying call for all American youth to get active and healthy. Its composition mirrors narratives of other black women public figures examined in this study who have centered youth within their political platforms. Maternity has been central in constituting Michelle Obama's iconicity in the national arena. More to the point, her advocacy for this project is steeped in her symbolic capital as the nation's First Lady, its most visible and vocal mother. Let's Move! fully actualizes and nationalizes her role as mom-in-chief, disrupting images of black women's pathologization in relation to maternity, including ideological tropes that proliferated throughout the final decades of the twentieth century, from the matriarch to the welfare queen. It is a project that constitutes her as a representative mother and prominent advocate and spokesperson for the nation's children as a collective. Within it, they are constituted as a barometer of the nation's health, whose fate is inextricably linked to the nation's well-being and survival. Similarly, as a mother, Beyoncé's projects have increasingly challenged and rewritten scripts of the black maternal body while constituting iconic models of motherhood that embody her as empowered and grounded within a unified family. Indeed, this book ends by describing Beyoncé as a figure in popular culture who has increasingly expanded her political voice and platform through her song lyricism and performances.

"Almost Like a Wedding": National Rebirth and Renewal and a New National Family

Acknowledging reactionary southern ideologies is indispensable as a backdrop for reading egregious raced, sexed, classed, and gendered representations of First Lady Michelle Obama that proliferated during her husband's tenure as president. To underscore her instrumentality in subverting racialist narratives of national femininity premised on white womanhood and in beginning to expand the prevailing models of national femininity and national family, I want to conclude my discussion by momentarily returning to the most ubiquitous and infamous texts in American and southern literary history and cinema that propagated white supremacist and nativist ideology to script American selfhood early in the twentieth century. In doing so, I aim to emphasize how assertively Michelle Obama and her family embodied a counternarrative to representations premised on dehumanized images of blackness and subverted the prevailing white-centered model of national femininity.

The deplorable images of the First Lady register as a throwback to egregiously racist representations of black masculinity and black femininity in literature, such as in *The Clansman: An Historical Romance of the Ku Klux Klan*, Thomas Dixon's 1905 novel, mainly set in South Carolina and the basis for D. W. Griffith's 1915 film *Birth of a Nation*, alongside *The Leopard's Spots* (1902). The residue of obviously racist and white supremacist melodramas in literature and film like *The Clansman* and *Birth of a Nation* was routinely apparent in representations of the First Lady, alongside the president, in the nation's public sphere. Such reactionary narratives in southern literary history and film are indispensable to draw on for analyzing some of the reactionary scripts of the First Lady, especially those that have ideologically emphasized her body. That Barack and Michelle Obama were residents in the White House as president and First Lady, along with their children and her mother, unsettled the raced, classed, and gendered social distinctions and hierarchies that were historically consolidated within a white supremacist social order in the U.S. South during the late nineteenth century, an ideology that, feeding on scientific ideas such as Darwin's, devalued blackness and construed it as pathological.

Birth of a Nation links the possibilities for national reunification in the wake of the Civil War to marriages that unite the novel's two main families from the North and South within its romance plot. I find it intriguing that marriage motifs and notions of national rebirth and revitalization were palpable during the 2009 Obama inauguration. Michelle Obama's fashioning for a series of ten inaugural balls, in the elegant, one-shouldered, Grecian-inspired embroidered white chiffon gown by twenty-six-year-old Asian designer Jason Wu, connoted purity and innocence and evoked the image of a bride. Wu gained international fame when he designed Obama's inaugural ball gown and is also a fascinating figure to consider when thinking of ex-slave Elizabeth Keckley's role as a White House seamstress in the nineteenth century. As Joan Kantor points out in *The Obamas*, the vision of Michelle Obama in this dress at the inauguration was bridal. Notably, Kantor describes the Obamas' relationship to the public as a symbolic marriage.[69] As a visual image, it symbolically reinforced the presentation of the Obamas on stage before the nation and the world that night as they were introduced as the nation's new first couple.

It embodied the promise of a new beginning filled with hope, change, renewal, and, most significantly, *rebirth* in the United States and around the world. As she wore this resplendent gown and they held hands and danced, the event seemed to re-wed them in the capital, as it introduced them together as the new president and First Lady, recasting and solidifying their marriage under the banner of a new and revived nation, and the White House in Washington as their new home. This moment was significant given that the intensive travel demands of Barack Obama's campaigns for the Senate, and then for the presidency, had given them limited time together, and that life in the White House promised more family time together. This gown's white color, also associated with purity, innocence, and femininity, reinforced the portrait of the new First Lady as a quintessential embodiment of womanhood in the conventional sense during her inaugural introduction, as well as presenting her as the symbol of an emerging new woman in the nation.

This image has been immortalized in the media and on magazine covers. On March 9, 2010, Michelle Obama donated the gown to the First Ladies Collection at the Smithsonian's National Museum of American History, the repository where the inaugural ball gowns of the nation's First Ladies have long been kept. The rendition of the classic Etta James love song "At Last" by the iconic singer Beyoncé as the backdrop for the first couple's first dance reinforced the connotations of this inauguration as a new beginning and created a climate of romance. André Leon Talley notes the significance of the styling of the gown and observes the song's linkages to the notion of starting over: "That night, I saw them again, she in her angel-white one-shouldered gown, he in his white tie, his first new tuxedo in fifteen years. After acknowledging the euphoric guests, the president said, 'Excuse me while I dance with my wife,' before leading her in a slow swirl to the strains of 'At Last,' a song about beginnings."[70] Even as they reinforced the nation's highly conventional definitions of marriage, family, motherhood, and womanhood, Michelle Obama's debut and dance as First Lady in this bright ensemble, which she had selected to wear from among several other available design choices, both confronted and unsettled the ideological detachments of black womanhood from notions of purity, femininity, marriage, and domesticity that have reigned in the national imagination, while performatively enshrining a black woman as a foremost model of femininity in the nation, revising and replacing the racist, reactionary script portended in *Birth of a Nation* with a new and more diverse national narrative inclusive of blackness.

This capstone moment reinforced the iconic force of Michelle Obama that had been building up to that point, and that has only been reinforced in the ensuing months and years. This 2009 inaugural image of Michelle and Barack Obama presents the Obama family as a new and model American family, following up and bringing full circle the framing of the Robinson family as a representative American family the night that Michelle Obama was introduced to a national audience for the first time at the DNC in 2008. The visual representation of the Obamas as the nation's new first couple challenged perceptions of black unbelonging in relation to the United States as a nation and the White House as a space. Significantly, in an interview with Oprah Winfrey, Michelle Obama herself links the mood of a wedding to the first weekend in the White House after the inauguration: "Well, we still had family here, so it was almost like a wedding. A huge, very complicated wedding. The last visitors didn't leave until Sunday. And then the first Monday was kind of weird."[71] The introduction of the nation's first black first couple through wedding tropes visually sanctioned and mirrored heteronormative couplings that potentially marginalized queer identities. On the other hand, this pageantry accords with the phenomenon of "the wedding complex," theorized by Elizabeth Freeman, that throws the queer impulses of weddings into relief as enacting intimacies in the public sphere that are distinct from marriage and monogamous heterosexual relationships. Read this way, this staging of a wedding paradoxically challenged the public to envision more diverse family models and ideals.[72]

In 2011, Michelle Obama hosted a White House screening of the 2011 film *The Help*, a cinematic production in contemporary popular culture that has helped to catalyze dialogue about the South in the national mainstream in recent years by highlighting the relationship between white women and black domestics during the era of Jim Crow and by revisiting civil rights history. The film is directed by Tate Taylor, based on Kathryn Stockett's 2009 novel of the same title, and stars Emma Stone, Viola Davis, and Octavia Spencer. Set in Jackson, Mississippi, during the 1960s civil rights era, *The Help* focuses on the experiences of black female domestics who work in the homes of white families. The film highlights indignities that black maids, such as Aibileen Clark, suffered in the private sphere that parallel the ones they suffered in segregated public facilities as mandated by the law of Jim Crow that prevailed in the South.[73]

The film *The Help* has been taken to task by numerous critics for presenting an ahistorical view of the civil rights movement and an unrealistic portrait of relations between white women and black domestics. Similarly, some are troubled by how the book, notwithstanding its many inaccuracies, has increasingly replaced history texts as a resource for teaching civil rights history. The vast profits that both the book and film have generated for Stockett have been problematic for some critics given allegations that she appropriated information about the life of her brother's maid, Ableen Cooper, in developing the novel and failed to compensate her. Cooper's case was dismissed by a judge in Mississippi in 2011 because he argued that the one-year statute of limitation had expired between the time that she received the book from Stockett, read it, and filed a legal case. As Patricia A. Turner comments in an op-ed piece in the *New York Times*, "The movie deploys the standard formula. With one possible exception, the white women are remarkably unlikable, and not just because of their racism. Like the housewives portrayed in reality television shows, the housewives of Jackson treat each other, their parents and their husbands with total callousness. In short, they are bad people, therefore they are racists. There's a problem, though, with that message. To suggest that bad people were racist implies that good people were not."[74]

The film's blind spots, including what some of its critics argue are stereotypical representations of black women, fueled a barrage of editorials, and even a statement by the Association of Black Women Historians, which argues that "*The Help* distorts, ignores, and trivializes the experiences of black domestic workers."[75] At the same time, *The Help* has been tremendously popular in and beyond the African American context. This popularity is signaled, for example, by the pilgrimages of black women's organizations, such as sororities and book clubs, to theaters to see it.

President Woodrow Wilson hosted one of the most infamous film screenings at the White House in 1915 for *Birth of a Nation* and commented thereafter that "it [was] like writing history with lightning, and my only regret is that it is all so true." What was truly regrettable was the endorsement by the president of this groundbreaking and technologically sophisticated film that was nevertheless riddled with racial propaganda. It gained notoriety for escalating violence against blacks, including lynching, along with a resurgence of the Ku Klux Klan, an organization that the film portrayed as heroic. This episode provides a cautionary tale about the power of the White House to shape the nation's discourses on race, for better and for worse, and the dire consequences that can conceivably result in the event of the latter.

Considering the contexts related to the unapologetically racist thematic content of *Birth of a Nation*, which was premised on notions of black inferiority and subjection, the screening of a film such as *The Help*, which grossly mischaracterized black female domestics, at the White House by the nation's first black First Lady seems intensely ironic a century later. Black labor has been historically associated with the White House as a domestic space. At the same time, this screening of *The Help* was subversive when presented in the White House for highlighting a film set in southern geography to meditate on the issue of race in this nation. The screening provides yet another compelling example of the salient and recurrent framing of Michelle Obama in relation to discourses on the South since her emergence on the national stage and her ongoing work in confronting painful racial histories linked to slavery.

The screening of the film was hosted in the plush red screening room at the White House and attended by several of its stars, including Emma Stone and Octavia Spencer, along with figures such as Marian Wright Edelman, the founder of the Children's Defense Fund. Carol Jenkins, a writer, producer, television journalist, and founding president of the Women's Media Center, was one of the forty figures on the guest list, and she described the event by remarking, "The First Lady, completely gracious and welcoming, introduced the film and its two stars before heading back into meetings. She explained that she and the girls and her mother watched the film last week—and she believes it to be instructive in the progress made in racial matters. Certainly the fact that we were at that moment staring at the first-Black-First-Lady in her private screening room at The White House was a counterpoint to the segregated, pre-Civil Rights setting of *The Help*."[76] As Jenkins's comments suggest, whatever the film's shortcomings, the screening of *The Help* coordinated by Michelle Obama at the White House serves as a measure of the journey of African Americans beyond the shadow of slavery and segregation in this nation's history, from being classified as servants in the White House to being recognized as leaders in the nation and world. Even beyond the recognition of the film's treatment of race relations, the event demonstrates a serious commitment to thinking about the material conditions and life histories of black domestics in this nation. They are, even in this day and time, sometimes reduced to old caricatures and stereotypes, such as the eponymous mammy, instead of being recognized in all their diversity and complexity.

Michelle Obama has emerged as perhaps the most iconic black female model of national femininity ever. Through representations of her family in the twenty-first century, she has broadened and radically redefined narratives of American selfhood and centralized blackness as a term in defining it beyond such ubiquitous images of black womanhood like the mammy. Her story as a descendant of slaves and ascendance to the role of First Lady disrupts white-centered notions of American identity at the same time that it upends the most toxic and long-standing political representations of blackness in the nation's cinematic history, along with prevailing stereotypes of black mothers, even as reactionary scripts of her persisted, suggesting that this nation is far from being postracial or colorblind. The sanctioning of a heteronormative black family model premised on idealization of home and place in the representational politics surrounding the Obamas was similarly limiting. It also obscured the alienation and inequality in black Chicago, as so many youth in the city were being victimized by homicides. While her popularity signaled a more inclusive nation, such persisting problems, along with white nationalist and white supremacist turns in politics in the era of Trump, underscore how much work still remains toward achieving a truly democratic and antiracist America.

Riché Richardson, *The Journey of Condoleezza Rice*, 2012. Photograph by Dave Burbank.

Conclusion

Beyoncé's South and the Birth of a
"Formation" Nation

From Beyoncé's emergence in her native Houston, Texas, in the late 1990s as the lead singer of the award-winning group Destiny's Child, and rise to fame alongside Kelly Rowland and Michelle Williams, her trajectory to international fame, superstardom, and a successful career as a solo singer, actress, clothing designer, and entrepreneur holds important implications for critical discourses on the U.S. South. It provides a poignant illustration in popular culture of the region's recurring impact on the nationalization and globalization of black femininity in popular and political contexts. Richard Iton reminds us of the intimate connection between popular culture and politics in the African American context in the post–civil rights era.[1] Themes related to Beyoncé's intersectional identity as a model of black and southern womanhood have recurred in her song lyrics, performances, and visual representations.

Beyoncé's performance at the 2009 inauguration of Barack Obama as the nation's forty-fourth president provided a platform for her to reflect on this aspect of her background with even more focus, by relating the conditions that made it possible to the experiences of her parents, Mathew Knowles and Tina Knowles, in the segregated South and black civil rights struggles. Beyoncé's performance at Obama's first inauguration ceremony expanded the foundations for the more salient and pronounced scripts of black southern identity, along with narratives related to her parentage, that have inflected her newer works beginning with her release of the song and video versions of "Formation" and continuing with the *Lemonade* album.[2] As various critics have pointed out, these new works have been more overtly political and, seemingly, designed primarily for a black and female audience. These observations suggest that these latest works eschew the narratives of postracialism and postblackness that grounded Beyoncé's inauguration performance; instead, they focus on her southern background, shaping a discourse on race and national femininity that decenters whiteness and that, in the words of Jamil Smith, "drip[s] with unapologetic black pride and power," making them visible for America.[3] It is a strategy that suggests the importance of examining her discourse on the U.S. South, which is only now more central and pronounced given the thematic and visual contours of *Lemonade*, in a more nuanced, complex, and panoramic way. This perspective will also help us recognize and appreciate the current intensity of her southern themes all the more.

In a June 27, 2011, interview with Piers Morgan on CNN's *Piers Morgan Tonight*, on location in London, Beyoncé described her performance of Etta James's classic song "At Last" at President Barack Obama's 2009 inauguration ball as the moment in her career of which her mother, Tina Knowles, has been proudest.[4] Beyoncé made this classic song her own when she starred in the 2008 biopic based on the life of James, *Cadillac Records*, in which she portrays the legend.[5] As Beyoncé performed the soulful song at the Neighborhood Inaugural Ball, Barack and Michelle Obama did a slow dance in a setting made to appear celestial, with bright sparkling lights that mirrored a starry sky. The singer capped off her performance by blowing a kiss to the new first couple.

The visual image of the new president Obama at the inaugural ball, like his oath of office during the day, was revolutionary to the extent that it dismantled the long-standing white and masculine visual imperatives of the presidency. The spotlight on the first black first couple dancing at the inaugural ball, along with the host, Denzel Washington, and a range of other black performing artists, such as Stevie Wonder, Jennifer Hudson, and Alicia Keys, who also featured prominently on the program, accorded black people an unprecedented salience in inaugural festivities and reinforced the democratizing impulse behind the Obama administration's introduction of the Neighborhood Ball. Beyoncé's nationally televised performance at the ball, complete with numerous close-up shots, reflected and extended the emphasis on the iconic images of Barack and Michelle Obama at the inauguration, which countered the typical marginality and invisibility of black bodies at such ceremonies, along with any sense of a mere "token" status of blackness in U.S. civic events.

In the interview with Morgan, Beyoncé frames her performance at this historic event as a reflection of a "new day" in the nation and as a triumph over her parents' experience of segregation in the South.[6] In describing this segregated southern background, she mentions how her father, Mathew Knowles, needed an escort daily as one of the first African Americans who attended his high school in Gadsden, Alabama, and the experience of her mother, Tina Knowles, a Galveston, Texas, native, of not being allowed to sit at the front of the bus.[7] Beyoncé draws on their past struggles to emphasize the significance of this monumental moment for her parents as blacks who grew up in the segregated South, underscoring that "it's a new day, and my parents saw me as being a part of that history."[8] As her biographer Daryl Easlea points out, "Beyoncé's upbringing is a tale of a new American South, a South very different from the one experienced by her parents just 30 years earlier. Beyoncé has only had to work hard to further her career, whereas her parents, father Mathew especially, had to work hard against Southern racism, segregation and colour bars."[9] By positioning her role at the inaugural ball as a culmination of this long struggle for her family, Beyoncé reads her journey to it as a triumph in American democracy. She describes her feeling prior to her performance that night by commenting to Morgan, "I can't believe I was there, and I can't believe that it was my voice for that moment, and [I was] so honored and [have] so many memories, so many stories from my father and my grandparents and my mother just all going through my mind, and it was really fantastic."[10] In the vein of the perspective with which many African Americans throughout the nation read the unprecedented election of the nation's first black president, by seeing it through the eyes of their elders, she observed, "It's great that my parents could live to see that, and it makes me very proud."[11] For many, the romantic tone of her performance and the *at last* refrain conveyed the magnitude of the breakthrough in electing Obama as the nation's first black president and having Michelle Obama, who grew up on Chicago's South Side in a family shaped by the Great Migration, as the nation's first black First Lady. The ballad's themes of triumph, breakthroughs, overcoming, and fulfillment resonated at a deeply personal level for Beyoncé, speaking to a triumph over past struggles as much as it suggested a new beginning, portended new possibilities for the nation, and introduced the new and youthful first couple.

Yet discourses related to postblackness and the postracial that gained popularity in the wake of Obama's election were equally evident in the interview.[12] For example, Beyoncé acknowledged that her small nephew, the son of her sister Solange, did not understand why people were identifying President

Obama as black because her nephew did not view the president in terms of color at all. These discourses were even more salient in Beyoncé's response to Morgan's question about whether she has ever experienced racism. She acknowledged that she has experienced it "a bit," but then quickly moved on to underscore the colorblindness with which her fans view her: "I feel like now . . . at least with my career, I've kind of broken barriers and I don't think people think about my race. I think they look at me as an entertainer and a musician, and I'm very happy that that's changing because I think that's how I look at people and that's how I look at my friends. It's not about color and race, and I'm just happy that that's changing."[13] This reflective moment, steeped in notions of colorblindness and postracialism, is telling. Her currency had also been advanced through advertising campaigns in cosmetics, emphasizing her "mixed" and "Creole" heritage and downplaying blackness. Indeed, her status as an "America's sweetheart" was among the factors that made her an ideal figure to perform at President Obama's inauguration in 2009. The tone of the song "At Last" reinforced this image all the more. I have argued myself that such backgrounds, like Beyoncé's earlier overlooked linkages to southern discourses, spanning back to her mirrorings of fellow Texan Farrah Fawcett in Destiny's Child's video for "Independent Women, Part I" (2000), along with their performance at a concert during the inauguration of George W. Bush in 2001, are crucial as points of reference to weigh against the epistemology of blackness that she scripts through song lyrics and visuals in more recent works, such as "Formation" and *Homecoming*.[14]

The occasion for Beyoncé's visit to London and the backdrop for her interview with Morgan was her performance at the Glastonbury Music Festival before an audience of more than 175,000 people, which made history in light of her status as the first black woman ever invited to the legendary annual musical event. Beyoncé's performance of "At Last" at the annual festival unfolded against a video montage featuring images from the inauguration and civil rights history.[15] Here, the linking of Obama's inauguration to civil rights history further reflected Mathew Knowles's and Tina Knowles's framing of the election as a triumph over a history of racism and oppression in the South. (That Beyoncé married hip-hop mogul Jay-Z [Shawn Carter] on April 4, 2008, the fortieth anniversary of the tragic assassination of Dr. Martin Luther King Jr., also underscores her investments in weaving civil rights narratives into her personal history.) At this level, Beyoncé's articulation of her identity through the lens of civil rights discourses accords with strategies for fashioning identity that have been recurrently associated with black women in the public sphere of politics. Standing before one of the largest audiences in Glastonbury's history, Beyoncé described the performance as the fulfillment of a dream because she "always wanted to be a rock star!"[16] This historic performance, as Morgan suggested, reinforced Beyoncé's status as "the most famous entertainer in the world." The performance attested to her global fame and iconicity.

Beyoncé was prominently associated with the nation's first couple in the media throughout Obama's presidency. It is significant that she and her husband, Jay-Z, are friends of the Obamas and were also sitting on the platform as the president took the oath of office in 2009. Beyoncé's participation in the inauguration ceremony for President Obama's second term on January 21, 2013, in which she sang a powerful rendition of the "Star-Spangled Banner" before a crowd of hundreds of thousands of people, further reinforced her linkages to the Obama administration, although the moment was shadowed by a public backlash when some of her critics alleged that she was lip synching during the performance. In Madison Moore's compelling short e-book, *How to Be Beyoncé*, he argues that the controversy about whether Beyoncé lip synched during her performance at the inauguration overshadowed the event itself.[17]

Moore has been at the vanguard among scholars working in queer and trans studies who are advancing the field's epistemologies on Beyoncé, while shaping emerging areas such as Beyoncé studies.[18] Black trans women have been foundational in promoting and mediating the iconicity of black femininity in popular culture and have played a central role in reinforcing and extending Beyoncé's, even as she has been primarily related to her narratives as a heterosexual wife and mother in the national arena in more recent years. A host of black queer and trans women, including impersonators and activists such as Riley Knoxx and Miss Shalae (who is also known as Michell'e Michaels), have played a salient role in helping popularize Beyoncé. Miss Shalae starred in a 2016 video remake of *Lemonade* by a collective of trans women known as the Glass Wing Group, entitled *Lemonade Served Bitter Sweet*. This project also resonates with the groundbreaking performance work of E. Patrick Johnson in *Sweet Tea*, which focuses on gay black men in the South.[19] Beyoncé has done outreach and collaborations with black queer and trans women, as illustrated in her work with Laverne Cox, the award-winning Alabama actress and activist who became popular through her role on the Netflix series *Orange Is the New Black*, and who serves as the face of Ivy Park, the active clothing brand cofounded by Beyoncé. Janet Mock has been foremost among black queer and trans women who have helped to expand and nuance analysis on Beyoncé within black feminist discourses.[20]

Beyoncé's performances at major political events both draw on and reinforce her iconicity as a pop singer. That a popular figure such as Beyoncé has been highlighted as a performer at presidential inaugurations is a reflection of how black women have gained visibility in the national public sphere and influenced notions of national femininity in popular and political contexts, ideals that have conventionally been associated with white womanhood, just as the notion of the national body has been correlated with white subjectivity. Her visibility at this level illustrates how black women as a category have increasingly challenged and expanded narrow notions of American selfhood, along with national narratives from which blacks have been conventionally excluded. Beyoncé's fashioning as a public figure with international fame and status as an icon of beauty in the first years of the new millennium registers the effect of popular culture in helping to envision a broader, more inclusive and racially and ethnically diverse notion of American democracy.

While embracing the unprecedented space that the Obama presidency opened for her as an entertainer, Beyoncé also saliently acknowledges new narratives of American womanhood and national femininity embodied in Michelle Obama's status as the nation's first black First Lady. Significantly, she has framed First Lady Michelle Obama as a model of quintessential American womanhood. On April 11, 2012, Beyoncé posted on Tumblr a handwritten open letter—billed by the press as a "love letter"—to Michelle Obama. The letter expresses gratitude to the First Lady for her example as a black woman and pride in having such a role model for Blue Ivy, Beyoncé's infant daughter:

> Michelle, is the ULTIMATE example of a truly strong African American woman. She is a caring mother, she's a loving wife, while at the same time, she is the FIRST LADY!!!! No matter the pressure, and the stress of being under the microscope—she's humble, loving and sincere. She builds and nurtures her family while also looking out for so many millions in so many ways. Michelle, thank you so much for every single thing that U do for us. I am proud to have my daughter grow up in a world where she has people like you to look up to.
>
> Love, Beyoncé[21]

While Beyoncé's comments here have the potential to reinforce the myth of the "strong black woman" at a rhetorical level, it is notable that Beyoncé underscores Michelle Obama's blackness in positing her as a representative and model woman. Here, in addition to emphasizing race and gender as primary factors in describing the First Lady, Beyoncé also frames her as a model wife and mother whose commitment to the first family mirrors her commitment to *all* American people. Beyoncé draws on the personal in framing the First Lady as a beacon by acknowledging her as an inspiration and role model for her daughter. In her thanks to the First Lady "for every single thing that U do for us," it is significant that Beyoncé positions herself as a representative and an intermediary to address Michelle Obama on behalf of the national body.[22] While Beyoncé circulated this letter digitally on an internet platform, the fact that it was a scan of her handwritten letter makes it more personal and heartfelt. Beyoncé's reference to the First Lady as Michelle also underscores the personal nature of their relationship and suggests the closeness of their friendship.[23] The mutuality in their sentiments was evident in the First Lady's equally public response on the social network Twitter two days later, in a tweet that read, "@Beyonce Thank you for the beautiful letter and for being a role model who kids everywhere can look up to.—mo."[24]

Significantly, this exchange builds on the collaboration that Michelle Obama established with Beyoncé in tandem with the Let's Move! campaign. The development of the song and video for "Move Your Body" (2011) revamps her song "Get Me Bodied" from her 2006 *B'Day* album and aims to motivate and energize American youth, just as remixes of its contemporaneous "Run the World (Girls)" from her 2011 album *4* have aimed to empower girls globally. Beyoncé's emphasis on children in her song and video work with Michelle Obama mirrors the political agendas and platforms centering children that have been disseminated by black women leaders into the twenty-first century. In 2019, on her website, Beyoncé similarly shouted out Janet Mock on a page highlighting the latter's activist history as part of the Black History Month series *We Good*.

The First Lady has been recurrently described as a South Side girl, reflecting her upbringing on Chicago's South Side, and her family roots in plantation slavery have been closely researched and were publicly acknowledged by her husband during his presidential campaign. Michelle Obama and Beyoncé both embody a model of national femininity that decenters whiteness and in which representative national subjects emerge as black and feminine, constituting black national femininities. Simultaneously, through their linkages to the Africana South, they embody new notions of southern subjectivity that were inconceivable and illegible in the past. Moreover, Beyoncé's hometown in Houston, Texas, makes it necessary to explore her through the critical lens and comparative methodologies of the Africana South(west).[25] Beyoncé's iconicity and global appeal in the pop arena show black women's capacity to interrupt and unsettle the prevailing white-centered narratives of American identity.

In "Formation," Beyoncé builds on thoughtful reflections on black southern identity that she offered in the wake of the 2009 presidential inauguration in the interview with Piers Morgan, and that have been manifest in her artistry since her days in Destiny's Child. She positions this identity as core to herself as a raced and gendered subject, drawing on it to challenge narrow and exclusionary notions of American selfhood. In the process, she makes legible new models of black southern womanhood that are sometimes imaginative and unmoored to geography, constituting new southern diasporas and identities.

These critical contexts are important and valuable, because much contemporary analysis that invokes Beyoncé in relation to the region often examines them in a vacuum, without tracing the relevant backgrounds. The typical methods in popular culture analysis are almost always urban centered, ungrounded, and uninformed by the important contemporary critical thinking in the field of southern studies, sometimes reinforcing notions of southern romance, along with other essentialisms.[26] Critical analyses of the Global and hemispheric South are the basis on which the U.S. South comes into geographic relief, as one of multiple Souths in the Western Hemisphere as a region inescapably shaped by colonialism, imperialism, and plantation slavery dialectically within the vast complex of plantation architectures iterated across its geographies, a critical perspective grounded in American studies that promotes interdisciplinary and comparative study of the region. My work on the U.S. South is rooted in such understandings, which accord with the new southern studies, critical methodologies that eschew the conventional geographic and temporal logics related to the region.

In "Formation," profuse invocations of black southern identity assert a narrative of Beyoncé's background that centers blackness, which complicates and, to some extent, contradicts the colorblind narratives of her history that had been circulated in the media. It shapes a subversive and inclusive notion of blackness that she boldly showcased in the video and during her performance before a national audience at the 2016 Super Bowl halftime show.

The release of the "Formation" video on the eve prior to her performance as part of the Super Bowl 50 halftime show heralded a radical turn in Beyoncé's repertoire and a more direct and assertive engagement with the U.S.

South. Its lyrics most saliently invoke the region by framing Beyoncé's identity in relation to her "Creole" mother's roots in Louisiana and her "Negro" father's in Alabama, autobiographically positioning Beyoncé as a byproduct of this geographic and genetic fusion, which she terms *Texas 'Bama*. As Jenna Wortham notes in her dialogue on "Formation" in the *New York Times*, this neologism is all the more significant because it unsettles the uses of the term *'Bama* as a "lethal insult."[27] Most typically, this term has been used in black urban contexts as an epithet to make fun of people regarded as tacky and "country," as illustrated in several scenes in Spike Lee's 1988 film *School Daze*.

The setting of the video "Formation" in post–Hurricane Katrina New Orleans, and featuring of the singer standing atop a police car that sinks as the video ends, critique the benign neglect of the city in the wake of the levee breakage in 2005 and the horrific losses of life in the aftermath. The tragedy there is foregrounded in a line sampled in the song from the late gender-nonconforming bounce rapper and local commentator Messy Mya questioning what happened there. The assertive voice that follows, of black queer hip-hop and bounce musician Big Freedia, also a New Orleans native, who does not appear in the video, establishes the tone of empowerment in the song, paradoxically by underscoring Beyoncé's fierceness among "bitches" and arrival to "slay." Such terms further link the song's message to black queerness linguistically; voice-over invocations of foods such as "cornbread" and "collard greens" root it in the South as a region through foregrounded sound dimensions that also signal Beyoncé's embrace of black queer and trans communities. It simultaneously indicts the pervasive killings of African Americans at the hands of law enforcement, which have typically gone unpunished. The camera pans through the areas of the city that were left most devastated by the storm and that have yet to recover, underscoring Katrina's continuing impact on the landscape. This visual dimension of the video helps to render Louisiana as a place that is visceral for viewers in the new millennium and signals it as a site of lingering trauma. Its history is further brought to life in Beyoncé's multilayered portraits of black women and girls dressed in white, recalling antebellum styles and traditions associated with black Creole women, invoking embodiments of black womanhood compellingly visualized by Julie Dash's film *Daughters of the Dust* (1991). Similarly, plantation-style architectures highlighted as settings invoke this history. As Jon Caramanica suggests in the aforementioned *New York Times* dialogue, "Beyoncé is both old South and new South."[28]

The singer's assertion that she has remained "country" despite her money, and references to soul food such as cornbread and collard greens, also play up southern themes. Beyoncé's acknowledgment of the "hot sauce in my bag" and images of a black marching band and black churches further emphasize southern heritage in the video. The culmination of the video with images of the sinking of the police car with Beyoncé atop it, a youth to whom officers raise their hands in surrender, and a wall that shows the words "Stop Killing Us" written in graffiti bring the video's themes regarding the abuses by law enforcement full circle. These bold themes fueled a backlash against the singer that resulted in the cancellation of several of her performances because police refused to provide needed security in protest.

The provocative contours of the video were the backdrop for Beyoncé's performance at Super Bowl 50, which, in a game featuring the Carolina Panthers and the Denver Broncos playing at Levi's Stadium in the San Francisco Bay Area, further emphasized the game's panther motifs by paying tribute to the Black Panther Party in the fiftieth anniversary year of its founding in Oakland, California. Beyoncé is featured alongside Coldplay and Bruno Mars, whose performances set the stage for her segment, which begins when she entreats her fellow women dancers, who are dressed in black leather bodysuits, afros, and berets, to "get in formation." This styling provides a direct paean to the Black Panthers, whose leather jackets and berets became iconic in photography and television media during the late 1960s. The dancers' afros also reference this period, when the black power movement helped popularize natural afro hairstyles and emphasized black beauty, while also visually building on Beyoncé's assertion of adoration for her daughter's afro hair in the song's lyrics. Notably, Beyoncé and her dancers configure their bodies to form an X, which pays tribute to the black Muslim leader Malcolm X, who played a key role in inspiring the organization's founding by Huey P. Newton and Bobby Seale in 1966. Their "formation" both enacts Beyoncé's opening entreaty and, with the song's lyric, echoes the militaristic formations in which the organization's members gathered as part of the drills that trained them for armed self-defense. The culmination of the halftime show against the backdrop of a video that includes black singers among several former Super Bowl halftime performers, such as James Brown, Stevie Wonder, Whitney Houston, Prince, and Michael Jackson, saliently invokes black history themes that aligned with the event's occurrence during Black History Month.

The juxtaposition of the visual economy of the video "Formation" and the song's performance at the Super Bowl as a paean to the Black Panthers underlined the long history of antiblack violence in policing. It connected the Black Panthers' founding to address abusive policing in black communities and its long-standing critique of police brutality with the work of political groups, such as Black Lives Matter and #SayHerName, in protesting contemporary police abuses. (Indeed, the latter hashtag echoes the popular song by Destiny's Child, "Say My Name," one of its anthems for women's empowerment.) Beyoncé's use of Black Panther Party iconography in her performance lies in a continuum with its citations within black popular culture, from Tupac Shakur's video "California Love" to musical performances and scenes in the television drama *Empire*. The roots of this organization in Alabama's Black Belt and the influence of the Lowndes County Freedom Organization on its emergence link it organically to the South and, in this sense, also reinforce the southern epistemology invoked in Beyoncé's "Formation."

This moment arguably rests in the continuum with John Carlos and Tommie Smith's famous salute to black power during the national anthem at the 1968 Olympics and anticipated the incendiary critiques of police violence staged later, in 2016, by Jesse Williams and Colin Kaepernick, the NFL player who launched #TakeAKnee by kneeling during the national anthem in protest of this issue and persisting racism. It suggested that it is important for American citizens to think more critically about law enforcement by recognizing abuses that they sometimes carry out, even when also invested in respecting their role as public servants who protect and serve communities, and to understand that such critiques should not be conflated with antipolice attitudes. It is also important to frame "Formation" in light of Mark Anthony Neal's critical acknowledgment of the historical and political dimensions of black popular music.[29] The backlash that Beyoncé experienced in the wake of this performance reflected discomfort with her validation of the black resistance movements most committed to confronting police violence in historical and contemporary eras. At the same time, her performance, which celebrated blackness and confronted persistent racism, unsettled the prevailing national fantasies of a postracial America. The video for the song "Freedom" on *Lemonade* anticipates "Formation" in paying tribute to the mothers of black men who have been victims of vigilante and police violence, including Wanda Johnson, the mother of Oscar Grant; Sybrina Fulton, the mother of Trayvon Martin; Gwen Carr, the mother of Eric Garner; and Lezley McSpadden, the mother of Michael Brown. These women also appeared with Beyoncé at the VMA awards in 2016 and have been called mothers of the movement, revealing Beyoncé's commitment to Black Lives Matter and another dimension of her advocacy for mothers and children at the national level, bridging this contemporary movement with earlier civil rights activism.

In "Formation," Beyoncé visualizes landscapes historically linked to African American subjectivity through a history of slavery and the lingering repercussions of this history, which conditioned the South as a symbolic ancestral home in the African American imaginary. For Beyoncé, the South's ongoing traumas are recollected in atrocities such as contemporary antiblack police violence. This song reflects a landscape haunted and shadowed by this painful past. It is not only a black southern history but stands in as American history itself, as she scripts herself as a representative and symbolic subject within the nation who has reached the pinnacle of success. She accomplishes the task of embodying national selfhood by remaining grounded in her Texas 'Bama identity and closely moored to her family of origin, while continuing to honor and pay tribute to southern legacies in her public claiming of her identity as a wife and mother.

In the "Formation" video and in her 2016 Super Bowl performance, Beyoncé underscores the utility of embracing alternative and hidden histories and challenges her audiences to envision the United States as a nation where white subjectivity is not always the center of its national selfhood. Increasingly, since the 2009 inauguration, Beyoncé's epistemology on the South has moved from margin to center in her artistry and increasingly informed its aesthetics, presenting a counternarrative to purist, nativist, white-centered notions of American identity and, in continuing to spotlight southern history, bringing her full circle from the earlier event. Beyoncé's subversive deployments of black southern identity and culture highlight their relevance and utility for advancing political activism. Invoking the South as an essential home in the project of constructing black authenticity, including black femininity, has some clear limitations and problems, such as risking the replay of nostalgic and romantic formulations of black identity, which repress the region as a site of lingering and continuing trauma and entrenched racial and social inequalities. Nevertheless, Beyoncé's "Formation" is valuable, and even revolutionary, in challenging her audience to think toward a new and more visionary and inclusive politics of race, sexuality, gender, and nation formation, in which she, and we, too, can sing "America."

While Phillis Wheatley is the earliest illustration of a black woman national icon during the late eighteenth century, in the years this nation emerged as a republic, figures such as Sojourner Truth and Harriet Tubman are among black women born in the antebellum era who crystallized as national icons during the era after slavery because of their courageous and daring work as abolitionists. This was a period during which the most ubiquitous and familiar images of black womanhood in the national arena were premised on gross stereotypes such as Aunt Jemima. Born in the post-Emancipation era, Mary McLeod Bethune heralded the litany of black women who would stand on their shoulders and establish platforms as political leaders that advocated for freedom and prioritized children. Like her predecessors, she challenged the prevailing pathological scripts of black mothers as mammies that gained popularity in the years after slavery, which were iterated in the matriarch by the postwar era, along with later stereotypes, from the welfare queen to the baby mama, premised on the disparagement of black mothers. Bethune's ubiquity as a symbol of the black freedom movement established foundations for the civil rights movement and for the emergence of a leader like Rosa Parks, whose iconicity as a mother figure and advocacy for children during the civil rights era resonated with Bethune's leadership legacy. Bethune's legendary friendship with the Roosevelts, participation in FDR's Black Cabinet, and emergence as an iconic mother who advocated for black children enabled her to help promote the concerns of African Americans on national agendas during the era of Jim Crow and to engage with policy issues in a way that served as an important precedent for the cabinet-level positions that leaders such as Colin Powell and Condoleezza Rice occupied by the end of the twentieth century and into the new millennium, models that nominally invoked civil rights but were paradoxically steeped in reactionary political agendas. The policy maneuverings of the Bush administration empowered the right wing and established foundations for the rise of Donald Trump; Rice played a primary role in advancing the Bush agenda. That his administration dropped the ball during Katrina is eerily similar to Trump's neglectful response to the Covid-19 pandemic.

Given Bethune's birth in the years after slavery and the specter of segregation that still loomed large at the time of her death, on the cusp of the civil rights movement, she could scarcely have imagined the election of a black president in the United States. She would likely see a figure such as Beyoncé as being uniquely advantaged and well positioned to make a difference, given her connections to the nation's first black president and First Lady. Bethune would readily recognize the potential of Beyoncé as a figure in popular culture to build on her special friendship with the president and First Lady to make a difference and promote policies to better the lives of African Americans and other people in the United States and around the world who still feel excluded from the nation's ideals of freedom and democracy and alienated within the national body.

As I conclude this book, I am amazed and inspired by how much a black and southern woman such as Beyoncé encapsulates the diverse contours of national femininity that I have explored in relation to black feminine figures in this study, including its liberatory and reactionary dimensions, its grounding in histories from slavery to Jim Crow to the civil rights era and beyond, and its investments in narratives related to family, children, and futurity. In recent years, Beyoncé's status as an iconic black mother, prominent voice advocating for the empowerment of black women and girls, and political activist has expanded her influence and made her all the more captivating for her audiences. Like her black female predecessors, her iconic force has been serviceable in making black femininity more legible and palatable in shaping more inclusive notions of American subjectivity in the new millennium. Increasingly, it has also helped to expand representational possibilities for black queer and trans women. Such dynamics render black feminine bodies less a premier marker of abjection when abstracted in contexts from global to national, and more entirely readable, believable, desirable, and imaginable as a quintessential embodiment of a new and more democratic kind of America, and as a symbol of all the greatest possibilities imaginable within its futures to come.

NOTES

Preface

1. For the text of Rice's speech, see "Rice's Speech to Republican National Convention."
2. See Olasky, *Compassionate Conservatism*; and Hall, "How Compassionate."
3. Frederickson, *Dixiecrat Revolt*; and Feldman, *Great Melding*.
4. Richardson, "Seen and Not Heard."
5. Michelle Obama, *Speeches*.
6. Adichie, "To the First Lady."
7. Cathy J. Cohen, *Democracy Remixed*.
8. Lorde, *Sister Outsider*.

Introduction

1. See Barbara Ortiz Howard and Susan Ades Stone, "The Petition," Women on 20s, May 11, 2015, http://www.womenon20s.org/the_petition.
2. Rooney, "Female Finalists."
3. Crenshaw, "Mapping the Margins," 1241–99; Collins, *Intersectionality as Critical Social Theory*; and Nash, *Black Feminism Reimagined*.
4. Democratic senator Jeanne Shaheen of New Hampshire also introduced legislation that urged the placement of a woman on the twenty-dollar bill and wrote President Obama in 2015 to advance the initiative. In 2016, treasury secretary Jack Lew announced the plan to place Tubman on one side of the twenty-dollar bill opposite Andrew Jackson by 2020, but the administration of Donald Trump has postponed the plan for the new bill until 2026.
5. Tillet, *Sites of Slavery*.
6. Toni Morrison, *Playing in the Dark*.
7. Dana D. Nelson, *National Manhood*.
8. On the fiftieth anniversary of Martin Luther King Jr.'s famous speech delivered at the March on Washington in 1963, *Time* magazine released a special double "I Have a Dream" anniversary issue in August 26/September 2, 2013, featuring an image of Dr. King on the cover and framing him as a founding father in the nation.
9. See, for example, hooks, *Ain't I a Woman*; Dorothy Roberts, *Killing the Black Body*; Jones, *Labor of Love, Labor of Sorrow*; White, *Ar'n't I a Woman?*; Giddings,

When and Where I Enter; Guy-Sheftall, *Daughters of Sorrow*; and Yaeger, "Circum-Atlantic Superabundance," 769–98.
10 Spillers, "Mama's Baby, Papa's Maybe," 454–55.
11 Snorton, *Black on Both Sides*.
12 Jacobs, *Incidents in the Life of a Slave Girl*.
13 Toni Morrison, *Beloved*.
14 Painter, *Sojourner Truth*; also see Sernett, *Harriet Tubman*.
15 Larson, *Harriet Tubman*.
16 Ferguson, *Aberrations in Black*.
17 Anna Julia Cooper, *Voice from the South*.
18 Manring, *Slave in a Box*.
19 For more on Aunt Jemima, see Witt, *Black Hunger*; Kern-Foxworth, *Aunt Jemima, Uncle Ben, and Rastus*; Diane Roberts, *Myth of Aunt Jemima*; Goings, *Mammy and Uncle Mose*; Patricia A. Turner, *Ceramic Uncles and Celluloid Mammies*; Manring, *Slave in a Box*; Wallace-Sanders, *Mammy*; Phil Patton, "Mammy"; James D. Anderson, "Aunt Jemima in Dialectics"; Cheryl Thompson, "I'se in Town, Honey"; Fuller, "Are We Seeing Things?"; Holbling, Rieser-Wohlfarter, and Rieser, *U.S. Icons and Iconicity*; Martin and Sublette, *Devouring Cultures*; McElya, *Clinging to Mammy*; and Cox, *Dreaming of Dixie*.
20 Christopher Robert Reed, "The Black Presence at 'White City': African and African American Participation at the World's Columbian Exposition, Chicago, May 1, 1893–October 31, 1893," Paul V. Galvin Library Digital History Collection, Illinois Institute of Technology, last updated March 8, 1999, http://columbus.iit.edu/reed2.html.
21 Wells, *Reason Why*. Also see Giddings, *Ida*.
22 Borgstrom, "Passing Over."
23 The film mirrored the reactionary narrative in mainstream historiography of the time, under the heading of the William Dunning school of thought, in propagating a nostalgic white supremacist narrative of the Civil War and Emancipation as having been historical changes that ravaged and destroyed the idyllic Old South as a land of peace and harmony, in which docile slaves had known their "place" under the supervision of their benevolent slave masters and caring mistresses, while empowering blacks in politics who were incompetent imbeciles during Reconstruction.
24 Jean Williams Turner, *Collectible Aunt Jemima*.
25 Patricia A. Turner, *Ceramic Uncles and Celluloid Mammies*, 11–12.
26 Horwitz, "Mammy Washington Almost Had."
27 For advertisements featuring these two slogans, see Quaker Oats (1917–1994), Boxes Q03 (1961–62) and Q04 (1963–65), J. Walter Thompson Company, Domestic Advertisements Collection, David M. Rubenstein Rare Book and Manuscript Library, Duke University. For related materials, also see the J. Walter Thompson Company Chicago Office, Quaker Oats Account Files, 1945–1965, in this repository.
28 Sharpless, *Cooking in Other Women's Kitchens*.

29 Berlant, "National Brands, National Body."
30 In the 1934 film version of *Imitation of Life*, which is based on Fannie Hurst's 1933 novel, the black woman character Delilah, who becomes the maid of the white model and saleswoman Bea Pullman as they raise their daughters, Peola and Jessie, respectively, and whose smiling image is later circulated on pancake boxes and emblazoned on a lighted marquee as Aunt Delilah to market her secret pancake recipe, ostensibly draws on the advertising legacy of Aunt Jemima. In 1939, the character Mammy portrayed by Hattie McDaniel in the film *Gone with the Wind* (1939), which was directed by Victor Fleming based on Margaret Mitchell's 1936 novel, is perhaps the most famous embodiment of the mammy stereotype in Hollywood history, a performance that garnered the actress an Academy Award for Best Supporting Actress, the first in history for an African American. On the other hand, early cinematic productions, such as *Birth of a Nation* and *Gone with the Wind*, idealized and romanticized southern white womanhood, propagating nativist and white supremacist notions of national identity premised on black women's devaluation and subjection, which had roots in antebellum slavery and were cornerstones of the ideology of the Old South. Its logic stressed white racial purity and the purity of white women, propagated antimiscegenation sentiment, and exalted white womanhood on a mythic pedestal. In McPherson's study *Reconstructing Dixie*, she discusses "lenticular" camera techniques that cinema routinely deployed to present a hierarchical juxtaposition of white and black feminine bodies, which mirrored the separatism of the southern segregated social order and was epitomized in the classic bifurcated imaging techniques of the characters Scarlett and Mammy in *Gone with the Wind*.
31 Toni Morrison, *Playing in the Dark*, 64.
32 Shimakawa, *National Abjection*.
33 Tipton-Martin, *Jemima Code*.
34 Richardson, *Black Masculinity and the U.S. South*.
35 Richardson, "Can We Please."
36 "Aunt Jemima Image to Be Removed and Brand Will Be Renamed, Quaker Oats Announces," NBC *Today Show*, June 17, 2020, https://www.today.com/video/aunt-jemima-image-to-be-removed-and-brand-will-be-renamed-quaker-oats-announces-85216837957.
37 See, for example, McPherson, *Reconstructing Dixie*; Jones and Donaldson, *Haunted Bodies*; Yaeger, *Dirt and Desire*; and Hunter, *To 'Joy My Freedom*.
38 Collins, *Black Feminist Thought*.
39 Lubiano, "Black Ladies, Welfare Queens," 323–63.
40 Collins, *Black Feminist Thought*, 76.
41 Williamson, *Scandalize My Name*.
42 Harris-Perry, *Sister Citizen*.
43 Braxton and McLaughlin, *Wild Women in the Whirlwind*.

44 Mohanty, Russo, and Torres, *Third World Women*; and Grewal and Kaplan, *Scattered Hegemonies*.
45 In France, while Marianne has historically functioned as a symbol of the French Revolution and values associated with it such as liberty, equality, and brotherhood, busts of her have been fashioned in the image of a range of famous French women, among them Brigitte Bardot, Catherine Deneuve, and Laetitia Casta.
46 Benedict Anderson, *Imagined Communities*.
47 McClintock, *Imperial Leather*.
48 Shome, *Diana and Beyond*, 20.
49 Shome, *Diana and Beyond*, 27.
50 Shome, *Diana and Beyond*, 6, 27.
51 Bhabha, *Location of Culture*.
52 See Richardson, "Mammy's 'Mules,'" 59.
53 Yaeger has pointed out how southern women are repeatedly linked to dirt in *Dirt and Desire*. In *Cane* (1923), Jean Toomer upends romanticized and naturalized imagery sometimes associated with white femininity. In "Portrait in Georgia," he uses imagery linked to the white feminine body, such as "Hair braided chestnut like a lyncher's rope" and a "slim body, white as the ash," to invoke the myth of the black rapist who preyed on white womanhood, which was exalted and sacralized in the southern imagination, serving as the primary rationale for the lynching of black men in the region and fueling antimiscegenation sentiment, in which sexual relations between blacks and whites were regarded as taboo and prohibited by law.
54 Fleetwood, *On Racial Icons*, 1.
55 Fleetwood, *On Racial Icons*, 3.
56 Berlant, *Queen of America*.
57 Holloway, "Body Politic," 484–95.
58 Baker and Nelson, "Violence, the Body, and the South."
59 Baker, *Turning South Again*; Baker, *Critical Memory*; and Fossett, Gussow, and Richardson, "Symposium of New Souths," 569–611.
60 Carl Gutiérrez-Jones, "Reimagining the Hemispheric South," University of California Humanities Research Institute, accessed August 1, 2016, https://uchri.org/awards/reimagining-the-hemispheric-south/.
61 Gutiérrez-Jones, "Reimagining the Hemispheric South."
62 See, for example, Curtin, *Rise and Fall of the Plantation Complex*. Also see Handley, *Postslavery Literatures in the Americas*; Smith and Cohn, *Look Away!*; Greeson, *Our South*; and Glissant, *Faulkner, Mississippi*.
63 See, for example, Hartman, *Scenes of Subjection*.
64 See Jones, "Southern Diaspora," 27–54; also see Gregory, *Southern Diaspora*; and Boyce-Davies, *Black Women, Writing, and Identity*.
65 Bobo and Hudley, *Black Studies Reader*.

1. Mary McLeod Bethune's "My Last Will and Testament" and Her National Legacy

1. The life story of Bethune has been addressed in several biographies. Among them are Sterne, *Mary McLeod Bethune*; Peare, *Mary McLeod Bethune*; Holt, *Mary McLeod Bethune*; Massie, *Legacy of Mary McLeod Bethune*; Long, *Life and Legacy*; and Martin, *Mary McLeod Bethune*. Furthermore, see Collier-Thomas and Franklin, *Sisters in the Struggle*.
2. For an elaboration of this phenomenon, see the chapter "The Trope of the Talking Book" in Gates's *Signifying Monkey*, 127–69.
3. It is a narrative that by implication positions Bethune at the forefront of one of the earliest waves of the Great Migration to the urban North, even prior to the second decade of the twentieth century, when black mass migration to cities such as Chicago intensified in light of the growing need for black labor in northern industries during World War I and conditions such as lynching and poverty in southern states making life in the region increasingly unbearable and bleak. See Litwack, *Trouble in Mind*, 482–83. Also see McCluskey, "We Specialize in the Wholly Impossible," 403–25.
4. See Dunbar, *Collected Poetry*.
5. Bethune, *Building a Better World*, xi.
6. Hanson, *Mary McLeod Bethune*.
7. Hanson, *Mary McLeod Bethune*, 161.
8. Giddings, *When and Where I Enter*, 230.
9. Bethune, *Building a Better World*.
10. Lindsey, *Colored No More*.
11. Bethune, "My Last Will and Testament," in *Building a Better World*, 59.
12. Elaine Smith, "Mary McLeod Bethune's 'Last Will and Testament,'" 105.
13. Bernstein, *Racial Innocence*.
14. John H. Johnson, *Succeeding against the Odds*, 157.
15. The Black Public Sphere Collective, *Black Public Sphere*.
16. Johnson, *Succeeding against the Odds*, 175.
17. Johnson, *Succeeding against the Odds*, 75.
18. Bethune, "My Last Will and Testament" (1955).
19. Du Bois, *Souls of Black Folk*.
20. McCluskey, "Representing the Race," 236; also see Elaine Smith, "Mary McLeod Bethune's 'Last Will and Testament,'" 109.
21. Franklin and Collier-Thomas, "Biography, Race Vindication," 164.
22. Johnson-Miller, "Mary McLeod Bethune," 337.
23. Johnson-Miller, "Mary McLeod Bethune," 340.
24. McCluskey, "Representing the Race," 237.
25. Elaine Smith, "Mary McLeod Bethune," 152–53, 163.
26. McCluskey, "Representing the Race," 236.

27 McCluskey, "Representing the Race," 237.
28 McCluskey, "Representing the Race," 243.
29 Benedict, Anderson, *Imagined Communities*.
30 Bethune, "My Last Will and Testament," 59.
31 Locke and Rampersad, *New Negro*.
32 Bethune, "My Last Will and Testament," 60.
33 Hubbard, *Sermon*.
34 Bethune, "My Last Will and Testament," 61.
35 Bethune, "My Last Will and Testament," 61.
36 Hughes, *Collected Poems*.
37 Elaine Smith, "Mary McLeod Bethune's 'Last Will and Testament,'" 105.
38 Elaine Smith, "Mary McLeod Bethune's 'Last Will and Testament,'" 111.
39 Elaine Smith, "Mary McLeod Bethune's 'Last Will and Testament,'" 109.
40 The president had become disabled as a result of being stricken in his late thirties with a disease thought to be polio, and he used a wheelchair to get around.
41 Long, *Life and Legacy*, 30.
42 See the brief biography on Bethune that serves as the opening page of Earl Devine Martin's *Mary McLeod Bethune*, 55. The Mary McLeod Bethune Home, which is also known as the Mary McLeod Bethune Foundation, located on the Bethune-Cookman College campus in Daytona, was dedicated as a U.S. national historic landmark later that year, on December 2, 1974.
43 In *Mary McLeod Bethune and the National Council of Negro Women*, Elaine Smith significantly sets the record straight regarding the assertion that Bethune advised four U.S. presidents, arguing, "Bethune was an informal presidential adviser—in the sense of personal access to the chief executive—to two presidents: Franklin Roosevelt and Harry Truman. Bethune's role as an adviser to FDR is generally known. And, Truman freely acknowledged that she counseled him" (338–40).
44 Height, *Open Wide the Freedom Gates*, 214.
45 In light of Bethune's presidency of the American Teachers Association in 1924, the National Education Association offered a special tribute to Bethune on the occasion of the monument's unveiling in the volume *Legacy of Mary McLeod Bethune*, which highlights sepia photographs covering various aspects of Bethune's story in juxtaposition with biographical paragraphs.
46 See Goode, *Washington Sculpture*; "BETHUNE, Mary McLeod: Memorial at Lincoln Park in Washington, D.C.," DC Memorials, last updated April 20, 2013, http://www.dcmemorials.com/index_indiv0000230.htm; "LINCOLN Park: Emancipation Memorial (ca. 1876) at Lincoln Park in Washington, D.C.," DC Memorials, last updated April 20, 2013, at http://www.dcmemorials.com/index_indiv0000222.htm; Kani Saburi Ayubu, "Mary McLeod Bethune Emancipation Memorial," *Black Art Depot Today*, September 7, 2011, http://blackartblog.blackartdepot.com/features/african-american-monuments-statues/mary-mcleod-bethune-emancipation-memorial.html; "Lincoln Park," National Park Service, accessed May 29, 2012, http://www

.nps.gov/nr/travel/wash/dc87.htm; "Lincoln Park," Capitol Hill Parks, last updated February 21, 2019, http://www.nps.gov/cahi/historyculture/cahi_lincoln.htm. Notably, Berks has also created a bronze bust of President John F. Kennedy, which was installed at the John F. Kennedy Center for the Performing Arts in Washington, DC, in 1971.

47 See Stephen A. Morrison, "Lincoln Park," 14.
48 Douglass, "Oration in Memory of Abraham Lincoln," 615–24.
49 Wiegman, *American Anatomies*.
50 Aishvarya Kavi, "Activists Push for Removal of Statue of Freed Slave Kneeling before Lincoln," *New York Times*, June 27, 2020.
51 Bethune, *Building a Better World*, xi.
52 Height, *Open Wide the Freedom Gates*, 212.
53 Butler, *Gender Trouble*.
54 Getsy, "Acts of Stillness," 8, 10–11
55 Getsy, "Acts of Stillness," 11.
56 *Wolf Trap Farm Park and Mary McLeod Bethune Council House: Hearing before the Subcommittee on Public Lands and Reserved Water of the Committee on Energy and Natural Resources, United States Senate*, 97th Cong., 2nd sess. (1982) (statement of Dr. Dorothy I. Height, President, National Council of Negro Women), 13.
57 *Authorizing Funds for the Mary McLeod Bethune National Historic Site and Land Conveyances in the State of Maryland, Hearing Before the Subcommittee on National Parks and Recreation of the Committee on Interior and Insular Affairs, House of Representatives*, 99th Cong., 1st sess. (1985) (panel consisting of Timothy Jenkins, Chairman, the Match Institution; and Nellie Longsworth, President, Preservation Action), 85.
58 Hanson, *Mary McLeod Bethune*, 167.
59 Hanson, *Mary McLeod Bethune*, 167
60 Hanson, *Mary McLeod Bethune*, 218–19.
61 *Wolf Trap Farm Park and Mary McLeod Bethune Council House* (opening statement of Hon. John W. Warner, a U.S. Senator from the State of Virginia), 2.
62 *Wolf Trap Farm Park and Mary McLeod Bethune Council House* (statement of Hon. Mark O. Hatfield, a U.S. Senator from the State of Oregon), 11.
63 *Wolf Trap Farm Park and Mary McLeod Bethune Council House* (statement of Vince De Forest, Afro-American Institute for Historic Preservation and Community Development), 42–43.
64 *Wolf Trap Farm Park and Mary McLeod Bethune Council House* (statement of Sue Bailey Thurmond, Founder and Editor, National Council of Negro Women, *Afro-American Women's Journal*, as presented by Dr. Bettye Collier-Thomas, Director, Historic Program, National Council of Negro Women), 39.
65 *Wolf Trap Farm Park and Mary McLeod Bethune Council House* (statement of Joseph Burstein, Attorney, Fried, Frank, Harris, Shriver, and Kampelman), 41.
66 Burstein statement, *Wolf Trap Farm Park and Mary McLeod Bethune Council House*, 42.

67 *Wolf Trap Farm Park and Mary McLeod Bethune Council House* (statement of Ira J. Hutchison, Deputy Director, National Park Service, Department of the Interior), 44.
68 Latimer, "Bethune Home."
69 *Authorizing Funds for the Mary McLeod Bethune National Historic Site* (statement of Hon. Mary Lou Grier, Deputy Director, National Park Service, U.S. Department of the Interior), 16–17.
70 See Davidson, "Preface," 444.
71 Republican Party of Bexar County, "Bexar Republicans Saddened by the Passing of Mary Lou Grier," press release, February 23, 2013.
72 *Authorizing Funds for the Mary McLeod Bethune National Historic Site* (statement of Hon. Mary Rose Oakar, a U.S. Representative from the State of Ohio), 17.
73 Oakar statement, *Authorizing Funds for the Mary McLeod Bethune National Historic Site*, 20.
74 *Authorizing Funds for the Mary McLeod Bethune National Historic Site*, 22–23.
75 *Authorizing Funds for the Mary McLeod Bethune National Historic Site*, 48–49.
76 *Authorizing Funds for the Mary McLeod Bethune National Historic Site* (panel consisting of Bettye Collier-Thomas, Executive Director, Bethune Council House National Historic Site; Richard Lyman, President, Rockefeller Foundation; and Roberta Anschutz, Vice President, National Council of Women), 51.
77 Panel discussion, *Authorizing Funds for the Mary McLeod Bethune National Historic Site*, 50.
78 Panel discussion, *Authorizing Funds for the Mary McLeod Bethune National Historic Site*, 50.
79 *Authorizing Funds for the Mary McLeod Bethune National Historic Site* (statement of Hon. Lindy Boggs, a U.S. Representative from the State of Louisiana), 84.
80 Witt, *Black Hunger*, 187.
81 Hanson, *Mary McLeod Bethune*, 203.
82 U.S. Congress, *Mary McLeod Bethune Council House*, 1.
83 U.S. Congress, *Mary McLeod Bethune Council House*, 1–2.
84 U.S. Congress, *Mary McLeod Bethune Council House* (statement of Denis Calvin, Associate Director for Planning and Development, National Park Service, Department of the Interior), 6.
85 Calvin statement, U.S. Congress, *Mary McLeod Bethune Council House*, 6.
86 U.S. Congress, Senate Committee on Energy and Natural Resources, *Authorizing the National Park Service*, 2.
87 U.S. Congress, Senate Committee on Energy and Natural Resources, *Authorizing the National Park Service*, 2.
88 Bettye Collier-Thomas and Committee to Save the National Archives for Black Women's History, "Save the National Archives for Black Women's History," press release, February 10, 2014.
89 Joseph, "Memo to Park Service."

90 Colbert I. King, "Dishonoring Bethune's Legacy."
91 In more recent years, historian Elaine Smith echoes Jenkins in explaining rationales behind the geographic establishment of the Council House in Washington, DC, and underscoring the importance of interpretive activities that emphasize Bethune's relationship with the capital city. Smith, *Mary McLeod Bethune and the National Council of Negro Women*, 335–36.
92 "100 Most Fascinating Black Women."

2. From Rosa Parks's *Quiet Strength* to Memorializing a National Mother

1 Durr, *Outside the Magic Circle*, 75.
2 Litwack, *Trouble in Mind*.
3 See McGhee, "Montgomery Bus Boycott," 253. Also see Greenhaw, "Rosa Parks," 8–15.
4 Quoted in "James F. Blake."
5 Theoharis, *Rebellious Life*, 65.
6 Brinkley poignantly draws on Parks's insights in describing Blake's notoriety for mistreating blacks and for insulting black women: "Blake was a vicious bigot who spat tobacco juice out of his bus window and cursed at 'nigras' just for the fun of it. 'He just treated everybody black badly,' Parks remembered. . . . Black women were prime targets for his slurs of 'bitch' and 'coon.' Rosa Parks never could understand the depth of Blake's malignity, but she knew evil in the Christian sense when she saw it." Brinkley, *Rosa Parks*, 58.
7 For more on the ungendering of blacks within the system of slavery, see Hortense Spillers's essay "Mama's Baby, Papa's Maybe," 203–29.
8 McGuire discusses the sexually charged view of southern black women and the routinized forms of violence and terror practiced against them during Jim Crow in *At the Dark End of the Street*. The story of how a white employer in Alabama attempted to coerce the eighteen-year-old Parks into a sexual encounter that she resisted and refused is included in a 1931 personal letter that was released to the public in 2011 as Guernsey's Auctioneers and Brokers prepared for a sale of her belongings. The Howard G. Buffett Foundation, run by the son of billionaire Warren Buffett, bought the archive in 2014 and loaned materials to the Library of Congress for a decade.
9 See Jo Ann Robinson, *Montgomery Bus Boycott*, xiv.
10 McGuire, *At the Dark End of the Street*, 43.
11 Theoharis, *Rebellious Life*, xv.
12 Theoharis, *Rebellious Life*, 16. Toni Morrison poignantly examines this problematic in fiction in her second novel, *Sula* (1973), in a scene on a train involving the character Helene, who has walked through a car designated for whites to get to the one for "COLORED ONLY" and smiles at a white conductor who had been abusive to

her. According to the narrator, the mystifying moment troubles Nel and two black soldiers who are standing nearby. See Toni Morrison, *Sula*, 21.

13 See Carlson, "Troubling Heroes," 51.
14 Hoose, *Claudette Colvin*.
15 U.S. Department of Labor, *Negro Family*.
16 See Brinkley, *Rosa Parks*, 207.
17 Events such as the Children's Crusade, which is sometimes referred to as the Children's March, and the deaths of the four girls at 16th Street Baptist Church, helped to consolidate this narrative of the civil rights era. The Children's Crusade was held in Birmingham, Alabama, on May 2–4, 1963, and organized by Rev. James Bevel in protest of segregation. Numerous black children who stayed out of school to march downtown to appeal to the mayor were attacked with dogs and fire hoses. Many youth were arrested, in some cases repeatedly.
18 Cooperman, Patterson, and Rigelhaupt, "Teaching Race and Revolution," 559.
19 Parks, *Rosa Parks*, 55–70, 59. In the chapter titled "Marriage and Activism," Parks describes witnessing the work of her husband, Raymond Parks, a member of the NAACP and "the first real activist I ever met," on the case involving the Scottsboro Boys, who were falsely accused and jailed for raping a white woman as they rode a train through Alabama and faced the threat of execution. It was a case in which he was deeply invested and that he regularly attended secret meetings to discuss, though women were not allowed to attend the meetings, and he shared no information with his wife to avoid endangering either her life or his. Parks goes on to chronicle her efforts to register to vote after meeting Edgar Daniel Nixon, the president of the Montgomery chapter of the NAACP and the Brotherhood of Sleeping Car Porters, in 1943, joining the organization, becoming secretary, and documenting cases involving racial abuses of blacks such as Recy Taylor, Elmore Bolling, and Jeremiah Reeves.
20 Kuofie, Stephens-Craig, and Dool, "Overview Perception," read Parks as an "introverted leader" and situate her reserved temperament in relation to that of other leaders who have transformed their societies, such as Martin Luther King Jr., Mahatma Gandhi, Mother Teresa, and Barack Obama. Also see Parks, *Rosa Parks*, 59.
21 Wade-Gayles, *Their Memories, Our Treasure*; and Wade-Gayles, Arnold, and SIS, *Their Memories, Our Treasure*.
22 Andrew Parker, *Nationalisms and Sexualities*.
23 Myrdal, *American Dilemma*.
24 Perry, *Looking for Lorraine*.
25 Cleaver, *Soul on Ice*.
26 Perkins, *Autobiography and Activism*, xv; and Ards, *Words of Witness*.
27 For example, my colleague Locksley Edmondson uses Pan-Africanist frameworks and teaches Rosa Parks's writings in juxtaposition with those of other radical black women writers, such as Shirley Graham Du Bois and Amy Jacques Garvey, of the diaspora.

28 Braxton, *Black Women Writing Autobiography*, 9.
29 Braxton, *Black Women Writing Autobiography*, 9.
30 Keys, *Our Auntie Rosa*.
31 Whitt, "Presentation for the Smithsonian Panel."
32 Parks, *Quiet Strength*, 11.
33 Parks, *Quiet Strength*, 21.
34 Parks, *Rosa Parks*, 182.
35 Parks, *Rosa Parks*, 133; and Whitt, "Presentation for the Smithsonian Panel."
36 Parks, *Quiet Strength*, 37.
37 Parks, *Quiet Strength*, 36.
38 Parks, *Quiet Strength*, 80.
39 Parks, *Quiet Strength*, 83.
40 Parks, *Quiet Strength*, 88–89.
41 Parks, *Rosa Parks*, 170.
42 Cooperman, Patterson, and Rigelhaupt, "Teaching Race and Revolution," 558.
43 Parks, *Dear Mrs. Parks*, 15.
44 Parks, *Dear Mrs. Parks*, 23.
45 See Cooks, *Exhibiting Blackness*; and Susan E. Cohen, *Mounting Frustration*.
46 Harris-Perry, *Barbershops, Bibles, and BET*, 3, 6.
47 Boyd, "A Layover in Detroit," 39.
48 Richardson, "Framing Rosa Parks," 54–65.
49 Prior to the establishment of the Rosa Parks Library and Museum, the renaming of Cleveland Avenue as Rosa Parks Avenue and its library as the Rosa Parks Avenue Branch Library in 1999 were the primary ways in which the city of Montgomery had paid tribute and established public monuments to Parks.
50 Dove, *On the Bus*.
51 Stewart is best known for portraying the mother of the nine-year-old girl raped by two white men in the 1996 film *A Time to Kill*, which is set in Mississippi in the post–civil rights era. Stewart also portrayed Johnnie Rebecca Carr as a character in the 2002 film *The Rosa Parks Story*.
52 It is also noteworthy that the Cleveland Avenue Time Machine in the Children's Museum is complemented by a physical timeline stenciled along the walls upstairs, which features major figures associated with the Montgomery bus boycott, beyond its major players such as Parks and King. Furthermore, an interactive computer extends the wall timeline and highlights programs such as the arrest records of a range of citizens who were arrested during the boycott.
53 The ship has been a long-standing metaphor associated with movement in the African American experience. For analysis, see Gilroy, *Black Atlantic*.
54 See Mark Dery, "Black to the Future: Afro-Futurism 1.0," shared by Art McGee, Rumori discussion list, November 4, 2002, http://www.detritus.net/contact/rumori/200211/0319.html.
55 See *Social Text* 20, no. 2 (2002); Everett, *Digital Diaspora*.

56 Alondra Nelson, "Introduction," 6.
57 See Hegel, *Introduction to the Philosophy of History*.
58 Benjamin, *Race after Technology*.
59 In recent times, Boni Wozolek has affirmed the value in linking black women leaders such as Bethune to Afrofuturism in educational contexts. See "Mothership Connection."
60 Brewington, "Thousands Pay Tribute."
61 A Concurrent Resolution Authorizing the Remains of Rosa Parks to Lie in Honor in the Rotunda of the Capitol, S.R. 61, 109th Cong., 1st sess. (2005).
62 See "Nation Hails Rosa Parks." Also see Janofsky, "Thousands Gather at the Capitol"; "U.S. Civil Rights Heroine"; Kurth, "Parks Will Lie in State"; Dvorak and Harris, "Washington Prepares"; Vaughn and Richter, "Nation Pays Tribute"; and "Thousands Attend Rosa Parks Funeral."
63 Orndorff, "Nation Bids Farewell."
64 See Millen, "In Her Debt."
65 Here I refer to the 1959 version of the film directed by Douglas Sirk and starring Lana Turner and Juanita Moore. The 1934 version was directed by John M. Stahl and starred Claudette Colbert and Louise Beavers. Both films are based on a 1933 novel of the same name by Fannie Hurst.
66 Hoffman, "Rosa Parks Honored."
67 Holloway, *Passed On*, 106.
68 Holloway, *Passed On*, 184.
69 Holland, *Raising the Dead*.
70 See Van Der Zee, Dodson, and Billops, *Harlem Book of the Dead*.
71 Theoharis, *Rebellious Life*, x, xii, 216.
72 Many political reactionaries questioned the value of posthumously honoring Parks at the U.S. Capitol building for very different reasons. For instance, neoconservative Jesse Lee Peterson argued in a *WorldNet Daily* editorial, "Using Rosa Parks," that "the legacy and name of Rosa Parks will continue to be used to advance the aims of the corrupt liberal elite, and specifically in the lead-up to the 2006 elections. Shame on them and their pretense of love for Rosa and for America." Reposted by New Destiny on the Free Republic discussion forum, November 16, 2005, http://www.freerepublic.com/focus/f-news/1523219/posts.
73 Theoharis, *Rebellious Life*, x.
74 Notably, Parks was also enshrined on a bronze bust by Artis Lane at the National Portrait Gallery in 1991.
75 White House, "President Bush Signs H.R. 4145 to Place Statue of Rosa Parks in U.S. Capitol," press release, December 1, 2005, https://georgewbush-whitehouse.archives.gov/news/releases/2005/12/20051201-1.html.
76 Southall, "Statue of Rosa Parks."
77 Canaday, *Straight State*; Puar, *Terrorist Assemblages*; Muñoz, *Cruising Utopia*; Warner, *Trouble with Normal*; Conrad, *Against Equality*; Farrow, "Is Gay Marriage

Anti-Black?"; Duggan, *Twilight of Equality*?; and Abdur-Rahman, *Against the Closet*.
78 Littlejohn, "San Pedro Artist's Bronze."
79 See description on "Rosa Parks," Architect of the Capitol, accessed March 20, 2020, http://www.aoc.gov/capitol-hill/other-statues/rosa-parks.
80 Littlejohn, "San Pedro Artist's Bronze." Also see Radin, "Kensington Artist."
81 Flock, "Sculptor Gives Behind-the-Scenes Look."

3. America's Chief Diplomat

1   For more insights on this topic, see the special issue of *American Quarterly* edited by Clyde Woods, "In the Wake of Hurricane Katrina," published in June 2010. Also see his co-authored study with Laura Pulido, *Development Drowned and Reborn*.
2   Jessica, "Condi Spends Salary on Shoes."
3   Rush et al., "As South Drowns, Rice Soaks in N.Y."
4   Patricia A. Turner, *I Heard It through the Grapevine*.
5   Jessica Robertson, "Kanye West Blasts Bush."
6   Condoleezza Rice, "Interview with *Essence* Magazine," U.S. Department of State Archive, May 25, 2006, https://2001-2009.state.gov/secretary/rm/2006/71813.htm.
7   Rice, *No Higher Honor*, 396, 399.
8   See Tatsha Robertson, "Being Condoleezza," 187.
9   For insights on black women and politics, see Mitchell and Covin, *Broadening the Contours*.
10 King and Riddlesperger, "Diversity and Presidential Cabinet Appointments," 97.
11 Boushee, "RNC's California Experiment."
12 See Vagnoux, "Introduction," 2.
13 See Bamberger, "Changing Face of Shoal Creek"; Myers, "Rice to Chair Champions Major"; and "Augusta National Slowly Changing."
14 Rice, *Extraordinary, Ordinary People*.
15 I explore additional representations of Rice in popular culture and art in unpublished essays that examine David Hare's play *Stuff Happens* and Sebastian Doggart's "Condi Trilogy" docudrama.
16 Spillers, "Long Time," 149–82.
17 Rice, *Extraordinary, Ordinary People*.
18 Prisock, "CEO of Self," 180.
19 See Bernstein, *Racial Innocence*; Wilma King, *Stolen Childhood*; Patton, *Spare the Kids*; and Nazera Sadiq Wright, *Black Girlhood*.
20 Kenney, "Condoleezza Rice Speaks to Grads."
21 Eugene Robinson, "Baghdad Isn't Birmingham."
22 Eugene Robinson, "Baghdad Isn't Birmingham."
23 Valerie Smith, "Remembering Birmingham Sunday," 180.

24 Valerie Smith, "Remembering Birmingham Sunday," 181. The ubiquity and recurrence of the narrative of "four little girls" to epitomize violence against blacks during the civil rights era also belies, for example, the individuality of the victims and does not have a rhetorical counterpart in the losses of "little boys" to racist terror and violence, including fourteen-year-old Emmett Till, who had been the same age as Addie Mae Collins, Carole Robertson, and Cynthia Wesley when he was lynched and mutilated in Mississippi in 1955. The narrative also obscures the injuries of others in the bombing, including Sarah Collins, the twelve-year-old sister of Addie Mae, who was blinded in one eye.
25 Mambry, *Condoleezza Rice*.
26 Rice, *Extraordinary, Ordinary People*, 5.
27 Berlant, *Queen of America*, 1.
28 Berlant, *Queen of America*, 28.
29 Prisock, "CEO of Self," 181.
30 Rice, *Extraordinary, Ordinary People*, 6.
31 The autobiography further registers the influence of a discourse on immigration, multiethnicity, and transnationality in relation to Rice in noting the Italian aspect of her ancestry on her maternal grandfather's side, which has inspired naming patterns across several generations, including her own name, which her mother chose based on Italian musical terms, such as *con dolce* and *con dolcezza*, a name that means "with sweetness."
32 Kaplan, Alarcón, and Moallem, *Between Woman and Nation*.
33 Royster, "Condi, Cleopatra," 103. Gilson makes similar observations about Hillary Clinton in "LOLZ with Hillz," 635.
34 Royster, "Condi, Cleopatra," 105.
35 See D'Ambruoso, "Norms, Perverse Effects, and Torture," 33–60.
36 Watkins, *On the Real Side*, 11.
37 Jackson, *Racial Paranoia*. The struggles in the comedy field, which led Chappelle to turn away from his successful comedy career because he felt mocked as a black person through his popular stage skits, are well known.
38 Wisniewski, *Comedy of Dave Chappelle*, 9.
39 The series of "Condi Comes to Harlem" skits also in effect speaks to Rice's potential to be a black radical. They are reminiscent of the portrayal of neoconservative Clarence Thomas as a closeted black radical in a skit on Keenen Ivory Wayans's popular television show, *In Living Color*, during the third episode of the third season. In the wake of Thomas's confirmation in 1991, in a skit entitled "Clarence Thomas's First Day," the actor David Alan Grier portrays Thomas acting like the obsequious Uncle Tom stereotype by serving the coffee of his compatriots and aligning with them against black interests as they review cases. Once he learns that his appointment is for life, he begins to speak in a radical voice that contradicts their perception of him as docile on race matters, describing himself as a true black

radical and their worst nightmare. The theme song to the blaxploitation film *Shaft* plays as the skit ends.

40 As Malcolm X famously commented in his 1964 speech "The Ballot or the Bullet," "Stop talking about the South. Long as you south of the—Long as you south of the Canadian border, you're south." See Malcolm X, *Malcolm X Speaks*, 23–44.

41 I consider this problematic in the fourth chapter of my first book, *Black Masculinity and the U.S. South*.

42 See Jennie Livingston's 1990 film *Paris Is Burning*. See related discussions by hooks, *Black Looks*; Butler, *Bodies that Matter*; and Steven Thrasher, "Paris Is 'Still' Burning." Also see Bailey, *Butch Queens up in Pumps*.

43 Baraka, *Somebody Blew Up America*.

44 Nas, *American Way*, Sony Urban Music/Columbia, 2004.

45 Manning Marable remarks, "In the field of foreign affairs, the leading race traitor, hands down, is Condoleezza Rice, Bush's national security adviser." See *Great Wells of Democracy*. One of the most sustained discussions of the black public sphere as a concept is available in the Black Public Sphere Collective's edited volume *Black Public Sphere*. Also see Habermas, *Structural Transformation*.

46 See Kern-Foxworth, *Aunt Jemima, Uncle Ben, and Rastus*; and Witt, *Black Hunger*.

47 Clayton Bigsby provided another useful illustration of the routine conflations of Rice with food when he remarked that "Condoleezza Rice, sounds like a Mexican dish. Maybe we should put her on a plate and send her to Mexico so the Mexicans will eat her" on the first episode of the first season of *Chappelle's Show* in 2003. More broadly, this phenomenon accords with the ideological identifications of African American women with food that have been analyzed by Witt in *Black Hunger*.

48 Latinx contexts are important to acknowledge, too, given Rice's background as provost at Stanford, California's premier private university. She spearheaded budgetary reductions and faculty and staff reductions that affected ethnic studies and garnered controversy on the campus. Her firing of Cecilia Burciaga, a Chicana dean of students and the top ranking Latina/x administrator, led to protests. See Barabak, "Not Always Diplomatic."

49 Kipnis, "Condi's Inner Life."

50 See Gilsdorf, "Luc Tuymans." Also see David Cohen, "Couch-Potato Painter"; and Knight, "Luc Tuymans."

51 Glenn Kessler notes in his study of Condoleezza Rice that Jim Wilkinson, one of Rice's aides, "decided to move Rice's news conferences with foreign officials upstairs to the ornate rooms of the seventh and eighth floors of the State Department. Rice would be photographed in front of a fireplace or walking fifty feet to a microphone evoking the spirit of presidential sessions in the White House." See Kessler, *Confidante*, 22.

52 See Malone, Allen, and Bentley, "I Love Her Very Much." Rice reports herself in *No Higher Honor*, the 2011 sequel to *Extraordinary, Ordinary People*, that during her

visit to Libya in 2008 as secretary of state, Gaddafi had shown her a slide show featuring photographs of her with various world leaders set to a song entitled "Black Flower in the White House," called her "Leeza," and given her gifts that included a diamond ring, a locket with an engraved photo of himself, and a lute. Rice, *No Higher Honor*, 702–3.

53 Patricia A. Turner, *Ceramic Uncles and Celluloid Mammies*.
54 Rice holds a book here inscribed with "Iraq," another salient artistic use of text in juxtaposition with image, as is the case in the images of Lloyd and Moor.
55 Boyce-Davies, *Black Women, Writing, and Identity*; also see Boyce-Davies, "CON-DI-FI-CATION"; Boyce-Davies, "Con-di-fi-cation."
56 Rooks, "Black Fashion," 4.
57 Rooks, "Black Fashion," 4.
58 Hannity, "Interview with Sean Hannity."
59 Greer, "This Is the Age of Power Pearls."
60 Givhan, "Condoleezza Rice's Commanding Style."
61 Lisa Thompson, *Beyond the Black Lady*.
62 Givhan, "Condoleezza Rice's Commanding Style."
63 Givhan, "Condoleezza Rice's Commanding Style."
64 Nadia E. Brown, *Sisters in the Statehouse*.

4. First Lady and "Mom-in-Chief"

1 Mundy, *Michelle*, 4. In general, Michelle Obama has been the subject of exclusive features or special issues in countless magazines, including *Essence, Vogue, Oprah, Today's Black Woman*, and *Life*. She has been the subject of several biographies and, as the nation's First Lady, has also emerged as a topic of great interest in genres ranging from style manuals to children's books. A number of texts on Michelle Obama and the Obama phenomenon are beginning to appear. Other works include Lightfoot, *Michelle Obama*; Michelle Obama, *In Her Own Words*; Michelle Obama, *Speeches*; Christopher P. Anderson, *Barack and Michelle*; and Slevin, *Michelle Obama*. The book by Anderson underscores the profound influence of Michelle Obama on her husband's thinking and the importance of her opinions to him, a point that has been recurrent in aspects of black feminist theory that have looked at the unacknowledged and obscured influence of the wives of major black leaders on the thinking of their husbands, as evident, for example, in Beverly Guy-Sheftall's project on Coretta Scott King, the wife of civil rights leader Martin Luther King Jr., and Ula Taylor's project on Amy Jacques Garvey, the wife of Universal Improvement Association leader Marcus Garvey. Within the growing body of publications on Michelle Obama, Nevergold and Brooks-Bertram's anthology *Go Tell Michelle* is important to mention in light of my interests in the national reach of Michelle Obama as a model of black femininity and the emphasis on black

women's voices in this project of national scope, along with the volume's inclusion of letters and poems honoring the First Lady and the articulation of issues of specific social and political concern related to black women.
2   Mundy, *Michelle*, 18.
3   Such scripts of Michelle Obama seem designed to assuage anxieties for some African American sectors that Barack Obama is "not black enough" given his birth in Hawaii and status as an interracial man born to a white mother from Kansas and a black father from Kenya. They also speak to anxieties in the national mainstream that he is "not American enough" given his father's Kenyan origins.
4   Crouch, "On Lady Obama."
5   Gwendolyn Brooks famously explored the feminine dimensions of the South Side through her title character's kitchenette apartment in her 1953 novella *Maud Martha*. The same is true of Lorraine Hansberry's 1959 play *A Raisin in the Sun*, in its characterizations of Lena, Beneatha, and Ruth Younger.
6   Jacqueline Jones, "Southern Diaspora," 27–54.
7   Allen, introduction in "Black/Queer/Diaspora," 211–48.
8   The release of the landmark television miniseries *Roots* in 1977, based on the epic book by Alex Haley, which traces his paternal lineage to his ancestor Kunta Kinte in West Africa, fueled the interest among African Americans in studying genealogy in the final decades of the twentieth century. In recent years, scholar Henry Louis Gates Jr., director of the W. E. B. Du Bois Institute for African and African American Research and the Alphonse Fletcher University Professor at Harvard University, has stood at the forefront in popularizing the study and teaching of genealogy through projects such as his book *Finding Oprah's Roots* and by hosting television series such as *African American Lives* (2006), *African American Lives 2* (2008), *Faces of America* (2010), and *Finding Your Roots* (2012). On the other hand, the research of scholars such as Alondra Nelson has also critiqued the popular contemporary fascination with genealogy and emphasized the limits and drawbacks entailed in the prevailing approaches to scientifically based methods of genetic testing in *The Social Life of DNA*. DNA testing has been among the research strategies that have been used in recent years to trace the family histories of both Barack Obama and Michelle Obama.
9   See Barack Obama, *Barack Obama's Speech on Race*.
10 Since the 1930s, the property has been owned by Frances Cheston Train's family, who turned it into a hunting preserve for rich northern tourists. Glanton and St. Clair, "Michelle Obama's Family Tree."
11 Swarns and Kantor, "In First Lady's Roots." Also see Swarns, "From Slavery to the White House."
12 Swarns and Kantor, "In First Lady's Roots."
13 Walsh, *Family of Freedom*, 209–10. Walsh describes the involvement of slaves in the construction of the White House from 1791, when its chief planner, Pierre L'Enfant, drew on slave labor in digging the building's foundation, and other slaves

in Virginia quarried stone used for its walls. According to him, "The slaves, along with free men, worked six days a week, twelve hours a day, from dawn to dusk, with a one-hour midday break for a meal, usually of salt pork or mutton, hoe cakes, and grease sandwiches. The slaves were not chained, but they were closely supervised" (7).
14. Swarns, *American Tapestry*.
15. Swarns, *American Tapestry*, 299.
16. Ellis and Ginsburg, *Cabin, Quarter, Plantation*.
17. Lusane, *Black History of the White House*.
18. Hancock, *Race and the Naming of the White House*.
19. In a 2009 interview with Oprah Winfrey, Obama discusses her approach to supervising the East Wing of the White House: "So in the first few days, I gathered my East Wing team and the residence staff—the folks who clean the chandeliers, the people in the kitchen, everyone—and thanked them for helping us transition through the move. Then I talked about our vision for this house: that it would be filled with life, that we'd have people in and out, that the kids would roam around. I want the kids to be treated like children, not little princesses. I told everyone that they should make their beds, they should clean their plates, they should act respectfully—and that if anyone on the staff sees differently, they should come to me. So the girls help set the table, they help bring the food out, they work with the butler staff, and they're in the kitchen laughing and making their toast in the morning. And everyone has adjusted to the rules." Winfrey, "Oprah Talks to Michelle Obama," 144.
20. Jeffries, *Paint the White House Black*, 120.
21. Michelle Obama, "Feed Your Children Well," 40.
22. Michelle Obama, *American Grown*.
23. Loizeau, "First Lady but Second Fiddle," 6.
24. Michelle Obama, *Becoming*, 284.
25. Michelle Obama, *Becoming*, 320.
26. Black feminist analysis that has considered the race and class politics of the Cult of True Womanhood has been provided by a range of scholars, including Guy-Sheftall, *Daughters of Sorrow*; Giddings, *When and Where I Enter*; and Collins, *Black Feminist Thought*.
27. This now infamous image appeared on the *Daily Kos* blog, May 19, 2008. It has since been removed from the site but as of June 2020 is still available at http://littlegreenfootballs.com/weblog/pictures/20080519DailyKosSouthernScreen.jpg.
28. Collins, *Black Feminist Thought*; and Lomax, *Jezebel Unhinged*.
29. Knuckey and Kim, "Evaluations of Michelle Obama."
30. Richardson, "Kara Walker's Old South."
31. Harris-Perry, "Defeating History's Demons," 72.
32. Feagans, "Georgian Recalls Rooming with Michelle Obama."
33. Feagans, "Georgian Recalls Rooming with Michelle Obama."
34. Feagans, "Georgian Recalls Rooming with Michelle Obama."

35 Even without knowledge of her roommate's reaction, the introduction to Michelle Obama's senior thesis had conveyed the sense of unbelonging that she felt sometimes at Princeton: "My experiences at Princeton have made me far more aware of my 'Blackness' than ever before. I have found that at Princeton no matter how liberal and open-minded some of my white professors and classmates try to be toward me, I sometimes feel like a visitor on campus, as if I really do not belong." Michelle La-Vaughn Robinson, "Princeton-Educated Blacks and the Black Community," 2. The project, which focused on the university's black alumni's feelings about race and commitments to black community and notions of giving back, also anticipated her ongoing commitment to the South Side in her career work and public service.

36 For more on black southern migration to Chicago and the South Side community, see, for example, Grossman, *Land of Hope*; and Wilkerson, *Warmth of Other Suns*.

37 *Michelle Obama: South Side Girl*, video, 6:28, uploaded by BarackObamadotcom, YouTube, August 25, 2008, http://www.youtube.com/watch?v=2Utt-6HumUU.

38 Craig Robinson, *Game of Character*, 35.

39 In a speech in Milwaukee, Wisconsin, on February 18, 2009, Michelle Obama remarked, "For the first time in my adult lifetime, I'm really proud of my country . . . not just because Barack has done well, but because I think people are hungry for change. . . . I have been desperate to see our country moving in that direction and not just feeling so alone in my frustration and disappointment." See "First Time Proud" in Michelle Obama, *Speeches*, 49–50.

40 Barack Obama, *Audacity of Hope*, 330.

41 This satirical political image, produced by Barry Blitt for the July 21, 2008, cover of the *New Yorker*, is entitled *The Politics of Fear*.

42 See the text of "One Nation," which was originally presented at the DNC on August 25, 2008, in Michelle Obama, *Speeches*, 79–88.

43 The official White House site profiling First Lady Michelle Obama notes, "The Robinsons lived in a brick bungalow on the South Side of Chicago. Fraser was a pump operator for the Chicago Water Department, and despite being diagnosed with multiple sclerosis at a young age, he hardly ever missed a day of work. Marian stayed home to raise Michelle and her older brother Craig, skillfully managing a busy household filled with love, laughter, and important life lessons." "Michelle Obama," White House, https://www.whitehouse.gov/about-the-white-house/first-ladies/michelle-obama/.

44 Krissah Thompson, "Leading Lady," 133.

45 Winfrey, "Oprah Talks to Michelle Obama," 143.

46 Talley, "Michelle Obama," 431.

47 Cheyfitz, *Disinformation Age*.

48 McDonald, "Racial Equity in the Farm Bill"; and Daniel, "African American Farmers," 3–36.

49 Shabazz, *Spatializing Blackness*.

50 Harper, *Sistah Vegan*.

51 Michelle Obama, "Feed Your Children Well," 40.
52 Michelle Obama, "Feed Your Children Well," 40.
53 Michelle Roberts, "Child and Teen Obesity."
54 Julie Hirschfeld Davis, "Closer."
55 Witt, *Black Hunger*.
56 Tipton-Martin, *Jemima Code*.
57 Hayden, "Michelle Obama, Mom-in-Chief," 14; also see Collins, *Black Feminist Thought*.
58 Hayden, "Michelle Obama, Mom-in-Chief," 16.
59 Grey, "Contesting the Fat Citizen," 566.
60 Michelle Obama, *American Grown*, 10.
61 Braxton, *Black Women Writing Autobiography*, 9.
62 Michelle Obama, *American Grown*, 19.
63 Ryan, "Changing the Conversation," 76.
64 Ryan, "Changing the Conversation," 86, 87.
65 Hayden, "Michelle Obama, Mom-in-Chief," 24
66 Cheyfitz, *Disinformation Age*.
67 Confessore, "How School Lunch Became the Latest Political Battleground."
68 Jansen, "Beyoncé Lends Star Power."
69 Kantor, *Obamas*, 42.
70 Talley, "Michelle Obama," 504.
71 Winfrey, "Oprah Talks to Michelle Obama," 143.
72 Freeman, *Wedding Complex*.
73 Stockett, *Help*.
74 Patricia A. Turner, "Dangerous White Stereotypes."
75 "An Open Statement to the Fans of *The Help*," Association of Black Women Historians, August 12, 2011, http://www.abwh.org/index.php?option=com_content&view=article&id=2%3Aopen-statement-the-help.
76 Silverstein, "Going to See *The Help*."

Conclusion

1 Iton, *In Search of the Black Fantastic*.
2 Beyoncé and Joseph, *Lemonade*.
3 Jamil Smith, "New Beyoncé Video."
4 For the full transcript, see Piers Morgan, "Interview with Beyoncé," *Piers Morgan Tonight*, aired June 27, 2011, http://transcripts.cnn.com/TRANSCRIPTS/1106/27/pmt.01.html.
5 "At Last" was written in 1941 by Mack Gordon and Harry Warren. It was initially popularized by the Glenn Miller orchestra and by Nat King Cole in 1957 before being adopted by James in 1961. It was reported widely that veteran singer Etta

James lashed out at Beyoncé in the wake the performance of the song at the inauguration and was upset that she was not invited to perform at the event. During a performance at the Paramount Theatre in Seattle, Washington, on January 28, 2009, James reportedly commented to the audience, "You guys know your president, right? You know the one with the big ears? Wait a minute, he ain't my president. He might be yours; he ain't my president. But I tell you that woman he had singing for him, singing my song—she's going to get her ass whupped." Furthermore, James is reported to have snidely commented, "The great Beyoncé . . . I can't stand Beyoncé. She has no business up there, singing up there on a big ol' president day, gonna be singing my song that I've been singing forever." Michaels, "Etta James." In an interview a few days later with the *New York Daily News*, James underscored that her comments were a joke. Melago, "Etta James Truly Miffed."

6   Morgan, "Interview with Beyoncé."
7   Morgan, "Interview with Beyoncé."
8   Morgan, "Interview with Beyoncé." In this interview with Morgan, Beyoncé further underscores the struggles that her parents endured by remarking, "My mother worked thirteen hours a day and I never heard her complain. She worked until her feet were calloused. . . . My father was an incredible entrepreneur and whatever he said he was going to have he worked until he had it." She also notes that she "grew up with a family that was successful but not born successful." Mathew Knowles also discusses the pain of Jim Crow in his memoir, *Racism from the Eyes of a Child*. I interviewed him at Cornell University alongside Harvard University scholar Marla Frederick in "A Conversation with Dr. Mathew Knowles," September 27, 2019. See https://www.youtube.com/watch?v=oUHMyS7odOI&t=2238s.
9   Easlea, *Beyoncé*, 1. Easlea goes on to say, "A true product of the American South, he [Mathew Knowles] saw at first hand segregation and the hatred from whites in a changing, troubled America. In his youth, the country was a cauldron of uncertainty and change, yet outwardly, it was almost impossible to notice. The world image of the country was one of a happy, smiling, white suburbia" (1). For additional biographical perspective on Beyoncé, see Arenofsky, *Beyoncé Knowles*; and Taraborrelli, *Becoming Beyoncé*.
10 Morgan, "Interview with Beyoncé."
11 Morgan, "Interview with Beyoncé."
12 Baker and Simmons, *Trouble with Postblackness*.
13 Morgan, "Interview with Beyoncé."
14 See Richardson, "Beyoncé's South and a 'Formation' Nation." Also see Richardson, "Forgetting Farrah."
15 See Halperin, "Beyoncé Delivers."
16 Halperin, "Beyoncé Delivers."
17 Moore, *How to Be Beyoncé*.
18 See, for example, Trier-Bieniek, *Beyoncé Effect*; Chambers, *Queen Bey*; and Brooks and Martin, *Lemonade Reader*.

19 See Johnson, *Sweet Tea*. Similarly, his *Black. Queer. South. Women.* has amplified the voices of black queer women in the South.
20 Mock, "My Feminist Awakening."
21 The post of the letter can be accessed directly at "Michelle Obama—The Ultimate Example," Beyoncé website, April 11, 2012, https://www.beyonce.com/article/michelle-obama-2/.
22 Beyoncé and Michelle Obama have been most prominently linked in the national arena through the First Lady's Let's Move! campaign, which was launched on February 10, 2010, and designed to combat childhood obesity by encouraging healthful eating in schools throughout the nation. The song "Move Your Body," which was composed by Beyoncé and hip-hop artist Swizz Beatz, was developed to promote the campaign and to encourage exercise; the video features Beyoncé dancing with children in the cafeteria at a school. Her support of this initiative draws on her celebrity and reinforces Beyoncé's visibility in the national political arena, providing her with a platform that will help make a difference in the lives of youth.
23 Beyoncé's letter to First Lady Michelle Obama picks up and mirrors the impulse that many African American women have had to reach out with missives to the First Lady, as evidenced in the rich compilation co-edited by Nevergold and Brooks-Bertram, *Go Tell Michelle*.
24 See Michelle Obama, Twitter, April 13, 2012, 12:04 PM, https://twitter.com/MichelleObama/status/190847977152188416.
25 See Steptoe, "Beyoncé's Western South Serenade," 183–91.
26 Baker and Nelson, "Violence, the Body." Baker's work, like my own and that of newer scholars in the field, has advanced critical reflection on black southerners. For example, see Zandria Robinson, *This Ain't Chicago*.
27 See Caramanica, Morris, and Wortham, "Beyoncé in 'Formation.'"
28 See Caramanica, Morris, and Wortham, "Beyoncé in 'Formation.'"
29 Neal, *What the Music Said*.

{ BIBLIOGRAPHY }

Abdur-Rahman, Aliyyah. *Against the Closet: Black Political Longing and the Erotics of Race*. Durham, NC: Duke University Press, 2012.
Adichie, Chimamanda Ngozi. "To the First Lady, with Love." *New York Times*, October 17, 2016.
Allen, Jafari Sinclaire. "Black/Queer/Diaspora at the Current Conjuncture." *GLQ* 18, nos. 2–3 (2012): 211–48.
Allen, Robert L., and Robert Chrisman, ed. *Court of Appeal: The Black Community Speaks Out on the Racial and Sexual Politics of Thomas vs. Hill*. New York: Ballantine, 1992.
Anderson, Benedict. *Imagined Communities: Reflections on the Origin and Spread of Nationalism*. New York: Verso, 1998.
Anderson, Christopher P. *Barack and Michelle: Portrait of an American Marriage*. New York: Morrow, 2009.
Anderson, James D. "Aunt Jemima in Dialectics: Genovese on Slave Culture." *Journal of African American History* 87 (2002): 26–42.
Angelou, Maya. *I Know Why the Caged Bird Sings*. 1970. New York: Bantam, 1993.
Applebome, Peter. *Dixie Rising: How the South Is Shaping American Values, Politics, and Culture*. New York: Mariner, 1997.
Ards, Angela A. *Words of Witness: Black Women's Autobiography in the Post-Brown Era*. Madison: University of Wisconsin Press, 2016.
Arenofsky, Janice. *Beyoncé Knowles: A Biography*. Westport, CT: Greenwood, 2009.
Ashmore, Susan Youngblood, and Lisa Lindquist Dorr, eds. *Alabama Women: Their Lives and Times*. Athens: University of Georgia Press, 2017.
"Augusta National Slowly Changing Its Discriminatory Tradition." *Sport Digest*, August 22, 2012. http://thesportdigest.com/2012/08/augusta-national-slowly-changing-its-discriminatory-tradition/.
Ayee, G. Y. A., J. D. Johnson Carew, T. N. Means, A. M. Reyes-Barrientez, and N. A. Sediqe. "White House, Black Mother: Michelle Obama and the Politics of Motherhood as First Lady." *Politics and Gender* 15, no. 3 (2019): 460–83.
Badas, Alex, and Katelyn E. Stauffer. "Michelle Obama as a Political Symbol: Race, Gender, and Public Opinion toward the First Lady." *Politics and Gender* 15, no. 3 (2019): 431–59.
Bailey, Marlon. *Butch Queens up in Pumps: Gender, Performance, and Ballroom Culture in Detroit*. Ann Arbor: University of Michigan Press, 2013.

Baker, Houston A., Jr. *Critical Memory: Public Spheres, African American Writing, and Black Fathers and Sons in America*. Athens: University of Georgia Press, 2001.

Baker, Houston A., Jr. *Turning South Again: Re-Thinking Modernism/Re-Reading Booker T*. Durham, NC: Duke University Press, 2001.

Baker, Houston A., Jr., and Dana D. Nelson, eds. "Violence, the Body, and 'the South.'" Special issue, *American Literature* 73, no. 2 (June 2001): 232–458.

Baker, Houston A., Jr., and Merinda Simmons, eds. *The Trouble with Postblackness*. New York: Columbia University Press, 2015.

Bamberger, Michael. "The Changing Face of Shoal Creek." *Golf Magazine*, August 2010.

Barabak, Mark Z. "Not Always Diplomatic in Her First Major Post." *Los Angeles Times*, January 16, 2005.

Baraka, Amiri. *Somebody Blew Up America and Other Poems*. New York: House of Nehesi, 2010.

Barnett, Rex, dir. *Mary McLeod Bethune: The Spirit of a Champion*. History on Video, 1996.

Basuli, Deb. "Cutting across Imperial Feminisms toward Transnational Feminist Solidarities." *Meridians: Feminism, Race, Transnationalism* 13, no. 2 (2016): 164–88.

Benjamin, Ruha. *Race after Technology: Abolitionist Tools for the New Jim Code*. Cambridge: Polity, 2019.

Berlant, Lauren. "Intimacy: A Special Issue." In *Intimacy*, edited by Lauren Berlant, 281–88. Chicago: University of Chicago Press, 2000.

Berlant, Lauren. "National Brands, National Body: *Imitation of Life*." In *Comparative American Identities: Race, Sex, and Nationality in the Modern Text*, edited by Hortense Spillers, 110–40. New York: Routledge, 1991.

Berlant, Lauren. *The Queen of America Goes to Washington City: Essays on Sex and Citizenship*. Durham, NC: Duke University Press, 1997.

Berlant, Lauren. "The Queen of America Goes to Washington City: Harriet Jacobs, Frances Harper, Anita Hill." In *Subjects and Citizens: Nation, Race, and Gender from Oroonoko to Anita Hill*, edited by Michael Moon and Cathy N. Davidson, 455–80. Durham, NC: Duke University Press, 1995.

Bernstein, Robin. *Racial Innocence: Performing American Childhood from Slavery to Civil Rights*. New York: New York University Press, 2011.

Bethune, Mary McLeod. *Building a Better World: Essays and Selected Documents*. Edited by Audrey Thomas McCluskey and Elaine M. Smith. Bloomington: Indiana University Press, 1999.

Bethune, Mary McLeod. "My Last Will and Testament." *Ebony*, August 1955, 105–10.

Bethune, Mary McLeod. *NYA and Negro Youth*. Washington, DC: Division of Negro Affairs, National Youth Administration, 1940.

Beyoncé and Kahlil Joseph, dirs. *Lemonade*. Parkwood Entertainment/Columbia, 2016.

Bhabha, Homi. *The Location of Culture*. New York: Routledge, 1994.

The Black Public Sphere Collective. *The Black Public Sphere*. Chicago: University of Chicago Press, 1995.

Blain, Keisha N., and Tiffany Gill, eds. *To Turn the Whole World Over: Black Women and Internationalism*. Urbana: University of Illinois Press, 2019.

Block, Ray. "Race, Gender, and Media Coverage of Michelle Obama." *Politics, Groups, and Identities* 5, no. 1 (2017): 161–65.

Bobo, Jacqueline, and Cynthia Hudley. *The Black Studies Reader*. New York: Routledge, 2004.

Borgstrom, Michael. "Passing Over: Setting the Record Straight in *Uncle Tom's Cabin*." PMLA 118, no. 5 (2003): 1290–1304.

Boushee, Nicholas. "The RNC's California Experiment: State and National Party Collaboration in Reforms to Minority Outreach." *California Journal of Politics and Policy* 8, no. 4 (2016): 1–16.

Boyce-Davies, Carole. *Black Women, Writing, and Identity: Migrations of the Subject*. New York: Routledge, 1994.

Boyce-Davies, Carole. "'Con-di-fi-cation': Black Women, Leadership and Political Power." *Feminist Africa* 7 (2006): 67–88.

Boyce-Davies, Carole. "CON-DI-FI-CATION: Transnationalism, Diaspora, and the Limits of Domestic Racial or Feminist Discourses." *Jenda: A Journal of Culture and African Women's Studies* 9 (2006): 1–39.

Boyd, Melba Joyce. "A Layover in Detroit, or Wherein Lies the Future of Black Studies?" *Souls* 2, no. 3 (2000): 37–42.

Bracey, Christopher Allen. *Saviors or Sellouts: The Promise and Peril of Black Conservatism, from Booker T. Washington to Condoleezza Rice*. Boston: Beacon, 2008.

Braxton, Joanne M., ed. *Black Women Writing Autobiography: A Tradition within a Tradition*. Philadelphia: Temple University Press, 1989.

Braxton, Joanne M., and Andree Nicola McLaughlin, eds. *Wild Women in the Whirlwind: Afra-American Culture and the Contemporary Literary Renaissance*. New Brunswick, NJ: Rutgers University Press, 1989.

Brewington, Kelly. "Thousands Pay Tribute—Rosa Parks Is the First Woman and Second African-American to Lie in Honor in the Capitol Rotunda." *Baltimore Sun*, October 31, 2005.

Brinkley, Douglas. *Rosa Parks: A Life*. New York: Penguin, 2005.

Brodie, Fawn. *Thomas Jefferson: An Intimate History*. New York: Norton, 2010.

Brooks, Gwendolyn. *Maud Martha*. New York: Harper, 1953.

Brooks, Kinitra D., and Kameelah L. Martin. *The Lemonade Reader: Beyoncé, Black Feminism, and Spirituality*. New York: Routledge, 2019.

Brown, Mary Beth. *Condi: The Life of a Steel Magnolia*. Nashville, TN: Thomas Nelson, 2007.

Brown, Nadia E. *Sisters in the Statehouse: Black Women and Legislative Decision Making*. New York: Oxford University Press, 2014.

Butler, Judith. *Bodies that Matter: On the Discursive Limits of Sex*. New York: Routledge, 1993.

Butler, Judith. *Gender Trouble: Feminism and the Subversion of Identity*. New York: Routledge, 1992.

Canaday, Margot. *The Straight State: Sexuality and Citizenship in Twentieth-Century America*. Princeton, NJ: Princeton University Press, 2011.

Caramanica, Jon, Wesley Morris, and Jenna Wortham. "Beyoncé in 'Formation': Entertainer, Activist, Both?" *New York Times*, February 6, 2016.

Carlson, Dennis. "Troubling Heroes: Of Rosa Parks, Multicultural Education, and Critical Pedagogy." *Cultural Studies—Critical Methodologies* 3, no. 1 (2003): 44–61.

Caroli, Betty Boyd. *First Ladies: From Martha Washington to Michelle Obama*. New York: Oxford University Press, 2010.

Carretta, Vincent. *Phillis Wheatley: Biography of a Genius in Bondage*. Athens: University of Georgia Press, 2011.

Chambers, Veronica, ed. *Queen Bey: A Celebration of the Power and Creativity of Beyoncé Knowles-Carter*. New York: St. Martin's, 2019.

Chatelain, Marcia. *South Side Girls: Growing Up in the Great Migration*. Durham, NC: Duke University Press, 2015.

Cheyfitz, Eric. *The Disinformation Age: The Collapse of Liberal Democracy in the United States*. New York: Routledge, 2017.

Cleaver, Eldridge. *Soul on Ice*. Crystal Lake, IL: Delta, 1968.

Clemons, Michael L. *African Americans in Global Affairs: Contemporary Perspectives*. Boston: Northeastern University Press, 2010.

Cohen, Cathy J. *Democracy Remixed: Black Youth and the Future of American Politic*. New York: Oxford University Press, 2012.

Cohen, Cathy J., Kathy Jones, and Joan C. Tronto, eds. *Women Transforming Politics: An Alternative Reader*. New York: New York University Press, 1997.

Cohen, David. "The Couch-Potato Painter." *New York Sun*, October 20, 2005.

Cohen, Susan E. *Mounting Frustration: The Art Museum in the Age of Black Power*. Durham, NC: Duke University Press, 2016.

Collier-Thomas, Bettye, and Vincent P. Franklin. *Sisters in the Struggle: African American Women in the Civil Rights–Black Power Movement*. New York: New York University Press, 2001.

Collins, Patricia Hill. *Black Feminist Thought: Knowledge, Consciousness, and the Politics of Empowerment*. New York: Routledge, 1990.

Collins, Patricia Hill. *Intersectionality as Critical Social Theory*. Durham, NC: Duke University Press, 2019.

Collins, Patricia Hill, and Sirma Bilge. *Intersectionality*. Cambridge: Polity, 2016.

Confessore, Nicholas. "How School Lunch Became the Latest Political Battleground." *New York Times*, October 7, 2014.

Conrad, Ryan, ed. *Against Equality: Queer Revolution, Not Mere Inclusion*. Chico, CA: AK Press, 2014.

Cooks, Bridget R. *Exhibiting Blackness: African Americans and the American Art Museum*. Amherst: University of Massachusetts Press, 2011.

Cooper, Anna Julia. *A Voice from the South*. 1892. New York: Oxford University Press, 1988.

Cooper, Brittney. *Beyond Respectability: The Intellectual Thought of Race Women*. Urbana: University of Illinois Press, 2017.

Cooper, Brittney. *Eloquent Rage: A Black Feminist Discovers Her Superpower*. New York: St. Martin's, 2018.

Cooperman, Rosalyn, Melina Patterson, and Jess Rigelhaupt. "Teaching Race and Revolution: Doing Justice to Women's Roles in the Struggle for Civil Rights." *Political Science* 49, no. 3 (2016): 558–61.

Cox, Karen L. *Dreaming of Dixie: How the South Was Created in American Popular Culture*. Chapel Hill: University of North Carolina Press, 2011.

Crawford, Vicki L., Jacqueline Anne Rouse, and Barbara Woods, eds. *Women in the Civil Rights Movement: Trailblazers and Torchbearers, 1941–1965*. Bloomington: Indiana University Press, 1994.

Crenshaw, Kimberlé Williams. "Mapping the Margins: Intersectionality, Identity Politics, and Violence against Women of Color." *Stanford Law Review* 43, no. 6 (1991): 1241–99.

Crouch, Stanley. "On Lady Obama." *The Root*, March 31, 2009. https://www.theroot.com/stanley-crouch-on-lady-obama-1790869171.

Curtin, Philip. *The Rise and Fall of the Plantation Complex: Essays in Atlantic History*. Cambridge: Cambridge University Press, 1998.

Daalder, Ivo H., and I. M. Destler. *In the Shadow of the Oval Office: Profiles of the National Security Advisers and the Presidents They Served—From JFK to George W. Bush*. New York: Simon and Schuster, 2009.

D'Ambruoso, William L. "Norms, Perverse Effects, and Torture." *International Theory* 7, no. 1 (2015): 33–60.

Daniel, Pete. "African American Farmers and Civil Rights." *Journal of Southern History* 1 (73): 3–36.

Dash, Julie, dir. *Daughters of the Dust*. Kino, 1991.

Davidson, Cathy N. "Preface: No More Separate Spheres!" *American Literature* 70 (1998): 443–63.

Davidson, Cathy N. *Revolution and the Word: The Rise of the Novel in America*. Expanded ed. New York: Oxford University Press, 2004.

Davis, Angela Y. *Women, Race and Class*. New York: Vintage, 1983.

Davis, Julie Hirschfeld. "The Closer: Michelle Obama." *New York Times*, November 5, 2016.

Davis, Thadious. *Southscapes: Geographies of Race, Region, and Literature*. Chapel Hill: University of North Carolina Press, 2011.

Dixon, Thomas. *The Clansman: An Historical Romance of the Ku Klux Klan*. 1905. Lexington: University Press of Kentucky, 1970.

Douglass, Frederick. "Oration in Memory of Abraham Lincoln." In *Frederick Douglass: Selected Speeches and Writings*, edited by Philip S. Foner, adapted and abridged by Yuval Taylor, 615–24. Chicago: Chicago Review Press, 2000.

Dove, Rita. *On the Bus with Rosa Parks: Poems*. New York: Norton, 1999.

Du Bois, W. E. B. *The Souls of Black Folk*. Edited by Henry Louis Gates Jr. 1903. New York: Norton, 1999.

Duck, Leigh Anne. *The Nation's Region: Southern Modernism, Segregation, and U.S. Nationalism*. Athens: University of Georgia Press, 2006.

Duggan, Lisa. *The Twilight of Equality?: Neoliberalism, Cultural Politics, and the Attack on Democracy*. Boston: Beacon, 2004.

Dunbar, Paul Laurence. *The Collected Poetry of Paul Laurence Dunbar*. Edited by Joanne M. Braxton. Charlottesville: University of Virginia Press, 1993.

Durr, Virginia Foster. *Outside the Magic Circle: The Autobiography of Virginia Foster Durr*. Edited by Hillinger F. Barnard. New York: Simon and Schuster, 1987.

Duster, Michelle, Paula M. Seniors, and Rose C. Thevenin. *Michelle Obama's Impact on African American Women and Girls*. Cham, Switzerland: Palgrave Macmillan, 2018.

Dvorak, Petula, and Hamil R. Harris. "Washington Prepares to Pay Rosa Parks Rare Tribute at Capitol." *Washington Post*, October 29, 2005.

Easlea, Daryl. *Beyoncé, Crazy in Love: The Beyoncé Knowles Biography*. London: Omnibus Press, 2011.

Elder, L., and B. Frederick. "Why We Love Michelle: Understanding Public Support for First Lady Michelle Obama." *Politics and Gender* 15, no. 3 (2019): 403–30.

Ellis, Clifton, and Rebecca Ginsburg, eds. *Cabin, Quarter, Plantation: Architecture and the Landscapes of North America*. New Haven, CT: Yale University Press, 2010.

Everett, Anna. *Digital Diaspora: A Race for Cyberspace*. New York: SUNY Press, 2009.

Farrow, Kenyon. "Is Gay Marriage Anti-Black?" *Colours of Resistance Archive*, 2004. http://www.coloursofresistance.org/552/is-gay-marriage-anti-black/.

Feagans, Brian. "Georgian Recalls Rooming with Michelle Obama." *Atlanta Journal and Constitution*, April 13, 2008.

Feldman, Glenn. *The Great Melding: War, the Dixiecrat Rebellion, and the Southern Model for America's New Conservatism*. Tuscaloosa: University of Alabama Press, 2015.

Ferguson, Roderick A. *Aberrations in Black: Toward a Queer of Color Critique*. Minneapolis: University of Minnesota Press, 2003.

Fernandes, Leela. *Transnational Feminism in the United States: Knowledge, Ethics, Power*. New York: New York University Press, 2013.

Finney, Nikky. *Head Off and Split*. Evanston, IL: Northwestern University Press, 2011.

Flanders, Laura. *Bushwomen: Tales of a Cynical Species*. London: Verso, 2004.

Fleetwood, Nicole R. *On Racial Icons: Blackness and the Public Imagination*. New Brunswick, NJ: Routledge, 2015.

Fleming, Victor, dir. *Gone with the Wind*. Metro-Goldwyn-Mayer, 1939.

Flock, Elizabeth. "Sculptor Gives Behind-the-Scenes Look at Rosa Parks Memorial: Sculpture Portrays Parks Sitting, but Not on a Bus Seat." *U.S. News and World Report*, February 27, 2013.

Fossett, Judith Jackson, Adam Gussow, and Riché Richardson. "A Symposium of New Souths: Houston A. Baker Jr.'s *Critical Memory* and *Turning South Again*." *Mississippi Quarterly* 55 (2002): 569–611.

Franklin, Vincent P., and Bettye Collier-Thomas. "Biography, Race Vindication, and African American Intellectuals." *Journal of African American History* 87 (2002): 160–74.

Frederickson, Kari. *The Dixiecrat Revolt and the End of the Solid South, 1932–1968*. Chapel Hill: University of North Carolina Press, 2001.

Freeman, Elizabeth. *The Wedding Complex: Forms of Belonging in Modern American Culture*. Durham, NC: Duke University Press, 2002.

Fuentes, Carlos. *La Silla del Águila*. Madrid: Punto de Lectura, 2002.

Fuller, Lorraine. "Are We Seeing Things? The Pinesol Lady and the Ghost of Aunt Jemima." *Journal of Black Studies* 32 (2001): 120–31.

Gaines, Kevin K. *Uplifting the Race: Black Leadership, Politics, and Culture in the Twentieth Century*. Chapel Hill: University of North Carolina Press, 1996.

Gates, Henry Louis, Jr. *Finding Oprah's Roots: Finding Your Own*. New York: Crown, 2007.

Gates, Henry Louis, Jr. *The Signifying Monkey: A Theory of African American Literary Criticism*. New York: Oxford University Press, 1988.

Gates, Henry Louis, Jr. *The Trials of Phillis Wheatley*. New York: Basic Civitas, 2003.

Getsy, David J. "Acts of Stillness: Statues, Performativity, and Passive Resistance." *Criticism* 56, no. 1 (2014): 1–20.

Giddings, Paula. *Ida: A Sword among Lions*. New York: Amistad, 2008.

Giddings, Paula. *When and Where I Enter: The Impact of Black Women on Race and Sex in America*. New York: Bantam, 1984.

Gilman, Sander. *Difference and Pathology: Stereotypes of Sexuality, Race, and Madness*. Ithaca, NY: Cornell University Press, 1985.

Gilroy, Amy, and William Verhoeven, eds. *Epistolary Histories: Letters, Fiction, Culture*. Charlottesville: University of Virginia Press, 2000.

Gilroy, Paul. *The Black Atlantic: Modernity and Double-Consciousness*. Cambridge, MA: Harvard University Press, 1993.

Gilsdorf, Bean. "Luc Tuymans: In His Own Words." *Daily Serving: An International Publication for Contemporary Art*, March 1, 2010.

Gilson, D. "LOLZ with Hillz: Neoliberal Power Circuits in the Divahood of Hillary Clinton." *Journal of Popular Culture* 48, no. 4 (2015): 627–38.

Givhan, Robin. "Condoleezza Rice's Commanding Style." *Washington Post*, February 25, 2005.

Glanton, Dahleen, and Stacy St. Clair. "Michelle Obama's Family Tree Has Roots in a North Carolina Slave Plantation." *Chicago Tribune*, December 1, 2008.

Glissant, Edouard. *Faulkner, Mississippi*. Chicago: University of Chicago Press, 1999.
Goings, Kenneth. *Mammy and Uncle Mose: Black Collectibles and American Stereotyping*. Bloomington: Indiana University Press, 1994.
Goode, James M. *Washington Sculpture: A Cultural History of Outdoor Sculpture on the Nation's Capital*. Baltimore, MD: Johns Hopkins University Press, 2009.
Gordon-Reed, Annette. *The Hemingses of Monticello: An American Family*. New York: Norton, 2009.
Gore, Dayo F., Jeanne Theoharis, and Komozi Woodard, *Want to Start a Revolution?: Radical Women in the Black Freedom Struggle*. New York: New York University Press, 2009.
Gossett, Reina, Eric A. Stanley, and Johanna Burton, eds. *Trap Door: Trans Cultural Production and the Politics of Visibility*. Cambridge, MA: MIT Press, 2017.
Greenhaw, Wayne. "Rosa Parks: One of Many Who Would Fight for Freedom." *Alabama Heritage* 85 (2007): 8–15.
Greer, Germaine. "This Is the Age of Power Pearls—And No One Exploits Their Potency Better than Condie Rice." *Guardian*, August 24, 2008.
Greeson, Jennifer. *Our South: Geographic Fantasy and the Rise of National Literature*. Cambridge, MA: Harvard University Press, 2010.
Gregory, James N. *Southern Diaspora: How the Great Migrations of Black and White Southerners Transformed America*. Chapel Hill: University of North Carolina Press, 2007.
Grewal, Inderpal. *Transnational America: Feminisms, Diasporas, Neoliberalisms*. Durham, NC: Duke University Press, 2005.
Grewal, Inderpal, and Caren Kaplan. *Scattered Hegemonies: Postmodernity and Transnational Feminist Practices*. Minneapolis: University of Minnesota Press, 1994.
Grey, Stephanie Houston. "Contesting the Fat Citizen: Michelle Obama and the Body Politics of *The Biggest Loser*." *Journal of Popular Culture* 49, no. 3 (2016): 564–81.
Griffin, Farah Jasmine. "At Last . . . ?: Michelle Obama, Beyoncé, Race, and History." *Daedalus* 140, no. 1 (2011): 131–41.
Griffin, Farah Jasmine. *Who Set You Flowin'? The African American Migration Narrative*. New York: Oxford University Press, 1995.
Griffith, D. W., dir. *Birth of a Nation*. Triangle Film, 1915.
Grossman, James. *Land of Hope: Chicago, Black Southerners, and the Great Migration*. Chicago: University of Chicago Press, 1991.
Guy-Sheftall, Beverly. *Daughters of Sorrow: Attitudes toward Black Women, 1880–1920*. Brooklyn, NY: Carlson, 1990.
Guy-Sheftall, Beverly, ed. *Words of Fire: An Anthology of African-American Feminist Thought*. New York: New Press, 1995.
Habermas, Jürgen. *The Structural Transformation of the Public Sphere: An Inquiry into a Category of Bourgeois Society*. Cambridge, MA: MIT Press, 1991.
Halberstam, Jack. *In a Queer Time and Place: Transgender Bodies, Subcultural Lives*. New York: New York University Press, 2005.

Halberstam, Jack. *Trans: A Quick and Quirky Account of Gender Variability*. Berkeley: University of California Press, 2018.
Haley, Alex. *Roots: The Saga of an American Family*. New York: Doubleday, 1976.
Hall, Nathan A. "How Compassionate Was George W. Bush's Conservatism?" *Inquiries* 2, no. 5 (2010): 1. http://www.inquiriesjournal.com/articles/243/how-compassionate-was-george-w-bushs-conservatism.
Halperin, Shirley. "Beyoncé Delivers Hit-Filled Glastonbury Performance: Video." *Billboard*, June 27, 2011.
Hancock, David Leslie. *Race and the Naming of the White House*. Hampton, VA: United Brothers and Sisters, 1992.
Handau, M., and E. M. Simien. "The Cult of First Ladyhood: Controlling Images of White Womanhood in the Role of the First Lady." *Politics and Gender* 15, no. 3 (2019): 484–513.
Handley, George B. *Postslavery Literatures in the Americas: Family Portraits in Black and White*. Charlottesville: University of Virginia Press, 2000.
Hannity, Sean. "Interview with Sean Hannity of Hannity and Colmes." Fox News, April 14, 2005.
Hansberry, Lorraine. *A Raisin in the Sun*. 1959. New York: Vintage, 2011.
Hanson, Joyce A. *Mary McLeod Bethune and Black Women's Political Activism*. Columbia: University of Missouri Press, 2003.
Hanson, Joyce A. *Rosa Parks: A Biography*. Santa Barbara, CA: Greenwood, 2011.
Harper, Amie Breeze, ed. *Sistah Vegan: Black Female Vegans Speak on Food, Identity, Health, and Society*. New York: Lantern Books, 2010.
Harrington, Walt. "Rosa Parks and the Montgomery Bus Boycott." In *The Civil Rights Movement*, edited by Paul A. Winters, 45–57. San Diego, CA: Greenhaven, 2000.
Harris, Duchess. *Black Feminist Politics from Kennedy to Trump*. Cham, Switzerland: Palgrave Macmillan, 2018.
Harris, Robert L. "Memorializing Dr. King: Interpreting His Memory." Paper presented at the Africana Studies and Research Center, Cornell University, March 9, 2011.
Harris, Trudier. *Summer Snow: Reflections of a Black Daughter of the South*. Boston: Beacon, 1993.
Harris-Perry, Melissa [Melissa Victoria Harris-Lacewell]. *Barbershops, Bibles, and BET: Everyday Talk and Black Political Thought*. Princeton, NJ: Princeton University Press, 2006.
Harris-Perry, Melissa [Melissa Victoria Harris-Lacewell]. "Defeating History's Demons: How Obama Shattered the Solid South." *Ebony*, January 2009, 72.
Harris-Perry, Melissa. *Sister Citizen: Shame, Stereotypes, and Black Women in America*. New Haven, CT: Yale University Press, 2013.
Hartman, Saidiya V. *Scenes of Subjection: Terror, Slavery, and Self-Making in Nineteenth-Century America*. New York: Oxford University Press, 1997.
Hayden, Sara. "Michelle Obama, Mom-in-Chief: The Racialized Rhetorical Contexts of Maternity." *Women Studies in Communication* 40, no. 1 (2017): 11–28.

Haynes, Christina S., and Ray Block. "Role-Model-in-Chief: Understanding a Michelle Obama Effect." *Politics and Gender* 15, no. 3 (2019): 365–402.

Hegel, Georg Wilhelm Friedrich. *Introduction to the Philosophy of History*. Translated by Leo Rauch. Indianapolis, IN: Hackett, 1988.

Height, Dorothy. *Open Wide the Freedom Gates: A Memoir*. New York: Public Affairs, 2003.

Henderson, Carol E. "Introduction: On First Ladies, Duchesses, and Bawses—Black Womanhood Rebooted." *Journal of American Culture* 42, no. 1 (2019): 3–9.

Henderson, Mae G. "'Where, by the Way, Is This Train Going?': A Case for Black (Cultural) Studies." *Callaloo* 19 (1996): 60–77.

Higashida, Cheryl. *Black Internationalist Feminism: Women Writers of the Black Left, 1945–1995*. Urbana: University of Illinois Press, 2013.

Higginbotham, Evelyn Brooks. *Righteous Discontent: The Women's Movement in the Black Baptist Church, 1880–1920*. Cambridge, MA: Harvard University Press, 1994.

Hoffman, Kathy Barks. "Rosa Parks Honored by Thousands at Funeral in Detroit." Associated Press, November 2, 2005.

Holbling, Walter, Klaus Rieser-Wohlfarter, and Susanne E. Rieser. *U.S. Icons and Iconicity*. Vienna: LIT, 2006.

Holland, Sharon. *The Erotic Life of Racism*. Durham, NC: Duke University Press, 2012.

Holland, Sharon. *Raising the Dead: Readings of Death and (Black) Subjectivity*. Durham, NC: Duke University Press, 2000.

Holloway, Karla FC. "The Body Politic." In *Subjects and Citizens: Nation, Race, and Gender from Oroonoko to Anita Hill*, edited by Michael Moon and Cathy N. Davidson, 481–95. Durham, NC: Duke University Press, 1995.

Holloway, Karla FC. *Passed On: African American Mourning Stories*. Durham, NC: Duke University Press, 2002.

Holt, Rackham. *Mary McLeod Bethune: A Biography*. Garden City, NJ: Doubleday, 1964.

hooks, bell. *Ain't I a Woman: Black Women and Feminism*. Boston: South End Press, 1999.

hooks, bell. *Black Looks: Race and Representation*. Boston: South End Press, 1992.

hooks, bell. *Bone Black: Memories of Girlhood*. New York: Holt, 1997.

Hoose, Phillip M. *Claudette Colvin: Twice toward Justice*. New York: Farrar, Straus and Giroux, 2009.

Horwitz, Tony. "The Mammy Washington Almost Had." *Atlantic*, May 31, 2013.

Houck, Davis W., and David E. Dixon, eds. *Women and the Civil Rights Movement, 1954–1965*. Jackson: University Press of Mississippi, 2009.

Hubbard, Dolan. *The Sermon and the African American Literary Imagination*. Columbia: University of Missouri Press, 1994.

Hughes, Langston. *The Collected Poems of Langston Hughes*. Edited by Arnold Rampersad. New York: Vintage, 1995.

Hull, Gloria T., Patricia Bell Scott, and Barbara Smith, eds. *All the Women Are White, All the Blacks Are Men, but Some of Us Are Brave: Black Women's Studies*. New York: Feminist Press at CUNY, 1993.

Hunter, Tera. *To 'Joy My Freedom: Southern Black Women's Lives and Labors after the Civil War*. Cambridge, MA: Harvard University Press, 1998.

Hurston, Zora Neale. *Their Eyes Were Watching God*. 1937. Urbana: University of Illinois Press, 1978.

Ikard, David, and T. Denean Sharpley-Whiting. *Lovable Racists, Magical Negroes, and White Messiahs*. Chicago: University of Chicago Press, 2017.

Iton, Richard. *In Search of the Black Fantastic: Politics and Popular Culture in the Post–Civil Rights Era*. New York: Oxford University Press, 2010.

Jackson, John. *Racial Paranoia: The Unintended Consequences of Political Correctness*. New York: Basic, 2008.

Jacobs, Harriet. *Incidents in the Life of a Slave Girl, Written by Herself*. Edited by Jean Fagan Yellin. 1861. Cambridge, MA: Harvard University Press, 1987.

"James F. Blake: Alabama Bus Driver Who Sparked a Social Revolution When He Ordered Rosa Parks to Give up Her Seat." *Guardian*, March 26, 2002.

Janofsky, Michael. "Thousands Gather at the Capitol to Remember a Hero." *New York Times*, October 31, 2005.

Jansen, Lesa. "Beyoncé Lends Star Power to Let's Move." CNN, April 11, 2011.

Jeffries, Michael. *Paint the White House Black: Barack Obama and the Meaning of Race in America*. Stanford, CA: Stanford University Press, 2013.

Jessica. "Condi Rice Spends Salary on Shoes." *Gawker*, September 1, 2005. https://gawker.com/123467/breaking-condi-rice-spends-salary-on-shoes.

Jette, S., K. Bhagat, and D. L. Andrews. "Governing the Child-Citizen: 'Let's Move!' as National Biopedagogy." *Sport Education and Society* 21, no. 8 (2016): 1109–26.

Johnson, E. Patrick. *Appropriating Blackness: Performance and the Politics of Authenticity*. Durham, NC: Duke University Press, 2003.

Johnson, E. Patrick. *Black. Queer. Southern. Women: An Oral History*. Chapel Hill: University of North Carolina Press, 2018.

Johnson, E. Patrick, ed. *No Tea, No Shade: New Writings in Black Queer Studies*. Durham, NC: Duke University Press, 2016.

Johnson, E. Patrick. *Sweet Tea: A Play*. Evanston, IL: Northwestern University Press, 2020.

Johnson, E. Patrick, and Mae G. Henderson, eds. *Black Queer Studies: A Critical Anthology*. Durham, NC: Duke University Press, 2005.

Johnson, John H. *Succeeding against the Odds: The Autobiography of a Great American Businessman*. New York: HarperCollins, 1993.

Johnson, Sherita. *Black Women in New South Literature and Culture*. New York: Routledge, 2009.

Johnson-Miller, Beverly C. "Mary McLeod Bethune: Black Educational Ministry Leader of the Early 20th Century." *Christian Educational Journal* 3, no. 2 (2006): 330–43.

Jones, Anne Goodwyn, and Susan V. Donaldson, eds. *Haunted Bodies: Gender and Southern Texts*. Charlottesville: University of Virginia Press, 1998.

Jones, Jacqueline. *Labor of Love, Labor of Sorrow: Black Women, Work, and the Family from Slavery to the Present*. New York: Basic Books, 2009.

Jones, Jacqueline. "Southern Diaspora: Origins of the Northern 'Underclass.'" In *The "Underclass" Debate: Views from History*, edited by Michael B. Katz, 27–54. Princeton, NJ: Princeton University Press, 1993.

Joseph, Peniel E. "Memo to Park Service: Don't Put Black Women's History Away on the Shelf." *Root*, February 18, 2014. https://www.theroot.com/memo-to-park-service-don-t-put-black-women-s-history-a-1790874621.

Kantor, Joan. *The Obamas*. New York: Little, Brown, 2012.

Kaplan, Caren, Norma Alarcón, and Minoo Mooalem. *Between Woman and Nation: Nationalisms, Transnational Feminisms, and the State*. Durham, NC: Duke University Press, 1999.

Keckley, Elizabeth. *Behind the Scenes, or, Thirty Years a Slave, and Four Years in the White House*. 1868. New York: G. W. Carleton, 1968.

Kenney, David. "Condoleezza Rice Speaks to Grads." *MS News Now*, May 16, 2003.

Kern-Foxworth, Marilyn. *Aunt Jemima, Uncle Ben, and Rastus: Blacks in Advertising, Yesterday, Today, and Tomorrow*. Westport, CT: Greenwood, 1994.

Kessler, Glenn. *The Confidante*. New York: St. Martin's, 2007.

Keys, Sheila McCauley, with Eddie B. Allen Jr. *Our Auntie Rosa: The Family of Rosa Parks Remembers Her Life and Lessons*. New York: Tarcher, 2015.

King, Colbert I. "Dishonoring Bethune's Legacy." *Washington Post*, February 22, 2014.

King, James D., and James W. Riddlesperger Jr. "Diversity and Presidential Cabinet Appointments." *Social Science Quarterly* 96, no. 1 (2015): 93–103.

King, Wilma. *Stolen Childhood: Slave Youth in Nineteenth-Century America*. Bloomington: Indiana University Press, 2011.

Kipnis, Laura. "Condi's Inner Life: What Freudian Slips Do—Or Don't—Tell Us about Politicians." *Slate*, April 26, 2004.

Knight, Christopher. "Luc Tuymans: Don't Take His Images at Face Value." *Los Angeles Times*, March 14, 2010.

Knowles, Mathew. *Racism from the Eyes of a Child*. Houston, TX: Music World, 2017.

Knuckey, Jonathan, and Myunghee Kim. "Evaluations of Michelle Obama as First Lady: The Role of Racial Resentment." *Presidential Studies Quarterly* 46, no. 2 (2016): 365–86.

Koncewicz, Michael. "The Gatekeepers Who Shaped the Modern White House." *Reviews in American History* 46, no. 1 (2018): 144–50.

Kulbaga, Theresa A., and Leland G. Spencer. "Fitness and the Feminist First Lady: Gender, Race, and Body in Michelle Obama's Let's Move! Campaign." *Women and Language* 40, no. 1 (2017): 36.

Kuofie, Matthew, Dana Stephens-Craig, and Richard Dool. "An Overview Perception of Introverted Leaders." *International Journal of Global Business* 8, no. 1 (2015): 93–103.

Kurth, Joel. "Parks Will Lie in State in Capital—Washington, D.C., Will Honor Civil Rights Icon in Lincoln Memorial; Burial Will Be in Detroit." *Detroit News*, October 27, 2005.

Larson, Kate Clifford. *Harriet Tubman: Portrait of an American Hero*. New York: Ballantine, 2013.

Lassiter, Matthew D., and Joseph Crespino, eds. *The Myth of Southern Exceptionalism*. New York: Oxford University Press, 2009.

Latimer, Leah. "Bethune Home Is Center of Historical Site Debate." *Washington Post*, May 26, 1982.

Lee, Spike, dir. *4 Little Girls*. HBO, 1997.

Lee, Spike, dir. *School Daze*. Columbia Pictures, 1988.

Lee, Spike, dir. *When the Levees Broke: A Requiem in Four Acts*. HBO, 2006.

The Legacy of Mary McLeod Bethune. Washington, DC: National Education Association, 1974.

Lewis, Jan Ellen, and Peter S. Onuf. *Sally Hemings and Thomas Jefferson: History, Memory and Civic Culture*. Charlottesville: University of Virginia Press, 1999.

Lightfoot, Elizabeth. *Michelle Obama: First Lady of Hope*. New York: Lyons Press, 2008.

Lindsey, Treva. *Colored No More: Reinventing Black Womanhood in Washington, D.C.* Urbana: University of Illinois Press, 2017.

Littlejohn, Donna. "San Pedro Artist's Bronze Statue of Civil Rights Icon Rosa Parks to Stand in Capitol Building." *Los Angeles Daily News*, February 25, 2013.

Litwack, Leon F. *Trouble in Mind. Black Southerners in the Age of Jim Crow*. New York: Knopf, 1998.

Locke, Alain, and Arnold Rampersad. *The New Negro: Voices of the Harlem Renaissance*. 1925. New York: Touchstone, 1999.

Loizeau, Pierre-Marie. "'First Lady but Second Fiddle' or the Rise and Rejection of the Political Couple in the White House: 1933–Today." *European Journal of American Studies* 10, no. 1 (2015). https://doi.org/10.4000/ejas.10525.

Lomax, Tamura. *Jezebel Unhinged: Loosing the Black Female Body in Religion and Culture*. Durham, NC: Duke University Press, 2018.

Long, Nancy Ann Zrinyi. *The Life and Legacy of Mary McLeod Bethune*. Cocoa: Florida Historical Society Press, 2004.

Lorde, Audre. *Sister Outsider: Essays and Speeches*. Berkeley, CA: Crossing, 1984.

Lubiano, Wahneema. "Black Ladies, Welfare Queens, and State Minstrels: Ideological War by Narrative Means." In *Race-ing Justice, En-Gendering Power: Essays on Anita Hill, Clarence Thomas, and the Construction of Social Reality*, edited by Toni Morrison, 323–63. New York: Pantheon Books, 1992.

Lusane, Clarence. *The Black History of the White House*. San Francisco: City Lights, 2011.

Lusane, Clarence. *Colin Powell and Condoleezza Rice: Foreign Policy, Race, and the New American Century*. Westport, CT: Praeger, 2006.

Malone, Andrew, Vanessa Allen, and Paul Bentley. "'I Love Her Very Much': Photographs Found in Gaddafi Lair of Condoleezza Rice, the Tyrant's 'Darling Black African Woman.'" *Daily Mail*, August 26, 2011.

Mambry, Marcus. *Condoleezza Rice and Her Path to Power*. New York: Modern Times, 2007.

Mann, Jim. *The Rise of the Vulcans: The History of Bush's War Cabinet*. New York: Viking, 2004.

Manring, M. M. *Slave in a Box: The Strange Career of Aunt Jemima*. Charlottesville: University of Virginia Press, 1998.

Marable, Manning. *The Great Wells of Democracy: The Meaning of Race in American Life*. New York: Basic Civitas, 2003.

Martin, Earl Devine. *Mary McLeod Bethune: Matriarch of Black America*. Bloomington, IN: Xlibris, 2004.

Martin, Jennifer, and Cammie M. Sublette. *Devouring Cultures: Perspectives on Food, Power, and Identity from Zombie Apocalypse to Downton Abbey*. Fayetteville: University of Arkansas, 2016.

"Mary McLeod Bethune and the Administration of the NYA." *Journal of Negro History* 40 (January 1975): 1–28.

Massie, Dorothy C. *The Legacy of Mary McLeod Bethune*. Washington, DC: National Education Association, 1974.

Matsuda, Mari J., Charles R. Lawrence II, Kimberlé Williams Crenshaw, and Richard Delgado. *Words that Wound: Critical Race Theory, Assaultive Speech, and the First Amendment*. Boulder, CO: Westview Press, 1993.

McCauley, Sheila Keys, with Eddie B. Allen Jr. *Our Auntie Rosa: The Family of Rosa Parks Remembers Her Life and Lessons*. New York: Tarcher, 2015.

McClintock, Anne. *Imperial Leather: Race, Gender, and Sexuality*. New York: Routledge 1995.

McCluskey, Audrey Thomas. "Representing the Race: Mary McLeod Bethune and the Press in Jim Crow America." *Western Journal of Black Studies* 23 (1999): 236–44.

McCluskey, Audrey Thomas. "'We Specialize in the Wholly Impossible': Black Women School Founders and Their Mission." *Signs: Journal of Women in Culture and Society* 22 (1997): 403–25.

McDonald, Noah. "Racial Equity in the Farm Bill: Context and Foundations." *NSAC's Blog*, December 1, 2017. https://sustainableagriculture.net/blog/racial-equity-in-the-farm-bill/.

McElya, Micki. *Clinging to Mammy: The Faithful Slave in Twentieth-Century America*. Cambridge, MA: Harvard University Press, 2007.

McGhee, Felicia. "The Montgomery Bus Boycott and the Fall of the Montgomery City Lines." *Alabama Review* 68 (2015): 251–68.

McGuire, Danielle L. *At the Dark End of the Street: Black Women, Rape, and Resistance—A New History of the Civil Rights Movement from Rosa Parks to the Rise of Black Power*. New York: Knopf, 2011.

McHenry, Elizabeth. *Forgotten Readers: Recovering the Lost History of African American Literary Societies.* Durham, NC: Duke University Press, 2002.

McKittrick, Katherine, and Clyde Woods. *Black Geographies and the Politics of Place.* Boston: South End, 2007.

McPherson, Tara. *Reconstructing Dixie: Race, Gender, and Nostalgia in the Imagined South.* Durham, NC: Duke University Press, 2003.

McWhorter, Diane. *Carry Me Home, Birmingham, Alabama: The Climactic Battle of the Civil Rights Revolution.* New York: Simon and Schuster, 2001.

Melago, Carrie. "Etta James Truly Miffed about Obama Snub, but Was Kidding about Disliking Beyoncé." *New York Daily News*, February 5, 2009.

Michaels, Sean. "Etta James: I'm Gonna Whup Beyoncé's Ass." *Guardian*, February 6, 2009.

Millen, Kate. "In Her Debt: Rosa Parks' Defiance Paved Way for Pilot to Earn His Wings." *Sun*, November 15, 2005.

Mitchell, Michael, and David Covin, eds. *Broadening the Contours in the Study of Black Politics: Political Development and Black Women.* Piscataway, NJ: Transaction, 2015.

Mock, Janet. "My Feminist Awakening and the Influence of Beyoncé's Pop Culture Declaration." Janet Mock (blog), September 3, 2014. https://janetmock.com/2014/09/03/beyonce-feminist-mtv-vmas/.

Mock, Janet. *Redefining Realness: My Path to Womanhood, Identity, Love, and So Much More.* New York: Atria, 2014.

Moghadam, Valentine M. *Globalizing Women: Transnational Feminist Networks.* Baltimore, MD: Johns Hopkins University Press, 2005.

Mogorovich, A. "African-Americans in the New Deal: The Federal Council on Negro Affairs between Institutions, Networks, and Rights." *Contemporanea* 22, no. 1 (2019): 29–50.

Mohanty, Chandra Talpade. *Feminism without Borders: Decolonizing Theory, Practicing Solidarity.* Durham, NC: Duke University Press, 2003.

Mohanty, Chandra Talpade, Ann Russo, and Lourdes Torres, eds. *Third World Women and the Politics of Feminism.* Bloomington: Indiana University Press, 1991.

Moody, Anne. *Coming of Age in Mississippi.* 1968. New York: Dell, 1992.

Moore, Madison. *How to Be Beyoncé.* Brooklyn, NY: Thought Catalog, 2013.

Morrison, Stephen A. "Lincoln Park: Evolution of a Landscape." *CRM*, no. 9 (1999): 14.

Morrison, Toni. *Beloved.* New York: Plume, 1988.

Morrison, Toni. *Birth of a Nation 'Hood: Gaze, Script, and Spectacle in the O. J. Simpson Case.* New York: Pantheon, 1997.

Morrison, Toni. *The Bluest Eye.* New York: Holt, Rinehart, and Winston, 1970.

Morrison, Toni. "Clinton as the First Black President." *New Yorker*, October 1998.

Morrison, Toni. *Playing in the Dark: Whiteness and the Literary Imagination.* New York: Vintage, 1993.

Morrison, Toni, ed. *Race-ing Justice, En-Gendering Power: Essays on Anita Hill, Clarence Thomas, and the Construction of Social Reality*. New York: Pantheon, 1992.
Morrison, Toni. *Sula*. New York: Vintage International, 2004.
Mundy, Liza. *Michelle: A Biography*. New York: Simon and Schuster, 2008.
Muñoz, José Esteban. *Cruising Utopia: The Then and There of Queer Futurity*. New York: New York University Press, 2009.
Murray, Pauli. *States' Laws on Race and Color*. Cincinnati, OH: Women's Division of Christian Service, 1950.
Myers, Alex. "Rice to Chair Champions Major at Shoal Creek." *Golf Digest*, March 22, 2011.
Myrdal, Gunnar. *An American Dilemma: The Negro Problem and Modern Democracy*. New York: Harper, 1944.
Nash, Jennifer C. *Black Feminism Reimagined: After Intersectionality*. Durham, NC: Duke University Press, 2019.
"Nation Hails Rosa Parks at Memorial Service." Associated Press, October 31, 2005.
National Education Association. *The Legacy of Mary McLeod Bethune*. Washington, DC: National Education Association, 1974.
Neal, Mark Anthony. *What the Music Said: Black Popular Music and Black Public Culture*. New York: Routledge, 1998.
Nelson, Alondra. "Introduction: Future Texts." *Social Text* 71, no. 20 (2002): 1–15.
Nelson, Alondra. *The Social Life of DNA: Race, Reparations, and Reconciliation after the Genome*. Boston: Beacon, 2016.
Nelson, Dana D. *National Manhood: Capitalist Citizenship and the Imagined Fraternity of White Men*. Durham, NC: Duke University Press, 1998.
Nevergold, Barbara A. Seals, and Peggy Brooks-Bertram. *Go Tell Michelle: African American Women Write to the New First Lady*. Albany: SUNY Press, 2009.
Obama, Barack. *The Audacity of Hope: Thoughts on Reclaiming the American Dream*. New York: Vintage, 2008.
Obama, Barack. *Barack Obama's Speech on Race: A More Perfect Union*. Thousand Oaks, CA: BN, 2008.
Obama, Michelle. *American Grown: The Story of the White House Kitchen Garden and Gardens across America*. New York: Crown, 2012.
Obama, Michelle. *Becoming*. New York: Crown, 2018.
Obama, Michelle. "Feed Your Children Well: My Fight against Childhood Obesity." *Newsweek*, March 22, 2010, 40.
Obama, Michelle. *Michelle Obama: In Her Own Words*. Edited by Lisa Rogak. New York: Public Affairs, 2009.
Obama, Michelle. *Speeches on Life, Love, and American Values*. Edited by Stacie Vander Pol. Seattle, WA: Pacific, 2009.
Olasky, Marvin. *Compassionate Conservatism: What It Is, What It Does, and How It Can Transform America*. New York: Free Press, 2000.

Olson, Lynne. *Freedom's Daughters: The Unsung Heroines of the Civil Rights Movement from 1830 to 1970.* New York: Scribner's, 2002.
"100 Most Fascinating Black Women of the Twentieth Century." *Ebony* 54, no. 5 (1999): 52–90.
Orndorff, Mary. "Nation Bids Farewell to Rosa Parks." *Birmingham (AL) News*, October 31, 2005.
Painter, Nell Irvin. *Sojourner Truth: A Life, a Symbol.* New York: Norton, 1997.
Parker, Andrew. *Nationalisms and Sexualities.* New York: Routledge, 1991.
Parker, Star. *Pimps, Whores, and Welfare Brats: From Welfare Cheat to Conservative Messenger.* New York: Pocket, 1998.
Parks, Rosa, with Jim Haskins. *Rosa Parks: My Story.* New York: Puffin Books, 1992.
Parks, Rosa, with Gregory J. Reed. *Dear Mrs. Parks: A Dialogue with Today's Youth.* New York: Lee and Low, 1997.
Parks, Rosa, with Gregory J. Reed. *Quiet Strength: The Faith, the Hope, and the Heart of a Woman Who Changed a Nation.* Edited by Elaine Steele. Grand Rapids, MI: Zondervan, 1994.
Patton, Phil. "Mammy: Her Life and Times." *American Heritage* 44 (1993): 78–87.
Patton, Stacey. *Spare the Kids: Why Whupping Children Won't Save Black America.* Boston: Beacon, 2017.
Peare, Catherine Owens. *Mary McLeod Bethune.* New York: Vanguard, 1951.
Perkins, Margo V. *Autobiography and Activism: Three Black Women of the Sixties.* Jackson: University Press of Mississippi, 2000.
Perry, Imani. *Looking for Lorraine: The Radiant and Radical Life of Lorraine Hansberry.* Boston: Beacon, 2018.
Perry, Imani. *Vexy Thing: On Gender and Liberation.* Durham, NC: Duke University Press, 2018.
Peterson, Jesse Lee. "Using Rosa Parks." *WorldNet Daily*, November 16, 2005.
Prisock, Louis. "The CEO of Self: Herman Cain, Black Conservatism and the Achievement Ideology." *Journal of African American Studies* 19, no. 2 (2015): 180.
Puar, Jasbir K. *Terrorist Assemblages: Homonationalism in Queer Times.* Durham, NC: Duke University Press, 2017.
Radin, Rick. "Kensington Artist Helps Bring Rosa Parks' Legacy to U.S. Capitol." *Contra Costa Times*, March 8, 2013.
Ransby, Barbara. *Ella Baker and the Black Freedom Movement: A Radical Democratic Vision.* Chapel Hill: University of North Carolina Press, 2005.
Reddy, Vanita. *Fashioning Diaspora: Beauty, Femininity, and South Asian American Culture.* New York: Fordham University Press, 2016.
Reiman, Richard A. *The New Deal and American Youth: Ideas and Ideals in a Depression Decade.* Athens: University of Georgia Press, 1992.
Rice, Condoleezza. *Extraordinary, Ordinary People: A Memoir of Family.* New York: Crown, 2010.

Rice, Condoleezza. *No Higher Honor: A Memoir of My Years in Washington*. New York: Crown, 2011.

"Rice's Speech to Republican National Convention." *New York Times*, August 2, 2000. http://partners.nytimes.com/library/politics/camp/080200rice-text.html.

Richardson, Riché. "Beyoncé's South and a 'Formation' Nation." In *Making Lemonade: Finding Art, Activism, and Community with Beyoncé*, ed. Christina Baade and Kristin McGee. Middletown, CT: Wesleyan University Press, forthcoming.

Richardson, Riché. *Black Masculinity and the U.S. South: From Uncle Tom to Gangsta*. Athens: University of Georgia Press, 2007.

Richardson, Riché. "Can We Please, Finally, Get Rid of 'Aunt Jemima'?" *New York Times*, June 24, 2015.

Richardson, Riché. "Forgetting Farrah." *HuffPost*, December 31, 2017. https://www.huffingtonpost.com/entry/forgetting-farrah_us_5a497203e4b06cd2bd03e12c.

Richardson, Riché. "Framing Rosa Parks in Reel Time." *Southern Quarterly* 50, no. 3 (2013): 54–65.

Richardson, Riché. "Kara Walker's Old South and New Terrors." NKA: *Journal of Contemporary African Art* 25 (2009): 48–59.

Richardson, Riché. "Mammy's 'Mules' and the Rules of Marriage in *Gone with the Wind*." In *American Cinema and the Southern Imaginary*, edited by Deborah Barker and Kathryn McKee, 152–78. Athens: University of Georgia Press, 2011.

Richardson, Riché. "Monumentalizing Mary McLeod Bethune and Rosa Parks in the Post-Civil Rights Era." In "The Genius of Black Women: One Hundred Years of Triumph," edited by Darlene Clark Hine and Paula Giddings, special issue, *Phillis: The Journal for Research on African American Women* 2, no. 1 (2014): 23–30.

Richardson, Riché. "Seen and Not Heard: Black Women's Voices Matter." *HuffPost*, April 10, 2017. http://www.huffingtonpost.com/entry/seen-and-not-heard-black-womens-voices-matter_us_58ebc729e4b081da6ad00673.

Roberts, Diane. *The Myth of Aunt Jemima: Representations of Race and Region*. New York: Routledge, 1994.

Roberts, Dorothy. *Killing the Black Body: Race, Reproduction, and the Meaning of Liberty*. New York: Vintage, 1998.

Roberts, Michelle. "Child and Teen Obesity Spreading across the Globe." BBC News, October 11, 2017.

Robertson, Jessica. "Kanye West Blasts Bush." *Rolling Stone*, September 6, 2005.

Robertson, Tatsha. "Being Condoleezza." *Essence*, October 2006, 187.

Robinson, Craig. *A Game of Character: A Family Journey from Chicago's Southside to the Ivy League and Beyond*. New York: Gotham, 2010.

Robinson, Eugene. "Baghdad Isn't Birmingham." *Washington Post*, September 26, 2006.

Robinson, Jo Ann. *The Montgomery Bus Boycott and the Women Who Started It: The Memoir of Jo Ann Gibson Robinson*. Edited by David J. Garrow. Knoxville: University of Tennessee Press, 1987.

Robinson, Michelle LaVaughn. "Princeton-Educated Blacks and the Black Community." Senior thesis, Princeton University, 1985.

Robinson, Zandria. *This Ain't Chicago: Race, Class, and Regional Identity in the Post-Soul South*. Chapel Hill: University of North Carolina Press, 2014.

Romano, Renee C. "Narratives of Redemption: The Birmingham Church Bombing Trials and the Construction of Civil Rights Memory." In *The Civil Rights Movement in American Memory*, edited by Renee C. Romano and Leigh Raiford, 96–134. Athens: University of Georgia Press, 2006.

Rooks, Noliwe, ed. "Black Fashion: Art, Pleasure, Politics." *NKA: A Journal of Contemporary Art* 37 (November 2015): 4–5.

Rooney, Ben. "Female Finalists to Be the New Face of the $20 Bill." CNN Money, April 8, 2015.

Royster, Francesca T. "Condi, Cleopatra, and the Performance of Celebrity." *Upstart Crow* 31 (2012): 103–14.

Rush, George, Joanna Rush, Jo Molloy, Chris Piazza, and Rovzar. "As South Drowns, Rice Soaks in N.Y." *New York Daily News*, September 2, 2005.

Ryan, Terre. "'Changing the Conversation': Contexts for Reading Michelle Obama's *American Grown: The Story of the White House Kitchen Garden and Gardens across America*." *Frontiers* 37, no. 2 (2016): 75–108.

Ryan, Terre. "The White House Kitchen Garden and the Aesthetics of Social Order." *Interdisciplinary Studies in Literature and Environment* 23, no. 4 (2017): 657–76.

Santamarina, Xiomara. *Belabored Professions: Narratives of African American Working Womanhood*. Chapel Hill: University of North Carolina Press, 2005.

Sedgwick, Eve Kosofsky. *Between Men: English Literature and Male Homosocial Desire*. New York: Columbia University Press, 1985.

Sernett, Milton C. *Harriet Tubman: Myth, Memory, and History*. Durham, NC: Duke University Press, 2007.

Shabazz, Rashad. *Spatializing Blackness: Architectures of Confinement and Black Masculinity in Chicago*. Urbana: University of Illinois Press, 2015.

Sharpe, Christina. *Monstrous Intimacies: Making Post-Slavery Subjects*. Durham, NC: Duke University Press, 2010.

Sharpless, Rebecca. *Cooking in Other Women's Kitchens: Domestic Workers in the South, 1865–1960*. Chapel Hill: University of North Carolina Press, 2010.

Sharpley-Whiting, T. Denean. *Pimps up, Ho's Down: Hip Hop's Hold on Young Black Women*. New York: New York University Press, 2007.

Sharpley-Whiting, T. Denean, and Joy James, eds. *The Black Feminist Reader*. Hoboken, NJ: Wiley-Blackwell, 2000.

Shimakawa, Karen. *National Abjection: The Asian American Body Onstage*. Durham, NC: Duke University Press, 2002.

Shome, Raka. *Diana and Beyond: White Femininity, National Identity, and Contemporary Media Culture*. Urbana: University of Illinois Press, 2014.

Silverstein, Michelle. "Cross-Post—Going to See *The Help* at The White House by Carol Jenkins." *Women and Hollywood*, August 12, 2011.

Simon, Jenni M., and Abby M. Brooks, eds. *Michelle Obama: First Lady, American Rhetor*. Lanham, MD: Lexington, 2015.

Sirk, Douglas, dir. *Imitation of Life*. Universal Pictures, 1959.

Slevin, Peter. *Michelle Obama: A Life*. New York: Knopf, 2015.

Smith, Elaine. *Mary McLeod Bethune and the National Council of Negro Women: Pursuing a True and Unfettered Democracy*. Washington, DC: Alabama State University, for the Mary McLeod Bethune Council House, 2003.

Smith, Elaine. "Mary McLeod Bethune and the National Youth Administration." In *Clio Was a Woman: Studies in the History of American Women*, edited by Mabel E. Deutrich and Virginia C. Purdy, 149–77. Washington, DC: Howard University Press, 1980.

Smith, Elaine. "Mary McLeod Bethune's 'Last Will and Testament': A Legacy for Race Vindication." *Journal of Negro History* 81 (1996): 105–22.

Smith, Jamil. "The New Beyoncé Video Is Nearly Five Minutes of Unapologetic Blackness." *New Republic*, February 6, 2016.

Smith, Jon. *Finding Purple America: The South and the Future of American Cultural Studies*. Athens: University of Georgia Press, 2013.

Smith, Jon, and Deborah Cohn, eds. *Look Away!: The U.S. South in New World Studies*. Durham, NC: Duke University Press, 2004.

Smith, Valerie. "Remembering Birmingham Sunday: Spike Lee's *4 Little Girls*." In *American Cinema and the Southern Imaginary*, edited by Deborah E. Barker and Kathryn McKee, 179–93. Athens: University of Georgia Press, 2011.

Smitherman, Geneva. *African American Women Speak Out on Anita Hill–Clarence Thomas*. Detroit, MI: Wayne State University Press, 1995.

Snorton, C. Riley. *Black on Both Sides: A Racial History of Trans Identity*. Minneapolis: University of Minnesota Press, 2017.

Sobel, Mechal. *The World They Made Together: Black and White Values in Eighteenth-Century Virginia*. Princeton, NJ: Princeton University Press, 1987.

Southall, Ashley. "Statue of Rosa Parks Is Unveiled at the Capitol." *New York Times*, February 27, 2013.

Spillers, Hortense, ed. *Black, White, and in Color: Essays on American Literature and Culture*. Chicago: University of Chicago Press, 2003.

Spillers, Hortense. "A Hateful Passion, A Lost Love." In *Black, White, and in Color: Essays on American Literature and Culture*, edited by Hortense Spillers, 93–118. Chicago: University of Chicago Press, 2003.

Spillers, Hortense. "Long Time: Long Lost Daughters and the New 'New South.'" *boundary 2* 36 (2009): 149–82.

Spillers, Hortense. "Mama's Baby, Papa's Maybe: An American Grammar Book." In *Within the Circle: An Anthology of African American Literary Criticisms from the*

Harlem Renaissance to the Present, edited by Angelyn Mitchell, 454–81. Durham, NC: Duke University Press, 1994.

Spillers, Hortense. "Views of the East Wing: On Michelle Obama." *Communication and Critical/Cultural Studies* 6 (2009): 307–10.

Spires, Derrick. *The Practice of Citizenship: Black Politics and Print Culture in the Early United States*. Philadelphia: University of Pennsylvania Press, 2019.

Spivak, Gayatri. "Three Women's Texts and a Critique of Imperialism." *Critical Inquiry* 12 (1985): 43–61.

Steptoe, Tyina. "Beyoncé's Western South Serenade." In *The Lemonade Reader*, edited by Kinitra D. Brook and Kameelah Martin, 183–91. New York: Routledge, 2019.

Sterne, Emma Gelders. *Mary McLeod Bethune*. New York: Knopf, 1957.

Stockett, Kathryn. *The Help*. New York: Berkley, 2011.

Story, Tim, dir. *Barbershop*. Metro-Goldwyn Mayer, 2002.

Stowe, Harriet Beecher. *Uncle Tom's Cabin*. Edited by Jean Fagan Yellin. 1852. New York: Oxford University Press, 1998.

Swarns, Rachel L. *American Tapestry: The Story of the Black, White, and Multiracial Ancestors of Michelle Obama*. New York: HarperCollins, 2012.

Swarns, Rachel L. "From Slavery to the White House: Michelle Obama's Roots Go Back to the Pre–Civil War South: The Five-Generation Journey of the First Lady's Family." *New York Times*, February 8, 2010.

Swarns, Rachel L., and Jodi Kantor. "In First Lady's Roots, a Complex Path from Slavery." *New York Times*, October 8, 2009.

Swarr, Amanda Lock, and Richa Nagar. *Critical Transnational Feminist Praxis*. Albany: SUNY Press, 2010.

Talley, André L. "Michelle Obama: Leading Lady." *Vogue*, March 2009, 431, 504.

Tanne, Richard, dir. *Southside with You*. State Street Pictures, 2016.

Taraborrelli, J. Randy. *Becoming Beyoncé: The Untold Story*. New York: Grand Central, 2016.

Taylor, Tate, dir. *The Help*. DreamWorks Pictures, 2011.

Theoharis, Jeanne. *The Rebellious Life of Mrs. Rosa Parks*. Boston: Beacon, 2013.

Thomas, Brook. *Civic Myths: A Law-and-Literature Approach to Citizenship*. Chapel Hill: University of North Carolina Press, 2007.

Thompson, Cheryl. "I'se in Town, Honey: Reading Aunt Jemima Advertising in Canadian Print Media, 1919–1962." *Journal of Canadian Studies* 49, no. 1 (2015): 205–37.

Thompson, Krissah. "The Leading Lady: Michelle Obama." *Essence*, September 2011, 133.

Thompson, Lisa. *Beyond the Black Lady: Sexuality and the New African American Middle Class*. Urbana: University of Illinois Press, 2009.

"Thousands Attend Rosa Parks Funeral." Associated Press, November 2, 2005.

Thrasher, Steven. "Paris Is 'Still' Burning." *Out*, May 22, 2011.

Tillet, Salamishah. *Sites of Slavery: Citizenship and Racial Democracy in the Post–Civil Rights Imagination*. Durham, NC: Duke University Press, 2012.

Tipton-Martin, Toni. *The Jemima Code: Two Centuries of African American Cookbooks.* Austin: University of Texas Press, 2015.

Toomer, Jean. *Cane: A Norton Critical Edition.* Edited by Darwin T. Turner. 1923. New York: Norton, 1988.

Trier-Bieniek, Adrienne, ed. *The Beyoncé Effect: Essays on Sexuality, Race, and Feminism.* Jefferson, NC: McFarland, 2016.

Tuck, Stephen G. N. *We Ain't What We Ought to Be: The Black Freedom Struggle, from Emancipation to Obama.* Cambridge, MA: Harvard University Press, 2010.

Tullos, Allen. *Alabama Getaway: The Political Imaginary and the Heart of Dixie.* Athens: University of Georgia Press, 2011.

Turner, Jean Williams. *Collectible Aunt Jemima: Handbook and Value Guide.* Atglen, PA: Schiffer, 1994.

Turner, Patricia A. *Ceramic Uncles and Celluloid Mammies.* New York: Anchor, 1994.

Turner, Patricia A. "Dangerous White Stereotypes." *New York Times,* August 28, 2011.

Turner, Patricia A. *I Heard It through the Grapevine: Rumor in African American Culture.* Berkeley: University of California Press, 1993.

"U.S. Civil Rights Heroine Rosa Parks Honored at Capitol Hill." *New York Times,* October 31, 2005.

U.S. Congress. Senate Committee on Energy and Natural Resources. *Authorizing the National Park Service to Acquire and Manage the Mary McLeod Bethune Council House National Historic Site, and for Other Purposes: Report (to Accompany H.R. 690).* Washington, DC: U.S. Government Printing Office, 1991.

U.S. Congress. Senate Committee on Energy and Natural Resources. *Mary McLeod Bethune Council House National Historic Site: Report (to Accompany H.R. 5084).* Washington, DC: Government Printing Office, 1990.

U.S. Department of Labor. *The Negro Family: The Case for National Action.* Washington, DC: Government Printing Office, 1965.

Vagnoux, Isabelle. "Introduction: North American Women in Politics and International Relations." *European Journal of American Studies* 10, no. 1 (2016). https://doi.org/10.4000/ejas.10463.

Van Der Zee, James, Owen Dodson, and Camille Billops. *The Harlem Book of the Dead.* Dobbs Ferry, NY: Morgan and Morgan, 1978.

Vaughn, Emma, and Paul Richter. "Nation Pays Tribute to 'Mother of the America We Grew to Be.'" *Seattle Times,* October 31, 2005.

Wade-Gayles, Gloria, ed. *Their Memories, Our Treasure: Conversations with African American Women of Wisdom.* Vols. 1 and 2. Atlanta: SIS Oral History Project, 2004.

Wade-Gayles, Gloria, Mykisha Arnold, and Spelman Independent Scholars (SIS). *Their Memories, Our Treasure: Conversation with African-American Women of Wisdom.* Vols. 3 and 4. Atlanta: SIS Oral History Project, 2006.

Wald, Priscilla. *Constituting Americans: Cultural Anxiety and Narrative Form.* Durham, NC: Duke University Press, 1995.

Walker, Clarence E. "Denial Is Not a River in Egypt." In *Sally Hemings and Thomas Jefferson: History, Memory and Civic Culture*, edited by Jan Ellen Lewis and Peter S. Onuf, 187–98. Charlottesville: University of Virginia Press, 1999.

Walker, Clarence E. *Mongrel Nation: The America Begotten by Thomas Jefferson and Sally Hemings*. Charlottesville: University of Virginia Press, 2009.

Wallace-Sanders, Kimberly. *Mammy: A Century of Race, Gender, and Southern Memory*. Ann Arbor: University of Michigan Press, 2008.

Walsh, Kenneth T. *Family of Freedom: Presidents and African Americans in the White House*. Boulder, CO: Paradigm, 2011.

Warner, Michael. *The Trouble with Normal*. New York: Free Press, 1999.

Washington-Williams, Essie Mae. *Dear Senator: A Memoir by the Daughter of Strom Thurmond*. New York: Harper Perennial, 2006.

Watkins, Mel. *On the Real Side: Laughing, Lying, and Signifying—The Underground Tradition of African-American Humor that Transformed American Culture, from Slavery to Richard Pryor*. New York: Simon and Schuster, 1994.

Wells, Ida B. *The Reason Why the Colored American Is Not in the World's Columbian Exposition: The Afro-American's Contribution to Columbian Literature*. 1893. Marlborough, Wiltshire: Adam Matthew Digital, 2016.

Wheatley, Phillis. *Poems on Various Subjects, Religious and Moral*. 1773. *The Collected Works of Phillis Wheatley*, edited by John Shields, xxvii–xxxii. London: Oxford University Press, 1988.

White, Deborah Gray. *Ar'n't I a Woman?: Female Slaves in the Plantation South*. New York: Norton, 1999.

Whitt, Mary Frances. Foreword to *Let My People Go!: The Miracle of the Montgomery Bus Boycott*, edited by Robert J. Walker. Lanham, MD: Hamilton, 2007.

Whitt, Mary Frances. "Presentation for the Smithsonian Panel in Observance of the 40th Anniversary of the Montgomery, Alabama, Bus Boycott." Presented at Walking Montgomery in Observance of the 40th Anniversary of the Montgomery Bus Boycott, National Museum of American History, Smithsonian Institution, January 13, 1996.

Wiegman, Robyn. *American Anatomies: Theorizing Race and Gender*. Durham, NC: Duke University Press, 1995.

Wilkerson, Isabel. *The Warmth of Other Suns: The Epic Story of America's Great Migration*. New York: Vintage, 2011.

Williams, Randall. *Johnnie Carr: A Life of Quiet Activism*. Montgomery, AL: Junebug, 2001.

Williamson, Terrion L. *Scandalize My Name: Black Feminist Practice and the Making of Black Social Life*. New York: New York University Press, 2016.

Winfrey, Oprah. "Oprah Talks to Michelle Obama." *O: The Oprah Magazine*, April 2009, 143–44.

Wisniewski, K. A., ed. *The Comedy of Dave Chappelle: Critical Essays*. Jefferson, NC: McFarland, 2009.

Witt, Doris. *Black Hunger: Food and the Politics of U.S. Identity*. New York: Oxford University Press, 1999.
Woodley, J. "'Ma is in the Park': Memory, Identity, and the Bethune Memorial." *Journal of American Studies* 52, no. 2 (2018): 474–502.
Woods, Clyde, ed. "In the Wake of Hurricane Katrina." Special issue, *American Quarterly* 61, no. 3 (2009).
Woods, Clyde, and Laura Pulido. *Development Drowned and Reborn: The Blues and Bourbon Restorations in Post-Katrina New Orleans*. Athens: University of Georgia Press, 2017.
Wozolek, Boni. "The Mothership Connection: Utopian Funk from Bethune and Beyond." *Urban Review* 50, no. 5 (2018): 836–56.
Wright, Nazera Sadiq. *Black Girlhood in the Nineteenth Century*. Urbana: University of Illinois Press, 2016.
Wright, R. Brian. "The Idealist Realist: Mary McLeod Bethune, the National Council of Negro Women and the National Youth Administration." Master's thesis, Virginia Polytechnic Institute and State University, 1999.
X, Malcolm. *Malcolm X Speaks: Selected Speeches and Statements*. Edited by George Breitman. New York: Grove Weidenfeld, 1965.
Yaeger, Patricia. "Circum-Atlantic Superabundance: Milk as World-Making in Alice Randall and Kara Walker." In "Global Contexts, Local Literatures: The New Southern Studies," edited by Kathryn McKee and Annette Trefzer, special issue, *American Literature* 78, no. 4 (2006): 769–98.
Yaeger, Patricia. *Dirt and Desire: Reconstructing Southern Women's Writing, 1930–1990*. Chicago: University of Chicago Press, 2000.
Zafar, Rafia. *Recipes for Respect: African American Meals and Meaning*. Athens: University of Georgia Press, 2019.

{ INDEX }

Page numbers in italics refer to figures.

Abrams, Stacey, xviii
"Acts of Stillness: Statues, Performativity, and Passive Resistance" (Getsy), 63–64
Adams, John, 3
Adichie, Chimamanda Ngozi, xvi
advertising, 14, 21, 48, 117, 157–60, 188, 191, 208, 224, 237n30
Afghanistan invasion, 142
African American literary history, 30; Bethune and, 45–46, 56–57, 85–86; black women in, 7, 21–23, 97–98, 135, 137, 210; Michelle Obama and, 211–12; Parks and, 94–95, 97–98; Rice and, 135, slave narratives, 135; talking book trope in, 41. *See also specific works*
Africana South, 33, 182, 227–28
Africana studies, 34
Afro-American Institute for Historic Preservation and Community Development, 70
Afrofuturism, 108, 109, 116–18, 155, 246n59
Alarcón, Norma, 146
Albright, Madeleine, 134
Alger, Horatio, 42
Allen, Eddie B., Jr., 98
Allen, Jafari Sinclaire, 182
American Dilemma, An: The Negro Problem and Modern Democracy (Myrdal), 96
American exceptionalism, 137–38, 145–47
American Grown: The Story of the White House Kitchen Garden and Gardens across America (Obama), 208, 209–10, 211–12
American Revolution, 3

American Tapestry: The Story of the Black, White, and Multiracial Ancestors of Michelle Obama (Swarns), 184–85
American Teachers Association, 240n45
"American Way" (Nas), 156, 159
ancestry, 182–83, 251n8
Anderson, Benedict, 24
Anderson, Christopher P., 250n1
Anderson, Marian, 47
Angelou, Maya, 135, 138
angry black woman stereotype, 187, 200
anticommunism, 48, 80
antimiscegenation laws, 237n30, 238n53
Ards, Angela, 97
Arkestra, 117–18
Association of Black Women Historians, 218
"At Last," 216, 223, 224, 254–55n5
At the Dark End of the Street (McGuire), 243n8
Audacity of Hope, The (Obama), 199
Auntie stereotype, 52–53
Aunt Jemima (DePillars), 157
Aunt Jemima and the Pillsbury Dough Boy (Donaldson), 157
Aunt Jemima stereotype, 18–19; black arts movement on, 157, 158; black maternal body and, 16; black stereotypes and, 18, 233; critiques of, 14; domestic labor and, 12, 13; film and, 13, 237n30; food and, 208; mammy stereotype and, 8–9; in material culture, 10, 11, 12, 16; national body and, 16; retirement of, 15; Rice and, 160–61
Austin, Elise, 69

Austin, J. L., 63
authenticity: Beyoncé and, 232; Barack Obama and, 199, 251n3; Michelle Obama and, 191, 204; Rice and, 149, 153, 158, 161–62, 166–67
autobiography. *See* African American literary history

baby mama stereotype, 18, 188
Baker, Houston A., Jr., 29, 30, 256n26
"Ballot or the Bullet, The" (Malcolm X), 249n40
Barack and Michelle (Anderson), 250n1
Baraka, Amiri, 156, 158, 159, 161
Barbershop, 106–7, 108, 115
Barbershops, Bibles, and BET: Everyday Talk and Black Political Thought (Harris-Perry), 107
Barnett, Rex, 39, 41–42, 45
Becoming (Obama), 190
Belafonte, Harry, 60
Belafonte, Shari, 60
Beloved (Morrison), 6
Benjamin, Ruha, 117
Berks, Robert, 58, 59, 241n46
Berlant, Lauren, 13, 28, 33, 144–45
Bernstein, Robin, 138
Bethune, Albertus, 52
Bethune, Mary McLeod, 39–86, *40*; Afrofuturism and, 246n59; anticommunism and, 48, 80; Beyoncé and, 233; Black Cabinet role, 43, 44, 47, 57; on black national family, 44, 46, 49, 53, 54, 62–63; Christianity and, 60; civil rights movement and, 47–48, 56–57, 85; contemporaries, 42–43; education and, 41–42, 43, 240n45; Great Migration and, 57, 239n3; iconicity of, 43–44, 75, 76; Jim Crow and, 47–48; Johnson and, 49–50; life of, 39, 41–42; maternal motifs and, 52; memoir and, 98; memorials to, 46, 58–65, 66, 67–68, 76, 126, 240n43, 243n91; "My Last Will and Testament," 45–51, 53–57, 60, 63, 80, 85–86, 99, 102; NCNW and, 68–69; Parks and, 98, 99; post-Emancipation era and, 41, 58, 62, 232–33; platforms for, 51–52; public sphere and, 22; on racial dignity, 55; Rice and, xi, 155; southern roots of, 39, 41, 42, 62; youth and, 46, 47, 51–52, 55–56, 57, 59–60, 61, 102
Bethune-Cookman College, 43, 240n42
Bethune Council House: Bethune's national influence and, 243n91; funding for, 71–73, 74–75, 78, 79; hearings regarding, 46, 64–65, 66–67, 69–70, 74–83, 85, 240n43; NABWH relocation and, 83–85; National Park Service management of, 80–82; national significance of, 70–71; property acquisition, 68–69; white-centered definitions of *woman* and, 67, 73–74, 78–79, 82
Bethune, Mary McLeod, Foundation, 54, 66, 240n42
Bethune, Mary McLeod, Memorial, 46, 47, 51–52, 55–65, 59, 69–71, 76, 102, 240n45
Bethune Museum and Archives, 82
Between Woman and Nation: Nationalisms, Transnational Feminisms, and the State (Kaplan, Alarcón, and Moallem), 146
Bevel, James, 244n17
Bey feminism, 213
Beyoncé, 214; Black Lives Matter and, 231; civil rights movement and, 221, 224–25, 231; fashion and, 225–26; iconicity of, 227, 228, 233–34; Michelle Obama and, 189–90, 213, 226–27, 256nn22–23; Obama inauguration performances, 212–13, 221, 222–23, 225, 254–55n5; postracialism and, 222, 223–24; queer/trans people and, 225–26, 229; U.S. South and, 222, 227–30, 231, 232
Bhabha, Homi, 25
Biden, Joe, xiii, xvii, xviii
Big Freedia, 229
Bigsby, Clayton, 249n47
Birthers, 191

Birth of a Nation (Griffith), 9, 26, 214–15, 218, 236n23, 237n30
Black, Barry C., 120
black arts movement, 156–58
Black Cabinet (Federal Council of Negro Affairs), 43, 44, 47, 57
"Black Fashion: Art, Pleasure, Politics" (Rooks), 172
Black History of the White House, The (Lusane), 185
"Black Ladies, Welfare Queens, and State Minstrels" (Lubiano), 18
black lady image, 18, 89, 175
Black Lives Matter, xviii, 14, 15, 29, 231
Black Madonna image, 92
Black Masculinity and the U.S. South: From Uncle Tom to Gangsta (Richardson), 14
black maternal body, 5–6, 11, 16, 45, 185, 214. *See also* mammy stereotype; maternal motifs and stereotypes
black national family. *See* national family
Black Panther Party, 155, 230–31
black power movement, 97, 118, 152, 157, 230, 231
black rapist myth, 15, 238n53
black South, 228–29, 256n26. *See also* U.S. South
black studies, 77
"Black to the Future" (Dery), 117
Blake, James, 89, 90, 94, 107, 108, 113, 118, 243n6
blaxploitation genre, 135–36, 150, 151, 153, 156, 177, 249n39
blues, 111, 181
Bluest Eye, The (Morrison), 211–12
Bochenek, Jan, 112
Boggs, Lindy, 79
Bolling, Elmore, 244n19
Bolton, Frances, 69
Bone Black: Memories of Girlhood (hooks), 138
Borat, 159
Borgstrom, Michael, 9

Boushee, Nicholas, 134
Boyce-Davies, Carole, 171
Boyd, Melba Joyce, 107–8
Bradley, Regina, 30, 108
Braun, Carol Moseley, xii
Braxton, Joanne M., 97–98, 210
Brent, Linda, 5
Brinkley, Douglas, 90, 243n6
Brooks, Gwendolyn, 251n5
Brooks-Bertram, Peggy, 250–51n1, 256n23
Browder, Aurelia, 91
Browder v. Gayle, 91
Brown, Alice, 194
Brown, Elaine, 97
Brown, Henry "Box," 113
Brown, James, 230
Brown, Michael, 130, 231
Brown, Nadia, 177
Brown v. Board of Education, 22, 47, 100, 137
Burciaga, Cecilia, 249n48
Burstein, Joseph, 72–73
Bush, George H. W., x, 173–74
Bush, George W.: Beyoncé and, 224; Hurricane Katrina and, xv, 130, 132; neoconservatism and, 130–31, 132; Parks and, 120, 123, 125–26; presidential campaign of, ix, x; Rice and, x–xi, 133, 142, 143, 147, 148, 151, 152, 153, 156, 163–64; in visual representations of Rice, 162–64, 163, 166, 167, 168; white masculinity and, 174
Butler, Judith, 63
Butler, Octavia, 116

Cabin, Quarter, Plantation: Architecture and Landscape of North American Slavery (Ellis and Ginsburg), 185
Cadillac Records, 222
Cain, Herman, 137–38
"California Love" (Shakur), 231
Calvin, Denis, 80–81
Cane (Toomer), 238n53
"Can We Please, Finally, Get Rid of Aunt Jemima?" (Richardson), 14

INDEX   283

capitalism, 2, 31
Caramanica, Jon, 229
Carlos, John, 231
Carnegie, Andrew, 42
Carr, Gwen, 231
Ceramic Uncles and Celluloid Mammies (Turner), 10
Chagoya, Enrique, 136, 166–67, *168*, 170
Chappelle, Dave, 148–49, 151, 154, 155, 248n37
Charleston murders (2015), 14, 29, 126
Chatelain, Marcia, 196
Chávez, Hugo, 162
Cheyfitz, Eric, 204–5, 212
Chicago: Bethune and, 41, 53; femininity and, 251n5; Michelle Obama and, 33, 36, 180–82, 187, 194–203, 206, 209, 210, 219, 223, 227, 253n43; political machine, xviii; Sun Ra and, 117–18. *See also* Great Migration
children. *See* Let's Move! campaign; youth
Children's March, 114, 244n19
Chisholm, Shirley, xi–xii, 76
Cho, Sumo, 137–38
Christian, Barbara, 30
Christianity, 60, 99, 100, 101, 111
cinema. *See* film
Civil Rights Act (1964), 22, 109, 133
civil rights movement: attempts to reverse, 83, 133, 137; Aunt Jemima stereotype and, 11; Bethune and, 47–48, 56–57, 85; Beyoncé and, 221, 224–25, 231; black arts movement and, 157; and black women's iconicity, 22, 23; club movement and, 10; male-centered nature of, 103–4; March on Washington, 56, 92, 103, 104; maternal motifs and, 92; Montgomery bus boycott, 87, *88*, 110, 114, 118, 245n52; monuments to, 85; national family and, 11, 65; national narratives and, 235n8; neoconservatism and, 65, 123, 134, 135, 137, 139–40, 144; Parks and, 22, 86, 93, 114; public sphere and, 22; Rice and, 133, 137, 139, 141, 155, 177; queer/trans people and, 92–93; space

race and, 109; youth and, 56, 92, 98–99, 100, 244n17. *See also* Cleveland Avenue Time Machine; Jim Crow
Civil War, x, 133
Clansman, The (Dixon), 214–15
Clark, Kenneth B., 47
Clark, Mamie, 47
Cleaver, Eldridge, 97
Cleopatra Jones, 150
Cleopatra motifs, 147, 150, 248n33
Cleveland Avenue Time Machine, 95, 108–19, 245nn51–52
Clinton, Bill, xiii, 119, 123
Clinton, Hillary, 2, 134, 162, 248n33
club movement, 9, 10, 21, 42
codes of respectability, 89
Cohen, Cathy, xviii
Cohen, Susan E., 105–6
Coldplay, 230
Cole, Johnetta B., xiii
collectibles, 10, 11, *12*, 16, 160, 167
Collier-Thomas, Bettye, 51, 70, 78–79, 84
Collins, Addie Mae, xv, 98–99, 135, 139
Collins, Patricia Hill, 2, 17, 18, 192, 208
Collins, Sarah, 248n24
colonialism/imperialism, 25, 146, 161, 166
colorblindness, 29, 83, 132, 158, 224
Colvin, Claudette, 91
comedy, 135–36, 147, 148–49, 248n37, 248–49n39
Comedy Central Presents, 159
Coming of Age in Mississippi (Moody), 138
compassionate conservatism, x
"Condi, Cleopatra, and the Performance of Celebrity" (Royster), 147
"Condi Comes to Harlem" (*Mad TV*), 135–36, 148, 149–56, 174, 176, 248n39
Condoleezza Rice: From Birmingham to the White House (Richardson), *128*
Condoleezza Rice and Her Path to Power (Mambry), 142
"Condoleezza Rice's Commanding Style" (Givhan), 175–76

284 INDEX

Confederate flags and monuments, 14, 15, 61–62, 126. *See also* Old South nostalgia
conservatism. *See* neoconservatism
"Contesting the Fat Citizen: Michelle Obama and the Body Politics of *The Biggest Loser*" (Grey), 209
Conyers, John, 120
Cooking in Other Women's Kitchens: Domestic Workers in the South, 1865–1960 (Sharpless), 12
Cooks, Bridget R., 105–6
Coolidge, Calvin, 51, 59
Cooper, Ableen, 217
Cooper, Anna Julia, 8
Cooper, Brittney, 30
Cooperman, Rosalyn, 94, 104
coronavirus pandemic, 29–30
Cotton Comes to Harlem (Himes), 149–50
Couric, Katie, 139–40
Covid-19, 29–30, 233
Cox, Laverne, 27, 225–26
Crenshaw, Kimberlé Williams, 2
critical race theory, 206
"Cross Road Blues" (Johnson), 111
Crouch, Stanley, 181
Cullors, Patrisse, xviii
Cult of True Womanhood, 5
cultural studies, 33

Daily Kos, 192–93, *193*
D'Ambruoso, William L., 147–48
Daniel-Barnes, Riché, 213
Dash, Julie, 229, 244n19
Daub, Eugene, 127
Daughters of the American Revolution, 47
Daughters of the Dust (Dash), 229
Davidson, Cathy N., 33
Davila, Yvonne, 197
Davis, Angela, 97, 138, 200
Davis, Julie Hirschfeld, 207–8
Davis, Ossie, 150
Davis, Thadious, 30
Davis, Viola, 217

Dawson, William L., 69
Daytona Educational and Industrial Training School for Girls, 41–42, 43
Dear Mrs. Parks: A Dialogue with Today's Youth (Parks and Reed), 94, 104–5
DePillars, Murray, 157
Dery, Mark, 117
Destiny's Child, 37, 212, 213, 221, 224, 228, 231
Diana (Princess of Wales), 24–25
Diana and Beyond: White Femininity, National Identity, and Contemporary Media Culture (Shome), 24–25
digital media, 111–12, 116–17, 161
Dirt and Desire (Yaeger), 238n53
"Diversity and Presidential Cabinet Appointments" (King and Riddlesperger), 134
Dixon, Thomas, 214–15
Dobson, Tamara, 150
domestic labor, 11, 12, 13, 49, 217–19
dominatrix, 174–76
Donaldson, Jeff, 157
Donnelly, Catherine, 194
Don't Ask, Don't Tell policy, xiii
double consciousness, 50
Douglass, Frederick, 42
Dove, Rita, 111
dream metaphor, 56–57
Dred Scott v. Sanford, 113
Drew, Charles, 70
Du Bois, Shirley Graham, 244n27
Du Bois, W. E. B., 42–43, 50
Dunbar, Paul Laurence, 42
Dunning, William, 236n23
Durr, Virginia, 89
Dyson, Eric, 130

Easlea, Daryl, 223, 255n9
Ebony magazine, 45, 48–49, 50, 51, 63, 86
Edelman, Marian Wright, 218
Edmondson, Locksley, 244n27
education: Bethune and, 41–42, 43, 240n45; black exclusion from national narratives and, 79; integration of, 22, 47, 100

Eisenhower, Dwight D., 62
Eisenhower, Mamie, 50
Elders, Joycelyn, xiii
Eliasoph, Nina, 211
Elliott, Charlotte, 201
Ellis, Clifton, 185
Enlightenment, 13, 117
Equal Justice Initiative, 106
Essence magazine, 131, 186
eugenics, 13
Everett, Anna, 117
evolutionary biology, 13
Extraordinary, Ordinary People (Rice), 135–46, 248n31

family history, 182–83, 251n8
Family of Freedom: Presidents and African Americans in the White House (Walsh), 184, 251–52n13
Farm Bill (2012), 205
fashion: Beyoncé and, 225–26; black power movement and, 230; Michelle Obama and, 215–16; Rice and, xiv, 172–77
Fawcett, Farrah, 224
Feagans, Brian, 194
Fear Mongering and Race-Baiting: Our New! Hi Tech! Southern Strategy (To Burn the Middle Class), Sponsored by the David Duke Fan Club (One Citizen), 192–93, *193*
"Feed Your Children Well: My Fight against Childhood Obesity" (Obama), 189, 207
feminism: Bethune and, 71; Beyoncé and, 213, 226; intersectionality and, 23, 73; Michelle Obama and, 191, 250n1; Parks and, 91, 94, 95, 123; Rice and, 174; transnational, 23, 146; white-centered definitions of *woman* and, 67, 83
Ferguson, Roderick A., 8
film: black stereotypes in, 13, 17, 237n30; Cleveland Avenue Time Machine and, 111; domestic labor in, 217–19; queerness in, 9; southern womanhood in, 25–26
Firmin, Rob, 127

"'First Lady but Second Fiddle' or the Rise and Rejection of the Political Couple in the White House: 1933–Today" (Loizeau), 190
First Lady role, xvii, 186–87, 188, 190–91, 211, 213–14, 215
Fleetwood, Nicole, 27
Fleming, Julius, Jr., 30
Fleming, Victor, 237n30
Floyd, George, 15, 61
food: black marginalization and, 205–6; Rice and, 159, *159*, 249n47; slavery and, 208; U.S. South and, 229–30. *See also* Obama, Michelle, childhood obesity campaign
"Formation" (Beyoncé), 224, 228–32
4 Little Girls (Lee), 140–41
Foxx, Redd, 148
Foxy Brown, 150
France, 238n45
Franklin, Aretha, 121
Franklin, V. P., 51
Freedman's Memorial, 59, 60–62, 76
"Freedom" (Beyoncé), 231
Freeman, Elizabeth, 28, 217
Freeman, Louis, 121
Fuentes, Carlos, 154, 162
Fulton, Sybrina, 231
funerary practices, 122–23

Gaddafi, Muammar, 166, 249–50n52
Game of Character, A (Robinson), 197–98, 199
Gandhi, Mohandas, 244n20
Garner, Eric, 231
Garner, Margaret, 6
Garvey, Amy Jacques, 244n27, 250n1
Garza, Alicia, xviii
Gates, Henry Louis, Jr., 251n8
Gates, Jobi Petersen, 197
genealogy, 182–83, 251n8
Getsy, David J., 63–64
Giddings, Paula, 43

Gilson, D., 248n33
Ginsburg, Rebecca, 185
Gish, Lillian, 26
Givhan, Robin, 175–76
Glanton, Dahleen, 183
Glass Wing Group, 225
globalization, 31, 33
Global South, 31–32, 34, 151–52, 187, 228
Goldberg, Whoopi, 148
Gone with the Wind, 237n30
Gordon, Bruce, 131
Go Tell Michelle (Nevergold and Brooks-Bertram), 250–51n1, 256n23
Grant, Oscar, 231
Gray, Fred, 91
Great Depression, 22, 43
Great Migration: Bethune and, 57, 239n3; matriarch stereotype and, 17; Michelle Obama and, 180, 182, 196, 200; Rice and, 143
Green, Nancy, 9, 188
Greer, Germaine, 173, 174
Grewal, Inderpal, 23
Grey, Stephanie Houston, 209
Grier, David Alan, 248n39
Grier, Mary Lou, 74–76, 77–78, 79–80
Grier, Pam, 150
Griffin, Farah Jasmine, 30
Griffith, D. W., 9, 26, 214–15, 236n23, 237n30
Guinier, Lani, xiii
Guston, Phillip, 167
Gutiérrez-Jones, Carl, 31–32
Guy-Sheftall, Beverly, xviii, 250n1

Halberstam, Jack, 34
Haley, Alex, 251n8
Hancock, David Leslie, 185–86
Hansberry, Lorraine, 17, 52, 96, 196, 251n5
Hansberry v. Lee, 196
Hanson, Joyce A., 43, 68, 87
Harlem, 151, 152, 177
"Harlem" (Hughes), 56–57
Harlem Book of the Dead (Van Der Zee), 122

Harlem Renaissance, 54–55, 152
Harper, Amie Breeze, 206
Harris, Kamala, xviii
Harris, Trudier, 30, 138
Harris-Perry, Melissa, 19, 107
Harvey, Steve, 148
Haskins, Jim, 94
Hatfield, Mark O., 70
Hayden, Sara, 208–9, 212
Healthy, Hunger-Free Kids Act (2010), 212
Hegel, G. W. F., 117
Height, Dorothy, 58, 59–60, 62, 64–65, 69, 70
Help, The, 217–19
Hemings, Sally, 163, 185
hemispheric South, 31–32, 162, 186, 187, 228
heteronormativity: Bethune and, 46, 53, 65; and black women's iconicity, 27; childhood narratives and, 28; maternal motifs and, 8; national family and, 127; Michelle Obama and, 189, 204; Old South nostalgia and, 15; Rice and, 152. *See also* queerness/transness; queer/trans people
Hidden Figures, 109
Hill, Anita, xiii, 18, 67, 137
Himes, Chester, 149–50
hip-hop, 106, 107–8, 162, 229
Hobson, Maurice, 30
Holland, Sharon, 30, 122
Holloway, Karla FC, 28–29, 122
Homecoming (Beyoncé), 224
Homestead Acts, 205
hooks, bell, 30, 138
Hoover, Herbert, 51, 59
Horwitz, Tony, 10
House Committee on Un-American Activities, 48, 80
Houston, Whitney, 230
How to Be Beyoncé (Moore), 225
Hudson, Jennifer, 222
Hughes, Langston, 56–57
Hunter, Tera, 30
Hurricane Katrina (2005), xv, 128–32, 147, 154–55, 177, 229, 233

Hurst, Fannie, 237n30, 246n65
Hutchinson, Ira J., 73
hybridity, 184, 185
hyperembodiment: mammy stereotype and, 9, 13, 208; Rice and, 132, 153, 157, 160, 165, 171

"I, Too" (Hughes), 57
iconicity, black women and, 19–20, 22–23, 26; early contributions, 7; heteronormativity and, 27; imperialism/colonialism and, 146; memoirs and autobiographies and, 97–98, 135, 137, 210; maternal motifs and, 21, 28; national body and, 21; national family and, 21; public sphere and, 22–23; U.S. South and, 26–27, 32–33; white femininity and, 25. *See also specific women*
"I Have a Dream" speech (King), 56, 92, 103, 104, 235n8
I Know Why the Caged Bird Sings (Angelou), 138
imagined community, 24
Imitation of Life, 13, 121, 122, 237n30, 246n65
immigration, 145, 146, 248n31
imperialism/colonialism, 146, 161, 166
"Independent Women, Part I" (Destiny's Child), 224
individualism, 13
infantile citizenship, 27–28, 145
"In First Lady's Roots, a Complex Path from Slavery" (Swarns and Kantor), 183
In Living Color, 248–49n39
intermixture: antimiscegenation laws, 237n30, 238n53; Beyoncé and, 224; Michelle Obama and, 184, 185; Rice and, 144, 163–64, 166
intersectionality, xviii, 2, 23, 29, 73–74, 90–91
intertextuality, 97–98, 105
Iraq War, xiv, 132, 133, 139–40, 142, 167, 250n54
Iton, Richard, 221

Jackson, John H., 148
Jackson, Mahalia, 92, 103, 121
Jackson, Michael, 230
Jacobs, Harriet, 5
James, Etta, 216, 222, 254–55n5
Jane Crow, xi. *See also* Jim Crow
Jarvis, Jonathan, 84
Jay-Z (Shawn Carter), 224, 225
Jefferson, Thomas, 3, 163, 185
Jeffries, Michael, 187
Jemima Code, The: Two Centuries of African American Cookbooks (Tipton-Martin), 208
Jenkins, Carol, 218–19
Jenkins, Timothy, 84, 85, 243n91
Jenner, Caitlyn, 174
Jet magazine, 48, 85
Jewell, Sally, 84
Jezebel stereotype, 192
Jim Crow: architecture and, 110; Beyoncé and, 223, 255nn8–9; challenges to, 47–48, 134–35; Cleveland Avenue Time Machine and, 113, 114; domestic workers and, 217; music and, 118; neoconservative obscuring of, 142; Michelle Obama and, 194–95; origins of, 113; *Plessy v. Ferguson* and, 47, 112–13; popular culture and, 217–18; Rice and, ix, 137, 139; sexual abuse and, 90–91, 243n8, 243–44n12; war on terror and, 142. *See also* civil rights movement
Johnson, Barbara, 64
Johnson, E. Patrick, 30, 225
Johnson, Eunice W., 49
Johnson, J. Bennett, Jr., 80
Johnson, John H., 48–50
Johnson, Katherine, 109
Johnson, Lyndon B., 47
Johnson, Robert, 111
Johnson, Sharita, 30
Johnson, Wanda, 231
Johnson Publishing, 48
Johnson-Miller, Beverly C., 51
Jones, Jacqueline, 33, 182

Jordan, Barbara, xii
Joseph, Peniel, 84
Journey of Condoleezza Rice, The (Richardson), 220
"Just as I Am" (Elliott), 201

Kaepernick, Colin, 231
Kantor, Joan, 215
Kantor, Jodi, 183
Kaplan, Amy, 33
Kaplan, Caren, 23, 146
Keckley, Elizabeth, 215
Kelley, Robin D. G., 30
Kelly, Emma, 69
Kessler, Glenn, 249n51
Keys, Alicia, 222
Keys, Sheila McCauley, 98
Killens, John Oliver, 30
Kim, Myunghee, 192
King, Colbert I., 84
King, Coretta Scott, 250n1
King, Francine, 39, 41–42
King, James D., 134
King, Martin Luther, Jr.: on black youth, 56, 92; Coretta Scott King's influence on, 250n1; memorials to, 110, 126; national narratives and, 235n8; Parks and, 98, 103; temperament of, 244n20
King, Wilma, 138
Kirby, 15
Knowles, Mathew, 221, 223, 224, 255nn8–9
Knowles, Tina, 221, 222, 223, 224
Knoxx, Riley, 225
Knuckey, Jonathan, 192
Ku Klux Klan, 218
Kurtzman, Harvey, 149

Lane, Artis, 246n74
Latinx contexts, 249n48
law enforcement, xviii, 15, 229, 230–31, 232
Lawless, Ben, 112
Lawrence, Martin, 9
Lee, Barbara, xii

Lee, Sheila Jackson, xii
Lee, Spike, 130, 140–41, 229
Legacy Museum and National Memorial for Peace and Justice, 106
Lemonade (Beyoncé), 213, 222, 225
Lemonade Served Bitter Sweet (Glass Wing Group), 225
Leopard's Spots, The (Griffith), 214
lesbians, 27
Let's Move! campaign, xvi–xvii, 187–90, 206–14, 227, 256n22
"Letter from a Birmingham Jail" (King), 56
Lew, Jack, 235n4
Lewis, John R., 82
liberalism, 13
Liberation of Aunt Jemima, The (Saar), 157
Lichtman, Abe, 69
Lightfoot, Lori, xviii
Ligon, Glenn, 162
Lincoln, Abraham, 10, 47, 59, 60–62, 76
Lincoln, C. Eric, 122
Lincoln Memorial, 10, 47
Lindsey, Treva, 44
literary history. *See* African American literary history
Livingston, Jennie, 27
Lloyd, Terry, 136, 159–62, 159, 166, 174
Lockard, John Onye, 157
Locke, Alain, 54–55
Loizeau, Pierre-Marie, 190
Lomax, Tamura, 192
"Long Time: Long Lost Daughters and the New 'New South'" (Spillers), 136–37
Lorde, Audre, xix
Love, Loni, 159
Lubiano, Wahneema, 18
Lusane, Clarence, 185
lynching, 9, 111, 218, 238n53, 239n3

MacDonald, Susie, 91
Madison, Dolley, 4
Mad TV, 135–36, 148, 149–56, 174, 176, 248n39

Magnificent Michelle Obama, Our First Lady, The: "Strength and Honor Are Her Clothing" (Proverbs 31:25) (Richardson), 178
Malcolm X, 230, 249n40
Mambry, Marcus, 142
mammy stereotype: Aunt Jemima stereotype and, 8–9; black arts movement on, 157; black maternal body and, 6, 17, 21; challenges to, 10–11, 14, 46, 52; in film, 13, 17, 237n30; food and, 208; national body and, 16; Michelle Obama and, 18, 188–89, 191, 194–95, 208–9; Old South nostalgia and, 8–9, 10, 13, 15, 237n30; queerness/transness and, 9–10, 12–13
"Mammy Washington Almost Had, The" (Horwitz), 10
Marable, Manning, 249n45
March on Washington (1963), 56, 92, 103, 104
marginalization: agriculture and, 205; education and, 79; historic sites and, 79, 85; memorials and, 125; modernity and, 114–15; national narratives and, 3–4; post–civil rights era, 134; space age and, 109; World's Columbian Exposition and, 9
Mars, Bruno, 230
Marshall, Thurgood, 47, 137
Martin, Trayvon, xviii, 231
Mary McLeod Bethune: One of America's Greatest Sweethearts and the World's Best Leaders (Richardson), 40
Mary McLeod Bethune: The Spirit of a Champion (Barnett), 39, 41–42, 45
"Mary McLeod Bethune's 'Last Will and Testament': A Legacy for Race Vindication" (Smith), 57
masculinity, 14, 111, 152, 162
mass communications, 22
material culture, 10, 11, 12, 16, 160, 167
maternal motifs and stereotypes, 7; Bethune and, 45, 52, 53; and black women's iconicity, 21, 28; in film, 17; heteronormativity and, 8; Michelle Obama and, 187–89, 197, 204, 208, 211, 212, 213; queer/trans people and, 9; Rice and, 143–44, 177; slavery and, 4–6. *See also* black maternal body; Parks, Rosa, as mother
Maud Martha (Brooks), 251n5
McCluskey, Audrey Thomas, 39, 43–44, 51, 52
McDaniel, Hattie, 237n30
McGhee, Felicia, 89
McGuire, Danielle, 90, 94, 243n8
McInnis, Jarvis, 30
McNair, Denise, xv, 99, 135, 139, 140
McPherson, Tara, 237n30
McSpadden, Lezley, 231
memoir. *See* African American literary history
Michaels, Michell'e (Miss Shalae), 225
Michelle: A Biography (Mundy), 180–81
"Michelle Obama, Mom-in-Chief: The Racialized Rhetorical Contexts of Maternity" (Hayden), 208–9
"Michelle Obama's Family Tree Has Roots in a Carolina Slave Plantation" (Glanton and St. Clair), 183
Mills, Florence, 122
minstrelsy, 9, 161
miscegenation, 237n30, 238n53
Miss Cleo, 14
Mississippi Burning, 108
Miss Shalae (Michell'e Michaels), 225
Mitchell, Margaret, 237n30
Moallem, Minoo, 146
Mock, Janet, 27, 34, 226, 227
modernity, 32, 114–15
Mohanty, Chandra Talpade, 23
Montgomery bus boycott, 87, *88*, 110, 114, 118, 245n52
monuments, 61–62, 126
Moody, Ann, 138
Moor, Ayanah, 136, 162–64, *163*, 166
Moore, Madison, 225
Moore, Stephen, 123

Morgan, Piers, 222, 223, 224, 225, 228
Morrison, Toni, 3, 6, 211–12, 243–44n12
Mother Emanuel murders (2015), 14, 29
mother motif. *See* maternal motifs and stereotypes
Mother Teresa, 244n20
Mount Rushmore, 127, 165
"Move Your Body" (Beyoncé and Swizz Beatz), 212, 213, 227, 256n22
Moynihan, Daniel Patrick, 17, 92, 97
Mundy, Liza, 180–81
Murphy, Eddie, 148
Murray, Pauli, xi, 52, 83, 93, 126
Mya, Messy, 229
"My Last Will and Testament" (Bethune), 45–51, 53–57, 60, 63, 80, 85–86, 99, 102
Myrdal, Gunnar, 96

NAACP (National Association for the Advancement of Colored People), 83, 90, 91, 101, 244n19
NABWH (National Archives for Black Women's History), 82, 83, 84
NACW (National Association of Colored Women), 10, 22, 68
Nas, 156, 159
national abjection, 13
National Archives for Black Women's History (NABWH), 82, 83–84
National Association for the Advancement of Colored People (NAACP), 83, 90, 91, 101, 244n19
National Association of Colored Women (NACW), 10, 22, 68
national body: African American literary history and, 21; defined, 20; mammy stereotype and, 16; Michelle Obama and, 209; Rice and, 135–36, 142, 153–54; romanticized femininity and, 125; white womanhood and, 24–26
National Council of Negro Women (NCNW): Bethune and, 22, 43, 52; Bethune Council House and, 68, 69, 70, 71–73, 74–75, 82; Bethune Memorial and, 58, 62; founding of, 68
national family: Bethune on, 44, 46, 49, 53, 54, 62–63; black power movement and, 97; and black women's iconicity, 21; civil rights movement and, 11, 65, 96; heteronormativity and, 127; matriarch stereotype and, 96; neoconservatism and, 65; Michelle Obama and, 181, 189, 200, 204, 216–17; Rice and, ix, 135, 136, 143–44, 146–47
national femininity, 23–24, 238n45
national historic sites, 70, 79. *See also* Bethune Council House
national narratives: black marginalization and, 3–4; civil rights movement and, 235n8; rebirth, 215–16; 16th Street Baptist Church bombing and, 141; transnational feminism on, 146; white womanhood and, 24–26. *See also* marginalization
National Organization for Women (NOW), xi, 83
National Park Service (NPS), 84, 85. *See also* Bethune Council House
National Youth Administration (NYA), 43, 49, 51–52, 58
NCNW. *See* National Council of Negro Women (NCNW)
Negro Digest, 48
Negro Family, The: The Case for National Action (Moynihan), 97
Nelson, Alondra, 117, 251n8
Nelson, Dana D., 3–4, 29, 33
neoconservatism: civil rights movement and, 65, 123, 134, 135, 137, 139–40, 144; Clinton administration and, xiii; immigration and, 146; infantile citizenship and, 144–45; Jim Crow and, 142; national family and, 65; national historic sites and, 72, 75, 78; Obama campaign and, 188; Parks and, 246n72; Rice and, ix–x, xii–xiii, xiv, 132, 137–38, 147, 149, 171, 249n45
neoliberalism, 25, 204–5
neonativism, 191, 192

Nevergold, Barbara A. Seals, 250–51n1, 256n23
Never Ignorant Getting Goals (Moor), 162–64, *163*, 166
New Deal, 43, 49, 51, 68, 75
New Jemima, The (Overstreet), 157
New Negro, 54–55
Newsome, Bree, 14, 29
new southern studies, 29, 33, 187, 226
Newton, Huey P., 230
9/11, xiv–xv, 132, 133
Nixon, Edgar Daniel, 96, 244n19
No Higher Honor: A Memoir of My Years in Washington (Rice), 131, 249–50n52
No More (Lockard), 157
Norman, Georgette, 110
Norton, Eleanor Holmes, 61–62
NOW (National Organization for Women), xi, 83
NPS (National Park Service), 84, 85. *See also* Bethune Council House
NYA (National Youth Administration), 43, 49, 51–52, 58

Oakar, Mary Rose, 76
Obama, Barack: authenticity and, 199, 251n3; and Chicago, 202; inaugurations, 212–13, 215, 221, 222–23, 224, 225, 254–55n5; national rebirth narrative and, 215; and Michelle Obama, 182–83, 197, 199, 250n1, 251n3; policy failings of, 204–5, 212; postracialism and, 158, 223–24; presidential campaign of, xvi, 18, 180, 182–83, 188, 189, 191, 192–93, 196; stereotypes and, 18; temperament of, 244n20; Women on 20s movement and, 1, 235n4
Obama, Michelle, 178–219, *178*; *American Grown*, 208, 209–10, 211–12; Beyoncé and, 189–90, 213, 226–27, 256nn22–23; biographical profile of, 189, 195–200, 209–10, 253n43; black national family and, 181, 189, 200, 204, 216–17; childhood obesity campaign, xvi–xvii, 187–90, 206–14, 227, 256n22; Chicago and, 194–99; controversial comment by, 199, 254n39; convention speech by, xvi, 201–3; fashion and, 215–16; First Lady role and, xvii, 186–87, 188, 190–91, 210–14, 215; iconicity of, xvii, 202–3, 209, 219; Joining Forces campaign, xvii; letters to, 250–51n1, 256n23; maternal motifs and, 187–89, 197, 204, 208, 211, 212, 213; neoliberalism and, 25, 204–5; Princeton experience, 194–95, 196, 253n35; professional background and, 206–7, 211; public sphere and, 22; reactionary narratives and, 192–93, *193*, 214–15; service and, 197, 253n35; slavery and, 182–85, 186, 200, 203–4, 210, 251n10; stereotypes and, 18, 188–89, 191, 194–96, 208–9; U.S. South and, 33, 180–82, 187, 191, 203–4, 218, 251n3; White House and, 185–86, 203, 209, 210–11, 252n19; writings on, 250–51n1
Obamas, The (Kantor), 215
Ogletree, Charles, 197
Old South nostalgia: Aunt Jemima stereotype and, 11; *Birth of a Nation* and, 236n23; critiques of, 14; gender ideologies and, 15; mammy stereotype and, 8–9, 10, 13, 15, 237n30; national reunification and, 215; paternalism and, 170; Rice and, 160; southern lady myth, 15, 89; white supremacy and, 236n23; white womanhood and, 15, 89, 237n30
Oliver, Luther, 92
On Racial Icons: Blackness and the Public Imagination (Fleetwood), 27
On the Bus with Rosa Parks (Dove), 111
On the Real Side (Watkins), 148
Open Wide the Freedom Gates (Height), 59–60, 62
Orange Is the New Black, 225–26
Our Auntie Rosa: The Family of Rosa Parks Remembers Her Life and Lessons (Keys and Allen), 98
OutKast, 106, 107–8
Overstreet, Joe, 157

Pan-Africanism, 97, 244n27
Paris Is Burning (Livingston), 27
Parks, Raymond, 107, 121, 244n19
Parks, Rosa, 87–127, *88*; archives of, 243n8; Bethune and, 98, 99; Christianity and, 99, 100, 101, 111; civil rights movement and, 22, 86, 93, 103–4, 114; *Dear Mrs. Parks*, 94, 104–5; honors and memorials, 119–27, 245n49, 246n72, 246n74; iconicity of, 22, 86, 93, 95, 109, 114, 115, 118–19; as lady, *88*, 89; literary voice of, 94–95; memoir and, 97–98, 99; Montgomery bus boycott and, 87, *88*, 110, 114, 118, 119; as mother, 86, 91–97, 104, 109, 114, 118, 119, 124; myths regarding, 94, 106, 107, 244n20; NAACP and, 90, 91, 101, 244n19; popular culture and, 106–8; public commemorations of, 95–96; public sphere and, 22; *Quiet Strength*, 94, 99–105; Rice and, xi; right-wing appropriation of, 123; sexism and, 88–90, 100, 108, 243n6; sexual abuse and, 90, 243n8; victimization, 101–2, 105; Women on 20s movement and, 2; youth and, 91–92, 93–94, 98, 99, 100–103, 105, 108–9, 114. *See also* Cleveland Avenue Time Machine
Parks, Rosa, Children's Museum. *See* Cleveland Avenue Time Machine
Parks, Rosa, Library and Museum, 110–11, 245n49. *See also* Cleveland Avenue Time Machine
Parks, Rosa and Raymond, Institute for Self-Development, 100–101, 104
partus sequitur ventrem, 4
Passed On: African American Mourning Stories (Holloway), 122
pastoral, 26, 238n53
Pathways to Freedom, 100–101
Patterson, Melina, 94, 104
Patton, Stacey, 138
PepsiCo, 15
performativity, 63–64, 85–86, 114, 123, 149, 174, 176

Perkins, Margo V., 97
Perry, Imani, 30, 96
Perry, Tyler, 9
Peterson, Jesse Lee, 246n72
Pigford v. Glickman, 205
Pinckney, Clementa, 14
plantation complex, 32, 170, 181, 182, 186
Plessy v. Ferguson, 47, 112–13, 114
police brutality, xviii, 15, 229, 230–31, 232
Politician Clipart #12206 (Vangsgard), 167, *169*
Poor George #3 (After P. G.) (Chagoya), 167, *168*, 170
Poor Richard (Guston), 167
popular culture: Jim Crow and, 217–18; Parks and, 106–8; Rice in, 135–36, 147, 148–54, 156, 248–49n39; white supremacy in, 26, 214–15, 218, 236n23, 237n30
"Portrait in Georgia" (Toomer), 238n53
postblackness, 29, 83, 158, 162, 222, 223–24
post–civil rights era: Beyoncé and, 221; black comedy and, 148; black organizing, xviii–xix; black women's memoirs and autobiographies and, 138; Chisholm and, xii; civil rights movement and, 93; color-blindness and, 132; education and, 79, 195; Parks and, 93, 107, 108, 114, 115, 123; Rice and, 22, 132, 133–34, 177; southern strategy, ix–x, 133, 192, 193–94; Thomas and, 137
postcolonial theory, 24, 95–96, 125
post-Emancipation era: Bethune and, 41, 58, 62, 232–33; domestic labor, 12, 217–18; food access, 205; material culture and, 10; violence during, 9, 193
posthumanism, 113
postracialism: Bethune Council House and, 83; Beyoncé and, 222, 223–24; Cleveland Avenue Time Machine and, 113, 117; intersectionality and, 29; Obama presidency and, 158, 223–24; Rice and, 134, 162
post–World War II era, 11, 49–50, 52, 96
Powell, Colin, x, 134, 149, 166
Preckwinkle, Toni, xviii

INDEX 293

Prince, 230
Prisock, Louis, 137–38, 145
Pryor, Richard, 148
public sphere, 22–23

Quaker Oats Company, 11, 15
Queen of America Goes to Washington City, The: Essays on Sex and Citizenship (Berlant), 28
queer diasporas, 182
queerness/transness: Clinton administration and, xiii; fashion and, 174, 176; invisibility of, 55; mammy stereotype and, 9–10, 12–13; nationalism and, 96; Rice and, 147, 150, 151, 152, 156, 160; slavery and, 5; wedding complex and, 217. *See also* heteronormativity
queer/trans studies, 8, 33, 34
queer/trans people, xviii–xix, 28; Beyoncé and, 225–26, 229; and black diasporas,182; Black Lives Matter and, xviii; and black women's iconicity, 27; civil rights movement and, 92–93; erasure of, 8, 10; matriarch stereotype and, 9; in post–World War II era, 52. *See also* heteronormativity
Quiet Strength: The Faith, the Hope, and the Heart of a Woman Who Changed a Nation (Parks and Reed), 94, 99–105

Race after Technology: Abolitionist Tools for the New Jim Code (Benjamin), 117
race traitor motif, 132, 136, 149, 151, 156, 158, 160, 161, 167, 249n45
race vindication, 51
"Racial Draft, The" (Chappelle), 148–49, 151, 154, 155
racial icons. *See* iconicity, black women and
Racial Paranoia: The Unintended Consequences of Political Correctness (Jackson), 148
racism. *See* white supremacy
Raising the Dead: Readings of Death and (Black) Subjectivity (Holland), 122

Raisin in the Sun, A (Hansberry), 17, 96, 251n5
Randolph, A. Philip, 93
Reagan, Ronald, 73, 75, 78, 155
Reconstructing Dixie (McPherson), 237n30
Reconstruction, 236n23
Reed, Gregory J., 94, 99, 104
Reeves, Jeremiah, 244n19
Rejman, Travis, 197
reverse discrimination, 83, 133
Rice, Angelena, 143
Rice, Condoleezza, 128–77, *128*, 220; American exceptionalism and, 145–47; authenticity and, 149, 153, 158, 161–62, 166–67; in Bush administration, x–xi, 133, 142, 143; civil rights movement and, 133–35, 137, 139–41, 155, 177; Cleopatra motifs and, 147, 150; conservatism and, ix–x, xii–xiii, xiv, 132, 137–38, 147, 149, 171, 249n45; family of, 143–44; fashion and, xiv, 172–77; food and, 159, *159*, 249n47; Gaddafi and, 166, 249–50n52; Hurricane Katrina and, xv, 128–32, 147, 155, 177; iconicity of, xiv–xvi, 131–32, 142–43, 147, 171; immigration and, 145, 146, 248n31; Iraq War and, xiv, 132, 133, 139–40, 142, 167; Latinx contexts and, 249n48; national family and, ix, 135, 136, 143–44, 146–47; performativity and, 149; in popular culture, 135–36, 147, 148–54, 156, 248–49n39; post–civil rights era and, 22, 132, 133–34, 177; power and, x–xi; press conferences and, 141–42, 165, 249n51; public sphere and, 22; segregation and, 134–35; southern roots of, 131, 139, 143, 151, 204; stereotypes and, 156, 157, 158, 159–61, *159*, 167, 249n39; visual representations of, 136, 142–43, 157–72; war on terror and, xv, 132, 135, 139–40, 142, 158, 162, 164, 167, 171
Rice, John, ix, 140, 143, 167
Riddlesperger, James W., Jr., 134
Rigelhaupt, Jess, 94, 104
Ringgold, Faith, 157

Rivera, Diego, 163
Roberts, Julia, 26
Roberts, Robin, 27
Robertson, Carole, xv, 99, 135, 139
Robinson, Craig, 179, 197–98, 199
Robinson, Eugene, 139–40
Robinson, Fraser C., III, 197, 200, 253n43
Robinson, Jo Ann Gibson, 90, 91
Robinson, Marian, 196, 197, 198, 200, 253n43
Robinson, Zandria, 30
Rock, Chris, 148
Rocker, Pamela, xviii
Roof, Dylann, 14
Rooks, Noliwe, 172
Roosevelt, Eleanor, 43, 47, 50, 58, 69, 70, 125
Roosevelt, Franklin D.: Bethune and, 42, 51, 58–59, 240n43; Black Cabinet of, 43, 44, 47, 57; disability of, 58, 240n40; fireside chats, 53
Roots (Haley), 251n8
"Rosa Parks" (OutKast), 106
Rosa Parks: My Story (Parks and Haskins), 94
Rosa Parks Story, The, 107, 245n51
Rosa Parks, Whose "No" in 1955 Launched the Montgomery Bus Boycott and Was Heard around the World (Richardson), 88
Ross, Betsy, 4
Rowland, Kelly, 221
Royster, Francesca T., 147, 150, 171
"Run the World (Girls)" (Beyoncé), 213, 227
RuPaul, 27
Russo, Ann, 23
Rustin, Bayard, 93, 126
Rutt, Chris L., 8
Ryan, Terre, 211

Saar, Betye, 157
#SayHerName movement, 2, 29, 231
"Say My Name" (Destiny's Child), 231
Scattered Hegemonies: Postmodernity and Transnational Feminist Practices (Grewal and Kaplan), 23

School Daze (Lee), 229
science fiction, 116, 153
Seale, Bobby, 230
Secretary of State, The (Tuymans), 164–66, *165*
Sedgwick, Eve Kosofsky, 33
segregation. *See* Jim Crow
separate spheres, 75
September 11, 2001, terrorist attacks, xiv–xv, 132, 133
sermonic tradition, 99
sexism: black power movement and, 97; civil rights movement and, 103–4; Parks and, 88–90, 100, 108, 243n6
sexual abuse, 5, 90–91, 243n8, 243–44n12
Shabazz, Rashad, 205
Shaft, 249n39
Shaheen, Jeanne, 235n4
Shakur, Assata, 97
Shakur, Tupac, 231
Sharpless, Rebecca, 12
Shetterly, Margot Lee, 109
Shimakawa, Karen, 13
ship metaphor, 115, 161, 245n53
Shome, Raka, 24–25
Silla del Águila, La (Fuentes), 154, 162
Simpson, Jessica, 26
Sims, J. Marion, 5
SIS Oral History Project, 95
Sistah Vegan: Black Female Vegans Speak on Food, Identity, Health Society (Harper), 206
Sister Citizen: Shame, Stereotypes, and Black Women in America (Harris-Perry), 19
Sites of Slavery (Tillet), 3
16th Street Baptist Church bombing (1963): American exceptionalism and, 146–47; black youth narrative and, 98–99, 244n17; childhood studies and, 138–39; contemporary narratives of, 140–41, 248n24; infantile citizenship and, 145; Rice and, xv, 135, 137, 139, 142, 177; war on terror and, iv, 142

Skipper, Joseph, 101–2, 105
slavery: black arts movement on, 163; black maternal body and, 5–6, 185; childhood studies and, 138; Cleveland Avenue Time Machine on, 113, 114, 115; comedy and, 149; economy of, 2, 16; food and, 208; labor under, 4–5; maternal motifs and, 4–6; narratives and, 3, 135; neoconservative appropriation of, 133; Michelle Obama and, 183–85, 186, 200, 203–4, 210, 251n10; plantation complex and, 32, 170, 181, 182, 186; Rice and, 139, 144–45, 156, 158, 161, 170; ungendering and, 5, 90; White House and, 185, 186, 210, 251–52n13; white masculinity and, 170. *See also* Old South nostalgia; U.S. South
Smith, Elaine M., 39, 43–44, 57, 240n43, 243n91
Smith, Jamil, 222
Smith, Tommie, 231
Smith, Valerie, 140–41
Smolenyak, Megan, 183, 184
Snorton, C. Riley, 5, 34
social Darwinism, 215
Social Life of DNA, The (Nelson), 251n8
"Somebody Blew Up America" (Baraka), 156, 158, 159
Soul on Ice (Cleaver), 97
southern belle myth, 15
southern diasporas, 33, 182. *See also* Great Migration
southern gentleman myth, 15
southern strategy, ix–x, 133, 192, 193–94
southern studies, 16, 29, 31–32
"Southern Turns" (Richardson), 14
southern white womanhood, 5, 15, 25–26, 89, 173–74, 237n30, 238n53
South Side (Chicago). *See* Chicago
South Side Girl (video), 189, 195–200, 201
South Side Girls: Growing Up in the Great Migration (Chatelain), 196
Southside with You (Tanne), 180
space age, 109, 114

Spatializing Blackness: Architectures of Confinement and Black Masculinity in Chicago (Shabazz), 205
Spencer, Octavia, 217, 218
Spillers, Hortense, 5, 30, 89, 90, 136–37
States' Laws on Race and Color (Murray), 52
statues, 63–64. *See also specific memorials*
St. Clair, Stacy, 183
Steele, Elaine, 99, 101, 105
steel magnolia motif, 174
stereotypes: angry black woman, 187, 200; Auntie, 52–53; baby mama, 18, 188; Bethune's challenges to, 44, 49, 52–53; black arts movement and, 157; comedy and, 149; domestic labor and, 12, 13, 218, 219; Jezebel, 192; Jim Crow and, 113; in material culture, 10, 11, 12, 16, 160, 167; matriarch, 9, 17, 45, 53, 92, 96–97; Michelle Obama and, 18, 188–89, 191, 194–96, 208–9; Rice and, 156, 157, 158, 159–61, *159*, 167, 249n39; slavery and, 5; welfare queen, xiii, 17–18, 72, 78; youth and, 99. *See also* Aunt Jemima stereotype; mammy stereotype
Stevenson, Bryan, 106
Steverson, Delia, 30
Stewart, Maria, 7
Stewart, Tonea, 112, 245n51
Stockett, Kathryn, 217
Stone, Emma, 217, 218
Story, Tim, 106
Stowe, Harriet Beecher, 9
strong black woman myth, 97, 226. *See also* maternal motifs and stereotypes
Subtlety, A, or the Marvelous Sugar Baby (Walker), 12–13
Succeeding against the Odds: The Autobiography of a Great American Businessman (Johnson), 48
Sula (Morrison), 243–44n12
Summer Snow: Reflections of a Black Daughter from the South (Harris), 138
Sun Ra, 117–18
Swarns, Rachel L., 183, 184–85

Sweet Tea (Johnson), 225
Swiss Family Robinson, The (Wyss), 199
Swizz Beatz, 256n22
Sykes, Wanda, 27, 148

#TakeAKnee movement, 231
talking book trope, 41
Talley, André Leon, 179, 203, 216
Tanne, Richard, 180
Taylor, Recy, 90, 244n19
Taylor, Tate, 217
Taylor, Ula, 250n1
Tea Party, 191
Terrell, Mary Church, 10, 70
Texas 'Bama, 229, 232
Theoharis, Jeanne, 91, 94, 122
Third World Women and the Politics of Feminism (Mohanty, Russo, and Torres), 23
30 Rock, 147, 148, 153
"This Is the Age of Power Pearls—And No One Exploits Their Potency Better than Condie Rice" (Greer), 173
Thomas, Clarence, xiii, 10, 67, 136 37, 248–49n39
Thompson, Dolphin, 69
thug motif, 162
Thurmond, Sue Bailey, 70
Till, Emmett, 85, 98, 248n24
Tillet, Salamishah, 3
Time Machine, The (Wells), 112–13
Time to Kill, A, 108, 245n51
Tipton-Martin, Toni, 208
Tometi, Opal, xviii
Toomer, Jean, 238n53
Torres, Lourdes, 23
torture, 147–48, 154, 162
transnational feminism, 23, 146
transness. See queerness/transness
Truman, Harry S., 59, 240n43
Trump, Donald: coronavirus pandemic and, 29–30, 233; neoconservatism and, 65, 167; right wing appropriation of Parks and, 123; southern strategy and, 194; white supremacy and, 191, 219; Women on 20s movement and, 235n4
Truth, Sojourner, 6–7, 19, 21, 126
Tubman, Harriet, 1, 2–3, 4, 6–7, 19, 21, 113, 235n4
Tubman, William S., 70
Turner, Patricia A., 10, 167, 217–18
Tuymans, Luc, 136, 164–66, 165

Uncle Ben, 160
Uncle Tom stereotype, 9, 14, 158, 159–60, 159, 167, 248n39
Uncle Tom's Cabin (Stowe), 9
Uncle Tom's Condi Rice (Lloyd), 159–62, 159, 166, 174
Underwood, Charles G., 8
ungendering, 5, 90
United Daughters of the Confederacy, 10, 17
Untitled (Snow White and the Seven Dwarfs) (Chagoya), 166–67, 168
"Using Rosa Parks" (Peterson), 246n72
U.S. South: activist movements in, 29; Afrofuturism and, 118; authenticity and, 204; Bethune and, 39, 41, 42, 62, 67, 86; Beyoncé and, 222, 227–30, 231, 232; binary of, 151–52, 249n40; Black Panther Party and, 231; and black women's iconicity, 26–27, 32–33; central role of, 18, 32–33; coronavirus pandemic and, 29–30; new southern studies on, 29, 33, 187, 226; Michelle Obama and, 33, 180–82, 187, 191, 203–4, 218, 251n3; Parks and, 86, 121; plantation complex and, 32, 170, 181, 182, 186; Rice and, 131, 139, 143, 151, 204; stereotypes and, 195. See also Great Migration; Old South nostalgia

Vagnoux, Isabelle, 134
Van Der Zee, James, 122
Vangsgard, Amy, 136, 167, 169
Vento, Bill, 74, 77
Vogt, Peter, 112
Voice from the South, A (Cooper), 8
Voting Rights Act (1965), 22, 109, 133

Wade-Gayles, Gloria, 95
Wald, Priscilla, 33
Walker, Kara, 12–13, 163
Walker, Maggie, 77
Walsh, Kenneth T., 184, 251–52n13
Ward, Jerry, 30
Warner, John W., 69–70, 73
war on terror, 132, 135, 139–40, 158, 162, 164, 167
Washington, Booker T., 42–43, 52
Washington, Denzel, 222
Washington, George, 3
Washington, Margaret, 6
Waters, Maxine, xii
Watkins, Mel, 148
Wayans, Keenen Ivory, 248–49n39
wedding complex, 217
We Good, 227
welfare queen stereotype, xiii, 17–18, 72, 78
Wells, H. G., 112–13
Wells, Ida B., 9, 193
Wesley, Cynthia, xv, 99, 135, 139
West, Kanye, 130
Wheatley, Phillis, 7
When the Levees Broke (Lee), 130
White, Thomas H., 42
white flight, 196
White House, 185–86, 203, 209, 210–11, 218, 251–52n13, 252n19
white masculinity, 15, 90, 123, 148, 153, 162, 166, 170
white supremacy, 185–86; Obama administration and, 214–15; police brutality and, xviii, 15, 229, 230–31, 232; in popular culture, 26, 214–15, 218, 236n23, 237n30; segregationist logic and, 194–96; social Darwinism and, 215; symbols of, 14, 15; Trump administration and, 191, 219; white womanhood and, 25–26
white womanhood: black rapist myth and, 238n53; Cult of True Womanhood on, 5; definitions of woman and, 67, 73–74, 78–79, 82, 83; fashion and, 173–74, 177; national narratives and, 24–26; pastoral and, 26, 238n53; romanticization of, 237n30; southern belle myth, 15
Whitt, Mary Frances, 98, 101
Who's Afraid of Aunt Jemima? (Ringgold), 157
Wiegman, Robyn, 33, 61
Wilkinson, Jim, 249n51
Williams, Jesse, 231
Williams, Mary Louise, 91
Williams, Michelle, 221
Williamson, Terrion L., 18
Wilson, Flip, 148
Wilson, Woodrow, 218
Winfrey, Oprah, 203
Wisniewski, K. A., 149
Witherspoon, Reese, 26
Witt, Doris, 208
woman: white-centered definitions of, 67, 73–74, 78–79, 82, 83
Women on 20s movement, 1–3, 4, 6, 24, 235n4
women's organizations, 9, 10, 21–22, 71. *See also specific organizations*
Women's Political Council, 90, 91
Women's Rights National Historical Park, 77, 78–79
Wonder, Stevie, 222, 230
World's Columbian Exposition (1893), 9, 10
World War I, 239n3
Wortham, Jenna, 229
Wozolek, Boni, 246n59
Wright, Nazera Sadiq, 138
Wu, Jason, 215
Wyss, Johann David, 199

Yaeger, Patricia, 238n53
youth: Bethune and, 46, 47, 51–52, 55–56, 57, 59–60, 61, 102; civil rights movement and, 56, 92, 98–99, 100, 244n17; Parks and, 91–92, 98, 99, 100–103, 105, 108–9, 114; studies on, 138; voices of, xviii

Zimmerman, George, xviii